Bard FICTION PRIZE

Bard College invites submissions for its annual Fiction Prize for young writers.

The Bard Fiction Prize is awarded annually to a promising, emerging writer who is a United States citizen aged 39 years or younger at the time of application. In addition to a monetary award of $30,000, the winner receives an appointment as writer-in-residence at Bard College for one semester without the expectation that he or she teach traditional courses. The recipient will give at least one public lecture and will meet informally with students.

To apply, candidates should write a cover letter describing the project they plan to work on while at Bard and submit a C.V., along with three copies of the published book they feel best represents their work. No manuscripts will be accepted.

Applications for the 2008 prize must be received by July 15, 2007. For further information about the Bard Fiction Prize, call 845-758-7087, send an e-mail to bfp@bard.edu, or visit www.bard.edu/bfp. Applicants may also request information by writing to the Bard Fiction Prize, Bard College, Annandale-on-Hudson, NY 12504-5000.

Bard College PO Box 5000, Annandale-on-Hudson, NY 12504-5000

COMING UP IN THE FALL

Conjunctions:49
A WRITERS' AVIARY

Edited by Bradford Morrow

From the mythic phoenix rising from the ashes to the bird of paradise, which, according both to legend and Linnaeus, remained in flight its whole life, birds have set imaginations soaring. The sacred quetzal, the industrious bowerbird, the authoritative bald eagle, the wise owl, the gothic raven, the plaintive whip-poor-will, the happy little blue-birds somewhere over the rainbow—there isn't a species that has failed to inspire us symbol-crazy, earthbound human observers. The fall issue of *Conjunctions, A Writers' Aviary*, collects a wide spectrum of works about birds by ornithologists and everyday birders, together with poets and fiction writers from several continents. Among the many contributors are British poet Tim Dee, Canadian writer Sylvia Legris, and Americans William H. Gass, Peter Orner, and D. E. Steward.

The issue also celebrates the distinguished half-century career of John Ashbery in a portfolio of essays, co-edited by Peter Gizzi and Bradford Morrow, addressing his oeuvre, book by book. Among the contributions: Reginald Shepherd on *Some Trees*, Peter Straub on *The Tennis Court Oath*, Charles Bernstein on *Rivers and Mountains*, Ron Silliman on *Three Poems*, Susan Stewart on *Self-Portrait in a Convex Mirror*, Ann Lauterbach on *As We Know*, Cole Swensen on *Hotel Lautréamont*, Harry Mathews on *Your Name Here*, and Robert Kelly on *Chinese Whispers*.

Subscriptions to *Conjunctions* are only $18 for more than eight hundred pages per year of contemporary and historical literature and art. Please send your check to *Conjunctions*, Bard College, Annandale-on-Hudson, NY 12504. Subscriptions can also be ordered by calling (845) 758-1539, or by sending an e-mail to Michael Bergstein at Conjunctions@bard.edu. For more information about current and past issues, please visit our Web site at www.Conjunctions.com.

CONJUNCTIONS

Bi-Annual Volumes of New Writing

Edited by
Bradford Morrow

published by Bard College

EDITOR: Bradford Morrow
MANAGING EDITOR: Michael Bergstein
SENIOR EDITORS: Robert Antoni, Peter Constantine, Brian Evenson,
   Micaela Morrissette, David Shields, Pat Sims, Alan Tinkler
WEBMASTER: Brian Evenson
ASSOCIATE EDITORS: Jedediah Berry, J. W. McCormack, Eric Olson
ART EDITOR: Norton Batkin
PUBLICITY: Mark R. Primoff
EDITORIAL ASSISTANTS: Jessica Loudis, Daniel Pearce

CONJUNCTIONS is published in the Spring and Fall
of each year by Bard College, Annandale-on-Hudson,
NY 12504. This issue is made possible in part with
the generous funding of the National Endowment for
the Arts, and with public funds from the New York
State Council on the Arts, a State Agency.

State of the Arts
NATIONAL ENDOWMENT FOR THE ARTS
A great nation deserves great art.

NYSCA

SUBSCRIPTIONS: Send subscription orders to CONJUNCTIONS, Bard
College, Annandale-on-Hudson, NY 12504. Single year (two volumes): $18.00
for individuals; $35.00 for institutions and overseas. Two years (four volumes):
$32.00 for individuals; $70.00 for institutions and overseas. Patron subscription (lifetime): $500.00. Overseas subscribers please make payment by
International Money Order. For information about subscriptions, back issues,
and advertising, call Michael Bergstein at (845) 758-1539 or fax (845) 758-2660.

Editorial communications should be sent to Bradford Morrow, *Conjunctions*,
21 East 10th Street, New York, NY 10003. Unsolicited manuscripts cannot
be returned unless accompanied by a stamped, self-addressed envelope.
Electronic and simultaneous submissions will not be considered.

Conjunctions is listed and indexed in the American Humanities Index.

Visit the *Conjunctions* Web site at www.conjunctions.com.

Cover design by Jerry Kelly, New York. Cover photograph by Rosamond Purcell
(detail) from *Dice: Deception, Fate and Rotten Luck* by Ricky Jay (Quantuck
Lane Press).

Available through D.A.P./Distributed Art Publishers, Inc., 155 Sixth Avenue,
New York, NY 10013. Telephone: (212) 627-1999. Fax: (212) 627-9484.

Printers: Edwards Brothers

Typesetter: Bill White, Typeworks

ISSN 0278-2324
ISBN 978-0-941964-64-7

Manufactured in the United States of America.

TABLE OF CONTENTS

FACES OF DESIRE

Congratulations to
Conjunctions founder and editor

Bradford Morrow

winner of the

2007 PEN/Nora Magid Award

for excellence in literary journal editing

The Agonized Face
Mary Gaitskill

A FEMINIST AUTHOR CAME to talk at the annual literary festival in Toronto, one of the good-looking types with expensive clothes who looks younger than they are (which is irritating even though it shouldn't be), the kind of person who plays with her hair when she talks, who always seems to be asking you to like her. She was like that, but she had something else too, and it was that "something else" quality that made what she did so peculiarly aggravating.

Before I go any further, it must be said that I arrived at the festival tense and already prone to aggravation. I have been divorced for five years. I am the mother of a ten-year-old girl. My ex-husband is stalwart in his child-support payments, but he is a house painter who is trying to be an artist, and out of respect for his dreams, his payments are not large. We met in graduate school where I was studying creative writing, a dream-cum-memory rolling monotonously near the bottom of the subthought ocean. After years of writing in-brief book reviews plus doing calendar composition for an online magazine, I have recently begun writing full-length reviews (which means a little more money and a lot less time for playing "The Mighty Michelle" with Kira); for the first time, I have been assigned to "do" something light and funny on the social scene at the literary festival. The idea of proximity to so many actual authors may've caused some more-intense-than-usual subthought rolling, which is perhaps why a fight with my daughter got nastier than it had to this morning. It did not help that it was a fight about whether or not she can, at ten, bleach her hair "like Gwen Stefani," and that the fight then had to turn into a discussion with Tom about how he had to be sure that while staying with him this afternoon, she did not somehow get hold of boxed bleach, and take charge of the bathroom. Or, furthermore, that she not be allowed to persuade him that red might be OK if blonde was not.

Still, for the most part, I was able to clear my mind of all this once I arrived at the festival. Writers from all over the world were there, people from Somalia, Greece, Israel, America, Italy, and Britain.

Mary Gaitskill

There were writers who'd been forced to flee their countries, writers from police states, writers from places where everybody was starving; writers who wrote about the daily problems of ordinary people, the obscenity of politics, and the pain of the lower classes; glamorous writers who wrote about the exciting torment of the fashionable classes. Writers with airs of gravity or triviality, well heeled or wearing suits they had probably rented for this event, standing at the bar with an air of hard-won triumph, or simply looking with childish delight at all the glowing bottles of delicious drinks and trays of foodstuffs. I glimpsed a smart blonde woman on the arm of a popular author and fleetingly thought of my daughter; if she could see me here, she would feel curiosity and admiration.

But getting back to the "feminist author": it is not really right to call her that as she was not the only feminist there, as in fact her presence may have annoyed other, more serious feminists. She was a feminist who had apparently been a prostitute at some point in her colorful youth, and who had gone on record describing prostitutes as fighters against the patriarchy. She would say stupid things like that, but then she would write some good sentences that would make people say, Wow, she's kind of intelligent! Some people may've said she should not have been at the festival at all, but why not? An event such as this is dazzling partly in its variety; it is a social blaze of little heads rolling by in a ball of light, and all the heads have something to say: "No one should ever write about the Holocaust again!" "Irony is ruining our culture!" Or in the case of the feminist ex-prostitute, "Women can enjoy sexual violence too!" *Well.* I had been asked to write something funny, and the feminist author sounded pretty funny. I pictured her in a short skirt and big high heels, standing up on the balls of her feet with her legs bowed like a samurai, her fists and her arms flexed combatively, head cocked like she was on the lookout for some patriarchy to mount. An image you could look at and go, OK, now for the author who says, "We live in an entertainment society and it's terrible!"

She was reading with two other people, a beautiful seventeen-year-old Vietnamese girl who wrote about rapes and massacres, and a middle-aged Canadian who wrote touching stories about his daughters. First the Vietnamese girl read about a massacre, then came the feminist writer. She immediately began complaining, but she did it in a way that made her complaint sound like a special treat we might like to have. Her voice was sweet with a sparkling rhythm that made you imagine some shy and secret thing was being

8

gradually revealed. I felt caught off guard; she wore a full-length skirt and little glasses and round-toed clog-style boots.

She wasn't going to read, she said; instead she was going to give a talk about the way she had been treated by the local media, as well as by the festival organizers who had described her in an insulting, unfair way in their brochure. I had not even read the brochure—I perhaps should've read it, but the information in such pamphlets is usually worthless—and from the looks on other people's faces, they hadn't read it either. The author, however, didn't seem to realize this. The brochure was not only insulting to her, she continued; it was an insult to all women, to *everyone*, really. They had ignored the content of her work completely, focusing instead on the most sensational aspects of her life—the prostitution, the drug use, the stay in a mental hospital, the attempt on her father's life—in a way that was both salacious and puritanical. "It isn't that these things aren't true," she said in her lilting voice. "They are. I was a prostitute for six months when I was sixteen and I spent two months in a mental hospital when I was eighteen. But I have also done a lot of other things. I have been a waitress, a factory worker, a proofreader, a journalist, a street vendor! I am forty years old and now I teach at Impala University West!"

There were cheers, applause, a woman in the back fiercely hollered, "You go, girl!" The author blinked rapidly and adjusted her glasses. "I can even understand it," she continued. "It's exciting to imagine such a kooky person off somewhere doing unimaginable stuff! I like the idea myself! But I am not that person!" It seemed to me that she kind of was that person, but right then it didn't matter. "And when we do that, when we isolate qualities that seem exciting, but maybe a little scary, and we project them onto another person in an exaggerated form, we not only deny that person their humanity, but we impoverish and cheat ourselves of life's complexity and tenderness!"

This wasn't funny. This was something wholly unexpected. We were all feeling stirred; like we were really dealing with something here, something that had just been illustrated for us by a magical, elvish hand. We felt like we were being touched in a personal place, a little like our mothers would touch us—a touch that was emotionally erotic. Like a mother, she seemed potent, yet there was something of the daughter there too, the innocent girl who has been mistreated by an importune boy, and who comes to you, her upturned face looking at you with puzzlement. Yes, she seemed innocent, even with her sullied, catastrophic life placed before us for the purpose of selling her.

She must've sensed our feelings, because she cut short her speech. We had been so kind, she said, that she wanted to give us something. She was going to read to us after all—in fact, she had her book right there with her, and she even had a story picked out. It was a story about a middle-aged woman dressing in sexy clothes to attend a party right after the death of a former lover. The party is for a woman who writes pornography and is held in a bar decorated with various sex toys. A good-looking boy flirts with the middle-aged woman, who allows that she is "flattered."

What had happened to the mother? Where was the injured girl? The voice of the author was still lilting and girlish, but her words were hard and sharp, the kind of words that think everything is funny. The middle-aged woman invites the young man to her home, gives him a drink, and then pulls his pants off while he lies there gaping. For the next several pages, she alternates between fellating him and chattering cleverly while he tries to leave.

This was the feminist author we had heard about, all right. Her readers smiled knowingly while the readers of the Canadian and Vietnamese authors looked baffled—baffled, then angry. And I was feeling angry too.

I am not really a feminist, probably because, at forty, I am too young to have fully experienced the kinetic surge of feminism that occurred in the seventies, that half-synthetic, half-organic creature with its smart, dry little mouth issuing books, speeches, TV shows, and pop songs. They are not stylish anymore, and in fact have come in for a lot of criticism from female pundits. Some of these pundits say that feminists have made girls think they have to have sex all the time, which, by going against their girlish nature, has destroyed their self-esteem, and made them anorexic and depressed. Feminists have made girls into sluts! Others, equally angry, say that feminists have imposed restrictive rules on nubile teens, making them into morbid neurasthenics who think they're being raped when they're actually just having sex. Feminists have neutered girls by overprotecting them! I don't know what I think of any of it; it's mostly something I hear coming out of my radio on my way to work. But I do know this: when I hear that feminism is overprotecting girls, I am very sympathetic to it. When I see my fashion-conscious ten-year-old in her nylon nightie peering spellbound before the beguiling screen at the fleeting queendom of some twelve-year-old manufactured pop star with the wardrobe of a hooker, a jerry-rigged personality, and bulimia, it seems to me that she has a protection deficit that I may not be able to compensate for. When she comes home wild with tears because she lost the spelling contest, or her ex-best friend called her fat or a boy said she's not the prettiest girl in class, and I press her to me, comforting her, even as that day's Amber Alert flashes in my brain, it is hard for me to imagine this girl as "overprotected."

Which is, in some indirect way, why the feminist author was so affecting and so disappointing. She was a girl who needed to be protected, and a woman standing to protect the girl. But then she became the other thing—the feminist who made girls into sluts. She sprouted three heads and asked that we accept them all! She said she had been a prostitute, a mental patient, that she tried to stab her father. She said it in a soft, reasonable voice—but these are not soft or reasonable things. These are terrible things. Anyone who has seen a street prostitute and looked into her face knows that. For her to admit these things without describing the pain she had suffered gave her dignity—because, really, she didn't have to talk about it. We could imagine it. But the story she read made what had seemed like dignity look silly and obscene. Because the voice of the story was not soft. It was dry and smart, and it showed its smartness like a dance step—but what it told of was not dry or smart. While the voice danced, making scenes that described the woman and the youth, an image slowly formed, taking subtle shape under the picture created by the scenes. It was like an advertisement for cigarettes where beautiful people are smoking in lounge chairs, and suddenly you see in the cobalt blue backdrop the subliminal image of a skull. Except the image behind the feminist author's words was stranger than the image of a skull, and less clear. It made you strain to see what it was, and in the straining you found yourself picturing things you did not want to picture. Of course, it can be fun to picture things you don't want to picture—but somehow the feminist author had ruined the fun.

After the reading we all went for refreshments in the hospitality lounge. The Vietnamese girl and the Canadian father as well as the feminist author were all there, signing books and talking with their readers. There were other authors present too, including an especially celebrated Somali author known for an award-winning novel of war and social disintegration, and an American woman who had written a witty, elegant, clearly autobiographical novella about a mother whose child is hit by a drunk driver and nearly killed. The feminist author appeared more relaxed in this setting than she had been on stage; she smiled easily and chatted with the mostly young women who approached her. And yet again I sensed a disturbing subliminal message bleeding through the presentation: a face of sex and woman's pain. The face had to do with disgrace and violence, dark orgasm, rape, with feeling so strong it obviates the one who feels it. You could call it an exalted face or an agonized face; in the context of the feminist author, I am going to call it "the agonized face." Although I don't know why—she doesn't look like she's ever made such a face in her life.

There was only one more person waiting to talk to her, an animated girl with ardently sprouting red hair. I got in line behind her. When I got up close, I saw that the author's eyes were not sweet, innocent, or sparkling. They were wary and a little hard. As she signed the animate red-girl's book, I heard her say, "Sex has been let out of the box, like everything is OK, but no one knows what 'everything' is."

"Exactly!" sprouted the ardent girl.

Exactly. "I liked the talk you gave," I said, "*before* the reading."

"Thank you," she said, coldly answering my italics.

"But I'm wondering why you chose to read what you read afterward if you didn't like what they said about you in the brochure you mentioned. I didn't read it but—"

"What I read didn't have anything to do with what they said."

No? "I'd love to talk more with you about that. I'm here as a journalist for *Quick!* Would you be able to talk about it for our readers?"

"No," she said. "I'm not doing interviews." And she turned her back on me to sign another book.

I stood for a moment looking at her back, vaguely aware of the Somali author talking into someone's tape recorder. With a vertiginous feeling, I remembered the days right after graduation, when Tom was an artist and I was a freelance journalist hustling work at various small magazines. We slept on a Salvation Army mattress; we ate and wrote on a coffee table. "The grotesque has a history, a social parameter," said the Somali author. "Indeed, one might say that the grotesque *is* a social parameter."

Indeed. I took a glass of wine from a traveling tray of glasses and drank it in a gulp. On one of those long-ago assignments I had interviewed a topless dancer, a desiccated blonde with desperate intelligence burning in other otherwise lusterless eyes. She was big on Hegel and Nietzsche, and she talked about the power of beautiful girls versus the power of men with money. In the middle of this power talk, she told me a story about a customer who had said he would give her fifty dollars if she would get on her hands and knees with her butt facing him, pull down her G-string and then turn around and smile at him. They had negotiated at length: "I made him promise that he wouldn't stick his finger in," she said. "We went over it and over it and he promised me, like, three times. So I pulled down my G-string, and as soon as I turned around, his finger went right in. I was *so* mad!" Then, bang, she was right back at the Hegel and Nietzsche. The combination was pathetic and yet it had the dignity of awful truth. Not only because it was titillating (though, yes, it was) but because, in the telling of it, a certain foundation of humanity was revealed; the crude cinder blocks of male and female down in the basement, holding up the house. Those of us who have spouses and/or children forget about this part—not because we have an aversion to those cinder blocks necessarily, but because we are busy on the upper levels building a home with furniture, decorations, and personalities in it. We are glad to have the topless dancer to remind us of that dark area in the basement where personality is irrelevant and crude truth prevails. Her philosophical chatter even added to the power of her story because it created a stark polarity: fine, intelligent words on one side, and mute, degraded genitals on the other. Between the poles there was darkness and mystery, and the dancer respected the mystery with her ignorant and touching pretense.

Which is exactly what the feminist author did not do. I drained my second glass of wine. The feminist author—she told and then read her degrading stories like she was a lady at a tea party, as if there was no mystery, no darkness, just her, a feminist author skipping along swinging some charming little bag and singing about penises, la la la la la!

Another server wafted past, a young woman with her mind clearly on something else. I reached for another glass of wine, then changed my mind. Of course, someone might say—I can picture a well-dressed, intellectual lady saying it—well, why not? And rationally there is no reason why not. These things are accepted now, these things are talked about in popular comedies on television. So why not? Because everyone knows such television shows are nonsense. Because such glib acceptance does not respect the profound nature

Mary Gaitskill

of the agonized face.

I reconsidered having another wine; looking for a server, I noticed that the Somali author, momentarily unpestered, was looking at me with a kindly expression. He was handsome, well-dressed, and elegant. Impulsively I crossed the room and introduced myself. His hand was long, dry, and warm. He had come from New York, not Somalia. He came every year. When I told him it was my first time he smiled.

"Are you enjoying yourself?" he asked.

"Yes," I said, "though it's been a long time since I had two quick drinks this early in the day."

He laughed, raised his wineglass, and sipped from it.

"And you?" I asked. "Do you enjoy this?"

"Oh yes," he said. "One meets such curious people. And of course interesting people too."

"What about her?" I indicated the feminist author, now chatting with her back to us. "What do you think?"

"Oh!" The Somali author laughed. "I've heard what she has to say many times—it's nothing new. But I did admire the panache with which she said it. Did you see Binyavanga speak on the power of place?"

But we were interrupted by more people wanting his signature, and then it was time for his reading. "I hope you will come," he said.

The Somali author read from his award winner, the novel about civil war and familial bonds. He skipped through the book, reading excerpts from several chapters, starting with a tender love scene between a husband and a wife who magically has two sets of breasts, the normal set augmented by a miniset located just under her rib cage. Their young son runs in and cries, "Are you going to give me a sibling?" Then the author jumped ahead and suddenly there it was again: the Agonized Face. The son, now grown, is being pursued by a fat, whorish girl who claims he owes her a baby, even though she has AIDS and he is engaged to someone else. We learn that this very girl, an orphan who was briefly taken in by the family when she was fourteen, once sexually attacked the grandfather, who responded by righteously kicking her in the face. When the mother learns that this slut is back again, she decides to get a gun, humiliate the girl, and then kill her. The grandfather, though, does not want the mother on the street during the escalating civil unrest. "Leave her to me," he counsels. "There is, after all, something unfinished between us." He goes to the son's house to lie in wait and, sure enough, the slut comes calling. She's looking for the son, but when she finds Grandpa, it doesn't matter; she wants his baby too. He pretends to be asleep while she masturbates him. She thinks, how beautiful his penis is! She longs for his children! She mounts him, and the grandfather reports, with a certain gentlemanly discretion, that he and the slut "went somewhere together." But, nonetheless, almost as soon as they are done, the girl is mystically stricken with discharge and gross vaginal itching; she runs down the road, scratching her crotch as she screams, "I itch! I smell!" The son is happily reunited with his fiancée, and the wife, his mother, finds new tenderness with her husband. The grandfather meditates on history.

If he had been an American or a Canadian man saying these things, he might've been booed as a misogynist. But an African man—no. It was wonderful, especially the way he read it—with the *earned* hauteur of a man who has seen war, persecution, and the two sides of the agonized face: the mother who is poignant in her open-legged vulnerability and the visage of the female predator. Because for all its elegance, that voice—unlike the voice of the feminist author—did not try to hide reality: the pain and anger of the unsatisfied womb grown ill from lack of wholesome use, a fungal vector of want, thick with tumors, baby's teeth, and bits of hair inside each fibrous mass. Pitiful, yes, but also nasty, though we in the antiseptic West don't say so.

"Motherhood is the off and on light in the darkness of night," concluded the author, "a firefly of joy and rejoicing, now here now there and everywhere. In fact the crisis that is coming to a head in the shape of civil strife would not be breaking in on us if we'd offered women-as-mothers their due worth, respect, and affection; a brightness celebrating motherhood, a monument erected in worship of women."

The audience went wild.

In the big reception hall we celebrated the Somali author with more drinks, and I caught up with the American novelist whose son had nearly been killed by a drunk driver. She was a good egg, hawk nosed and plainly dressed, and she was having a stiff one. When I asked her she said she'd disliked writing about the accident, but that if she hadn't, she never would've been able to pay the medical expenses. We gossiped; we admired the Somali author. "I can't imagine an

American writer saying something like that," she said. "'A monument erected in worship of women.'"

"I know," I said, "it was lovely." *As long as you're the right kind of woman,* I didn't say. I glimpsed the feminist author across the room from us, standing by herself eating a fistful of grapes. The American writer was saying something about how irony is the most human of artistic methods, but I was thinking of something else. I was thinking of a girl I had known in high school named Linda Phoenix. She was a thin girl with a stark, downy back, who fucked every boy plus some girls. Jeff Lyer, an angry fat kid, brought pictures to school of Linda drunk and sucking someone's penis with her legs open. Apparently Linda did not know these pictures had been taken. Because during lunch, when a picture was passed to her, she ran out the cafeteria door, knocking down a condiment and kicking it across the floor as she ran.

Across the room two reporters approached the feminist author with their tape recorders. I thought of Linda Phoenix's stumbling fleeing form. I thought of my daughter, standing before the mirror, pushing her lower lip out, making seductive eyes. I thought of her sitting at the kitchen table, drawing scenes from her favorite book, *Magic by the Lake.* I thought of her frightened awake from a nightmare crying, "Mommy, Mommy!" I remembered washing her as a baby, using the spray hose from the kitchen sink to rinse shit from the swollen petals of her infant slit—a hole she will fall down if she opens it too early, a black Wonderland of teeth and bones and crushing force. The hole in life, a hole we cannot see into, no matter how close we look.

I had had too much to drink and too little to eat, and for a drunken instant the hall became a courtroom, the authors and journalists members of a jury overspilling the box to cry out: Now hold on a minute! Are you completely out of your mind? It is one thing to express disdain for this so-called feminist, who may deserve it. Even the muddled atavism about rotten wombs full of baby teeth—well, it is loony and gross, but in the locked closet of our inmost heart, we can see how you might feel that way. But your daughter? What kind of mother are you? Leave her out of this nonsense, please!

And of course the imaginary jury was right. I would love Kira no matter how many boys she did what with, or girls for that matter. Things are not like they once were. *Sex in the City* is on TV. Still, when I think of her as she will be—dripping with hormones and feelings, nursing the secret hurt of a seed about to burst into flower—it makes me uneasy. It's true that to think of her opening her warm spring darkness to any lout who wants it makes me feel a surprising surge of anger and contempt. (Anger that includes an even more surprising burst of sympathy for my mother's anger, sympathy even for the time she slapped my face after she caught me and Donald Parker doing it in the rec room.) But even as I feel the anger, even with my mother's anger crowding behind it—my mother, also single, now a mild alcoholic in old age, calling me to give me a piece of her mind about the latest nonsense on the news—even as I feel the anger, love rises up to enclose it. Inside love anger still secretly burns—but it is a tiny flame. I can hold it like I once held my daughter in my body, a world within a world.

But just now I allowed myself to enter the little flame and feel it all the way. I did it in the spirit of the feminist author—and to show her up too. So, she can be the innocent girl and the prostitute and the author, eh? Well imagine a full deck of cards, each card painted with symbols of woman: the waif, the harlot, the mother, the warrior, the queen—until the last card, on which we see Medea, a knife in her raised, implacable hand. Yes, there I am and there any woman can be, even though we don't stand up on the stage and make a fuss about it. And we can skip lightly back through the deck, carelessly touching each card as we do, before returning to the card of the good mother, or the lover, or, in my case at this moment, the stolid female worker in my brown skirt and flat shoes. Every woman knows all about everything on those cards, even if her knowledge is wordless and half conscious. It is wordless knowledge because it is too big for words. Sometimes it is too big for us. Stand up on stage and put words on it and you make it small—and then you say it's sexist when people don't like it.

Except that, if I am going to be honest, I have to admit something that weighs in on the side of the feminist author *just slightly.* The anger and contempt that I let myself feel, that mere hot pinprick in the ardent wetness of love—when you let yourself feel it, when *I* let myself feel it, it was, is, very strong. Strong and primitive. Enter in through that tiny spot of fire and come out in a hell of shape-shifting and destruction. In that hell lives a beast that will devour anything in front of it, and that beast is especially partial to woman; she already has a hole in her body, why not make it bigger? Why not split her open all the way, just for the pure animal joy of rending and

17

tearing? For a woman even to skirt this place is dangerous because she has the open part. She needs rules, structures, intact shapes to make sure the openness doesn't get *too* open. For a man it is different—he can align his strength with the monster and ecstatically tear the prey with its teeth. For a second he can walk triumphant in a place of no place. Then he can say the woman lured him there.

That is why the grandfather in the Somali author's book wants to fuck the slut. He tells his son that because she has no children he feels sorry for her, that he is fucking her out of sympathy. But he does not seem to feel sorry for her. He wants her, you could even say he needs her, for through her he can descend into a terrible, thrilling world and then come back in his suit and tie and be good. The Somali author almost acknowledges this with his frank fascination in the slut. For if she was not there, how could he go to that place of no place? He would have to discharge his anger and contempt on mom-with-double-boobs and this would be more than anybody could bear—for like me, he has more love than anger. How unfair that men get to go to this mysterious place and come back whole. How noble that the feminist author stands up on stage and tries to speak for the sluts they go there with, even if she fails. Even if her story makes something terrible into something light and silly, even if she herself is light and silly.

This is what I was thinking as I sat in the hospitality lounge, nursing a seltzer water with lemon, after attending a reading by a man from the prairies who had written a prize-winning novel about a heroic woman who rescues an orphan from an abusive foster parent. I was sitting by the window, and, in the sunlight, the room seemed composed of impossible purple and mahogany hues. People stood in little groups, looking game, but worn out by their own personalities, and the effort it took to keep them in place. Caterers discreetly moved in and out, replacing platters of food and trays of drinks.

Soon I would leave, pick up my daughter, and take her for pizza. We would go home and watch *Buffy the Vampire Slayer*. And then maybe that strange anime show, the one we stumbled on last week; a show where the heroine, the good girl, had no arms and the sexy villainess was powerful and crude. It looked like the cartoon slut was trying to kill the heroine and steal her boyfriend. But instead, in the middle of a gun battle between hero and villain, the slut (admiring the armless girl's purity) took a bullet to save her and died with the heroine in her arms. When the embrace broke, the good girl magically stood up with arms of her own and proceeded to beat the crap out of the bad guy. "There's going to be some changes around here!" she announced. Rock music played.

"Weird," said Kira, and it really was.

I drank my seltzer water and reviewed my notes.

Early in my career, I did a piece on the then-burgeoning phenomenon of TV talk shows, focusing on a particular show, a show that at that time had made its reputation by sympathetically telling the stories of victims, stories that had once been too shameful to tell. Rape was a mainstay of the show, and I was present on the set for an episode that featured two women who had been raped by coworkers in the workplace, one of whom had succeeded in pressing charges and the other who had lost her case. The successful woman was a flamboyant redheaded beauty who came on yelling, "I just want to say I've got a shotgun ready for any sumbitch who tries it again!"

But first came the defeated one, a chubby middle-aged woman who tried to hide her identity by sitting with her back to the camera and wearing an ill-fitting wig. The man she'd accused of raping her was there too, and he had a lot to say. "She go like this!" he said. "On the desk!" He stood up and bent over, putting his hands out like he was bracing himself. "And I say, no! I don't want that!"

The awful thing was, you could totally picture her bent over the desk. Even from the back we could see her bending nature; the mild, gentle slope of her shoulders, the sweetness of her excess flesh, the way she turned in her chair to yell, "No! That's not the truth!" Her anger was like a clumsy animal, and you could hear in it the soft puzzlement of a person who does not understand cruelty.

"You are an alcoholic!" screamed the accused rapist. "Everybody knows!"

"I offered you one drink!" she cried. "I thought you were lonely!"

"You are a whore! You give VD!"

"No!" cried the woman. "No!" And then she just wept.

A stout little woman came on to talk about rape. She planted her feet, set her small barrel body in a "no bull" stance, and gave it to us straight: rape was bad, and she was prepared to duke it out with anyone who said it wasn't.

"I agree!" yelled the accused rapist. "I agree!"

The wigged woman continued to weep. Nobody looked at her.

19

In swept the triumphant redhead who bellowed about her rights. "And I just hope the rapists who are watching the show right now understand that we aren't going to take it anymore!" she cried. The audience cheered. The wig woman wept. The talk show hostess strode about the set, blonde and bristling with savoir faire. She had featured progress but she had not forgotten the agonized face. Unlike the feminist author, she had put it right up there on the screen.

But wait! The feminist author was not talking about rape, was she? Being a prostitute is not the same thing as being raped, is it? And of course they are not the same. But for the purposes of my discussion here—for the deepest layer of my discussion—they are close enough! The rape victim on TV was treated like a prostitute on an official pro-victim show, and the feminist author—well, it probably wasn't fair to talk about her that way in the pamphlet, even if nobody read it, even if it was true. Can you blame her for not wanting to be like the poor, hurt woman on the talk show, preferring to prance around swinging her little handbag instead? Can you blame her for trying to put a good face on it? For talking so loudly about things that have been used to shame women for centuries? Wordless knowledge can be heavy and dark as the bottom of the ocean. Sometimes you want the relief of dryness, of light, bright words. Sometimes you might be on the side of a smart aleck middle-aged woman who thumbs her nose at the agonized face and fellates a snotty, sexy man, just for a dumb little thrill. Sometimes you wish it could be that easy.

I looked at my watch. I drank my seltzer and felt myself return to sobriety. I listened to the prairie author entertain a group with a story about how he had been so drunk the previous night that, in a muddled attempt to find the bathroom, he had left his hotel room naked and had roamed the hills until a "beautiful woman" from room service had escorted him back. Everyone laughed. A harried caterer, bearing a platter of torn-at grapes and wilted cheeses, wiped her hand on her rumpled white shirt and made a disgusted little face. I looked out the window; people strolled the sidewalks like sensitive grazing animals, full of trust that what they needed was to be found here on the grounds of the hotel. From across the room, I heard the prairie writer cry, "And she had the most incredible ass!" There was delighted laughter.

Suddenly, I was flooded with goodwill toward the feminist author. I didn't even care that she had refused to speak with me. She wrote well enough and she was an articulate, perhaps even socially

20

significant figure. Why should she be dismissed while a man who ran around naked in public and yelled about people's asses was coddled? And yet . . . some part of me was still troubled by the issue of the agonized face. Because the face is not only about rape and pain.

I remember how it was with my husband sometimes, or rather how it was on occasion, or really, maybe just once. It was before I became pregnant with Kira. We had not been getting along, and we were trying to have a special time together. We lit a candle and we undressed and lay on the bed outside the covers. We rubbed each other with oil. It was relaxing and awkward too—it would feel really good and then he would have a sneezing fit. Or I would turn his foot at a strange angle during the foot massage and he would open his eyes and tactfully try to pull it a more comfortable way. When he touched between my legs, I wasn't even thinking about sex anymore. His presence was physical and insistent, like the smell of a wild animal, like a bear, grunting and searching for food, picking berries with the elegant black finger of its tongue—but my mind had wandered away. It wandered like someone browsing a junk store, its attention taken this way and that by each gewgaw, the faded, painted face of each figurine: an argument with my sister, a birthday gift for a friend, the novel I was supposed to review, and, like a tiny reflection on the curve of a glass, a scene from the novel (hero and heroine in tense conversation on a fire escape at dusk, red flowers climbing the wall, traffic darting below). Every few moments my attention would return to my husband, and I would feel what he was doing, and caress his rough fur and then dart away again. Except with each return, I darted away more slowly, and then I didn't dart at all. His touch had entered my nervous system without my knowing it. The images in my head softened and ran together, colorful, semicoherent, and still subtly flavored with the novel. The blunt feelings of my lower body came rolling up in dark, choppy waves. He put his hand on my abdomen and said, "Breathe into here." I did. He didn't have to touch me anymore; the flesh between my legs was hot and fat. He touched me with his genitals. I took his large bony head in my hands. We kissed, and the kiss went down layers. We entered a small place sealed away from every other place. In that place, my genitals were pierced by a ring attached to a light chain. He held the chain in his hand and we both looked at it, smiling and abashed—*Whoa! How did that get there!?* Then I became an animal and he led me by the chain. We entered into stunning emptiness; we emerged. He moaned and bit my shoulder with his hot, wet mouth.

Afterward, we smiled, rolling in each other's arms, laughing at ourselves, laughing at the agonized face. But we couldn't laugh at the emptiness. It was like entering an electrical current, passing first into a landscape of animate light, and then into pitch-darkness, warm with invisible life, the whispering voices, the dissolving, re-forming faces of ghosts and the excited unborn. Everything horrible to us, everything nice to us. We did not conceive Kira at that time; I think that happened one sleepy morning when there was no special massage, no sudden dropping into a hidden place. Without even realizing it, we entered emptiness again and brought a tiny female out of it.

My husband and I are not friends, but we are amicable. Once, after we split up, I called him late at night, after I'd had a terrible dream, and I was glad for his kind response. But I have never called him like that since, and I'm sure he is glad of it. He is now another wholly separate creature with whom I can negotiate, chat, joke, fight, cooperate with or not. But I remember that moment between us, and it is represented to me by the agonized face. It is easy to be ashamed of the face—and sometimes the face is shameful. But it is also inextricably bound up with the royalty of female nature. It symbolizes our entry into emptiness because it is a humiliation of our personal particularity, the cherished definition of our personal features. Men don't go there because they can't or because they are too scared. So they pretend to look down on us for it—but, really, they know better.

It is this weird combination of pride and shame that makes you want to snap at the feminist author, like a dog in a pack. Perhaps it is also what gives her an audience; I don't know. But for her to raise the issues that she sweetly raised in her earnest elf voice—the humiliated middle-aged woman pretending that humiliation is an especially smart kind of game, together with the casual mention of her experience with prostitution—and yet to leave out the agonized face? No way. If she had told the same story, even with the prostitution attached, and let us see the face—that would've been one thing. We could've sat back and nodded to ourselves, a little contemptuous maybe, yet respecting the truth of it. But to tell that story and pretend there's no agony—it makes you want to pinch her like a boy in a gang, following her down the street while she tries to act like nothing's wrong, hurrying her step while someone else reaches out for another pinch. It makes you want to chase her down an alley, to stone her, to force her to show the face she denies.

Which in a metaphorical sense is what I did with my article. When I turned it in, the managing editor said, "Whew! She sure pissed you off, didn't she?" And I said, "Do you think it's too much?" And the editor said, "No, if that's what you feel. . . ." Although of course, I didn't say what I "feel." I couldn't because it could not be printed in a newspaper. I had to speak in the fast brute code of public discourse and count on people to see the subtler shapes moving in the depths below the conventional grid of my words.

The day after my piece appeared, there was some discussion among the younger girls at *Quick!* who did not like it that I had failed to "support" a woman artist, who felt that I used unfair, sexist language. And, privately, when I think of the feminist author, standing there at the podium in her long skirt and her glasses, blinking nervously, I almost agree that it was not fair. But fair or not, I was right. The agonized face and all it means is one of the few mysteries left to us on this ragged, earthen planet with its gutted heart of dirt and its veils of gas and ether. It must be protected, even if someone must on occasion be "stoned." Even if that person is someone for whom we feel secret sympathy and regard.

And, besides, she wasn't really stoned. She will probably go on writing her books, making her money, standing up on stages. She will probably do better than I. I think of the night Kira and I watched the strange anime story about an armless heroine, and the villainess who dies. As Kira was getting ready for bed, I asked her if she found the story scary.

"No," she said, yawning. "But it was sad the other girl had to die." She paused, climbing into bed. I bent to pull the covers up to her chin. "But even if she died, she won anyway," she continued. "Because it was her arms that beat the bad guy."

"That's right," I said, and kissed her and turned out the light. *That's right.* I kissed her again.

23

Pornografía

H. G. *Carrillo*

I.

ITS WORKING TITLE is *La firma de María_del_Pilar*, the director told her over lunch at a restaurant that served tiny portions on oak planks. No plates. Unpolished cotton napkins, Sugar in the Raw. Her organically farmed fresh CoHo salmon was not only bright red but a bit frozen at the center.

That was sure to change, he said. Before it wraps it will be called something like *La Firma* or *María del Pilar* or something else, something romantic, evocative as the character is evocative; besides the Spanish puts some folks off—Fools!—but that too is changing.

He had spoken with a mouth full of remoulade, teeth flecked with bits of caper.

Those kinds of changes always occur, he said. That's immaterial because what they'll be doing will be incredible. This will be beautiful, he said. We are about to say something in the vast wasteland of film that says so little.

The producer was very famous, the director's name vaguely familiar when he had called earlier in the week. She had never heard of the writer. The actress—who, according to what the director said the producer said, would soon be even bigger when all was said and done—had gained thirty pounds for the role, and had worked the past year with three separate language coaches at her own expense, and was pretty much doing whatever it took to bring María del Pilar to life.

They were counting on her, the director said into his cell phone at the same time that he pointed to something on the menu called mango brulée, indicating to the waiter without consulting her that they would take two.

We're counting on you, he repeated. And Lupe had no idea whom he was talking about until, without so much as a goodbye, he dropped the phone onto the plank of spent red sauce in front of him, teetered all the stemware to grab both her hands and bring them over the table to his chest.

Tears filled his eyes as he told her that of all the set designer-slash-decorators he could think of, she was the only one he felt was up to it, the only one who could do what really needed to be done. Your talents are boundless, he said of the three shorts and the reel of twenty or so commercials and music videos that she had done. And when she began to question his enthusiasm, he was quick to interrupt, telling her that this is not Hollywood, it's Chicago; this is not Big Budget, it's Independent; if they were looking for the slick, the overblown, the produced, he knew exactly where to find it. He had been it, done it, lived it, bought a house there, sold it, and moved.

Fuck all that other shit that you might be thinking about, he said as he stuck his spoon into her mango brulée without asking; a smooth, flesh-colored cream coated his lips, his tongue, and the tip of his nose as he nearly shouted, This, m'dear, goddamn it, is art!

And she took it over the industrial she'd been offered that would have paid more in the long run because she saw it as an opportunity to show what she could do.

A friend—more a colleague, really—who was a food designer with whom she had worked a few times shrieked into the phone that night that she was so jealous she could kill her.

Lup, you have no idea, something like this could change your whole career . . . your whole life! And for more than an hour she talked about the director's reputation, and what working with people like that could mean to her future. Lupita, I just hope you remember who your friends are, perra, when your shit is so hot not even you can stand it.

Try and see if you can't get me on, her friend asked.

Within three weeks of revisions, e-mails, and heated phone conversations, her agent approved a contract and sent her to their lawyer's office on Ohio near Michigan Avenue.

She hadn't thought about what she'd wear that day. It wasn't really a meeting. The director had phoned to apologize for not being there even though he really wanted to be. He thought that it was important that he was there for every step of the process. Like family, they were all his to nurture and care for.

He was sorry, he said—and then asked if he should say Lo siento or Descúpeme—and she said, I'm sorry will do. Lo siento, he said, he would really have preferred to be there, but needed to give testimony that morning in Los Angeles.

It seems he had been victim of a gay bashing the year before, and even though he wasn't gay he wanted to make sure these mother-fuckers got exactly what was coming to them.

Jesus Titty Fucking Christ! he shouted in Lupe's ear. Can't a man in this day and age dress nicely without . . .

But he stopped and told her that happier days were on the way, that it was a green light on his end of it, everything all signed; the lawyer was just there as a glorified notary.

After the heat and noise from the street, the quiet cool of the lawyer's office was welcome.

The receptionist went for the Pellegrino he'd offered while she waited, Lupe applied fresh lipstick, powdered the shine from her forehead and cheeks, unpinned and shook her hair down.

The carpets were Turkish, and an extremely well-preserved old, if not antique. The lighting was incandescent from brass and rosewood sconces that seemed to grow out from the paneling and a halogen tube that was recessed into a fold in the ceiling that ran the perimeter of the waiting area and was diffused by an opalescent cap of milk glass. She was seated on a very fine black leather Italian sofa and behind her was a teak étagère on top of which sat a table lamp the base of which was an illuminated green marble slab and up out of which floated sculpted bronze sea grass and angel fish.

The wall behind the receptionist's desk was an aquarium—where hundreds of red and blue tetras had set up individual schools in contrary directions, and a coral reef sprouted an entire forest, through which sailed very light pink, round flat fish, big as faces—that seemed to mock the lamp simply by its movement.

She had started to count the tiny squares inlaid in a checkerboard pattern that bordered the dark hardwood floor, and wanted to go home and change into something more elegant or businesslike. She had had nothing to put the contract in that would keep it flat. No briefcase, a purse wouldn't have done, so she had slipped it into one of the plastic sleeves of her portfolio.

Hours later, headed home, she was walking up Michigan Avenue toward the subway and caught herself reflected in a storefront full of tuxedos and pink and black dresses. She felt good, pretty, in her worn huaraches and the light orange, two-year-old sundress that she had bought off the street in Mexico City, and wondered why she had been worried at all.

The lawyer had come out to the reception area to greet her, both his arms extended. She had been unsure if he wanted to be hugged or if this was just his way. His big round face went pink as gum when she grabbed both his hands the way the director had hers and shook them in the air between them.

In his office, they talked about the upcoming project long enough to find out that he was an investor—this was the first time he had done anything like this; it made him feel so much like a real patron of the arts, he said—and with a director of this caliber and reputation, there was no telling what anyone involved would be doing next.

After he had stamped his witness to her signature, he told her that her dress was lovely, really set off her skin, her eyes, hair, and the lapis beads she wore around her neck. That color orange like that, he said, reminded him of where the air meets over the Gulf of Mexico.

She told him how she got the dress and about the toothless woman in the street market who had told her that if she could still get her big, fat body into it, neither she nor it would be there now.

But the lawyer had fallen backward into one of the twenty or more times that he had traveled to Mexico. It was a reverie that took him through the gardens of Xochimilco and introduced him to the woman who took him there. The woman had had the darkest and most deep-set eyes he had ever had the pleasure of getting lost in. And when he told Lupe that the woman too had only worn the lightest shade of orange—orange nearly pink, orange almost not orange at all, something else, he said—Lupe seized the opportunity to tell him that she was Cuban and hadn't realized the dress had been made in Taiwan until she had gotten it back to her hotel room.

The after-work traffic had died down considerably and she was able to find a window seat in a cool car with very few passengers. She rested her head against the window and the smell of her own body— warm and sweet—so that when the lawyer had stopped in midsentence to comment on the fragrance that she was wearing—It reminds me of something vanilla-y, yet with an underhum of ripening fruit, he said—she hadn't had the heart to tell him it was probably her underarm deodorant.

His scalp had gone bright pink and seemed it would bleed out the tips of his longish blond hair as he stretched out across his desk, hanging his head over the edge. Without disengaging, she had turned her back to him and with each of her knees tucked into his sides pushed herself all the way the way down until he whimpered like a puppy.

Little sounds. Soft, guileless, frightened, lost as she pulled up again.

Reflected in the glass of a photograph of a woman she assumed to

27

be his wife at the far end of the desk, Lupe had watched her body swallow and spit his fat pink prick over and over again and again. Leaning backward, flattening him immobile by pinning his shoulders with the heels of her hands, so that thousands of times over in the faceted copper polished ceiling, she had seen herself—breasts, belly, hips rocking as she threw her hair, opened her mouth—nearly make him disappear.

With just his hairy legs sticking out from underneath her—still in his shoes and socks, pants, too eager, too excited to be embarrassed by the skid mark in his underwear to either notice or try to hide it from her—unfamiliar, dislocated, strange yet at the same time compelling as a found object.

The train trudged out of the ground up to the elevated when a thin pale boy with a pointed face with an unfortunate splatter of freckles and topped with a carrot-colored flurry of dreadlocks that she hadn't noticed before began muttering to himself. It wasn't until he yelled, Bitch! that she saw the earpiece and plastic tube heading toward his mouth.

He stood and his eyes sharpened out to green chinks bright as bottle glass as he began to scream, Why you think, Bitch . . . cause you my bitch, Bitch, and I love you, Bitch! Well why you think? he yelled and stopped and listened long enough for Lupe to attribute the smell of patchouli that permeated the air back to him.

Oh, like I roll like that? he demanded confirmation, and announced to a spot on the ceiling above the handrails that This bitch must have went and lost her entire motherfuckin mind!

As the train drew closer to her stop, Lupe had reached under her sundress and slipped her panties down over her feet. The boy went red-faced, starting a fire under all those spots with wanting to know, If I didn't love you, Bitch, why would you be my bitch, Bitch? And he yelled la-la-la-la-la-la-la-la until the doors opened at Lupe's stop and she dropped her underpants into the seat in front of him.

She stood on the platform as the doors closed behind her. The boy's mouth was open, but it was clear no sound was coming out as the train pulled away. He was holding her underwear. She knew he'd bury them in a pocket only later to bring them to his nose not knowing that he smelled the lawyer too.

The lawyer hadn't been sure if it was water lilies or some kind of orchid—Jasmin-y . . . lemon-y, he said—the woman had shown him as they rowed around the gardens at Xochimilco. And Lupe had reminded him again that she was Cuban, knowing he wouldn't hear and it really didn't matter.

She hadn't wanted him. No desire at all. She hadn't even bothered to fake an orgasm. It was because he was so hungry that she couldn't resist, knowing that he would forever feel foolish around her afterward, attempt to avoid her if their paths crossed on the street.

That night she made a light supper and cleared her drawing table and sharpened pencils before she read the script from beginning to end for the eighth and ninth times.

Despite the title, the protagonist's name was Carolina. Very beautiful, very bright, the script described her as a woman well aware of those relationships we make do for love sometimes.

She leaves her family's poor farm in Camagüey to be a prostitute in La Habana and then, through the generosities of a wealthy Swiss businessman, a prostitute in Miami. All the action, however, takes place when she is married, in her forties, and living in Chicago with a husband who thinks that he pulled her out of a cannery in Florida. The only truth he knows about her past is that she arrived on the shores of Miami in a boat with some others when she was nineteen.

Page after page before the actual script begins is dedicated to what she wears and how she moves. What she uses to decorate the various places she lives before she meets the man who becomes her husband.

Carolina and her husband raise a daughter who only knows the stories her mother tells her of where she's from, and Carolina has used existing laws as an excuse for why they can't go back. What her husband and daughter know of Cuba is seen only through Carolina's eyes.

Yet after her daughter leaves for college, instead of the longing for a Cuba that has passed, or a Cuba of nostalgia, or a lost homeland, or a desire to come clean, it is for an audience for the Cuba that she can make come out of her head anytime and in any way she wishes. And she finds it one night on the Internet with one of the many who write to her, like Titi Kitty:

De: lavirgencitadelcobre <lavergencitadelcobre@hotmail.com>
Para: titi_kitty <titikitty@yahoo.com>
Asunto: RE: Mis Amores
Fecha: Miércoles, 28 de Julio de 2004 22:39 PM

H. G. Carrillo

queritisma virgencita:

forgive my inglés, i know we made a pact to write to help keep our spanish,

pero nenita, i've had yet to figure out what i'm still doing here in buenos aires now that it is over between aníbal and me. so i have done nothing about getting a computer or anything. just that furnished apartment on charcas that he set me up in that i sent you pictures of when i first came down here that gets grimier every day now that i don't have aníbal's support and can't have the maid come in once a week anymore. so, i'm still at that cybercafé on colonel díaz that i told you about last time and that toady, pimply tipo that likes to read over my shoulder is working tonight.

i don't know what you're going to do. are you sure that edu's mother is really dying this time? when we met, what was it, three years ago?, she was on her last leg and you two were headed down to la habana. then six months later, edu was getting all of those calls from his primo, and then you were going again. and then just, what was it, four months ago? how long can a woman with pancreatic cancer, if she really does have pancreatic cancer, last? is she really dying this time? if she is, nena, i really hope that she's dying this time, if only for your sake.

think of it this way, at least you have been back. mi madre sometimes cries for no reason at all no reason that she can explain to me. but i know it has something to do with fleeing to EE UU as if it would change her life radically, having me in Miami with some tipo that was just like all the tipos back home that she was trying to escape, and never looking back.

we get the news about us going back to cuba here hard and heavy. it's not like what we get in miami. you can't make a turn on a street corner in barrio palermo without running past a kiosk that él aborolito is not splattered across it wearing some sort of metaphorical devil's horns. though i'm sure knowing that doesn't make it any better for you. so i'm sorry, but i'm not.

i'm sorry because i'm sure edu is worried sick, and making your life a living hell wondering how he is going to get back to his dying mother. that can't be any fun at all. i'm not sorry because it leaves you in the position of not knowing. not knowing anything as far as i can see. i know when aníbal stopped touching me in those last few months i was nearly crazy with rage. i'd go into bars and sit here and drink too much and flirt with any man . . . y nena, i mean any man who was good-looking . . . just to make sure i still existed. i knew he was still fucking his wife, even though he said he wasn't. they always do, say they aren't even when they are. they think it makes you feel better.

and i told you the last time i saw them coming out of the teatro colón together, but i didn't tell you, maybe because i didn't want to see it at the time, about the way that he looked at her. had i let myself know then that he was still in love with her and would probably always be in love with her, maybe i wouldn't be this way now. but really, i knew coming into this, coming down here, would probably nearly kill me but just because you know the pain is coming doesn't mean that it hurts any less.

y tu tambien, to be in your situation? well, hermana, i can tell you you're more woman than me. three years without anything, or little more than nothing, and i'm not sure that i'd be able to find my face in the mirror to make it up. and maybe that has something to do with why i came down here, and why i got so hung up on aníbal.

i need to go now. my time is nearly run out and i need to conserve funds. besides, i think the pimply one is rubbing himself under the counter. and even though i'm in sore need of a lot of attention, that's not really the sort of thing i'm looking for right now. or ever. what do they think?

i'm sick as I've ever been for miami right now. when i get back, and i will be coming back, virgencita, we need to meet face-to-face finally. from the way you describe it, your house isn't far from my mother's in coral gables, and that's where i'll be when i get back, because i will not have a penny to my name, and will have to become that relative that everyone detests. pero, we should finally meet one of these days. it's funny that we haven't. i have come to feel you're like a sister to me, or another self. funny, ¿no?

i imagine you dark haired and pale skinned with roses under your cheeks. roses, funny, ¿no? life under the surface, you know, like when winter turns into spring. nice figure, of course, but that i can tell by your pictures. i think you probably have a wonderfully engaging laugh, and before all these problems that you and edu have been having over the past couple of years, you were fond of dancing and entertaining and were often the life of the party.

i can't begin to tell you how dear you have been to me, being a married woman and all and not judging me for what happened between me and aníbal. i imagine that one day we might sit down to a cafecito together or drinks somewhere. we can wear hats and gossip like girlfriends who have known each other for years, telling each other everything that's happened. maybe you might introduce me to some cute guy that works in your office.

someone who isn't married that might want to stay with me for a while. i can't tell you how much i miss miami, i miss hearing cubano. i took the greengrocer's wife, trust me we have nothing in common, just to hear her talk. i miss the long talks we have never had, virgencita, and the walks along the beach where we take each other into our confidence, and the long cries about nothing, and the shopping trips for just the right shoes.

i've only a couple of minutes left on my card and so much to say though i have no idea of what it is.

by the way, my real name is ángelina. funny, ¿no? going all this time without knowing what my real name is. maybe one day you will tell me yours, virgencita?   maybe one day.

cuidate, virgencita, cuidate. if you don't who will?

besitos, teeny tiny besitos until then,

```
                       *.
titi-kitty             .
   ^..^     ~~      . . .
     miooo...xxxx
        **       *
                    *
```

Out of a Philadelphia investment banker's desire to cruise El Malecón in a baby-girl pink 1958 Oldsmobile Ninety-eight Holiday Sedan—Jetaway Hydra-Matic, sleek, with modified wings, he writes—and a Sunnyvale housewife's wish for stories about her birthplace from someone who knows it as well as she remembers it, and through the dedication of an unflagging Guadalupe Yoli fan—a woman in Wisconsin who has every record, on vinyl, on CD, on cassette—and whose mother never taught her Spanish, María_del_Pilar is born.

She answers e-mail with the name lavirgendelcobre and is the— dark-eyed, the blue-eyed, the sea green–eyed—near virgin or sage all-knowing vieja. And it's with a magpie's lust to discriminate the shiniest objects that she sweeps over the island in the dark for what they are looking for.

A sixty-three-year-old woman widowed earlier in the year is only comforted by a yeasty smell that she remembers finding between a lost abuela's breasts, and María_del_Pilar sends back a photograph of a glade caught in impeccable light. A fourteen-year-old boy who inherited a wristwatch from a tío he's never met is sent three prayers and a limpia he's to perform on the second Sunday of each of the succeeding six months. Photos she has of a cane field, the Teatro Nacional, and a recipe for the definitive ropa vieja are ready in a file on her computer.

The opening credits are to roll over an overhead shot of an early morning in the Sierra de los Organos that in quick time rolls through La Plaza de Armas to a glistening, sunny Miami Beach noon and heads upward through a snow-covered Lake Shore Drive evening dressed for Christmas and over an icy Lake Michigan as it moves across the expansive grounds of a lakefront Winnetka estate and into a window where Carolina reads one of the at least thirty e-mails she gets each night addressed to lavirgendelcobre, and as she begins to type, four instant-message windows pop up on the screen, asking, María_del_Pilar, por favor.

Really a gorgeous opening, the director has said. Though he had also told Lupe he had no idea where that money was going to come from, and if any of it happened at all, El Yungi would have to serve as La Sierra de los Organos, and Old San Juan could work for La Plaza de Armas as long as they didn't focus in on any one thing too clearly. Stock footage and C.G.I. would get them through Miami and into Chicago and the lawyer she had met with earlier was allowing them to shoot in his North Shore home—beautiful place . . . a really great guy—in exchange for a cut.

Before bed, Lupe sat on the back porch of her building and had a glass of wine. Across the alley, between the buildings, directly above the moon, she realized it was the first time she had seen Mars and thought she knew what it was that she was looking at.

II.

I can do no wrong, Lupe told her friend the food designer late the following January.

The two women had agreed to meet for lunch, but it seemed that her friend's New Year's resolution had had something to do with not eating.

I've lost fourteen pounds already, she told Lupe as she looked through racks of size 5 dresses at Filene's. It wasn't about the weight, she explained, it was really more about a kind of aestheticism, a way of finding comfort and solemnity in your life—don't worry, nena, I'm not anorexic or nothing—it's something nearly religious, just without God and all, you know, given the time church and that sort of thing takes up, it's much more efficient. And if she was going to believe in something she couldn't see, she preferred that it was a lightness around her hips and waist that gave her the kind of confidence to walk into one of those places where everything has spaghetti straps.

In the months since taking the job, Lupe had bought her sister's children exorbitant Christmas presents, had her apartment repainted, broken it off with the man she had been seeing, and done 397 drawings for the rooms Carolina was to inhabit in the film,

33

each of which the director praised as brilliant for her genius and her clairvoyance.

Overindulged and at times indifferent, her niece and nephew responded to the gifts of a year's worth of swimming and violin lessons as if she had forgotten them, but she knew that it was the kind of gift she and her sister had always dreamed of getting—something that would last a long time, change them, make them better—and as the children had gone on to other packages, Lupe looked across the room as her sister mouthed a tearful Gracias, gracias, muchas gracias, and thought it had been worth it.

Shortly afterward, in bed, while he was still in her, she told the man whom she had been seeing, Let's not do this anymore.

He said, OK, and got up and went to the bathroom, and while he was peeing wondered out loud if they could get back the deposit for New Year's Eve. He brightened a bit when she suggested that he might take someone else, and before he left told her he would send her a check for her half.

She hadn't been sure what it was that she had expected from him. Tears? Regrets? Or just for him to acknowledge that she had made a declaration that separated her from assumption. With him, no matter what their arrangement, she was always someone's girlfriend, could be claimed, tagged, questioned about motives. It was a new year coming and with it disruptions between what was seen and what was expected when she walked into a room.

And it really wasn't until after he was gone that she realized all the searching she had done and the hundreds of chips she had collected in her bag to make comparisons with her rugs and the wood floors that she had painted nearly the same colors as her apartment had been before. The pale yellows and oranges were warm against the cool, crisp, clean white of the wainscoting and kickboards; the dark stain on the floor made the grain glow.

Weeks later she ran into the man she had been seeing with the woman who took her place New Year's Eve, and then she ran into them again a couple of days afterward. The three of them decided that the coincidence was somehow fated and decided to get together that following Friday. They had had drinks, and Lupe, liking this new woman for him so much, thinking he had made the right choice for himself, later found herself pushing her up against a stall door in the ladies' room, and rubbing her breast against hers. Lupe felt the woman's fingers moving toward her groin, and had no idea where it would have led had someone else not come in.

The woman called and left messages for nearly a week afterward to which Lupe didn't respond. Her former boyfriend had sent the check as promised, but instead of cashing it she shredded it along with an offer for roofing.

Her days were mostly spent with the script or at her drawing board.

The writer, a woman named Bell or Beal or Ball or Beryl—Lupe never got it right when people would ask what she was doing lately and inevitably they would correct her—was British and had been very helpful in directing Lupe toward the books and paintings she had been looking at and songs she had been listening to when she wrote lines like Carolina lives in a shrine to Changó.

The woman—Bell or Beal or Ball or Beryl?—had e-mailed that she was confident Lupe would get it right.

You won't encounter the same problems realizing the settings for the character that I did, the woman wrote, and it was the phrase Lupe highlighted when she replied, asking the woman what did she mean by that? Three times with no response before the woman had outright ignored the question and wrote, asking if Lupe had met Mongo Zuniga.

Lupe finally e-mailed the director, who phoned to let her know that he read e-mail, though he was proud to say that he was yet to initiate or respond to one. And he told her the writer was a bit super-fluous at this point, if you think of it. Work through what you can, he said, I'll be in Chicago at the end of the week to see how things are coming along and to clear up any questions you might have.

Yet his jaw had dropped at a sushi restaurant on Damen as he was passed across a librarylike table pages of purple and red encaustic bleeds that ran the yellows and oranges into rooms the script read looked as if they smelled like passion and orchid. Pleasant rooms, though washed with a dangerous pea-colored light, where Carolina brews root teas, turns cards, and her erect nipples can be clearly seen through the sheer indigo robe she wears as she tells a long series of men she is unsure if this is a ghost story or a love story.

Thirty-two unnamed men—Lupe had counted—that the director told her would appear in montage. And men named Augusto, one for each place Carolina has lived: Augusto, her father's best friend while she was still a girl in Cuba, who first seduces her with a pink dress and then rapes her while she is wearing it; Augusto, with one black eye the other milk covered and an infectious laugh—easy as water—who lets go of her hand in a crowd one afternoon and is never seen again; the one she meets when she gets to Miami who treats her as if she were the eighth of his seven daughters before he dies of a heart attack in front of her house. This is either a love story or a ghost story, I'm unsure, she says to the last of the Augustos—either her husband or her pimp, or a husband who looks and sounds like a pimp—on a snowy night before cutting his throat from ear to ear.

The moon, in nearly all its phases, was a series of wax resists clear down to bare paper that Lupe had painted black windows around. Sometimes crescent, half and full in the same room, on the same page, as she found herself at her drawing table wondering what it was, what it would take to want to kill somebody.

Splendid . . . absolutely splendid, the director exhaled over the drawings, moving his hand against their surfaces as if he might push through, fall into them.

Again with the tears? her friend the food designer had asked over the phone that night. What's with this guy? Is he practicing to be a woman or something?

Carolina or María_del_Pilar, or La Virgen del Cobre, one, Lupe responded flatly.

Carolina? the friend giggled in disbelief.

Carolina, Lupe repeated, Carolina.

As Flaubert was to Emma Bovary, soy Carolina, the director had said.

And Lupe had nodded as though she knew what he meant. It would be easier if she needed something from him that she hadn't contracted for if he thought they both thought of him as the woman. She had once dated a man who would occasionally wear her underwear. He could just as easily have stolen it and worn it alone at home, she supposed, but there had been something about his knowing that she knew—was sitting across the table in a restaurant or beside him in the movies in identical thongs and matching teddies under their clothes—that made it real for him.

The director had cradled the drawings as if they were a child and brought them to his bosom as he asked if he might take them to show to Mongo Zoo. Mongo Zuniga, he added when she had clearly failed to hide the puzzlement that hearing that name again brought about. He had said it was like Flaubert and Emma Bovary, and then named the actress and the writer, so again she had nodded.

The day before, when lunch had turned into an afternoon of looking at dresses that would fit a doll at Filene's with her friend the food designer, Lupe had met with the producer for the first time.

Nothing like you would think he would be like, she told her friend, who had moved over to the size 1 rack, stopping to hold what looked like a doll's dress in front of her.

Warm, gracious, Lupe described him. Very kind, very down to earth.

Not a lunch or a dinner, not even coffee. He had met her on a settee in the lobby of the Drake. Very tall and very pale under a mop of dark hair—angular and puppetlike as he seemed to gather all his bones, stand, and shake her hand—up close, where she could see the creases in his face. He gave the impression of a very old boy.

His manner of getting her to sit and, as he said, to the business at hand, had been officious and accurate. He told her that he had spoken with the director and the location scout would be in touch with her as soon as she had a full doctor's release. The word *budget* was written under the word *scout* on his legal pad. He checked off *scout* and then told her that she should take advantage of the opportunity to work with the scout, but reminded her that their per diem would be small so it would be helpful if she kept the scout within budget before he checked that off too.

The best really, he said. This particular scout had worked on the last two films he had done that were in postproduction and he named another that she had seen. The best, really, the best, just . . . the nervous type, and then suggested that Lupe carry her own maps and a portable GPS device while the two of them were out. Just in case, he had said, but clearly elaborating on any topic or questions that he might have had were not on his list.

Lupe's drawings were spectacular, unbelievable; the writer claimed she was beside herself with tears when she saw the color photocopies that had been made of them, the producer had told her.

Everyone was excited, and he asked her if she weren't close to tears knowing that she had brought the writer, the creator of this magnificent work, close to tears? And Lupe had responded that just knowing that color Xeroxes had been made of her work was reason enough.

They even shut Mongo Zoo up for a while, the producer told her, which he had said he couldn't help but equate with approval because The Zoo was the voice of dissent on nearly everything.

You've met Manny Zoo? the producer asked.

And before Lupe could answer, he had said, Mongo Zuniga, this is La Lupe of whom our director says she—and I tend to agree—can do no wrong.

37

With the excitement and bustle that was going on in the lobby, she hadn't noticed the man standing behind the producer.

Underwhelmed, she told her friend the food designer who had produced a tape measure from her purse and was clearly calculating the number of inches she would need to lose before a size zero would fit her.

All this time everyone had been asking me if I had met this Mongo Zoo, like he was some big deal or something, she told her friend. The director, the producer, the woman who's working on the costumes and whatnot are all like: have you asked Mongo Zoo?

Has this been cleared by Mongo Zoo; has Mongo Zoo seen this; are you consulting with Mongo Zoo?

Even when she turned around only to see this small, round, mustachioed Pancho Villa–looking vato standing next to her with his hand out, Lupe still couldn't believe that this was The Zoo from whom everyone was seeking approval.

Sex with The Zoo had been perfunctory and accurate without celebration. Lying in bed next to him afterward, she thought, like a barbecue dinner, satisfying and hardy, nothing special, no surprises, all it had needed was Wetnaps. As with his job on the film as technical consultant, he either knew what to do or knew how or whom to ask.

The Zoo's impressions of both the director and the producer were accurate and very funny. He could do both their voices accurately, but he could also pull the same kind of fraught facial expressions that would begin with the director rubbing his chin before he would ask something like, Look, Zoo, I'm not Latin but if I were, would I . . .

And for a few seconds it seemed to Lupe that she had found an ally—she felt warm and comfortable, and as if someone else understood the situation she was in by taking this movie; and there they were lying together, lying next to each other, brown face to brown face dressing in browner face—until they had stopped laughing and were lying there for a few moments, and instead of silence, she noticed a ticking. It wasn't like one of those loud Swatches, you know, she told the food designer. No, more like someone clicking his tongue against the roof of his opened mouth. Hollow, constant, regular.

Through all the hair on The Zoo's chest, Lupe hadn't noticed the scar that had bisected The Zoo's breastbone. A mechanical valve, two years ago, The Zoo told her, a complete surprise to me. . . . No history, never smoked, ate well, exercised, an aneurysm, now this.

She found out he was almost ten years younger than she, had once owned a sailboat but lost it in a poker game, he wanted to make documentaries about public policy but never offered his politics nor did he give any indications as to where he stood politically, and she found herself increasingly afraid to ask.

She was thinking, You can't stay, just as he said I better get going. As he dressed, she asked what Mongo stood for, and he told her, Just Mongo. My father loved Cuban jazz, he said. I'm Mexican. She said she knew, but she hadn't really thought of it before she had slept with him. And after he had left, she had lain there in her bathrobe thinking about the hand attached to the arm stuck forever outside his chest that made his heart move and how her whole mouth tasted like unwashed cock.

I don't care, I'll fuck The Zoo if I have to too, the food designer said. Just get me on.

And because Lupe could do no wrong and Carolina eats in an outdoor café after weeks of looking for a job in Havana—pays for her first good meal with the money she makes from a man who wants her to put her hair into braids, play on the floor with a doll in a very short dress, not wear panties, and call him Papi—and eats in a fancy Miami restaurant in a borrowed Dior gown, and throws the entire Thanksgiving dinner at her husband the first time in years that they are celebrating alone, she was able to get the food designer three days for each of the six weeks of shooting.

III.

Seven weeks before they were to begin shooting, on the morning of the first of two meetings of all the principle players, the director wanted to know if anyone in the room was gay.

Lupe, the actress playing Carolina, her assistant, her coach, her makeup artist, and her own personal—brought in at the actress's own cost—wardrobe consultant, the actor who plays her husband, one of the Augustos, the actor playing Leandro_Suave, the producer, The Zoo, the cinematographer, his assistant, a lighting guy, the two ADs—particularly the one whom it had been clear the director was sleeping with, a very pretty blonde who was doing it for credit for a course she was taking at CalArts—had all looked around for the possibility of a raised hand.

The other AD—also blond, also a CalArts student; a gangly young man with a scraggly beard and a cloud of cologne-masked body odor—stammered a series of w's that could have been the start of a why or a what that the director interrupted by saying he was sure that they were all well aware that he was involved in a high-profile gay-bashing case, and that had brought him to a new level of consciousness, and he had been talking to as many gay people as possible to see if the new state of awareness he had acquired had validity. And it turned out that r's, l's, and w's were a constant source of problem for the AD, and his question was Where is the washroom? Other than some fidgeting, no one else had a suggestion after the actress offered that perhaps the director should try sucking dick for a while.

For two days they all met in a double suite on a high floor of the Drake that overlooked Lake Michigan. Breakfast and lunch were catered. They went out for dinner only to return and meet late into the night. Lupe never got home before two the next morning.

The actress had moved to the city and was paying for the lawyer and his family to live in a hotel for the next four months so that she could get the feel of what it was to really be Carolina, how she lived, and what she did in that space. The lawyer's guesthouse had been turned into her offices, and she had had her staff and tanning bed moved in.

She had asked Lupe where she got her hair done and who did her nails, and when she found out that Lupe did her own nails she asked if Lupe might show her assistant how she did them. By the morning of the second day, extensions had been added to the actress's head and she and her assistant had run up to Lupe together to compare something she called deep chestnut to Lupe's hair. After that, anytime Lupe answered one of the actress's questions, the actress would respond by saying, Bueno, and rolling the fingers of a hand away from her face and back toward an ear as if it were a manila folder.

They had been assembled together to—as the director had put it— "nail down" principle photography on what he believed to be the heart—or el corazón, he said, looking in the direction of The Zoo, who nodded yes—of the film. He had told them that he always believed in shooting the most difficult part first; that way we all know where we are coming from, he said.

Our beloved Carolina, he gestured toward the actress, will begin by having to age herself twenty—Twenty-five, the actress corrected— twenty-five years, the director corrected himself. And he had lifted a sheet of paper covering a radial chart at the center of which was a color Xerox of the drawing Lupe had done of the room from which

Carolina sends María_del_Pilar into the world.

On the way out from the ray that leads back to Carolina's birthplace in Camagüey is a room in which a young woman thinks of dying every night. Her name is Angelnenita88 and she writes in a pop-up window:

> dulce virgencita, what is it that i long for?
> i have no idea, i don't want a man or
> children or any of the things my mother says
> that a good cubana should want. growing
> up mostly in minnesota, i can't say that i
> have any idea what a good cubana is.

And María_del_Pilar writes back:

> Save every penny even when you're just aching
> for that new dress. . . . Save. You have no idea
> how easy it is to get away even when you think
> getting away is impossible.

And the screen fades to the small dirt farm where Carolina grew. It's an overhead shot of the land and a donkey and a cistern but very few plants. In the distance, there are palm trees that seem still in the hot air as the camera pushes into the tiny kitchen where the young Carolina is bent over, clawing the edge of a wooden table. Her dress is pulled up over her back, underwear at her ankles as she repeatedly takes the strap from her mother.

The director announced that he wanted everyone to rally their support for the actress; he was asking her—within the first week of shooting—to hit the highest emotional arc of the picture. Daring and very unconventional of me, I know, the director had said, but it's the kind of shove in the deep end that this film needs, that we all need.

And he had pointed to the center of the radial, and said, This is where we'll begin. In the room in which:

María_del_Pilar watches.

And Leandro_Suave runs an index finger around the neckband of his T-shirt.

She waits for the next set of pixels to align.

A tiny rip appears.

He swirls the hair where his throat and chest met.

Mi amor, he had written that afternoon.

41

Now, his stomach tight, his hairy navel hugged his fingertip.

The words I can no longer wait, appear on her screen.

Edu was talking to his sister in the other room, she responds.

And she watches as Leandro_Suave puts three fingers into his mouth, and then passes the hand through the hair on his chest. Then again—to the knuckles—he puts his fingers into his mouth, traveling them around his lips, down his throat, and around the back of his neck.

Why do we do this to ourselves? his e-mail said earlier that afternoon. Why? he asks now, when we already know so much about each other that, already belonged to each other, are already tied in a way that never lets go or eases up.

And for most of the first day the director had focused their attention on the third to the last scene in the film right before she cuts her husband's throat, as Carolina asks: And did María_del_Pilar believe him? I wonder. There's no Edu in the next room, no mother still in Cuba dying of pancreatic cancer, she says. George is a fifty-three-year-old investment banker with an enlarged prostate. She looks around the room and wonders out loud what her own dreams of Cuba might look like.

Leandro_Suave looks like the picture he had sent to her. Somewhere between thirty and thirty-five she would have guessed had he not already told her thirty-two. The white in the salt-and-pepper hair that he advertises in his profile, later apologizes for—wrote, once: Virgencita, forgive it, it makes me look older than my years—is undetectable. It looks black and is longish as it passes through his fingers, nearly to his shoulders.

The eyes that he had written were green she discovers are what she had grown up hearing called island eyes: ocean clear, squeezing the color of sand—white, brown, black, gray—through them. Now she was free to imagine them stilled and set off in the distance. He can't see her—she would disappear if she set a camera up—and she is free to imagine those eyes wet and moving, starting at her head, opening her legs against her will, burns from razor stubble across her cheeks and her neck.

He brings his fingers to his mouth again, and she can't help but part her knees a little as he scans the camera down to his erect prick.

Right here. . . . Right here! the director had shouted on the morning of the second day of meetings right before they were going to break while lunch was brought in. This is where Carolina makes her decision to end her oppression, this is the pinnacle, moving toward an end of a life in crisis. . . .

And Lupe had not been surprised—she had been thinking it since the moment that she had first met with the director, since she first read the script—but it had been the intense moment of something hot and sudden as bile as the word White! came out of her mouth.

Once it was there in the room with them, like a spilled satchel of birdseed—the scatter and the rattle—that Lupe had been certain that Leandro_Suave would have only described it as being akin to being laughed at by someone you desperately loved as they all examined the line of drool that ran from his lips that connected them to his left nipple.

Lupe took advantage of their collective blotchy silence to clarify that the room should be white. All of it. Everything in it, she had said, And their words—María_del_Pilar's words, the words of those on the other end—should be projected on the walls, each letter, one at a time, first bold then fading into white, she had said. And she had either been regaining control over her voice or the rush and pound of blood in her ears is what had made it sound calm, faraway and calm.

She had watched the eyes in the room travel toward The Zoo, but not even The Zoo helped her or anyone in the room—he had just sat there, head down, one arm across his chest, the other pinching the bridge of his nose—to step away from what to Lupe sounded like a steel ball circling a tin funnel of silence that she had set off, that she had suddenly begun to wish would rattle on and on and deafen them all to madness. She had closed her eyes and imagined them tripping over each other, falling over their own limbs to get away from it—a tattering of rough edges ripping against soft, pampered flesh—when all of a sudden she had heard the director say, Brilliant, Lupe, that's absolutely brilliant.

There were lots of buts raised around the table—preplanning, pre-production, script consistencies, Lupe had watched as the word symbology passed among them with the same inconsistencies and ill-fitting awkwardness that they had had trying on Cuban expressions from the script the day before—but when it was confirmed by the producer that the costs of the change were most likely negligible and, in fact, might result in the kind of savings that would put them under budget, everyone had quickly agreed that it was a brilliant idea. Everyone, that is, except the actress, who demanded to know from the director what she was going to do, how was she going to relate, how could she be convincing in an all-white room. And Lupe had answered for him, saying, I suppose you'll have to act as brown as you can.

Yet there was little satisfaction that everyone in the room had agreed with her and rallied around the white room. But she had not been able to take pride in the responsibility she had in the actress's sudden sullenness or the fact that throughout the rest of the production she only spoke to Lupe through her assistant.

She had exposed nothing, done nothing, said nothing, and had not even the benefit of an inside joke. It was The Zoo who had taped white sheets of paper over the center of the radial while they had eaten lunch. At dinner, instead of sitting next to the actress and occasionally whispering in her ear as he had the night before, the director had sat next to Lupe, rubbed his knee against hers, and in a low voice—as if he were speaking into his chest—had asked her if she wanted to have a drink in his room.

But he had seemed to have either forgotten or refocused his attention on the actress by the time they were ready to break for the evening. He hadn't noticed Lupe leaving with the smelly second AD. And never mentioned that she had stood him up or acted like he had ever invited her to his room that night.

She had taken the second AD to a tiny obscure jazz club near the lake. A sweet boy really, she thought. By the end of that night he had been the only one who remembered that the white room had been her idea; after dinner it had seemed as if it had always been there. The actress had had her assistant make a note that she wanted to have a bracelet, necklace, and earrings made from tiny plastic banana bunches for the scenes shot in it.

It had been all the smelly AD had to talk about as they sat through the last set at the club and took the drinks offered by the bartender at last call. He thought she was brilliant, he had repeated it in the director's voice, and wondered how she had thought of it. And in the cab back to his hotel, she had given him a hand job to shut him up.

IV.

From his own pocket, the producer had had the Pump Room shut down for the wrap party. The prebuzz around this is already incredible, the director had yelled in her ear over the merengue band, and that was the last she saw of him unless he was being interviewed on television. There had been mojitos and authentic ropa vieja and something called ropa vieja vegan made with tofu. There were empanadas, papusas, plaintains, natilla, and picadillo criollo, frijoles negroes, chicken and yellow rice, tofu and yellow rice, frituras and yucca. The dance floor had been lit with strands of colored lights, and a woman, dressed as an old-time cigarette girl, passed out an array of illegal cigars. The credenza, normally in the center of the dining room, had been replaced with a shiny white 1958 Chevy Impala Coupe with red interior.

Lupe had spent too much money on a black silk sheath that forced her to go braless, and she had worn it with sheer black hose and the highest heels she could find that she could still walk in. She had parted and sliced her hair close to her head, pulling the rest back in a twist. The only makeup she wore was a gash of red lipstick. No earring, no necklace, no bracelet. Men had asked her to dance all night. Men asked her to come back to their rooms, out to dinner sometime, for her phone number, asked her to fuck them.

But there was no one there she wanted to fuck. She smiled though she was sick through to her soul at what she had done, at what she had been part of, sick also with knowing that she would be asked to do it again, and she would miss it, miss it so much that she had no idea when or if she would ever start to say no. She had let them push her around the room, though over their shoulders she whispered— virgencita, María_del_Pilar, decúlpame, lo siento, I'm sorry—a wish that seemed somehow miscalculated and headed moonward.

The Master at St. Bartholomew's Hospital 1914–1916

Joyce Carol Oates

I.

IT WAS TO BE the crucial test of his life.

He will remember: arriving at St. Bartholomew's Hospital by taxi and in a haze of apprehension ascending the broad stone steps and entering the foyer that even at this early hour was shockingly crowded. Medical workers, men in military uniform, civilians like himself looking lost—"Excuse me? If you could please direct me?"—but his gentlemanly manner was not forcible enough to make an impression, his cultured voice was too hesitant. Hospital personnel passed him by without a glance. St. Bartholomew's was a great London hospital in a time of national crisis and its atmosphere of urgency and excitement was a rebuke to him, a solitary civilian figure of a certain age. His large deep-set blinking eyes took in the dismaying fact, as so often they did in recent years, that he was by far the oldest individual in sight. He lacked a uniform of any kind: neither medical nor military. Though surely he knew better, with a kind of childlike vanity he had halfway expected that someone might be awaiting him in the foyer, the eagerly obliging, friendly chairwoman of the volunteers' committee to whom he'd given his name perhaps. But no one resembling this woman was anywhere to be seen. And no one resembling Henry himself was anywhere to be seen. Perplexed, on the edge of being alarmed, he saw that the foyer was oval in shape and that corridors led off it like spokes in a wheel. There were signs posted on the walls he had to approach to read with his weak eyes. He noted that the floor was made of marble that, very worn and grimy now, must have been impressive at one time; high overhead was a vaulted ceiling that gave the foyer the air of a cathedral. Directly above his head was a large dome that yielded a wan, sullen light and trapped against the inside of the dome were several small tittering birds. Poor trapped sparrows, in such a place!

He caught sight of a harried porter making his way through the crowd and dared to pluck at the man's sleeve to ask where volunteers to aid the wounded were to report, but the porter passed by without seeming to have heard. He asked a harried young nurse where he might find Nurse Supervisor Edwards but the young woman muttered something scarcely audible in passing. Keenly he felt the insult: he had not been addressed as *sir*. He was being jostled by impatient strangers, without apology. Medical workers, hospital employees. Men in military uniform. It seemed that new admissions were being brought into the hospital for emergency medical treatment, newly arrived soldiers shipped to London from the besieged French front. Was there a smell of—blood? Bodies? Human anguish? In another part of the hospital, what scenes of suffering were being enacted? Henry was concerned that he might become faint, this was so alien a setting for a man of such inwardness: the Master, as he was fondly, perhaps ironically, called, for the finely nuanced artistry of his mature prose style, which rebuked all simplicity, that is to say all that was raw and unformed, in what he knew to be the Byzantine complexity of the human heart. Now, in this bedlam of a foyer, his breath became short. Since boyhood he'd had a dread of noise, something of a phobia, fearing that his thoughts might be rendered helpless by noise, his soul would be extinguished within it. For our souls are speech, and mere noise cannot be speech. He felt a constriction in his chest, that tinge of pain that precedes an angina attack, and was resolved to ignore it. Sternly he told himself, *You will not succumb! You have come here for a purpose.*

"Sir!"

His sleeve was plucked, somewhat impatiently. It appeared that a woman had been speaking to him; he had not heard amid the noise and confusion. She was an attractive woman of youthful middle age in a dark serge dress or jumper suggestive of a uniform, though she did not wear a starched white cap as nurses did, nor was she wearing rubber-soled shoes. She asked if Henry had come to be a volunteer in the "wounded ward" and quickly he said yes and was led away along one of the corridors. "How grateful I am, that you discovered me! I was feeling quite . . ." His heart beat quickly now at the prospect, at last, of adventure; even as his sensitive nostrils pinched at the acidulous odor of disinfectant, which grew stronger. He was having some difficulty keeping up with the woman in dark serge, who seemed to assume that he was capable of following her at a rapid clip though clearly he was not young, and walked with a cane, favoring his left knee. In both legs he suffered from gout pain and edema; he was a large, portly gentleman who carried himself with a kind of pinched

47

caution, like Humpty Dumpty fearing a sudden spill.

"Please wait here, sir. The nurse supervisor will be with you shortly. Thank you!"

The waiting room was rather a blow to Henry's pride: a makeshift space with but one grimy window looking out onto an airshaft, where some ten or twelve fellow volunteers—sister volunteers, for all were women—were waiting nervously. This was so very different a setting from Lady Crenshaw's Belgravia drawing room where, in the company of others, the Master had joined the Civilian Volunteers Hospital Corps with such excitement. He did not recognize a face here from Lady Crenshaw's gathering yet he steeled himself for the inevitable *Is it—Mr. James? What an honor! I am one of your greatest admirers*—and was both relieved and somewhat disappointed when no one seemed to recognize him. Courteously he greeted the women, without singling out any individual, at once seeing that these were ladies of the privileged class to which, at least by reputation, Henry James belonged; though judging from the fussy quality of their clothing and footwear, and by the opulence of their wedding rings, he understood that they were surely richer than he. All the straight-back chairs in the waiting room were taken and when one of the younger women stood to offer her chair to him, quickly Henry thanked her and murmured it would not be necessary.

The Master's face throbbed with indignation. As if he were so very infirm, at the age of seventy-one! Pointedly he remained standing just inside the doorway, leaning on his cane.

In the corridor, hospital workers were carrying patients on stretchers, some of them unconscious, if not comatose, into the interior of the building; pushing them in wheelchairs and on gurneys, in a ghastly procession at which it was impossible not to stare, with mounting pity and alarm. Here and there were ambulatory young men hobbling on crutches, escorted by nurses. Some were still wearing their badly bloodied uniforms or remnants of uniforms. There were bandaged heads, torsos, and limbs wrapped in blood-soaked gauze; there were hideous gaps where limbs were missing. Henry turned away, shielding his eyes. So this was war! This was the consequence of war! He had quite admired Napoleon, at one time— the *gloire* of military triumph and, yes, tyranny; precisely why, he would have been ashamed to speculate. *Because I am weak. Weak men bow to tyrants. Weak men fear physical pain; their lives are stratagems for avoiding pain.* He felt the tinge of angina pain, like a schoolboy taunt.

He'd had such attacks. He was not in perfect health: his blood pressure was high, he was overweight, easily winded. In his inside coat pocket he carried a precious packet of nitroglycerine tablets, to swallow quickly should the pain increase.

Prudently, Henry retreated from the doorway. From somewhere a crude footstool was found for him, which he consented to accept, with gratitude; not wishing to note, in the women's eyes, that veiled concern one might feel for an older relation. Awkwardly Henry sat on the stool, gripping his cane. Almost, he'd forgotten why he was here, in this cramped place; for whom he, along with these ladies with whom he was not acquainted, seemed to be waiting. He did not join with them as they murmured anxiously together, complaining of being rudely treated by the hospital staff, and lamenting the latest news of German aggression. News of further atrocities wreaked by the Imperial German Army in Belgium, the fear that England would be invaded next. Much was being made in the newspapers of the fact that, in this hellish war of the new century, many numbers of civilians were being deliberately killed. That morning, Henry had not been able to finish reading the *Times* but had had to set the paper aside at breakfast, and then, feeling very weak, he had not been able to finish breakfast. Since the outbreak of the war in late August, now nearly five weeks ago, he had taken to reading a half-dozen papers, both dreading the lurid news and eager for it. His own so finely textured prose he had set aside, he was transfixed now by the banner headlines, the astonishing photographs unlike any previously published in British journals, the vividly described battlefield scenes, accounts of the bravery of British officers and soldiers and of their tragic woundings and deaths, that quite outshone the newspapers' interior, editorial pages with their reasoned analyses of the political situation. His nerves were raw, wounded. He slept but fitfully. He did not wish to think that, from this new wartime perspective, all of the Master's efforts might be seen as but the elegant flowering of a civilization that had, all along, been rotting from within, and was now in danger of extinction. He thought, *I have outlived my life.* And yet: he'd signed up as a hospital volunteer. He'd given money: to the Belgian Refugee Relief Fund organized by a wealthy woman friend, to the International Red Cross, and to the American Volunteer Motor-Ambulance Corps. Since the outbreak of this hideous war with a rapacious Germanic aggressor, Henry had been almost reckless in giving away money that he could scarcely afford to give away; his earnings for 1913, as for 1912 and preceding years, were scarcely more than one thousand pounds.

So scorned by the vast, plebeian reading public yet, so ironically, designated in literary circles the Master! Though his heart was broken, yet Henry was resolved to see the humor here.

"Ladies. You will come with me to Ward Six." A nurse of some authority, about forty-five, rather stout, with flushed cheeks, appeared abruptly in the doorway: Nurse Supervisor Edwards. Seeing the lone gentleman in the waiting room, Nurse Edwards amended, with more annoyance than apology, "And you, sir. Now."

Again, Henry felt the sting of insult. His large somber face darkened with embarrassment as, with the assistance of one of the women, he heaved himself to his feet.

With no more ceremony, Nurse Supervisor Edwards led the contingent of volunteers along the treacherous corridors, scarcely taking notice if they were able to keep pace with her. The nurse supervisor was a stalwart woman who carried herself with a military bearing. She wore a starched white blouse and a white apron over a navy blue skirt that fell nearly to her ankles; on her feet were white rubber-soled shoes. Her gray hair was tightly coiled into a bun and on her head was a starched white cap. Her brusque manner suggested nothing sociable or yielding, as one might expect of a woman of her class, in the presence of her superiors, for Nurse Edwards seemed not to consider the volunteers her social superiors, which was disconcerting. Henry, at the rear of the wavering procession, was made to feel uneasy by any such breach of decorum, which did not bode well for his first morning of volunteer work. The congestion of the hospital alarmed him and such odors!—he could not allow himself to identify.

Yet more dismaying, in the midst of such rank smells, attendants were pushing trolleys laden with food trays, smelling of rashers, grease, sweet baked goods.

Ward Six was, at the very first impression, a hive of sheer noise: a vast open space like a hall, crammed with cotlike beds so close together you could not imagine how the medical staff might ease between them. The volunteers were being told that all that was wanted from them, at least initially, was to "comfort"—"visit with"—the wounded men who were capable of communication. Those who could speak French were urged to seek out the French-speaking Belgians. Volunteers were not to offer any sort of medical opinion or advice but to defer to the medical staff exclusively. They were not to register alarm, or horror, or pity, or disgust, but only to provide solace. At the rear of the group that stood out so awkwardly, in civilian clothes, there was the elderly gentleman volunteer leaning on his cane, his large, regal, sculpted-looking head held erect even as Henry desperately fought a sensation of nausea. The smells in Ward Six were repulsive, terrifying: rank animal smells, bodily wastes, a powerful stink as of rancid, rotting flesh: gangrene? And yet Henry was being led—where? What was expected of him? How had he stepped, as in a mocking dream, from the splendor of Lady Crenshaw's drawing room to this hellish place?

In one of the narrow, badly stained beds, a young man looking scarcely more than eighteen lay motionless between thin covers, head wrapped in gauze, eyes covered like a mummy's, if indeed he had eyes any longer; at a ragged, red-stained hole where a mouth, or a jaw, should have been, a nurse was inserting a tube, with some difficulty, that the wounded man might be fed. Henry looked away, panicked. In a bed at his very elbow, another young man lay raving with pain, his features feverish and distended, his right leg missing. On all sides were cries of pain and fear, moans, maddened eyes of terror. Henry stumbled forward, led farther into the ward. What was this—flies brushing against his face? And on the discolored ceiling overhead, clusters of black flies, glistening. There were loud voices, male voices of authority. Henry was deeply grateful to see at least two doctors on the scene but he dared not approach them. Another time he stumbled; he was being led forward perhaps to visit with one of the Belgian soldiers, quite distracted by seeing in a tangle of bed sheets what appeared to be a disfigured male torso, raw moist flesh like a side of beef, and the young man's head wrapped in gauze, lying at an unnatural angle as if the neck had been broken. Someone was calling, *Sir!* with an air of concern. Henry turned to see who it was, and what was wanted of him, in that instant seeing on a trolley in the aisle, in what appeared to be a porcelain bedpan, or a container very like a bedpan, bloody human vomit yet writhing with white grains of rice—maggots? Had one of the stricken men been infested with—maggots? Henry stumbled forward, the skin of his face taut and cold and his lips fixed in a small dazed smile very unlike the aloof, poised smile of the Master in public settings; one of the young nurses was leading him to the bedside of a ravaged-looking young man with pale blue dazed eyes, and dimly he was aware that his fellow volunteers did not appear to be having so much difficulty as he was and in protest he thought, *But they are women, they are accustomed to the horrors of the body.* Henry's vision was

51

rapidly narrowing, he seemed suddenly to be peering with difficulty through a darkened tunnel. At the bedside of the dazed-looking young man he began to stammer, *"Pardonnez-moi? S'il vous plaît, je suis—"* but a black pit opened suddenly at his feet, he fell into it, and was gone.

II.

Unspeakable. Beyond shame. As civilization itself crashes.

That shameful day at St. Bartholomew's he would mark in his diary with a tiny black-inked cross: †.

Scattered through the diary, most concentrated since the outbreak of the war, were these mysterious black-inked crosses, to indicate, in secret code, Days of Despair: † † † ††††.

The rare Day of Happiness the diarist noted with a tiny red-inked cross: †.

He'd had to devise a code, for secrecy's sake. So very much of the Master's passional life was secret, subterranean. No biographer would ever plumb the depths of his soul, he vowed.

"Except perhaps it is a shallow soul, after all. And will become more shallow with age."

How disappointed he was with himself! How poorly the Master had performed, put to the test.

In dread of what he would discover, Henry glanced back through the diary. On numerous pages there were cryptic black crosses. Not very frequently, red crosses. The last red cross seemed to have been months ago, in June: friends had come by motorcar to have lunch with Henry in Rye, at Lamb House. Since then, only just unmarked days, or days marked in black.

The elderly gentleman has fallen. Revive him quickly and get him out of here.

Somehow, they'd gotten Henry onto his feet. Strapping male attendants. He'd been half carried out of the ward and to the front entrance of the hospital and by taxi he'd been delivered back home to the brownstone near the river from which, earlier that morning, in such hopeful spirits, he'd bravely departed.

In the privacy of his flat for days afterward Henry heard the nurse supervisor's uplifted voice that had registered rather more vexation than concern or even alarm. The terrible woman, trained as a nurse, and no doubt a very skilled nurse, who would not have greatly cared if the elderly volunteer had died, so long as he didn't die in her ward.

Elderly gentleman. Out of here. Quickly!

What erupted from the Master's pen, scrawled in his notebook, was but shrieks of raw animal pain.

    brute matter/ brutes

    atrocities against unarmed civilians, children & the elderly

    rot/ gangrene/ *gloire* of history

    private wounds, mortification: teeth extracted

    angina/ jaundice/ shingles/ food loathing

    migraine/ malaise

    crash of civilization/ sickness unto death

    the world as a raw infected wound

    the world as a hemorrhaging wound

    Ward Six, St. Bartholomew's Hospital: an anteroom of hell

    damned dentures ill fitting / overly shiny/ costly

    failure of the New York Edition

    piteous royalties, after a career of four decades

    Imperial German Army: marching columns of voracious ants

    deep inanition & depression

    "not to wake—not to wake": my prayer

    "avert my face from the monstrous scene"

Yet how to avert his face, when the *monstrous scene* enveloped him on all sides, like rising sewage!

Here is a secret of the Master's early life: how in 1861, as a boy of eighteen living in Newport, Rhode Island, with his family, at a time of mounting war excitement when men and boys were eagerly enlisting in the Union Army to fight against the rebellious Confederates, Henry had claimed to have suffered an "obscure hurt"—a "prevailing pain" in the region of his back, which made enlisting as a soldier, for him, not possible.

And so, Henry had been spared further bodily harm and even the possibility of harm. So sensitive a young man!—so clearly unfitted, as both his parents discerned, for any sort of "masculine" endeavor like the army, or marriage; he'd been spared even accusations of *coward, malingerer.*

And yet it was so. He was a coward, and a malingerer. At the age of seventy-one, as at eighteen. He had hidden from the great, grave dangers of war while others of his generation had gone off to fight to preserve the Union and to end slavery. Some had died on the battlefield, some had returned maimed, crippled. Some had returned without evident injury yet altered, matured, and "manly." Henry had hidden away and very soon then Henry had traveled to Europe, to inaugurate his destiny.

In the bay window of his London flat, in the attenuated light of autumn, he thought of these matters obsessively. Stiffly he sat on a leather divan poised to write, pen in hand and a notebook on his knees, his brooding eyes turned toward the river in the near distance where tugboats and barges passed with ever more urgency in this time of war. In his right hand he gripped a pen, but he could not write. He could not concentrate to write. Thoughts ran helter-skelter through his mind like that lightning. Why had that nurse supervisor woman taken so immediate a dislike to him? Why to *him*? That by his clothes and bearing he was a gentleman and Nurse Edwards was hardly of the British genteel class, he could understand; yet the woman's animus had seemed personal. His heart beat in resentment and fear of her, as though she were close by, in this very room with him.

Elderly gentleman. Out of here!

Each time Henry heard the voice, more clearly he heard: the gratification, the malicious satisfaction in it.

"She has triumphed over 'the Master.' There is nothing to be done—is there?"

Henry was not one to drink. Not alone. Yet now in this season of hell 1914, with ever more distressing war news in the papers and this personal shame gnawing at his bowels, to steady his shredded nerves and to allow him to sleep, very deliberately Henry poured a glass of heavy Madeira port for himself, to sip as he brooded. Recalling then, as the port began to warm his veins, a memory he had quite suppressed: how, some years ago when he'd first acquired Lamb House in Rye, to live a more concentrated and a more frugal bachelor-writer existence than seemed possible in London, he'd been kept awake one summer night by a hellishly yowling creature and had gone outside, in a rage quite uncharacteristic of him, located the creature, a cat, a large black-and-white mottled cat, spoke at first cajolingly to the cat to win its trust, and then, to his own astonishment, struck the cat with his cudgel with such force that the poor creature died on the spot, its head broken.

Immediately then, Henry had backed away, beginning to vomit.

Yet in recalling the incident, as the port so warmly coursed through his veins, he felt rather differently about it: more astonishment than horror, and a thrill of exultation.

III.

"Why, sir. You are back with us."

The voice was flat, unwelcoming. The mineral eyes stared and the clenched bulldog jaws suggested how badly Nurse Supervisor Edwards wished she might forbid him entry to Ward Six, but of course a mere member of the nursing staff, regardless of her rank, had not that authority. For the volunteer program had proved popular in the understaffed hospital and Henry, this time acknowledged as "Mr. James," was being escorted into the ward by one of the senior physicians on the hospital staff, a close friend of Lady Crenshaw.

Henry murmured yes, he was back: "I want so badly to be *of use,* you see. As I am rather too old to sign up as a soldier."

Under the wing of the physician, one of the administrators of St. Bartholomew's, Henry knew himself invulnerable to the nurse supervisor. He would not challenge the woman's authority but simply avoid her, for Nurse Edwards was that most disagreeable of females: one who cannot be charmed. A younger and more congenial nurse had been assigned to oversee the morning's volunteers and was leading Henry forward to introduce him to patients who were not so desperately injured or in such delirium that volunteers were discouraged from approaching them. Ward Six did not seem, to Henry's relief, to be so chaotic as it had several days before, though the odors were as discomfiting as before, and it was an ominous sight that opaque white curtains had been set up around several of the beds to hide what was taking place inside.

This time, Henry was better prepared for his visit to St. Bartholomew's: he'd thought to bring a basket of soft, chewable fruits and chocolates, small jars of jam, crossword puzzles, and slender books of verse by Tennyson, Browning, Housman. (He had considered bringing Walt Whitman's more robust yet controversial verse, but had decided against it; for he was not altogether certain that he approved of this "barbaric" American poet entirely.) Greeting the first of his patients, a sullen-faced young man who lay stiffly propped against what appeared to be soiled pillows of his narrow cot of a bed, Henry tried not to be distracted by the young man's deep-shadowed eyes and haggard face but to speak in an uplifted manner, as the female volunteers were doing.

"Hello! I hope that I am not disturbing . . ."

With a grimace of dissatisfaction, or pain, the young man lifted his eyes toward the gentleman volunteer stooping over his bed like a hulking bird of prey, but, as if the effort were too much for him, his gaze stopped at about the shiny top button of the gentleman's vest. His thin lips twitched in a mechanical smile in mimicry of the sort of polite behavior youth is expected to exhibit in the presence of elders for whom they have not the slightest feeling. Henry had been informed that the young man was a "shrapnel case" but he couldn't see what the young man's injuries were at a quick glance; he was relieved that, unlike many of his comrades, he didn't seem to have suffered a head injury and was not missing an eye. Henry asked what was the young man's name?—and was told in a dispirited mumble what sounded like "Hugh"; Henry asked where was the young man from?—and was told what sounded like "Manchester." To this, Henry could think of no response: unconsciously he was pressing a hand against his chest, as if to contain his heart, which beat and lurched like a drunken thing.

Other inquiries into Hugh's background, his position in the army, were answered in the same way, curtly, rather sullenly, with that same fixed mock smile, while the bloodshot gaze held steady, not rising to Henry's face. Henry wanted to plead, *But, my boy, look at me: my eyes! How yearning I am, to give comfort to you.* Fumbling to say, as if such expressions were common to the Master, "And where, Hugh, did you 'see action' in France?—I assume it was France?" Now the young man's face stiffened, his shoulders began to quiver as if he were very cold. Blundering Henry had said the wrong thing, had he? Yet what else might one say in these circumstances? Clearly Hugh wished now to talk, in a hoarse, anguished voice, telling Henry a not-very-coherent story of himself and several other soldiers in his platoon, at Amiens; where someone seemed to have been killed, and where Hugh had been wounded; the last thing Hugh remembered was a deafening explosion. More than two hundred shrapnel fragments had penetrated his legs and lower body, he'd been told afterward. He'd almost died of blood poisoning, "sepsis." Now Henry saw that the young man's legs beneath the thin blanket didn't look normal; the muscles appeared wasted, atrophied. And Hugh spoke so slowly, with such a distortion of his face, Henry had to wonder if he'd suffered some sort of brain injury, too, or had become mentally unbalanced by his ordeal. Now Hugh's eyes snatched at his, in unmistakable misery and anger. He was trying not to cry; tears ran down his cheeks. Not knowing what he did, Henry fumbled to grip the young man's hands, which shook badly. The fingers were icy cold yet closed eagerly about Henry's fingers. "Dear boy, take courage.

You are safe now on British soil, you will get the very best medical care in this hospital and be sent home to your family in . . ." These words, which might have issued from a politician's smiling mouth, somehow issued from the Master's mouth; he had no idea where they'd come from, or whether in any way they might be true. He was shaken by the fact that for the first time in his life he had reached out to touch another person in this way, and this person a stricken young man, a stranger.

"You will be well! You will walk again! I am sure of it."

Only the watchful mineral gaze of Nurse Supervisor Edwards, elsewhere in the ward, prevented Henry from sinking to his knees beside the young man's bed.

Also that day in Ward Six, smiling gravely and moving with portly dignity from bedside to bedside, pulse quickened in excitement he took care to conceal, the Master visited with young wounded soldiers named Ralph, William, Nigel, Winston. They were from Newcastle, Yarmouth, Liverpool, Margate. He read comforting verse to them ("Loveliest of trees, the cherry now / Is hung with bloom along the bough"), and he offered gifts from his basket, like a doting grandfather. How fatigued he was, as if he'd been awake for a day and a night, or had traveled a great distance. He had not become accustomed to the shock of seeing so many young, injured, and incapacitated men, and to the strange, unsettling intimacy of their being in their beds, and in hospital attire; nor had he become accustomed to the flies, and roaches underfoot, and the odors of human waste, gangrenous flesh. He was chastised to think how there were simply no names for such things in the literary works he and his companions wrote, as in their conversations with one another; in all of the Master's lauded fiction, not one individual, male or female, inhabited an actual physical body, still less a body that *smelled.*

Walking with a handkerchief pressed against his nose, as Henry left Ward Six he managed to avoid several of the other volunteers who were also leaving, for he was impatient to be alone with his thoughts. The ladies' warmhearted but banal chatter, after Ward Six, would be intolerable.

The Master returned home by taxi. Staggered up the steps of the brownstone building, sank heavily onto the leather divan in the bay window. How exhausted he was, and yet—how exhilarated! That evening he wrote in his diary, *It is as if my skin had been peeled off, and all my nerves exposed.* He marked the day with a red cross, the first in months, and beside the tiny cross the enigmatic initial *H.*

*

For weeks, months in succession in the quickly waning year 1914 the oldest of the volunteers at St. Bartholomew's Hospital moved like one entranced. Each time he stepped into the tumult of Ward Six the vision was a revelation and a shock to him. So many wounded! Maimed! Such pain, grief! Such a spectacle of suffering seemed to the Master a rebuke of him, as of his ornate, finely spun art for which the world had lauded him. Half in shame he thought, *This has been the actual world—has it?*

He had not seen Hugh again.

Hugh, you. To whom he might have given his (aging, ailing) heart.

Entering Ward Six the morning after his initial visit and with a fluttering pulse he saw a hellish sight: a white-curtained screen around the young soldier's bed, hiding what took place inside. Henry stopped dead in his tracks. Henry could come no nearer.

"You must not become attached to the young men, sir. You will see why."

Sharp-eyed Nurse Supervisor Edwards had noted the look on Henry's face. She spoke sternly yet not without sympathy.

Henry mumbled a reply. In truth, he could think of no reply.

If there was not to be Hugh, there remained Ralph, William, Nigel, Winston. The newly arrived wounded from the front line, dazed with pain, missing arms, legs, eyes, red-haired Alistair, blue-eyed Oliver, to these as to others Henry would read verse, and he would read from the newspapers; he who had made it a practice to dictate to a stenographer for years, to ease the painful writer's cramp in his right hand, found himself now delighted to "take dictation" and to write letters to soldiers' families, in the most legible and elegant hand of which he was capable. Often it was a painfully emotional experience, writing such a letter; both the young man, and his elderly stenographer, were moved to tears. At the conclusion, if the young man could not see to sign his name, or could not manage a pen unassisted, Henry would grip the young man's hand to aid him in signing.

He paid for postage, he posted letters. He brought his usual gifts, to be passed around the ward. He brought adventure novels: Sir Walter Scott, R. D. Blackmore, Wilkie Collins. (For quickly he'd seen how unlikely it was that any of these young men, even the more intelligent among them, would wish to stumble through the Master's highly refined, relentlessly analytical and slow-moving prose, that focused exclusively on the gossamer relations of men and women of privilege who had never suffered even the mild violence of a slap to the face.) He spent money rather recklessly, buying such items of clothing as underwear, socks, bathrobes, even pillowcases and linen, warm shawls, blankets, slippers, shoes. Though his heart sometimes pounded with the strain, he helped young men rise from their beds, adjust themselves to crutches or into wheelchairs; he was an eager volunteer to push the wheelchair patients to a sunroom at the rear of the building, overlooking the hospital grounds. On sunny days, he pushed them outside along the graveled paths beneath exquisitely beautiful plane trees, though the effort was considerable, leaving him short of breath.

If he died in the effort—in a young man's arms, perhaps!—it would not be so very tragic a death.

In this winter of 1914–1915 the diary was riddled with red-inked crosses beside such initials as *A., T., W., N., B.*

"My secret! My happiness, no one must know."

For there seemed to him, in the very tumult of his blood, something sinful, indeed vulgar and demeaning, about happiness.

Now reading to the young wounded men, in the richly modulated tone of one who can barely keep his voice from quavering, the thrilling, suggestive verse of his great countryman Walt Whitman:

> Shine! shine! shine!
> Pour down your warmth, great sun!
> While we bask, we two together.

And these hypnotic words pulsing with the surge of his own awakened blood:

> O camerado close! O you and me at last, and us two only.
> O a word to clear one's path ahead endlessly!
> O something ecstatic and undemonstrable! O music wild!
> O now I triumph—and you also;
> O hand in hand—O wholesome pleasure—O one more desirer
> and lover!
> O to haste firm holding—to haste, haste on with me.

In his diary the wistful plea *Who would be Master, if he could be—"Camerado"?*

Pushing one of the young men in his wheelchair, along the crowded corridors of St. Bartholomew's, suddenly he might confide, daringly: "D'you know, my ghost will haunt this place, I think! Long after the Great War has ended, and you have all been discharged, my melancholy figure will continue to haunt this site—the 'ghost lover.'"

Ghost lover. This was daring. This was risking a great deal. But the hospital so thrummed with noise, whichever young man he happened to be pushing in a wheelchair at this time, lost in a disturbing dream of his own, grimacing with physical discomfort, wouldn't trouble to ask the elderly volunteer to repeat his curious words.

"Oh! What has . . ."

Hastily Henry laid aside his copy of *Leaves of Grass* to stoop over the stricken young man in the wheelchair whose name, in this terrifying moment, he'd quite forgotten, as the young man began shuddering and convulsing. Out of his anguished mouth blood welled, running down his chin and splashing onto his chest; Henry, in a panic, fumbled to remove from his pocket and to unfold, with trembling fingers, one of his monogrammed spotless white linen handkerchiefs, to attempt to wipe away the ghastly welling blood.

". . . dear boy, what has happened? O God, don't let . . ."

An alarm went up, hospital workers intervened. The stricken patient was wheeled away for emergency treatment and the elderly volunteer, looking somewhat distraught, was sent home.

. . . must for dear life make our own counterrealities.

In the seclusion of his London flat on a quiet street, in the privacy of his bedchamber the Master reverently unfolded the linen handkerchief and for a long time stared at the damp crimson stain that seemed to him star shaped, symmetrical. "Dear boy! I pray that God is with you." Though the Master was not a religious man, nor in the habit of murmuring such prayers, even in private. He kissed the crimson stain. Carefully he placed the handkerchief, unfolded, on a windowsill to dry. And when it was dry, that evening before he retired to bed, he tenderly kissed the stain again, and placed the handkerchief, still opened, beneath his heavy goose-feather pillow, as he would place it for many nights to come; taking care each morning to remove the handkerchief, and to hide it away, that his housekeeper, Mrs. Erskine, would not discover it and think, to her horror, that the Master had been coughing up blood in the night.

In his diary for these somber days so fraught with emotion, Henry would record, in delicious code, that no biographer might ever decipher, both black-inked and red-inked crosses: † † † † †.

"Sir! You have suffered a shock, I see."

Formidable Nurse Supervisor Edwards seemed, by her stance, to be blocking the entrance to Ward Six. Stolidly she stood with her strong, compact arms folded across her large, hard-looking bosom. Her spotless white-starched nurse's cap, her spotless starched-white blouse and white apron, like the navy blue skirt that flared at her wide hips and dropped nearly to her ankles, gave her the look, both austere and willful, of a Roman Catholic nun. Nurse Edwards's voice was one of seeming sympathy belied by the ironic twist of her lips and the accusatory stare of her close-set eyes.

"A—shock? I? But—"

"Yesterday. Here. A sudden hemorrhaging, I was told. You—meant to give aid. You are the most devoted of our volunteers, sir? We do thank you, we are most grateful." Still the nurse supervisor fixed the Master with her ironic, accusatory gaze, which provoked him to but a stammering and faltering reply, curtly interrupted by Nurse Edwards as she turned away, to allow him passage:

"Such shocks show in the face, sir. Be warned."

She knows! She has seen into my heart. The woman is my enemy: nemesis. How can I prevail upon my nemesis to take pity on me!

It was so, in Henry's eyes there had come to be an unnatural glisten, and in his lined, flaccid cheeks a ruddy blush, as if his face had been slapped. Like an opiate, the spell of St. Bartholomew's Hospital had worked its way into his bloodstream.

"Not I! The least likely of 'addicts.' "

How disapproving the Master was of such weaknesses in others:

heavy drinking, eating, tobacco smoking; lethal absinthe, and yet more lethal opium (in its genteel guise beloved by many fashionable women, as "laudanum"); above all, illicit, reckless, and demeaning liaisons with persons of a questionable rank or class. (The Master had had no sympathy, indeed, for the "squalid tragedy" of his younger contemporary Oscar Wilde whose scandalous trial for "unnatural acts" with young men had captivated London in the 1890s, and had primly refused to sign a petition to alleviate the harsh condition of Wilde's prison sentence.) Yet Henry had to concede, removed from the febrile atmosphere of St. Bartholomew's, that he had become— to a degree!—"addicted" to it: to the young, wounded, and so often maimed and crippled soldiers of Ward Six. Awake and asleep he was haunted by their faces: no less powerfully in the privacy of his London flat than in their actual presence. How innocent they seemed to him, in the freshness of youth! How like boys, like mere children, fearful of what had happened to them, the terrible, perhaps irremediable alterations of their young bodies, yet, somehow, so heartrendingly susceptible to hope. Henry's relations with them were rarely other than formal for he dared not touch them lingeringly; if, assisting the nurses, he aided in feeding those incapable of feeding themselves, yet he took care not to press too near, and not to stare too avidly, with eyes of yearning. Only in the privacy of his bedchamber might the elderly volunteer murmur aloud: "I would die for you, my dear boys! If I could—somehow—take your place. These old, ailing legs I would give you, who have lost your legs! My breath, my heart, my very blood: if I could fill you with my life, and make you fit and whole again, my dear boys, I *would*."

Such proclamations made him breathless, light-headed as if he'd been drinking. Pacing about in his bedchamber, striking his fists lightly together, whispering, flush-faced, and eyes glistening and his collar torn open at the throat, that he might breathe more freely.

In secret, in this bedchamber, in a closet with a lock to which Mrs. Erskine had no key, Henry had set up an altar: on a beautifully carved mahogany box he had placed two votive candles to illuminate what he'd come to call his "sacred relics," which consisted, so far, of several handkerchiefs monogrammed *HJJ*, stiffened with dried blood; strips of medical gauze stained with blood and/or mucus; clumps of hair; a signet ring; a sock; several photographs (of young, smiling uniformed men taken in the happier days before they'd been shipped away to war); even a rosary, of shiny black beads, left behind by a discharged soldier. It was not discreet of him, Henry knew, to purloin such items at the hospital, nor was it discreet to assemble them in such a way, and in moods of wild exhilaration to kneel before the makeshift altar by candlelight and kneel and clasp his hands together in an attitude of prayer. The Master did not believe in prayer, as the Master did not believe in God. Yet his lips moved in the most giddy prayers: "Dear boys! My loves! You live in me. I live in you. But no one must know of you. Not even *you.*"

Art is long and everything else is accidental and unimportant.

So the Master wrote to a prominent literary acquaintance, an elder of distinction like himself. Smiling to think how biographers of decades to come, in reverence for his genius, would seize upon such pronouncements with little cries of discovery.

IV.

"My blood is bad. Like my soul."

His name was Scudder: bluntest of names. His face creased in repugnance should anyone call him by his first name: Arthur.

Scudder was an amputee, a new arrival on Ward Six. You could see that he'd had a boy's face at one time, now scarred, scabbed, furrowed, his skin so very pale as to seem greenish. Scudder had had a head wound, his hair was shaved close to his scalp, which was luridly crisscrossed with scars. For all Scudder's misery he had an air of authority, and so the elderly gentleman volunteer who read to him from the London *Times* and the Manchester *Guardian* and from the less sentimental poets, provided him with math-puzzle books and licorice twists, and pushed him, in reasonably good weather, along the graveled paths behind the great hospital, wished to honor him by calling him "Lieutenant Scudder."

For Scudder was an officer, or had been. But now Scudder sneered: "Not here. No more bloody 'Lieutenant.' Scudder will do."

Scudder had rebuffed the other volunteers. Scudder was dismissive and rather rude to the hospital staff and even to the physicians of Ward Six and Nurse Supervisor Edwards herself and so Henry did not take it personally that Scudder might speak contemptuously to him.

"'Scudder.'" Henry pronounced the name as if tasting it: so uncommonly blunt.

This opiate, St. Bartholomew's Hospital! The smells of men's bodies, in cramped intimacy. Body perspiration, body wastes, flatulent gases like noxious fumes. Enamel bedpans, soiled sheets. On soiled pillowcases, minuscule lintlike dots: bedbugs. And amid all this, such astonishing individuals as Scudder, from Norwich.

In all of the Master's prose, not one Scudder. From Norwich.

Henry's angina heart beat heavily. Henry's large unsteady hand pressed against the front of his vest, grasping.

Scudder breathed harshly, at times laboriously. But Scudder was shrewd. Fixing Henry with a frank, rude stare: "And you? What is your name?"

"Why, I've told you, I think—Henry."

"Henry is what someone has baptized you. Tell me what, in your blood, you *are:* your surname."

Seated close beside Scudder's cot, in a smelly, fly-buzzing corner of the ward, Henry stammered, "My s-surname? It scarcely matters; I am not wounded."

Irritably Scudder said, "What matters to me, about me, is not that I am 'wounded.' 'Wounded' is a damn stupid accident that happened to me, as it has happened to so many. My identity is not bloody 'wounded' and my intention is to outlive bloody 'wounded.'"

Scudder's accent suggested middle class: father a tradesman? butcher? Not a public-school background but military school.

"Of course! I see . . ."

Henry felt his face burn in embarrassment. Nothing is so annoying as condescension, in the elderly for the young. He had hardly meant to insult this outspoken young army officer and could not think how on earth to apologize without further blundering.

"Well, then? Henry?"

This was the first time in his months as a volunteer at St. Bartholomew's that one of the young men of Ward Six had asked Henry his surname, as it was the first time that a young bedridden man had made it a point to turn to him, to look him full in the face, as if actually seeing *him.*

Ah, the effect of those eyes! Bloodshot eyes, jeering eyes, sunk deep in their sockets, yet moist and quivering with life. Shyly, Henry murmured: "James. My surname is—James."

Scudder cupped his hand to his ravaged ear, to indicate that Henry must speak louder.

"My surname is—James."

It was uttered! Henry was overcome by a strange, wild shyness. A deep flush rose in the face that had been described more than once as sculpted, monumental; his cheeks throbbed with heat.

"James. Henry James. Has a ring to it, eh? You are something to do with—journalism?"

"No."

"Politics?"

"Certainly, *no*."

"Not an MP? House of Lords?"

"No!" Henry laughed, as if rough fingers were tickling his sides.

"Retired gentleman, in any case. Damned good of you, at your age, to be mucking about in this hellhole."

Henry protested: "St. Bartholomew's is not a hellhole—to me."

"What is it, then? Paradise?"

Gravely Henry shook his head no. He would not contradict this argumentative young man. Though thinking, as Scudder laughed, a harsh laugh that shaded into a fit of prolonged bronchial coughing: *This is paradise; God has allowed me entry before my death.*

In Henry's diary for that day not one but two red-inked crosses beside the initial *S*. And on the altar, a stiff mucus-and-blood–stained strip of gauze, into which the lieutenant had coughed.

"How reckless you are, dear Henry! I mean, of course, with your health."

Chidingly his friend spoke. With shrewd eyes she regarded him, the elderly bachelor man of letters who had long been an ornament, of a kind, at her Belgravia townhouse and at her country estate in Surrey, now, so mysteriously and so vexingly, since the previous fall, disinclined to accept her invitations, and with the most perfunctory of apologies. Henry could only smile nervously, and murmur again how very sorry he was, how all consuming this hospital volunteer program was; he regretted not seeing his old friends any longer but truly he had no choice: "The hospital depends upon its volunteers, it is so understaffed. Especially Ward Six, where some of the most badly injured and maimed men are housed. I must do what little I can, you see. I am painfully aware, my time to be 'of use' is running out."

"Henry, really! You speak as if you are ancient. You will make yourself ancient, if you persist in this—" His friend's beautiful inquisitive eyes glanced about the drawing room as if to seek out, through the thickness of a wall, the locked closet, the secret altar, the precious relics laid upon that altar, "—devotion."

The most subtle of accusations here. For a woman senses: a woman knows. You cannot keep awareness of betrayal from a woman. Henry laughed. His large, so strangely plebeian hands lifted, in a gesture of abject submission, and fell again, onto his trousered knees.

"My dear, in this matter of 'devotion'—have we a choice?"

In Ward Six in the chill rainy spring of 1915 there was young Emory, and there was young Ronald, and there was young Andrew, and there was young Edmund; and there was Scudder, who did not wish to be called Arthur.

"Scudder. From Norwich."

Henry learned: Scudder had been "severely wounded" in a grenade attack, given up for dead with a number of his men in a muddy battlefield north of the Meuse River, in Belgium; and yet, bawling for help amid a tangle of corpses, Scudder had not been dead, quite. In a field hospital his shattered right leg had been amputated to the knee. His left leg, riddled with shell fragments, was of not much use. His wounds were general: head, chest, stomach, groin as well as legs and feet. He'd nearly died of blood poisoning. He suffered still from acute anemia. He suffered heart arrhythmia, shortness of breath. He suffered "phantom pain" in his missing leg. His scarred and pitted skin had yet a greenish pallor. His ears buzzed and rang: he heard "artillery" in the distance. His tongue was coated with a kind of toad-belly slime. (Which turned oily black, when he sucked the licorice sticks Henry brought him.) His shoulders were broad yet thin boned, like malformed wings. His legs, when he'd had legs, were somewhat short for his body. His head, covered in scar tissue, was somewhat small for his body. He was not yet twenty-eight but looked years older. No one came to visit him here: he wished to see no one. He had some family in Norwich, he'd even had a girl in Norwich; all that was finished, he refused to speak of it. He did not want the hospital chaplain to pray for him. Rudely he interrupted Henry reading to him from the London *Times*, how sick he was of war news. Interrupted Henry reading to him from one of Henry's slender books of verse, so very sick of verse. He did not want "uplift"—he despised "uplift." His teeth had never been good and were now rotting in his jaws. He could not feel sensation in the toes of his useless left foot. He'd bred maggots in the more obscure of his wounds, he claimed. Here at St. Bart's he'd been scrubbed out and scrubbed down, but there were flies here, too: "Big fat bastards, eager to lay their eggs." He laughed, showing angry teeth. He laughed without mirth as if barking. The wilder Scudder's laughter, the more likely to become a fit of coughing. Such violent fits, such paroxysms, can cause hemorrhaging. Such fits can cause cardiac arrest. He was ashamed, forever bleeding through gauze bandages, "leaking." His damned stump of a leg "leaked." His groin, too, had been "messed up." He hated it that the elderly gentleman volunteer so readily wiped his face as if he were a baby, wiped his wounds that leaked blood and pus, and pushed him in the damned clumsy wheelchair like a baby in its pram, even outside on the mud-graveled paths, even in cold weather.

"Should have left me there, in the mud. Should have shot me between the eyes, bawling like a damned calf."

"Dear boy, no. You must not say such things."

"Must I—not? Who will say them, then? *You?*"

It was a bleak April afternoon. Rain-lashed daffodils and vivid red tulips lay dashed against the ground in a tangle of green leaves. The hospital grounds were nearly deserted. There was a sharp rich smell of grass, of wet earth. The heavy wheelchair stuck in the gravel, the rubber-rimmed tires stuck, Henry pushed at the contraption with a pounding heart as Scudder kicked and laughed in derision. So painful was the moment, so suddenly revealed as hopeless, a bizarre elation swept over Henry, of the kind a man might feel as he leaps impulsively from a great height into the sea, to sink or to swim; to drown or to be borne triumphantly up. In the muddy gravel Henry was kneeling in front of the aggrieved man in the wheelchair, trying clumsily to embrace him, murmuring, "You must not despair! I love you! I would die for you! If I could give you my—my life! My leg! What remains of my soul! What money I have, my estate—" Abject in adoration, scarcely knowing what he did, Henry pressed his yearning mouth against the stump of Scudder's mutilated leg, which was damp, and warm, and bandaged in gauze, for the raw wound was healing slowly. At once Scudder stiffened against him, but did not push Henry away; to Henry's astonishment, he felt the other man's hand tentatively against the fleshy nape of his neck, not in a caress, not so forceful nor so intimate as a caress, and yet not hostile.

In the chill dripping garden behind St. Bartholomew's Hospital in April 1915 Henry knelt before his beloved in a trance of ecstasy, his soul so extinguished, so gone from his body, he could not have said his own illustrious name.

67

*

"Mr. James!"

Guiltily he started: yes?

"You must come with me, sir."

"But I am just returning Lieutenant Scudder to—"

"An attendant can do that, Mr. James. You are wanted elsewhere."

With no ceremony, Scudder in the heavy wheelchair was taken from the Master's grip, pushed away along the corridor in the direction of Ward Six. With yearning eyes Henry stared after him but saw only the broad stooped back of the attendant and a movement of rubber-rimmed wheels; nor did Scudder glance back. In a hoarse voice Henry called, "Goodbye, Lieutenant! I will see you—I hope—tomorrow."

Lieutenant. Though Scudder had forbidden Henry to address him by his rank, Henry could not resist in Nurse Edwards's presence. He took a peculiar pride in the fact that his young man was a British Army lieutenant, and wondered if, in secret, Scudder did not take some pride in it, too.

"You are very close with the lieutenant, Mr. James. You will have forgotten my warning to you, not to become attached to the young men of Ward Six."

It was so; Henry had long forgotten Nurse Edwards's admonition. He was the sole volunteer remaining of the original group, all the rest of whom had been women; as these others had dropped away, pleading fatigue, melancholy, ill health of their own, new volunteers had appeared in Ward Six, as newly wounded men were continually being admitted into the ward. No bed remained unused for more than a few hours, even beds in which men had died of hemorrhaging, for space was at a premium.

Henry murmured an insincere apology. His lips twitched, badly he wanted, like an insolent boy, to laugh in the woman's face, which seemed almost to glare at him, as if it had been polished with a coarse cloth.

"Very well, sir. You must come with me."

Walking briskly ahead, Nurse Edwards led Henry into a shadowy alcove several doors beyond the entrance to Ward Six, and into a small, overheated room. "Inside, sir. I will shut the door."

Henry glanced about, uneasy. Was this the nurse supervisor's office? A small maplewood desk was neatly stacked with documents, and there was a large, rather battered-looking filing cabinet; yet also a deep-cushioned chair and an ottoman, a lamp with a heavy fringed shade, on the wall a framed likeness of Queen Victoria, and on the floor a carpet in a ghastly floral pattern, as one might find in the bed-sitter of a shabbily "genteel" female. As Henry turned, with an air of polite bewilderment, he saw Nurse Edwards lift her arm: there was a rod in her hand, perhaps three feet long. Before Henry could draw back, Nurse Edwards struck him with it several times in rapid suc-cession, on his shoulders, on his head, on his uplifted arms as he tried to shield himself against the sudden blows. "On your knees, sir! Your knees are muddy, are they? And why is that, sir? Your gentle-man's trousers, why are they splattered with mud, sir? Why?"

Henry whimpered in protest. Henry sank to his knees, on the floral-print carpet. Henry tried feebly to protect himself against Nurse Edwards's grunting blows, yet could not avoid them, head bowed, wincing, red faced with guilt, he who had never been disci-plined as a child, nor even spoken harshly to by his dignified father or his self-effacing mother or by any tutor or elder, until at last, fatigued by her effort, Nurse Edwards let the rod drop to the floor and panted, in a tone of disgust, "Out of here, sir. Quickly!"

Like a man in a trance, the Master obeyed.

V.

In the bay window of the London brownstone that overlooked, at a distance, the mist-shrouded Thames, the Master lay part-collapsed on the uncomfortable leather divan, in a kind of stupor. How long had he been lying there, feverish and confused? Had he taken a taxi home from—where? The train station? The hospital—St. Bartholo-mew's? And his left arm tingled from the shoulder to the wrist. And how warm he was!—he'd had to tear open the stiff-starched collar of his shirt. His housekeeper, Mrs. Erskine, had been summoned by the taxi driver, to help her dazed master up the stone steps of the brown-stone, but that had been several hours ago and Henry was blessedly alone now, and could take up his diary to record, for this tumultuous day, two small red-inked crosses linked with the initial *S*; and to write, in a shaky but exhilarant hand, *This loneliness!—what is it but the deepest thing about one? Deeper about me, at any rate, than anything else: deeper than my "genius," deeper than my "discipline," deeper than my pride, deeper, above all, than the deep countermining of art.*

*

The flat mineral eyes widened: "Why, sir. You are back with us."

Another time, the elderly gentleman volunteer had quite astonished Nurse Supervisor Edwards. He murmured yes in a deferential tone, with a small grave, frowning smile. "As you see, Nurse Edwards. I report to you, to be of use."

"Very well, then! Come with me."

For the Master had no choice, it seemed. Only just to stay away from St. Bartholomew's Hospital, which was unthinkable.

To be allowed reentry into Ward Six, the gentleman volunteer Mr. James had to demonstrate, as Nurse Edwards phrased it, his "good faith" as a hospital worker. What was needed in this time of crisis, with so many more wartime casualties than the government had predicted, and a severe shortage of staff, was not poetry and fine sentiments, but *work*. Mr. James would have to take on tasks of a kind not to be expected of the lady volunteers: he would have to prove himself a true hospital worker, a willing aide to any of the medical staff, including nurses and attendants, who required him. "You must not decline any task, Mr. James. You must not be loath to dirty your hands—or you will be sent away from St. Bartholomew's." And so, with a stoic air, the elderly volunteer donned a bulky coverall over his tailored serge suit and spent the remainder of that day aiding attendants as they pushed a meals trolley from ward to ward and carried away uneaten food and dirtied plates afterward; in the hot, foul-smelling kitchen where the trolleys were unloaded, where garbage reeked and black-shelled roaches scuttled on every surface, Henry was nearly overcome by nausea and light-headedness, but managed to rally and did not collapse and completed his assignment. Next day, Henry aided attendants who pushed a linens trolley from ward to ward, delivering fresh linen and taking away dirtied, sometimes very filthy linens to deliver to the hot, foul-smelling hospital laundry in a nether region of the vast building. "Sir, you will want gloves. Ah, sir!—you will want to roll up your sleeves." The hospital laundresses laughed at the elderly volunteer, made to stand at a vat of steaming, soapy water and with a wooden rod, so very clumsily, nearly falling into the vat, stirring befouled sheets in a tangle clotted and obdurate as, his fanciful brain suggested, the Master's distinguished prose. *Only go through the movement of life that keeps our connection with life—I mean of the immediate and apparent life behind which all the while the deeper and*

*darker and unapparent in which things really happen to us learns
under that hygiene to stay in its place* and what determination in
this resolve! what joy! he would carry with him, secret and hidden
as the nitroglycerine tablets in his inside coat pocket, through his
travails at the hands of Nurse Supervisor Edwards, and he would not
be defeated. Next day, the elderly gentleman volunteer who had
never in his life wielded any household "cleaning implement" was
given the task of sweeping floors with a broom and using this broom
to clear away cobwebs, some immense, in which gigantic spiders
lurked like wicked black hearts and crazed flies were trapped; following this, Henry was given the task of mopping filthy floors stained
with spillage of the most repulsive sort: vomit, blood, human waste.
And another time though the Master staggered with exhaustion he
had not succumbed to vomiting or fainting; he smiled to think that
surely his coworkers would report back to Nurse Supervisor Edwards
that he had completed his tasks for the day. Thinking with childlike
defiance, *The woman has put me to the test; I will not fail the test.
The woman wishes to humble me; I will be humbled.* On his way
out of the hospital in the early evening Henry could not resist pausing at the threshold of Ward Six, to peer anxiously in the direction of
his young friend's cot at the farther end of the room, but he could not
make out whether Scudder was there—or perhaps that was Scudder,
in a wheelchair?—but quickly Henry turned away, before one of the
staff recognized him, to report on him to Nurse Supervisor Edwards.

Next morning, though he'd awakened with a hopeful premonition
that his exile might be over and he would be allowed reentry into
Ward Six, Henry was assigned his most challenging task thus far: the
bathing of bedridden patients. These were not the comely young
men of Ward Six but patients in other wards of the hospital, most of
them older, and some of them obese; they were gravely ill, disfigured, senile, drooling, leaking blood from orifices, comatose, inclined
to unpredictable outbursts of rage. They were covered in bedsores
and they smelled of their rancid, rotting bodies. No task had more
depressed Henry than this task, which filled him with revulsion
where he so badly wished to feel empathy, or pity. He could not comprehend how anyone could perform such work day following day as
the nursing staff did, energetically, and capably, and seemingly without complaint. "Why, sir! You are becoming very handy!"—the
young nurses praised their elderly assistant, or teased him. Henry
blushed with pleasure at the attention. It was his task to haul away
buckets of soapy, dirty water to dump into an open drain near the

latrines where every bit of filth accumulated: garbage, clotted hairs, floating human excrement, roaches. (Everywhere in the hospital these shiny hard-shelled roaches scuttled, ubiquitous as flies.) When Henry returned to the nurses' station there was Nurse Supervisor Edwards to regard him with coolly assessing eyes that signaled approval—grudging approval, but approval nonetheless. "Mr. James, my staff has been telling me that you have not declined any task, and have executed most of them quite capably. This is very good news."

In a gentlemanly murmur Henry thanked the woman.

"Yet you are still an American, Mr. James, are you? And not one of *us?*"

Henry stood stricken and silent, as one accused.

Next day, Henry knew himself fittingly punished: he was given the lowliest and most repulsive of hospital tasks, more disgusting even than bathing patients' bodies, or carrying away their no longer living bodies: latrine duty.

In his now filth-stiffened coverall, Henry was enlisted to help collect bedpans from the wards, and to set them, often brimming with unspeakable contents that lapped out beneath their porcelain lids, onto a wobbly trolley to be pushed to the latrines. He was to assist a gnarled, misshapen, and morose individual who exuded an air of hostility toward the gentleman volunteer, and refrained from praising him as the nurses had done. When Henry's hand shook and reeking waste slopped out onto the floor, it was Henry's responsibility to mop it up immediately: "Your move, mate!" Repeatedly, Henry was overcome with nausea and faint-headedness, swaying against the trolley, so that the attendant chided him harshly; in addition to his fear that he would collapse on the job, Henry worried that the attendant would report him to Nurse Edwards, and he would never be allowed reentry to Ward Six. Bedpans were to be emptied in latrines in the nether region of the hospital, a labyrinth of corridors in which one might wander lost for a very long time; through this endless day, Henry was made to think, *In all of the Master's prose, not one bedpan.* Not excrement of any kind, nor the smells of excrement. Wielding a long-handled brush to scrub the emptied bedpans clean, trying not to breathe in fumes from a chalky white cleanser, Henry swayed, slumped, nearly sank to his knees. More and more frequently that day the sharp angina pain teased him, for in his coverall he could not readily reach into his coat pocket to seize his nitroglycerine tablets.

"Eh, mate? It's fresh air you're wanting now, is it?"

Henry must have been looking very sickly, for the dwarflike attendant seemed now to be taking pity on him. With a rough hand he urged Henry in the direction of a door as feebly Henry protested, "No, I am to report to"—he fumbled to remember—"Ward Six. I am taking a young soldier home to live with me, where he will have full-time nursing care."

The attendant whistled through his teeth. Impossible for Henry to judge whether the man was mocking him or genuinely admiring.

"Crippled and maimed, is it? Ward Six? Bloody good of you, mate."

Henry protested, "They are not all crippled and maimed. Some of them—a few of them—may yet be well again, and whole. I am not a rich man, but—"

"A disting'ished thing you are doing here, mate. At last."

The man spoke with a strange somber emphasis, *disting'ished, at last,* Henry could not comprehend, for a dazzling sensation seemed to have come over his exhausted brain as of strokes of lightning, very close, yet making no sound. Henry murmured gratefully, "Yes. It is. I hope—I hope it is." He stumbled, and would have fallen, except the man grasped Henry's hand firmly in his gnarled hand and held him erect.

28 July 1915. Mr. Henry James, 72, the internationally acclaimed man of letters, has surrendered his American passport and sworn the oath of allegiance to King George V, to become, after decades of living in London, a British citizen. Mr. James has been a faithful participant in the St. Bartholomew's Hospital Volunteers Corps since last autumn.

The cruel rumor was, an emergency amputation had had to be executed in Ward Six. One of the amputee soldiers whose "good" leg had begun to turn gangrenous from poor circulation. At the threshold to the ward the elderly volunteer hesitated. For at the far end of the ward was a white-curtained screen, hiding what was taking place inside, and his eyes, which watered with tears, were not strong enough to determine which bed it was the screen was hiding. And how crowded the long ward was, how dismaying its sights, how disgusting its smells, and there was an incessant buzzing of flies, and commingled moans and whimpers and cries of the wounded, so very demoralizing. Now the Master had been allowed reentry to Ward Six, he'd been eager to resume his duties here, eager to see his young friend Scudder again, whom he had not seen in more than a week; yet at the threshold to the ward he hesitated, for he was seeing unfamiliar faces, it seemed to him; the ward appeared to be larger than he remembered, and more congested. Preparing for this visit Henry had brought more gifts with him than usual, and special treats for Scudder; he'd debated with himself whether to show the young lieutenant the news item from the London *Times*, for Scudder would be surprised to learn that his devoted volunteer friend Henry James was an "acclaimed"—still less, "internationally acclaimed"—man of letters, and worse yet, that Henry was seventy-two years old, for surely Scudder would have guessed him to be a decade younger, at least. A white-clad woman was plucking at Henry's sleeve asking, "Sir? Are you unwell?" even as Henry drew prudently back, stammering, "Excuse me—I can't—just yet—Goodbye—"

VI.

You would not call it a *deathbed*. For it was not a *bed*.

Not a bed but a leather divan overlooking the Thames. And not death but a sea voyage the Master had arranged for his young friend the lieutenant and for himself. The Great War had ended, the oceans were again open. On the leather divan in the bay window overlooking the river he was suffused with such childlike yearning, and yet such joy, almost his heart could not bear the strain except the young lieutenant remained at his side, and guided his hand, which moved as if he were writing with only just his fingers; as his rather parched lips shaped words he seemed to be speaking, if not audibly; and sometimes, to the astonishment of his observers, whose faces he could not identify, the Master requested paper and pen in his old, firm voice, and his eyeglasses, that he might read what he'd written for no one else, save the Master himself, and his young friend the lieutenant could make out the Master's scrawling hand. His high-domed and near-hairless head was regal as a Roman bust. The strong, stubborn bones of his face strained against the parchment skin. The deep brooding eyes were sometimes glazed with dreaming and yet at other times alert with curiosity and wonder: "Where will we be disembarking this evening, Lieutenant? You have been so very inspired, arranging for these surprises."

It was so: the young lieutenant from Norwich, son of a trades-man, had quite taken charge. So deftly now walking with one of the Master's canes, maneuvering himself on his "good" leg (which had been saved from amputation by the head surgeon at St. Bartholomew's) and on his "peg leg" (the costly prosthetic leg purchased for him, by Henry).

In a warm lulling breeze they stood against the railing on the deck of an ocean liner. Henry thought it so strangely charming, that the vast ocean, which must have been the Atlantic, was as companionably crowded with small craft, even sailboats, as the Thames on a balmy Sunday in peacetime. And now Henry was settling into his lounge chair; his young friend tucked a blanket around his legs. They planned to disembark at only the most exotic of the foreign ports. They would travel incognito. Henry would continue to read to his young friend the verse of Walt Whitman, of surpassing beauty. Now they were lounging at the prow of a smaller ship: a Greek ferry perhaps. The wicked black smoke issuing from the discolored smokestack had a look of Greek smoke. For there was the unmistakable aquamarine of the Mediterranean. Beneath a cloudless sky, floating Greek islands. *O sir!* a jarring and unwelcome voice intervened: an awkward young woman in a white nurse's uniform was leaning over Henry on the divan with tablets on a small plate for him to swallow. Politely he'd tried to ignore this rude stranger, now with a glance of exasperation at the lieutenant he swallowed the first of the tablets with a mouthful of tepid water, but the second tablet stuck like chalk in his throat and, ah! he began to cough, which was dangerous; the brittle bones of an elderly rib cage can be cracked in a paroxysm of coughing, the heart can be overstrained. Yet the Master was hotly furious suddenly! Demanding to know why they'd been brought back to dreary London when they'd been so happy on their Mediterranean idyll! And where exactly was this place? Who were these uninvited people? The goose-feather pillows against his back were uncomfortable. He had never liked the damned leather divan; it had long been one of those pieces of furniture that is simply in the household as if rooted to the floor. In fact, Henry preferred to travel at the prow of the ship where, if there was discomfort, there was adventure at least. *Sir, you are very stubborn, are you?* In place of the awkward girl nurse was an older, fleshier female who wore a formidable white-starched cap on her head and nurse's attire formal as a military uniform. *I have warned you, sir, but you never listened, did you?* Yet there was approval here, even admiration, as between equals. The Master saw, to his relief, that it must be now an earlier time: this careless thing that had happened, so like a stroke of lightning entering his brain, had not yet happened. He would write about it in his diary, and then he would fully comprehend it. For there is no mystery that, entered into the diary, in the Master's secret code, eludes the Master's comprehension. Speaking forcefully as in his old life he instructed the woman: "You see, I must give blood. For that is all that I can give." The woman frowned in hesitation as if such elderly blood might not be worthy of her needle but the Master prevailed upon her for the Master could be most persuasive when he wished to be. And so, the Master was told to lie down, to lie very still, to hold out his arm, as the woman in glimmering white drew near and in her hands was a "hypo-dermic" needle device for the piercing of skin and and the drawing of blood. The Master shut his fluttering eyes, in a swoon. He was very frightened. Yet he was not frightened but courageous: "I will. I must. My blood is mine to give to—" The young man's name would come to him shortly. Which of the young wounded men whose blood had been poisoned, the Master's blood would restore to health. "Ah!"—Henry steeled himself as a white shadow glided over him and the sharp needle sank into the soft raddled flesh of the inside of his elbow. Swiftly the woman drew blood out of the Master's ropey vein, with capable hands attached a thin tube to the tiny wound, that the blood would continue to drain out, into a saclike container, in a most ingenious way. A comforting numbness as of dark rising water came over Henry, as he lay on the lounge chair, on the deck of the mysterious ship, a blanket tucked over his legs. This day, these many days, he would mark with a red-inked cross: he was so very happy. The young lieutenant, his scarred and scabbed face ruddy with renewed strength, stood at the foot of the lounge chair holding out his hand: "Henry! Come with me."

NOTE. "The Master at St. Bartholomew's Hospital 1914–1916" is a work of fiction drawing, in part, upon passages from *The Complete Notebooks of Henry James*, edited by Leon Edel and Lyall H. Powers, and *Henry James: A Life* by Leon Edel.

Deep Breathing
David Shields

WE HIKE AND HIKE and hike. The moon hangs above us like a floater in the eye. Thin, lighted disc, electric lamp, perfectly circular moon—I hate it. I don't want to see her face. I don't want her to see mine. The moon seems accessible to me, bothersome and ceaseless, and I hate it. I want darkness and earth. Clouds, if possible. Not the moon. I crave eclipse.

The moon burns and we hike on, up hills, down hills, further into the recesses of the mountain. The moon sucks trees into its light and paints our faces green, turning us into clowns. I imagine I'm a harlequin, dance about, tell jokes. Carla says she's heard the stories before; they're not funny. I disagree. We look into each other's glasses, see ourselves, and wave. We exchange glasses and stumble. She's nearly blind. I wear glasses to feel detached and look intelligent. She thinks I'm brilliant. She tells me so. I'm not brilliant.

The moon is brilliant. Luminous even. It cuts through the sky, the hills, the trees. It throws thick tunnels of light at us. The sky stretches itself out for miles around us, faceup. The moon doesn't move. We do. Carla says it's a full moon. I agree. "We're lost," she says. I agree again and tell her not to worry. She asks me, please, not to patronize her. I apologize.

Carla doesn't like the idea of being lost. I, obviously, revel in it. In her backpack she has a toothbrush. The moon tells us where to go. Away. Way away. Carla says it's a full moon. I agree. "Wolves," she says. "Yes," I say. "I'm scared," she says. "That's absurd," I say, "we'll protect each other." "That's absurd," she says.

The path ends. Tree limbs shake at us like parents' fingers. Bushes jump out at us like animals. We're lost. I'm wearing jeans, a torn green turtleneck, boots. I'm carrying a sleeping bag, a backpack. "Let's go back," Carla says. I have no intention of going back. I don't want to go back. I want to hike. Carla wants to sleep. She's tired. I offer to carry her backpack for her. Her sleeping bag. Her head. The moon. She walks ahead of me, moving her arms like pistons.

My eyes focus on her ass. I try to avert my attention. I stare at her backpack, her head bobbing up and down. I look up at the moon, down at the dirt. Moon like an attenuated traffic light, dirt like waves. I squint toward the treetops, peer into labyrinths of entangled tree limbs. They're all of only passing interest. My eyes are riveted on her ass.

Carla asked me if I thought her ass was too large. I couldn't decide. With my tongue I took her temperature. I was worried. She seemed feverish. Her ass stared me in the face like balloons. She lay facedown on the mattress on the floor. She chewed the pillowcase. Her shirts hung like straitjackets above us on the backs of chairs, from the lightless chandelier. She asked me if I thought her ass was too large. I rubbed balloons until they squeaked. I licked them until they shined. I pulled the balloons apart, rubbed them some more. I took her temperature. 98.6 was obliterated. I untied the knots in the balloons, let the air out. Carla turned on her side, away from me. She asked me if I thought her ass was too large. I told her no. I lied. I accommodated.

She asks me to promise we'll stop at the first clearing we come to. I promise. "I'm tired," she says, "you have to respect that." I tell her I do; I'm tired, too; sleep is inevitable and natural, like the moon. I want to remove the moon, rebel against sleep. I want to hike until the moon fades, until the sun rises, until my backpack slips off my shoulders.

We walk into a black meadow that's dominated by plants as tall as I am. The plants dwarf Carla. We walk in wet soil and whip whorls of long, pointed leaves out of our way. "Culver's root," she says. I disagree. I hate displays of knowledge. Carla slips and pulls clusters of leaves with her. The moon surveys the field, withholds comment. We turn our hands into scythes, trample Culver's root, tear off leaves.

Carla watered the plants with a coffee pot. She cluttered the sunroom, the kitchen, the bathroom, the bedroom with plants. She played music for the plants on cheap speakers. Like a child she loved Mozart, Brahms. She talked to the plants. Nights, naked, she walked around the house, watering. Dry dirt caked. Dead leaves crumbled. The plants begged for more water. I flooded the plants. "Don't," she said. Potted plants toppled over. Soil became mud. Roots stretched like legs. Leaves turned into huge hands. Hanging plants swayed. "You'll ruin the plants," she said, "leave them alone." I bought new music like candy. Mahler. Nothing else. Only Mahler. Only the symphonies. I turned up the volume all the way. The plants sprouted up like arms, brought the ceiling down a foot or two. The plants took over the house, dominated rooms. The sunroom was transformed into a greenhouse. Carla said she felt suffocated by the plants, that they were out of control. She threw out the plants. She played Mozart. Early Mozart. Very quietly.

The meadow curves upward. We use plants like walking sticks. The meadow straightens its back, stands straight up. The meadow becomes a hill, becomes a seventy-degree angle. Our backpacks hang on our shoulders like vaults. Carla's sleeping bag slips out of her hand, unrolls into mud, opens flat like a mattress. I suggest we stop hiking, take advantage of the mattress. She rolls up the sleeping bag like a tongue. She stands up and walks ahead of me. I quote a passage from Camus so banal that it's the text of a fairly popular poster: do not walk ahead of me, do not walk behind me, walk next to me and be my friend, etcetera. She hurries away from me. I run after her. Climbing the hill, carrying my backpack and sleeping bag, I run after her and overtake her.

Until I was twelve years old I was the fastest person I knew. I ran to the store, around the block, to school, up the stairs, around town, across highways, away from people, with people, toward people, on dirt, on sand, on asphalt, on the beach, in bare feet, in sneakers, in sandals, in boots, in good thin tight shiny laced black shoes. I was twelve and had no hair on my legs, had legs hard as rubber, tanned as an Indian. My girlfriend was twelve and ran, too. We ran together. We ran into each other, into trouble, around lakes. We raced. She won. I thought, perhaps, she won because of a false start. I demanded a rematch. She said no. I took off my sneakers, threw them into the lake, stepped on twigs, rocks, glass in my bare feet. She ran away from me. She started smoking cigarettes, lost her wind, became a cheerleader. We broke up, returned identification bracelets, found out who we were.

The top of the hill curves toward us like a lip. The moon flashes off the plants like lightning. We make crunching sounds, snap twigs, step on snails. We kiss the hill's lips. We make it to the top. The white moon ensconces itself in a cloud, hovers casually. We look around, at the sky, the mountains in the very far distance, down below us at a river and, beyond that, to a dark flat field.

"A clearing," Carla says. I agree. "A place to sleep," she says. "Yes," I say. We run down the hill like goats. Carla trips, tastes dirt. I lick topsoil off her mouth. I swallow earth. I spit out pebbles and dry terrain. "You don't love me," she says, "I swallow you." "They're of different consistency," I say. She nods. She loves scientific answers like that. I wish she'd push handfuls of mud past my throat.

At the bottom of the hill we catch our breaths, suck in the soft summer night. The moon climbs higher into the sky. The river's wider and deeper than I thought it would be. Many things turn out that way. Carla, for instance. She says the water's filthy. I drink gallons of the river. "You'll destroy yourself," she says. Like a child, I blow bubbles. I look into the river, stare into murky water. Carla recounts the myth of Narcissus. "Boring," I say, "obvious," and slurp water. The moon bounces off the stream like flashbulbs.

In a secluded glade, surrounded by woods and the deep dark verdant shadows of cypress trees, I played with the camera, twisted the f-stop dial, adjusted the black plastic strap. I undressed Carla in my mind. I thought about the softness of infinity, the violence of the close-up. I thought about undressing her. "We don't have much sunlight left," I said. Shadows splashed across her face like paint. I read the light meter, tinkered with the f-stop. She made a pile of her clothes like laundry. She stood in the shade, folding her arms across her breasts. "Put your arms down," I said. "I feel naked," she said. "You should," I said. I put the camera down, jumped out of my clothes, made a pile of clothes like a picnic. "Better?" I said. "Yes," she said. I looked into the viewfinder: her breasts hung like pinecones. Her arms were pinned to her bare legs like pickets. Shadows warped the picture. Sun streamed through the trees, throwing my light reading off. "Take off your glasses," I said, "they refract light." "No," she said, "I can't see without them." "There's glare," I said. "I don't care," she said. The rhyme gave rise to laughter, to frolic, to my ripping her glasses off her face. I spoke of the poetry of blindness, the clarity of an oblique vision, our need for distortion. "Give me back my glasses," she said. Shadows cut off the sun, stretched like ladders. "Step out of the shadows," I said. Hands on bony hips, Carla walked out of the penumbra, sprawled out on the grass, chewed blades like a cow, spread her legs, rocked, fingered herself, arched her back like a cat. "Better?" she said. "Yes," I said, "hold it." I toyed with the range finder. Shadows sprayed her body like a water hose. I turned the f-stop to 2.8. I switched the shutter speed to 1/25th of a second. "It hurts," she said. I straddled her, crouched down, turned the camera vertically, focused. "It hurts," she said again. I spoke of the need, now and then, to suffer. I photographed through her body: I ducked between her legs and shot from her thighs to her face. Shadows fell like walls.

The river stretches itself out in front of us for years, winds its way through meadows, trees, bushes for as far as we can see in either direction. It presents itself to us like a broken arm, some nagging ugly contorted barrier. The water, hissing, ceaseless, kisses the rocks and banks of its own chasm. Carla says we have to turn back; we certainly can't cross the river. "Of course we can," I say.

I throw our sleeping bags and backpacks, one at a time, onto the flat land of the empty dark field on the other side of the river. The backpacks clank like prisoners. The sleeping bags fly like bullets. I run to the foot of the hill behind me, stare up at triangular acres of Culver's root. The moon recedes, climbs higher into the black sky, turns down its light, waits for the stars to dance. "Don't go leaping over the river," she calls, "athletics repulse me."

In the pastels of early morning, on quiet empty black-tar courts, I served yellow tennis balls and Carla swung at air. I rushed the net, made chalk cough. I smashed cross-court shots at wicked, impossible angles. I sliced drop shots that bounced back onto my side of the court. I arched lobs that tickled the sky, landing inches inside the back line. I served hard, like a cannon, deep, into corners. "You serve too hard," she said. She held her tennis racquet like a guitar. She hit backhands with two hands, spun around, lost her balance. She played in a white tennis dress. Emily Dickinson was buried in a white casket. Every other game, we exchanged sides, slurped orange juice, kissed, intertwined racquets like serpents' heads, like hands, tugged at shorts. "Don't," she said, "I'm trying to concentrate." Like an athletic genius she concentrated. We played hundreds of games. She rarely won a point. I aimed for the bottom of the net and she won a game. She danced around the court and flung her racquet into the trees. She kissed me until I could taste the salt of her sweat. She gripped me like the handle of her racquet. "I let you win," I said. "I won," she said. "I let you." "You didn't." "I did." She twisted my racquet, poked me in the stomach, broke my strings.

"Don't jump," Carla says. I'm not committing suicide. I'm jumping over a river, shallow stream of murky water. I crouch low, feel light, feel bounce and spring in my legs. I want to land on dry earth, open up my sleeping bag, connect zippers with her. The moon twists around like a dangling yo-yo. I clench my fists, tug at dirt, run hard. She waves her hands, shakes her head. "You'll kill yourself," she says. The river's as wide as two tables. I'm willing to risk it. She looks away, hides her face from the moon. As I near the river, I stutter-step. My feet chop at the ground like piano keys. I bounce off the last clump of earth before the river and lift—arms outstretched, hands clapping air, stomach tight as a fist.

As if I'm gliding forward in a swing, I kick my legs out ahead of me. I savor altitude, flight, proximity to the moon. As if I'm riding a bicycle, I pedal air. Air leads to earth. Below me is water. I make it. My right foot lands on level ground; my left foot, on the steeped bank. I lunge forward, lose my balance. As I slide down the hill, belly up, I clutch crazily after rocks, twigs, things to hold onto. I slip into the scummy edge of the river. I roll away from the water like a crocodile into mud. I scramble up the hill onto flat land, take off my wet shoes and socks, my soaked pants. Otherwise I'm bone dry.

Carla laughs. It's the kind of event that entertains her. She thinks I'm clumsy. She thinks I have no sense of myself in relation to things around me. The things around me at the moment are weeds, rocks, backpacks, sleeping bags, clumps of bushes. I feel in union with them. With all of them, with each of them. In touch.

I loped around the kitchen like a gazelle, making a lavish breakfast in honor of Carla's birthday. "These are dessert forks," she said, thumbing the Sunday paper, twanging the fork like a Jew's harp. I ignored her. The distinction seemed spurious. A fork is a fork, I thought. You shovel food with it. I patted the omelets, threw cold cinnamon bagels into the oven. "These are dessert forks," she said again. Like a magician I switched forks. Like a gourmet I made breakfast. I poured milk, stirred orange juice, boiled water. "Coffee," I said. "Tea," she said. I whipped out tea bags like condoms. I hated tea. Polite weak tea. Healthy herbal tea. Carla sipped tea. I inhaled coffee. I was addicted to coffee. I lived on bitter black essence. She folded the paper around her like a dressing room, occasionally poked her head out over the headlines, lost herself in new places to travel, new marriages, new books. I despise the temporal. Food isn't temporal; it's substance. Like a waiter I served omelets, crisp bagels. Like a fountain I spilled orange juice, tea, coffee. I slapped butter on a plate. "These forks are dirty," she said. "Fuck the forks," I said, "eat with your hands." I pushed omelets past my face, swallowed bagels like sugar doughnuts, drank coffee, orange juice, cold milk. "You're a pig," she said, crumpling her newspaper. I rubbed my finger in butter, smeared her lips, kissed her until I smelled smoke. "The oven's on," she said.

The moon turns on its side, noses its way into oblivion. The moon, alone, bored with its own waning light, surrounds itself with stars. I can't see Carla on the other side of the river. I clap my hands, call to her. "Carla," I say. "Carla, Carla." She howls like a dog. "I'm not a dog," she says, "don't you dare clap your hands at me." I applaud. I whistle. I cluck my tongue. I snap my fingers. Across the river she yells at me. "Come on, Spot," I say, "jump over the river."

Carla fed her dog the morning mail. She threw a rubber ball at its nose. Now and then she walked the animal, wrapping the leash around her wrist like a bracelet. The dog, in heat, chased a Great Dane. On the front lawn, at night, beneath Carla's window, a Great Dane and Carla's dog copulated. The Great Dane pranced away like a pimp. A few seconds later, months before it could have puppies, Carla's dog chased a bird across the street. The bird flitted up to telephone wires. The dog barked. A car flipped its high beams, honked, slammed brakes. The dog put out its right front paw, waved, swallowed tires. The car dropped into third, then fourth, while Carla and I, undressed, unfinished, ran down the stairs and into the street. I rolled the dying, dead animal into the gutter. The dog wheezed like an air conditioner. Carla said she couldn't stand to look at the animal; she loved it too much. "If that were true," I said, "you wouldn't have left the door open all night." She pleaded with me not to put my guilt trip on her. She adored the terms of popular psychology, spat them out like bubbles. "You couldn't stand the bitch," I said. "Liar," she said. "Kiss it," I said. "What?" she said. I was undressed, but I meant the dog. "The dog," I said. "No," she said. "Kiss it." "No." I held her by the arm, pressed her face into the still wet crotch of the animal, into its wine-colored rib cage. She cried. Not for the dog but for her own desolation she cried. Man-to-man I shook its paw, said goodbye, crossed its legs. The driver of the white van unlocked the door of the cage and scooped up Ubu like fish.

"Run back," I say, "and jump." Carla's light. Even with her ass she weighs 114 pounds. It's conceivable to me the wind will simply pick her up, carry her across the river, and deposit her neatly in the limbs of one of the trees on my side of the river. The dichotomy bothers me. Her side. My side. It suggests two people, married, turned away from each other, sleeping. "I'm afraid," she says. "Don't be," I say. "Basically," she says, "at heart, I'm a coward." "Basically," I say, "so is everybody." "I can't do it," she says, "I can't, I can't." She sits down and holds her head in her hands, thinks about things. She pounds dirt.

If, momentarily, she's inaccessible, her clothes are not. I undo the knots in her backpack, fold back the flap. I squeeze her clothes into a ball, smell them, breathe in their musty odor, spill them across the ground. The moon fades and descends slowly. Falling, but in control, the moon wraps itself in the curtain of night. The moon retreats into the bottom of the sky. "What are you doing?" she asks. Worry is imbedded in her voice like gallstones. I say nothing and tie cloth into cloth, turn jeans into outstretched arms, knot her clothes into a rope. Her fat woolen socks. Her patched pairs of jeans with their stuck corroded zippers. Her stained silken panties. Her navy blue sweatshirt, inside out. Her 34B lace bra.

I hold onto Carla's panties and, holding onto my soft pink end of the clothesline, throw the other end across the river to her. "Catch," I say, and the clothes nose through the night like an eel. She catches her clothes. A line tight as wire stretches between us. "Hold on," I say. "Now what?" she says. "Hold on tight and swing across," I say. "You're brilliant," she says. I am brilliant. The moon isn't brilliant. Not even close. The moon sits on top of a cloud like a dime caught in a coin slot. The cloud drifts away, threatens rain, and the dime falls, clanks silently, disappears.

Carla, awake for hours, played music, walked around the room, hung up clothes. She lifted up the covers, pinched my ass, and whispered. "Got change?" she said. She never had change. She hated to break a dollar. She hated to be late for work. With all the walking around the room she did, she could have walked up and back to work twice. She changed records, tucked in the covers, bent hangers. "Close the shade," I said. I didn't want to see the sun or hear the alarm clock. I wanted to sleep. She sat down on the edge of the bed, opened up her yellow bathrobe, and kissed me, checked if I had tonsils, until I was awake. "I need bus fare," she said. She lay on top of me, felt soft as soap, smelled like toothpaste. I pulled out my toothbrush, lathered up. She turned my pants pockets inside out, spilled coins onto the rug. "Don't be a whore about it," I said, "don't just take money." "Oh, pretty-pretty-please, Father, mightn't I borrow a pittance," she said, "pretty-pretty-please?" "At least play fair," I said, "flip a coin— double or nothing." "What do you mean?" she said. Carla wasn't a gambler. "I'm late," she said. "Flip a coin," I said. "Call it," she said. "Tails," I said. She caught the coin in midair, jammed it into her pocket, snapped the shade open, kissed me on the ear. "Get up," she said, then pulled the blankets off, jingled change. "You denigrate the act," I said. She rang the alarm clock, slammed the door behind her. "What act?" she said.

Carla tugs on her end of the clothesline. "Just jump?" she asks. "Yes," I say, "hold on tight and jump." "I can't," she says. "Swing across," I say. I pull on my end. "Don't," she says. She tiptoes to the edge, sizes up the river. "Are you holding on?" I ask. "Yes," she says. "Tight?" "Yes." I yank the clothesline like a bed sheet.

At first I think she's going to make it. She swings through the air like a wrecking ball. She clings to her clothes, screams, kicks her feet. I hold tight. With two clenched hands I hold tight. She's only a few feet away from me, on the upswing, when she loses her grip. The clothes slip through her hands and she plops backward into the river like an enormous fish. "Carla," I call. She's gone.

The river sucks her up, sends her downstream, flows on. She seeks the surface, coughs water. She cries for help. She slaps at water. Like a buoy she bobs above water. Like a suitcase she sinks to the bottom. Virginia Woolf placed a good-sized rock in her coat pocket to make sure. Carla struggles for survival: one moment, alive, determined, searching; the next, hidden, drowned, dead.

I run toward her, in bare feet, downstream, away from the moon. I hurdle bushes and pick up speed. I dive. Headfirst I dive. I cut the water like a knife. I hit the soft muddy bottom of the river, jet to the surface. I spot her, swim toward her furiously, wrap one arm around her waist. She weighs a ton. With my free arm I dog-paddle toward the bank. The river splashes foam at us and the undertow carries us downstream while the moon diminishes to a pale empty disc and the bank recedes a couple hundred yards every time I reach for it so that I have a fairly strong sense of doing battle with nature. I win. I swim through the current, lunge and thrash my way across it, then claw at roots, dig my fingernails into dirt. I pull her to me. I hold onto her, crawl out of the river, drag her onto the soft slime at the edge of the river.

I lie down on top of her unconscious body and breathe into her blue pale paper lips. I breathe into her mouth like the wind. I press my wetness to her wetness like rags. I pound on her chest, want to know if anyone is home. Breathe, you bitch. The bottom of the moon touches the earth at the end of the meadow. I rub her neck like masturbating, tear open her shirt. My feet chip at pebbles, sink into mud. Cold courses through my body like wet wires. I lick her teeth, the back of her tongue. I bite her lips like hard candy till they bleed. Breathe. I thump her chest like applause. I kiss and kiss and kiss. Only the top edge of the moon is still visible. I sit on her legs, rock up and back like a horse. I open her mouth like a cave, enter. Her legs shake, kick at the ground. I sway from side to side, swing my hips forward, squeeze my thighs tight to her cheeks. Water sprays out of her mouth like a geyser. She coughs. She pukes. Carla breathes.

The moon falls like a bomb.

The Aim of All Nature Is Beauty
Anne Tardos

—*For Jackson Mac Low*

My religion is to live—and die—without regret.
—Tibetan poet saint Milarepa

I. INTRODUCTION

I do the dishes
I double-click
I stand clear of the closing doors

Bottom-dollar gorgonzola
Bigelow jumping gigolo bump

An adventure.

The ganglionated arch of
Johann Gottlieb von
Goodgirl, who is really a
very bad girl, an angry girl,
whose almond-cake
seduction via her bocca,
her thumbsucking bocca,
such a furious, pissed-off
girl.

Her sibilant juicy sister, left alone amid all the senseless
debris, contemplates the schmerz of her lorgnette, her
effortlessly lovelorn fairy-tale suicide as she is pedaling in the
darkness that amplifies her task.

"Has she not made a scene?"
"No, she is not scenic."

Filial duties, artery cloggers

You're right   I'm wrong   Whatever

Are you sure you're warm enough?
Try this visor if that one's too loose.
Please let me read my book in peace.
No, I'm not hungry today. I'll never be hungry again.

What's that smell? Is it food?
How come your feet are so big?
I can't stand it anymore.

Poor lonesome loon out on the lake, singing that
mournful tune. All this rain is making me crazy.
I would much prefer being lazy in the sun.

Motorists see more tourists see more hair

A certain pride   a certain dignity
A certain above-it-all that is genuine

Above the bickering the petty dusty petty lowly nasty
little small-minded little beneath and little beneath

The agriculture of it all!
And the interactiveness of it all!

Topographically speaking a genuine representation of a
human sentiment

The universe I inhabit versus the one that inhabits me
  The voice in the morning
  The first one to speak

Down a precipice
Off course

We need oblivion to escape oblivion
We need plants around us, and large pockets of time
wherein nothing much happens

Then maybe something can happen

II. NOW THAT YOU'RE GONE

Now that you're gone

I can't read what I've written
I can't see it
I lost the ability to write
I can barely say my own name

What happens now

What happens now can only be the result of everything
that has preceded this moment

This moment, the present, can only be seen as something
that's very close to what has just been happening

The immediate memory of the just elapsed moment
is the closest we come to experiencing the elusive present

Immediate memory allows us to notice what our mental
processes have just been, and thus, becoming includes being

Now that you're gone

Unrelenting-yearning-and-grief-consistently-benefitting-
evidence-of-mental-reality-theorizing-small-pedestals-with-a-
growing-and-grueling-exertion-facilitated-briefly

Now that you're gone

Libertine gigolo vis-à-vis
Have a madeleine, it's good for the memory

Sedimentation fiber organism bedrock intensity lingo
formidable network realization flipside stratification data
delinquency meditation

Gotta be careful   always
We're in the midst of an explosion and think it's just
everyday life

III. INTERMEZZO BY A LAKE

We were headed for a cabin by a lake in a pine forest that I
had found on the Internet
All around us clockwork resolution happiness and conflict

We were headed for a cabin by the Internet of the lake
without a key to our consciousness

Headed as we were into an organizing notion of conflict and
happiness

We are sitting by a lake along the Internet, holding hands
and playing cards without a key

We are sitting at the window of a pine forest
Sitting in the lake of our happiness
Playing cards that we were given
holding keys in our hands
sitting on the notion of our minds within the years of
consciousness without a card
Holding hands

Headed to a cabin by a lake in a pine forest where we find
each other's happiness

IV. GOING AWAY

My life takes time.
I realize that my life takes up a certain amount of time, which
is the only reason I can refer to this particular state of being,
as life.

> He may go away.

Without the concept of time, I'd be like the animal that does
not concern itself with labeling its life "life." It concerns itself
with food and shelter and survival. This is good, it feels good,
that, on the other paw, is bad. Not good. Don't go there.

> He may be going away.

Temporal organization is of no
conscious concern to the animal,
although a cat will follow a
very strict routine during
the day, by preference.

> He is going away.

But without a hierarchical agreement on temporal units and
their applications, we could not have assembled here today.

He avoids going away.

Temporary eunuchs are an impossibility. The operation that
produces a eunuch is irreversible. Did Greer, when coining
the phrase "the female eunuch," imply that women's situation was
hopeless?

He wants to go away.

From temporal units to temporary eunuchs. Sorry.

He may have gone away.

One question in writing could be: when do you hit the Enter
key and when do you not? When do you open a new document? What do you call your file when you save it? One option
is to leave it Untitled1, Untitled2, etc., as in e-mailing, when
nothing is entered into the Subject field, and the program
volunteers the theme: "No Subject." But such evasiveness has
no virtue. When given an opportunity to say something,
say something!

He may be going away.

The difficulty can lie in resisting the integration of the self into
the surrounding environment, for fear of losing one's identity or
individuality. And yet, of such a nonassimilation and failure to
become an integral part of the entire perceived universe,
nothing good will come.

He may avoid going away.

As usual, I return to myself with a sigh of relief.

He may want to go away.

My face needs to be animated by expression. My gaze should be colorful, my smile defiant. I need to take a bath. What am I waiting for? I'm used to my life. I talk to myself out of a need to formulate my thoughts. A woman presses her forehead against a mirror.

He has been going away.

To write. To face the blank page. Une feuille blanche, where blanc does not equal blank. A white page, or a blank document page on a screen, staring back at you blankly.

He has avoided going away.

The periodic need to note, to paint . . . to find that flexible, glistening, and fleeting adjective. It's an urge.

He has wanted to go away.

To be hungry and see oranges flung about.

He is avoiding going away.

We're OK together here, aren't we? Nothing to think about
for years, just let life take care of everything. To think of
nothing.

He is wanting to go away.

I recognize his impeccable looks and perfect pronunciation.
Where will they lead me to? No one knows anything. I might
as well be sitting on the moon.

He avoided wanting to go away.

To suffer, to regret, to prolong the night by insomnia, by
solitary wanderings into the deepest, darkest hours of the
night. I see it coming, yet I march bravely toward it.
I hide my fears and tears with a dark eyeliner.

He may have been going away.

Nobody is waiting for me. I have no glory, no love, no money.
No birds sing in the deep forest. How puzzling is that?

He may have avoided going away.

Years of marriage. A good chunk of my existence spent with a
man who paints portraits of women, specializing in showing
their velvety flesh. A scoundrel of the worst kind.

He may have wanted to go away.

My friends would say: well what did you expect, dear child,
what did you expect?

He may be avoiding going away.

I had enough. The next day I didn't return and neither did I
the next, or the one after that. And this is where my story
ends, or rather begins.

He may be wanting to go away.

I won't dwell on the brief and morose period of transition that followed. There were consolations and felicitations. In any case I cut myself off and chose complete isolation, give or take a few close friends. My solitude is my freedom, which allows me to work hard.

He has been avoiding going away.

Sunday again. And how cold it is. My dog and I took our constitutional in the park after lunch. This animal will be my ruin. I spend more on her than on myself. But it's worth it just to be near her shiny coat glistening in the sun.

He has been wanting to go away.

Beautiful Sunday in a beautiful park. My dog and I think of this park as our own forest. She runs faster than I do, but then I walk faster than she does. A thin, pink haze filters the sun, a defanged sun you can actually look at. Flowers and mushrooms and violets in the grass on a bright winter day. I surge forward, feeling an elastic exhilaration and animalistic joy.

He is avoiding wanting to go away.

She is a born theatrical dog. She loves to run up on stage.
I'm telling you all this so you understand her better. This is a
dog who doesn't care about money, and who's been living in
the garden—and in my heart—for a long time.

He may have been avoiding going away.

Extensive success and artistic ambition lead to silence, as
does failure.

He may have been wanting to go away.

Nellie, a performing dog, drops by my dressing room. She
seems to say to me, yes I know, you love me, you pet me,
yes, you have a box of cookies waiting for me, but tomorrow
or the day after, we're leaving and I probably won't see you
again. So don't ask anything of me. The luxury of tenderness,
peace, and security, is not available to the likes of me.
Adieu then, Nellie, adieu.

He may have been avoiding to go away.

Gertrude Stein: A vegetable garden in the beginning looks so
promising and then after all little by little it grows nothing but
vegetables, nothing, nothing but vegetables.

He may have wanted to go away.

So many things could go wrong, I'm afraid to ask. But a good
day can sneak up on you as unexpectedly as a bad one.
Silence in the garden.

He may go away.

My friends, the real ones, the faithful ones, are tied to me by
their solidarity. But I can hardly believe it. Friendship should
not be a ring through anyone's nose. Stripped by some, hit
on by others, you might want to imprison yourself inside a
gloomy serenity, made of incurable goodness and silent
contempt. Do not form that habit.

He has gone away.

Disclosures of Don Juan
Robert Kelly

Somewhere there's a wife who commands him to write.
Discovering her identity will take his whole life.

The Confessions of Don Juan are the confessions of Faust.

Don Juan becomes the doctor, Doctor Faust. We suffer from all his
degrees. Titles. Names of his novels, operas, plays, poems. Pregnant
with fame from the beginning, a smug licentiate. Diplomas rolled,
phallic tubes. A bundle of perversions. Speak!

The story of Faust must appear incoherent and tragically chaotic,
the way *Faust II* appears at the end of Goethe's life, clarified into
marble and gold, daytime and meadow, a radiant perplexity.

There is nothing more seductive than permission: I am permitted.
Nothing more seductive than Thou may'st. But not for long.

A window on her sleeping form.

His story must demonstrate how *this* time is as fragmented,
unruly, disturbed, as the era of the industrial revolution was—
that gave birth to *Faust I,* and that Goethe tried in some curious,
copious way to respond to all through *Faust II*—

or the enterprising merchant-pirate era that saw the first
Faustbuch and Marlowe's play in a time of exploration, slavery,
landgrab as a root of war.

Because Faust always has to be *the* hero of his age, this age.

*

But his own age: Faust was old to begin with.

Before that, he was Don Juan. And after, again. A cycle. The young libertine ages into the old phallosopher of love, and becomes, just as Plato prophesied, only a philosopher itself. Who then, restless in wisdom, seeks to wield the fist of youth. Reclaim his youth. For, despite the plant that Gilgamesh found and lost, it is not to be young *again* that Faust wants, but to claim his eternal youth. Or, more exactly, eternal adolescence.

Faust is the haughty child-man always seeking *gravitas*, seeking *auctoritas*, seeking *dynameis*, powers, and only 'at the end of the day'

(but the end of his day is Easter morning, when our play or opera begins)

realizing that it is *pulchritudo et voluptas*, beauty and pleasure, that he wanted, we wanted all along.

Only a child could make this mistake, only a child could be healed of his error by falling into the mud puddle and remembering what feeling feels like when it is actually feeling and not thinking about mastery and goal.

Mozart never grew old enough to forget this: Don Giovanni falling down the octave into hell is the child falling, half willingly, into the mud puddle.

A child lacks power and authority more than he lacks anything else.

The Will to Power is the will to be Old.

Faust is about Age. Aging. Age in the sense of being old and then not wanting to be the thing you spent your whole life working so hard to become: master, doctor, learned, grave, severe.

And about Age in the sense of epoch, in this age of the world and not another. This age 'of ours' discovered Age as an issue.

Robert Kelly

*

There was no Faust before alchemy, no Faust before mercantilism.
Banks and trading companies are the direct inventions of alchemy—
the transmutation of labor into gold, of paper into gold, of ordinary
land into 'owned' land—property—turning landscape into states
and boundaries. *Turning experience into commodity*—that is the
alchemy housed in hell's real estate by Dante. But put in charge of
the state by Louis XIV and Cromwell alike.

The instruments of power, as of *voluptas,* are infinite.

No end of pleasure, no end of sin, no end of mastery. There is
always someone left to subject, to make into a subject, to control.
Subjèct: make someone into a serf or monarch's thrall. Sùbject:
a mental commodity you study in school: botany or economics.

*

Goethe's Faust becomes the hegemon of the sea in Part II—
powerful old man against the world. Liquidity of money. The
colonial moment at its height.

The will to power, like the will to pleasure, is unchanging, an
invariant energy, a variable goal. Fatiguing to have to be close to
someone who wants. Marguerite does not succumb to her own
desires but to his. We faint into the power of another.

Faust wore a business suit in college. He disdained the flute and
the guitar. He leaves that to Mephistopheles, to pluck the lute, the
apron strings, the delicate tracery of the bra. Stripped bare by mere
magic, the woman stands revealed to Faust. Instant nude. The
urgency of his own desiring makes him think she's beautiful.

Faust speaks: I will teach you how to be old. Disdain anything that
children love. That is enough.

Spend your life secretly yearning for what children have every day.

Dreams of power are commonplace. The will to power (in and out
of Nietzsche's sense) is rare.

Heidegger explains that the Will to Power is the Will to Being.

A verb on pilgrimage to the noun. Change of state. Desire's alchemy: to become the thing you desire to possess. The element.

Midas: what he embraces becomes him.

*

(thinking about Busoni's opera *Doktor Faust*)

I heard it last night from Berlin, a new production. Take it by ear. It's years since I heard it last, even more years since I last read the libretto. A lot stays in mind, though, cries, dreams, passageways, a sly, high devil, a woman in love. To hear music at night is to be an island, thinking.

Wille = "will," *Welle* = "wave."

There is a dialectic, or certainly a tension, between *Wille* and *Welle. Ich, Faust, ein ewiger Wille,* he cries. [I, Faust, an eternal Will!] But also another cry, one I have so many times arising in me, that I have joined with him in making, pompous as it is: *Arbeit, heilende Welle, in dir bad' ich mich rein!* [Work, healing wave, in you I bathe myself pure!]

Work, and the determination to work, and the valuation of work— the word 'opera' itself means work—are all prime signifiers in the phallocratic realm. Yet this very self-important work, this Opus Magnum of the self becoming itself (*himself*), this archetypal masculine industry, the Work itself, is 'bathed' in a remarkably feminine image: the wave, the waves. We think of Virginia Woolf's great novel of lost, shared, found identities, we think of Undine, of Mörike's *schöne Lau*, Anna Livia Plurabelle, and all the rest of it. So Busoni construes Work as itself immersion in the woman. Penetration of the wave, yes, to that extent characteristically virile, but it is the wave that 'does the work,' the healing.

Yet the first time he cries out about the healing wave of Work,
he seems to be abandoning the quest for demonic guidance or
demonic companions. And at the very moment that the voice (high
as a countertenor, feminine in its caress) of Mephistopheles calls
him. And the last time Faust cries out about how he will immerse
himself in the redeeming Work, it is just as he sinks down dead—
only to be reborn (or to have someone be born). He falls and a
young man stands up, sassy as a Blake drawing of glad youth,
and springs away.

With Faust's wave of healing, wave of work, Busoni at least frees
Faust a little from the Christian value system. It is not the lance
that heals Amfortas, no spear, no sword. Not even the Cup of the
Grail—it is the uncontained, uncontainable *water itself,* water in
its most active form: the wave, the overwhelming. It is the pure
water itself—water that the lance can jab and stir but never wound,
water that the cup can try for a time to contain. Water is the grail
beyond the grail. Though the letters of grail spell 'a girl,' and confuse
him for most of his life, what he really wants is beyond any one or
any thing he craves. His *désir* on the other side of his *demande.*

Best of all things is water, sings Pindar.

*

Faust's wager is not with the devil, but with reality itself. His
wager is: Let what I have imagined become real. I make reality.

*

The penis is the only woman a man really has. The foreskin
retracting during erection rolls over the glans the way a snug skirt
peels off the round hips of a woman. Deep origin of fascination
with striptease and unveiling, Salome's dance. Think of Helen
veiled in *Doktor Faust,* veiled but *übrigens nackt* [naked, by the
way]. The woman who is naked and clothed at once. A woman's
body is the real penis, of which the little one-eyed fellow between
the legs is just a sad, yearning symbol. When the alchemists (for
example, Michael Maier in *Atalanta Fugiens*) say, "Bring fire to
the fire," this is much of what is meant; bring the body to the body.

102

Dream within dream within desire. More than any music I know (here I think only of the sound of the orchestra and of *her* voice, I forget, if ever I knew, the words in her voice, the words that are just another part of her body's fugue), the sleepwalking monologue of the Duchess of Parma is the sound of someone in love, disastrously, wondrously, in love, drifting by the power of pure desire alone through the sea of what she—she too is an eternal Will!—wants to feel, wants to receive. It is the Duchess, the more or less real-world figure (rather than the fantasized Helena, or the ditzy maiden Gretchen in whom Busoni does not find much to interest him), she, the Duchess, who is the Faust among women, the power and self-delusion of her own *"ewiger Wille"* to feel, love, desire, be possessed.

Balzac says in a notebook somewhere: "Any woman who can no longer be tricked by a love letter is a monster." I think of that as I listen (over memory's ardent but unreliable radio) to the Duchess's long dreamy scena, hearing it already though the actual Internet broadcast hasn't yet reached that scene in the opera. The actual is hurrying to keep up with my memory.

The Duchess is Faust's counterpart, the projection of his self-delusion. She is his penis, wandering out of control down a night of desires, encounters, abandonments—however intense the excitement, the penis eventually falls, detumesces. The will sleeps. The penis is the sleepwalker—*La Sonnambula* in yet another opera.

*

Lacan's sense that the penis only does its work when veiled. It is the veil of the foreskin I want to talk about, no less than the symbolic castration of the penis "lost into" the woman, the veil of flesh—isn't it Geza Roheim who carries on about the foreskin as the vagina? Woman as veil, Salome dances. For this dance, a man pays with half his kingdom.

In Busoni's manuscript of the text—of course he wrote the libretto himself—(4 Oktober 1917—what else was happening that day? The Battle of Broodseinde, part of that half-year-long massacre called Passchendaele), Busoni writes *ich Faust, ein ewiger Begriff,* then crosses the last word out, writes in *Geist* instead, then crosses that

103

out in turn, writes *Wille.* 'Concept' becomes 'Mind' becomes 'Will.'

Very important this point: the Christian—uncircumcised—Lacan discusses the veiled (preputial) penis. To link it with and contrast it with the circumcised Freud's insistence on symbolic castration.

Freud seems to locate castration everywhere except in the most obvious wound of circumcision itself. Strange how the early Jewish (but unbelieving) analysts seem to pay little attention to circumcision as an issue. The shyness of Freud? The tacit assimilation? Perhaps Freud's determined resistance to Rank's root doctrine of the birth trauma is fueled not just by Freud's conceptual preference for his "own" Oedipus complex as explanation, but also by an awareness that *the issue of birth trauma would open the door to a consideration of 'circumcision trauma'*—which immediately introduces (as Freud nowhere seems to allow) a *radical rupture in psychic topography* between male and female, Christian and Jew . . . naively one wonders how the pain of infant circumcision could possibly fail to constitute trauma—with consequences to follow, if indeed trauma explains anything.

I wish I knew Freud better. What *does* he say about circumcision? I keep thinking he doesn't want to know anything about it, about anything that would so profoundly and incurably separate patients into inalterable categories—isn't a great part of the beauty of the noble construction of his life work exactly his insistence, everywhere implicit, on the unity and integrity of the human psychic organization, same in all people?

*

Faust, dreaming:
I was always young. It needed no transformation music, pretty as it is, for me to seem so again. My beard and fusty robes sprang away from me the way leaves rush from a lawn, cleaned away by an invisible wind.

'To seem so again.' To seem to myself young, and seem so to you. To her.

I was the devil I sold myself to.

*

And Germany is calling again.—Johannes Faust

Latin *faustus* is a contraction of *favustus* = fortunate, favored, favored by fate.—Lucky John

German *Faust* = fist.

Which do I mean, my force or my fate? Am I agent or am I angel'd?

Spoused fun. Faust pun. He needs a wife I need a wife. What's true for him truer for me. Comparative of bliss.

He goes from woman to woman, not out of licentiousness but to seek the perfect wife. No matter how many he has. Marriage is no obstacle to married bliss. Find her, whoever she is. Whoever he seems to be.

Marguérite = *margarita*, 'pearl.' A string of pearls. He finds her, smooth, simple, pale. One after another. The serial infatuation of the empty hand.

Because he is a perfect husband he must marry everyone he meets. Everyone who seems as if she might be the perfect wife.

His desire is the fire in which they're both to be refined. Defined. They are transformed by what he wants. A hoax, like the hoax of poetry.

This is not adultery but its opposite.

This is not infidelity. It is a pilgrimage of faith itself.

Faith is belief in the perfectibility of person, in the perfectibility of relationship.

Adultery, adultery is settling for imperfection. Settling. It is as when we say of a substance that is not purely itself, it has been adulterated. Something is adulterated when it is not utterly true to itself.

Adulteration destroys the alchemic process. Aborts it. In clear crystal spheres the true essences ripen as colors and hold the colors firm. But in the adulterous alembics the brewed elixir becomes a venom, a sad mistake. He thinks.

*

And so on Easter morning:
I am a bottle, dark blue glass, barely translucent but translucent.

In me is a message carefully and neatly written, on sturdy paper with decent ink, screwed tight and stuffed into the bottle's neck.

Name, personality, history, so forth—all those are just the cork snugged into the mouth of a little phial.

The red message is intact inside. I am in the sea.

I wait for you, wave. I wait for you, shore.

Certainty was never my business. A puff of smoke, greenish, from my chalice. A few dead leaves, scarlet symmetries. That's sure enough. Enough to go on.

*

She knew she was in trouble when she felt his eyes all over her body, not just her face. Not just his glances that smooched along her cheeks to linger on her lips. Lips open, moving. To speak. His eyes were on her body. Body: midriff, loins, nape of neck, socket of knee, small of back, hollow of throat, curve of belly, *chute de reins.* She knew she was in trouble when she could feel him reading her skin. Her cautious smile—he had measurements for that. He had a musical notation for her shallow quick breaths.

He stole her feelings. Shanghaied them into his complicated design. There he worked them into the pattern—her feelings, so important to him, as if he had none of his own.

Faust has no feelings. Something to bear in mind.

The autistic will.

His phantom city he built around her. Live in me, he seemed to be saying. But he *had* no in.

A perfectionist has no peace, ever.

He was a pilgrim through a world not yet finished. Never finished. He was to go on. He called that living, sometimes he called that loving.

She was afraid of him, so she took him in her arms. Maybe he would be so close to her that he could not hurt her. Lacking the leverage that distance gives.

She could see him: he studied her the way a blind man faces the rising sun.

She thought: how does what he sees have anything to do with me?

Open me, open me and read! He would say things like that, even the devil could make no sense of such jargon.

The language of enthusiasm is always inexact. If you truly knew the thing you wanted, you would not go on wanting it. Want means a consciousness of deprivation, whereas knowing is consciousness of possession.

Enthusiasm speaks from deprivation, always approximates, blurs, yearns.

The shadow adds dimension to the man. She studies his shadow in turn, trying to know the thing he makes happen, the thing of which he cannot be fully aware.

No man knows his whole shadow, she said, and he thought her clever for saying so. It made him more determined to possess her. Or not so much possess her as possess that power that simultaneously summons, appropriates, and dismisses all such images into and from the slim chapel in the world, in his mind, that she occupied. Her amber yellow hair.

Faust dreaming:
I am a lover of chastity. I yearn for chastity the way a poor man hungers for money—anxiously, energetically, dreamily, in vain. The metabolic turbulence I bring to my quest for the object of that desire annihilates the very quality I seek.

In the story of Midas his fingers found the same quality in everything, and everything he touched became the same. The same. His so-called gold.

When I touch her, my touch imbues even the freshest virgin skin with my own weary experience, a kind of sour taste that after a moment I recognize as the taste of my own mouth, my sour old kisses, left as defilement on her skin.

I make unclean. Parable of the leper: he goes through the world ringing his bell. In the old dictionary, he is illustrated by a woodcut of a woeful figure tottering along, wearing a huge heart on his shirt. The leper comes along and promises: what I am, I make you too.

Immundus. Unclean. As if: un-world, un-worlded. The world is clean. The only chastity (he is told) is everything that is, left just the way it is. The unclean lover takes his love out of the world. In French *immonde* means sordid, unclean. A world is ordered. A world is what is clean.

*

Come home with me.

I want to wake and see you beside me on the bed, your head pillowed in the bedding I have left bare for you. I have saved you from the world. I study morning light on your cheek, the stain of shadow along your throat. I hear you breathe. Not meaning to, you have saved me from the world.

There is a strange ancient novel called *The Recognitions.* It begins with a sentence that haunts me all my life: "I, Clement, a native of the City, have been all my life a lover of chastity."

Clement, whom we call of Alexandria, says of himself, I am a native of the city of Rome. I feel utterly known a thousand years before I'm born.

This book translates me. But in vain again. For Clement in the book achieves that which he sought, finds it because he already is it.

Is Socrates wrong, then? Love, far from being penurious and full of hungry wanting, is love actually all Surfeit and *satis* and serene with its own fulfillments?

He found what he was, and he found it in everyone.

If you must be chaste to find chastity, must I be or become the woman I desire?

Is Faust Marguérite? (No wonder she has little to say for herself. He has all the lines.) Faust looks (and what a sad story this is going to be), he looks for that quality he desires, looks for it in a person who is enough like him to support the inference: "this person is a lover of chastity," but also enough like him to warrant a foundational impurity, a looseness, a door somewhere in the back of the house slamming open and shut in the hot prairie wind. Through that portal, unclean lust slouches in and out.

*

Faust writes on a piece of stiff cardboard: Never doubt your desires or your entitlement to them. Doubt is loud, and others will hear it, and come to doubt you too. Faust looks at what he's written and doubts it too. It seems childish, cynical, adolescent, accidental, merely true.

Faust in his dealings with men and women much prefers civility to truth. Truth changes with situations, while civility is permanent.

Faust in his dealings with angels and demons is much more likely to give and expect truth, imagining (wrongly) that angelic beings perceive situations better than humans, however wise. This is superstition, of course, and will get him into endless trouble.

Angels and devils are in the situation too. Or they are the situation. How can someone in a situation see the whole situation, which itself is part of an endlessly proliferating network of situations. Each situation brackets all the others, and is bracketed in turn.

Faust knows this too, of course, because he's smart. But because he is still a little boy, he believes that telling the truth is the civility we owe to angels. And true enough, it is. It is superstition, however, to expect truth from them in return. Because pure Presence alone is the only civility we can expect from angels, the only gift they have to proffer or withhold.

Faust feels the warm pearls slip through his fingers.

Pearl after pearl. Such a long string of beads. Has he ever counted them? How many pearls is forever? Can he tell the pearls that are his past from the ones that are to come? Pearls of identity.

What if this one warm lustrous pearl in his fingers now, round, sensuous, faintly exciting, between slope of thumb and fingertip, what if this one were the last pearl of all? Would he know he had come to the end of the rosary and started round again? How can he tell? Would it be again if he didn't know it was again?

How warm a pearl is. It never loses a certain animal warmth or spirit. You can tell it was alive once, before it was slain by admiration, desire. By being possessed. It may still be alive. Or capable of summoning (or is it only simulating?) life from the body with which it rests in contact.

Is the warmth coming from the pearl or from the skin? From her or from him? Maybe it is a product of contact itself.

Faust remembers a Russian mystic who taught that the sun gives no light and no heat. Space beyond earth's kindly atmosphere is dark and cold. What we call heat and light are earth's response to the distant diamond icon of the sun. Light and heat are response.

They are the friction of earth's love song, earth's welcoming the sun's invisible ardent ray, the spill of glory from the touch of love.

Or maybe earth is just us, ourselves. Maybe heat and light are our answer, billions of humans metabolizing all their lives, marrying the sky.

This heat comes from me, Faust thinks. When he thinks this, all at once it becomes bearable for him to remember that after all is said and done, the pearl borrows its warmth from the skin. As once it borrowed its substance from the tender self-regard of the oyster, the anxiety that spoke and spoke around a core of doubt.

Its luster is its own.

Where does the skin go to get its heat? From the pearl, surely. We feed one another. I am Faust and you are Marguérite, and the other way round.

All the properties of all the pearls are complete in any pearl. A praise of monogamy!

Except for the allness of them. The many. If one were enough, once would be enough. If once were enough, there would only be one sunrise in the world. Then one sundown and no more kisses.

*

This must be why, on Easter morning, when the bells are clanging and the fools of the town, those ordinary people, are putting on their fuzzy pink cloth spring coats and their lime green sports jackets and their two-tone shoes, Dr. Faust himself is slumped in his armchair, his hands, weary of pearls for the moment, toying with a small blue bottle.

This is the poison.

He doesn't propose to drink it in order to become young again. He is always young again. He can't grow old, he can't grow out of his adolescence, desires, requires, skin and silk and flying through the air, all the Witch Sabbaths that a young man dreams and an old

111

Robert Kelly

man, he is an old man, can no more stop dreaming than he can stop breathing.

Breathing too is a young man's folly. Hence the bottle. Breath and folly, youth and desire, all can be escaped at once.

But what image will be the last one to form in his mind's eye, clear or murky, looming there as his consciousness, such as it is, dims down for the endless night, dims out, yields, stops. What image last will lurk inside the mind? He remembers asking that question when he was young, eighty years ago he asked it and still he doesn't know.

What is the final image?

And suppose it is her, the last one, the one who still is waiting for his answering letter, the phone call, the promised necklace, the book of Sufi proverbs he borrowed, the weekend in the mountains, all the feints of love? Can he leave her so unsatisfied?

Why should she be more satisfied than I, Faust wants to know. That is crabby and selfish of him, even to think it. He knows that, he unthinks it, the thought turns into Well, at least I can satisfy her, a little, maybe, now if not later, now if not forever.

But he'll have to stay around to do that. He puts down the blue bottle and picks up the green telephone.

*

It is strange, or not so strange that in the West, in love as we are with masks and those who wear them, we have never noticed that all our principal heroes are just different stages, different ages, of the same man.

Don Juan—who has often been the one speaking here—is an immature version of Dr. Faust.

And Faust is he now; run out of steam, he can be described as learnèd, *doctus*, doctor. That is, he can be defined by what happened to him, his *hap*. The weary wisdom that accumulated in his heart. It stifled his passion without in the least extinguishing desire.

Don Juan and Faust are respectively the middle-aged and old-aged stages of the young hungry happy hero we call the Grail Knight, *pierce-the-veil.* Parsifal is the larval stage of Faust.

But maybe the man, the hero, does not age at all. His society changes around him. Some crafty angel out of Adorno could tell us, but doesn't it seem that when the chivalric age ends, Parsifal's quest for the Holy Grail makes him a different person, since there is no Christ, no blood, no cup to fill with it, no company of love in the mercantile protobourgeois world—Philip II's Spanish Empire, Vermeer's Delft. The Grail Knight must become the Girl Knight and seek out women, who alone remain prized, mysterious, imaginably holy, and who—unlike the Grail—remain multiple, sacred in each instance, each instance compelling to the next, the whole holiness graspable *only when all the instances have been embraced.* Women are many. Manifold as the opportunities for grace in a godly world, manifold as the opportunities for profit in a merchant world.

And then Faust is a very old youth indeed, and the spirit of his quest is alive enough in him to make him uncomfortable with his wife, displeased serenity. Serenity means night music. And he doesn't want to go to bed yet. Not yet.

*

Faust teaches how to relax into ardor. His pupils come up the stairs one by one most days, he embraces them one by one as they come in. Hour after hour, life after life. When they leave they take the wax of his candle, leaving him to keep his flame alive as well as he can. They take the glass of his glasses, the sand of his hourglass, the Christ off his crucifix, the words out of his books, so at midnight he has to pray to an empty wall.

All they leave him is geometry. All they leave him is empty pages and a still keen urge to fill them.

Robert Kelly

In his discomfort with his stillness, he writes essays on Nomadic Poetics, on the Art of Exiles. He rediscovers in the curlicues of his wet fleshly brain the lost Germanic epic the poet Ovid wrote during his exile among the Goths. He argues that literature reveals its truth best in translation, when it is estranged from what it supposes to be itself and becomes the other, or at least the other's. Undistracted by the sound of its own voice, the smell of its own breath, it is candid in translation.

*

Faust thinking:
I have achieved the transmutation. The work of thirty-seven years has finally, quietly, been completed. The stone. Bred in mind then banished to the world of objects, returns and recognizes itself a subject again. Returns to my body. To be my bones. Every bone renewed. Every integument by which one bone knows another.

Then he takes out a postcard of the Tour Saint-Jacques and turns it over. He writes in Latin on the message half of the card. In translation, he has said: This erection in Paris not far from the Town Hall, the Woman's Cathedral, the River, this upthrust emblem tells much of my story. Stonework, the little lizards who run down from the sun, the girls who make waterspouts of their hands so that the rain says something to the street below. He has room only to sign: *your Faust*. But he does not write anything in the name and address side of the card. He does not know to whom to send it. He turns the card over again and admires, above and on either side of the mysterious tower the uninflected vivid blue of the sky.

I have achieved the stone. It has come home and claimed me.

I belong to all the things I ever said.

He crosses that out and tries again: I belong to all the things I never made.

Awake now, he gets up with a stiffness in which he imagines he can distinguish the muscular torpor of recent sleep from the clumsy stiffness of old age. He goes across the room, away from

114

the window, and pours himself a glass of liqueur, green pastis, and pours some water onto it, so that the clear emerald green turns yellow and grows turbid. He drinks some of this, and goes back to his chair, balances the glass on the chair arm.

They know my name but they do not call me. I know their names but do not touch them. We are even in our sad desuetude. We are equals.

*

Faust puts maps up on his walls—stained, wrinkled, discolored sheets that represent, usually ineptly, the glorious landscapes of the earth that once were women, stayed women long enough for the eye of the artist to observe them, and recognize their lineaments afterward in the habit of sea and the haberdashery of rock and cloud.

A map on the wall is always a woman in disguise. He writes this and thinks about crossing it out.

Then he fears that doing so will make it all the truer, since the hidden is worth more than the evident, isn't it?

Elle, qui fût la belle heaulmière. The woman who once was beautiful, another man's wife. A woman lost. Or still here, hidden in time. Heart hidden in mocking ribs.

Faust thinks of a woman standing at a window, taking in a view of the city, perhaps giving the city a view of herself. Which comes first, to see or to be seen? How are they different?

Sometimes he sees her as if he were looking up at her from the sidewalk several stories below. Sometimes, though, he is in the room with her, watching from behind, observing what little of the sky and house roofs and steeples is not obscured by the graceful curve of her opaque and curious body.

She stands there against the light. She who used to stand for the light. The only light he needed. Once.

115

Robert Kelly

Sometimes he sees her as from a window directly across the street from hers. At those times, their eyes seldom meet. But sometimes they do, and they dare to stare. There, each thinks, that is the one they call the other.

And when they stare, then it is that Faust, not she, is the first who looks away, shy not of the woman (I think) but shy of the sudden suspicion that he is looking into a mirror, and that she is he.

Or that the only woman left to him is the one projected from his eyes.

A woman is a mirror, he writes, and crosses it out.

Maybe she is the only woman he ever knew, even though he successfully courted one thousand and three of them in Spain. Were they just the several, separate breaths of his sighing, his desiring? Maps, walls, women—all symbols of one another. But of what else?

That too he thinks about crossing out, and does, then realizes—as if a moment too late—that Else is a woman's name too.

He wonders: the poison in the little blue phial, warm from my touch now, a blue pearl, a blue rose of forgetfulness, haven't I drunk it already, many times, haven't I died many times?

And then he forgets. He forgets, just as he has forgotten many times before. Only in forgetting can he go on.

Startles, wakes, starts again. The blue poison is surely my ink. Why didn't I know it long ago? The clear poison took color from the bottle in which it lived so long.

Now he writes the world dead. Word by word.

Death lives in glass.

Faust is almost sleeping now. Blue ink.

I have used this ink to poison the world, infect you. Love letter by love letter, poem by poem, treatise by treatise, I have infected you with my own virus, with me, with me, with the view from my window I made you once, once, think was your own. And in that rapt moment when you knew me as yourself, we lay down together as it always was, became as close to one as two can get

> and this love lasted till the light faded from both our windows
> and all our doors were banging in the wind
> and one of us got up to shut them and the other was alone
> and never came back and still am alone.

Faust is sleeping. The blue bottle rolls out of his fingers and drops, unbroken, into the skirts of his warm robe that bunch at the foot of his chair.

Errantry

Elizabeth Hand

I WAS HANGING OUT in Angus's apartment above the print shop, scoring some of his ADHD medication, when Tommy Devaraux ran upstairs to tell us he'd just seen the Folding Man over at the Old Court Grill. This was some years after the new century had cracked open and left me and my friends scrambled, even more feckless than we'd been thirty years earlier when we met as teenagers in Kamensic Village. The three of us had been romantically involved off and on during high school and for a few years afterward, held together by the wobbly gravitational pull exerted by adolescence and the strange, malign beauty of Kamensic, a once-rural town that had since been ravaged by gentrification and whose name had recently been trade-marked by a domestic housewares tycoon.

Angus had never left Kamensic; he'd spent the last three decades nurturing a musical career that never quite took off, despite a minor 1977 hit that continued to generate residuals and a ringtone that now echoed eerily across the floor of the New York Stock Exchange. His most recent job had been with a brokerage firm absorbed by MortNet. The three kids from his first marriage were grown, but the younger ones, twins, had just started school, and child support and legal bills from the second divorce had stripped him of almost everything.

His ex-wife Sheila and the twins remained in the McMansion out by Kamensic Meadows, but Angus lived in a third-floor flat he rented from another old friend who owned the struggling printing company below. The entire rickety wood-frame building smelled of dust and ink, the faintly resinous odor of paper mingled with acrid chemical pigments and the reek of melted plastic. In bed at night in Angus's room, with the old presses rumbling on the floor below, it felt as though we were on a train. Walls and floors vibrated around us and a sallow street lamp coated the window with a syrupy greenish light. A few yards away, real trains racketed between the city and the outer exurbs.

I lived sixty miles north of Kamensic, in the next county, but spent more time in my old stomping grounds than reason or propriety allowed. Angus was my half brother, the result of what Shakespearean scholars term a bed-trick. We didn't know of our complicated parentage when we first slept together, but once we learned about it we figured it was too late and what the hell. Few people besides us ever knew, and most of them are now dead. My own career, as assistant professor of Arthurian studies at a small college upstate, had flamed out due to accusations of sexual harassment (dropped when a student recanted his story) and drug and alcohol abuse (upheld). Despite my dismissal, I found work as a private tutor, coaching rich kids on their college admissions essays.

"Vivian," Tommy said breathlessly when I opened the door. "Angus here?"

I brushed my cheek against Tommy's as he swept inside and crossed to where Angus sat hunched over his computer. Tommy peered at the monitor and frowned. "Where's Estelle?"

Tommy had a little obsessive thing that dovetailed neatly with Angus's frenetic energy, as in their latest collaboration, a thirty-seven-song cycle Angus was writing about Estelle, an imaginary woman based on a real woman, a stockbroker Tommy had dated once. He became obsessed with her, and she eventually hit him with a restraining order and moved to Vermont.

Angus scowled. "I'm taking a break from freaking Estelle."

"Well, sacrifice that Voidwalker and log off," said Tommy. "I just saw the Folding Man."

"At the Old Court?" Angus ground out his cigarette and lit another. "He's there now? Why didn't you just call us?"

Tommy glanced at me imploringly. He was tall but sparely built, softer than he'd been but still boyish, with round tortoiseshell glasses on a snub nose, his long dark hair gone to gray; slightly louche in a frayed Brooks Brothers jacket and shiny black engineer's boots. He was a special ed teacher at a private school and dealt with autistic teenagers, many of them violent. He'd been attacked so often by kids bigger and stronger than he was that he'd started to have panic attacks, and now took so much Xanax just to get through the working day that his customary expression was a rictus of mournful, slightly hostile chagrin—he looked like the Mock Turtle after a lost weekend.

"Well, he left," he said. "Plus my cell phone died. But he gave me this—"

He sank into a swivel chair beside Angus, hands cupped on his knees as though he held a butterfly. The illusion held for an instant when he opened his hands to display a tiny diadem of russet and yellow petals that fluttered when he breathed upon it.

"Nice," said Angus grudgingly. "He'll be gone by now."

I crouched beside Tommy and stared at it. "Can I see?"

"Sure."

I picked it up and weighed it tentatively in my palm. Angus's Focalin was starting to have its way with me, a diffuse, sunny-day buzz that meshed nicely with the day outside: midafternoon, early May, lilac in bloom, kids riding bikes along the village sidewalks. I drew my hand to my face and caught a whiff of the Old Court's distinctive odor, hamburgers and Pine-Sol, but also, inexplicably, a smell of the sea, salt, and hot glass.

I blew on the bit of folded paper. It fell onto the floor. Angus grabbed it before I could pick it up again.

"He gave it to me," Tommy said in an aggrieved tone.

But Angus was already opening it. Tommy and I stood beside him as he carefully unfolded wings, triangles, unveiling creases in once-glossy paper, swatches of azure and silver, topaz, pine green. The yellow and russet-colored petals must have sprung from the other side of the page, torn from a magazine or brochure.

"Someone's been to the beach." Angus held up a finger dusted with glittering specks, spilled sugar or sand; licked it and smoothed out the paper on his desk.

"What does it say?" asked Tommy.

"'YOU ARE HERE.'"

I edged between them to get a better look. The paper was four or five inches square, crosshatched with grayish lines indicating where it had been folded countless times. It was almost impossible to imagine it had ever had a shape other than this one, and impossible to remember just what that shape had been—an insect? tiger lilies?

"Beach roses," said Tommy. "That's what it's a picture of."

"How the hell can you know that?" demanded Angus.

"It's a map," I said.

Angus's cell phone buzzed. He glanced at it, muttered, "Sheila," and turned it off. "Let's see."

I adjusted my glasses and frowned. "It's hard to see, but there—those lines? It says Route 22."

"That's the Old Court there," Tommy agreed, squinting at a blotch on a smudge of shoreline. "Those dotted lines, that's the old road that runs parallel to it, out toward that apple farm where they want to put the development."

Ashes dropped from Angus's cigarette onto the ersatz map. When he blew them away, a tiny spark glowed in one corner.

"There." Tommy stubbed out the ember with his finger. "It ends there."

"Like I said." Angus finished his cigarette. "X marks the spot. Let's go check it out. Who wants to get stoned?"

Angus had retained a company car, I never understood how. The back was filled with his stuff, sheet music, CDs, manila envelopes, Happy Meal toys, a guitar case. I sat in the front with Angus's hand on my knee. Tommy shoved stuff aside and slumped in the back, his face pressed against the window. He looked like a kid on a long drive, at once resigned and expectant. I thought, not for the first time, how little had changed since we really were kids: still bombing around on a Saturday afternoon, drunk or stoned or generally messed up, still screwing each other when no one else would have us, still singing along with the radio.

"Is there a channel just for your songs?" asked Tommy as we drove over the railroad tracks and headed north to old Route 22. Angus tapped the radio screen until he found something he liked. "Like, is there a satellite that just beams 'Do It All Day'?"

"That would be the Burnout Channel."

"This is the Cowsills," I said. "That song about the park and other things."

"*And then I knew,*" chanted Tommy, "*that she had made me happy.*"

"Happy, happy," echoed Angus. He began to sing his own words.

> "*I love the Folding Man*
> *He may be just a drunk*
> *And I'm a worn-out skunk....*"

Outside, the remnants of old Kamensic slid past, stone churches; the sprawling Victorian where Angus had grown up, now a B and B; the ancient cemetery with its strange stone animals; Deer Park Inn, a former dive that had been cleaned up and christened the Deer Park Tavern, its shattered blacktop newly paved and full of SUVs and Priuses. It was easy to blame these changes on Marian Lavecque, the domestic maven whose reign had redrawn the town's aesthetic and cultural boundaries.

But I knew the decline stretched back longer than that, to the years when Angus and I had first become entangled. So it was hard some-times—for me anyway, since my academic background had trained me to see patterns everywhere, a subtle tapestry woven into the grungiest Missoni knockoff—not to feel that our folie à deux had broken something in the place we loved most.

One upshot was that we had to go farther afield now to find a bar that suited us. I'd never heard of the Folding Man being anywhere but the Old Court.

I reached to touch Tommy's knee. "You OK back there?"

"Sure," he said. "We're on a quest." He smiled as Angus's voice filled the car.

> *"I love the Folding Man*
> *He may be just a geek*
> *And I'm a burned-out freak. . . ."*

Tommy was the one who'd always believed in things. Even though he could never really explain to you exactly what those things were; only trace circles in the air when he was drunk, or go into long, ram-bling exegeses of conspiracies between real estate developers and the Zen Buddhists who'd built a retreat house on what had once been old-growth forest, or the purported sexual relationship, based on a mutual desire to make artisanal cheese, that existed between Estelle, the woman he'd been obsessed with, and a dot-com millionaire who did in fact now live in Vermont. I felt protective of Tommy, although when drunk he could become bellicose, even violent. Asleep he resembled a high-school athlete fallen on hard times, his T-shirt rid-ing up to show a slack torso, gray hair, an appendectomy scar like a wincing mouth, a bad tattoo of a five-pointed star.

Whereas Angus retained the body he'd had as a teenager, his skin smooth and unblemished, pale as barley; he slept curled on his side and breathed softly, like a child, occasionally sighing as in some deep regret he couldn't acknowledge in waking life. Then the deep lines on his face seemed to fade, and his eyes, closed, held no hint of what burned there when he stared at you.

"Let's stop for a minute," I said as we crested the hill overlooking the Old Court.

"He won't be there." Angus glanced into the rearview mirror. "You said he left."

"Yeah, he left." Tommy opened his window. A green smell filled the car, young ferns and the leaves of crushed meadowsweet. "But stop anyway."

Inside, the Old Court was sunlit, its curved oak bar glossy as caramel and warm to the touch. A few elderly bikers sat drinking beer or coffee and watching the Golf Channel. We sat at the far end, where it was quieter, in front of the brass bowl that held the Folding Man's handiwork.

"Back already?" Nance, the bartender, smiled at Tommy, then glanced out the window to see whose car was parked there: not Tommy's, so she could serve him. "You want the same?"

Tommy and I had red wine, Angus a rum and Coke. Tommy drank fast—he always did—and ordered another. I drank mine almost as quickly, then shut my eyes, reached into the brass bowl, and withdrew a piece of folded paper.

The Folding Man's work isn't exactly origami. Tommy has showed some of it to a woman he knows who does origami, and she said it was like nothing she'd ever seen before. The Folding Man doesn't talk about it either, which is probably why Tommy became obsessed with him. Nothing gets Tommy as revved up as being ignored—Angus says he's seen Tommy get a hard-on when a woman rejects him.

Not that Tommy had ever actually met the Folding Man, until now. None of us had, even though he'd been a fixture at the Old Court for as long as we'd been drinking there. We first began to notice his work in the early 1980s when, before or after a wild night, we'd find these little folded figures left on the floor near where we'd been sitting.

"This is like that guy in *Blade Runner*," said Tommy once. He'd picked up something that resembled a winged scorpion. "See?"

I looked at it closely and saw it had the face of Anjelica Huston and, instead of pincers, a pair of spoons for claws.

But then Tommy carefully unfolded it, smoothing it on the bar.

"Don't get it wet," warned Angus.

"I won't." Tommy looked puzzled. He slid the crumpled paper to me. "It's gone."

"What's gone?"

I looked at the paper, and saw it was a square taken from an ad for Yves Saint Laurent Opium perfume—the word OPIUM was there, and part of the bottle, and I could even smell a musky trace of the fragrance.

But there was no woman anywhere in the ad. I turned the paper over: nada. No spoons, either.

"Edward James Olmos."

Tommy and I turned to stare blankly at Angus.

"That's who played that character." He took the paper and scrutinized it, then flicked his cigarette lighter and set it on fire and dropped it in his ashtray. "In *Blade Runner*. Edward James Olmos. Great actor."

The Folding Man's stuff was always like that. Things were never quite what they seemed to be. Sea anemones with eyes and wheels, body parts—vulvas were a popular theme—that sprouted fingers, exotic birds with too many heads and hooves instead of feathers, a lunar lander printed with a map of the Sea of Tranquility, the extravagant effects produced by some infernal combination of paper folding and whatever was actually printed on the paper. None of them was any larger than the area I could circumscribe with my thumb and forefinger, and some were much smaller.

But if you unfolded them, they were never what they *didn't* seem to be, either—you ended up with nothing but a page from a magazine or travel brochure, or a paper menu from McDonald's or the Kamensic Diner, or (in the case of the lunar lander) a fragment of the Playbill for *Via Galactica*. They were like origami figures from the Burgess Shale, beautiful but also slightly nightmarish.

And what made it even stranger was that no one except for me and Tommy and, to a lesser degree, Angus, ever seemed to think they were weird at all. No one paid much attention to them; no one thought they were mysterious. When Tommy started asking about who made them, Nance just shrugged.

"This guy, comes in sometimes to watch the game. I think maybe he used to smoke or something, like he wants to do something with his hands. So he does those."

"What's his name?" said Tommy.

Nance shook her head. "I don't know. We just call him the Folding Man."

"You don't know his name?" Angus stared at her, his tone slightly belligerent, as it often was. "What, he never puts down a credit card? You know everyone's name."

"He drinks rail whiskey, and he pays cash. Ask him yourself if you really want to know."

But before now we'd never seen him, not ever, not once, though over the years Tommy had chased down customers and bartenders to receive detailed descriptions of what he looked like: older, paunchy, gray hair, weathered face, unshaven, eyes that were usually described as blue or gray, glasses, faded corduroys, and a stained brown windbreaker.

"He looks like a fucking wino, Tommy," Angus exploded once, when the hundredth customer had been quizzed after a thumbnail-sized frog with match-head eyes and the faces of the original Jackson Five had materialized beneath Tommy's barstool. "Give it a fucking break, OK?"

But Tommy couldn't give it a break, any more than he could keep from getting obsessively fixated on women he hardly knew. Neither could I, and, after a while, neither could Angus, though Angus was the one who made the ground rule about never taking any of the folded paper figures out of the Old Court.

"There's enough crap in my apartment. Yours too, Tommy."

Nance didn't like customers taking them from the brass bowl, either.

"Leave them!" she'd yell if someone tried to pocket one at the end of the night. "They're part of the decor!"

I knew Tommy had nicked some. I found one under his pillow once, a lovely, delicate thing shaped like a swan, or a borzoi, or maybe it was a meerschaum pipe, with rows of teeth and a tiny pagoda on what I thought was its head (or bowl). I was going to make a joke about it, but Tommy was in the bathroom, and the longer I lay there with that weird, nearly weightless filigree in the palm of my hand, the harder it was to look at anything else, or think of anything except the way it seemed to glow, a pearlescent, rubeus color, like the inside of a child's ear when you shine a flashlight behind it.

When I heard Tommy come out of the bathroom I slipped it back beneath the pillow. Later, when I searched for it again, I found nothing but a crumpled sale flyer from the old Kamensic Hardware Store.

Now I set my wineglass on the bar, opened my eyes, and looked at what I had picked from the brass bowl. A fern, gold rather than green, its fiddlehead resembling the beaked prow of a Viking ship.

"Let's go." Tommy stuck some bills under his empty glass and stood.

"We just got here," said Angus.

"I don't want to lose him."

Angus looked at me, annoyed, then finished his drink. "Yeah, whatever. Come on, Vivian."

I replaced the fern and gulped the rest of my wine, and we returned to the car. I sat in the back so Tommy could ride up front with Angus and navigate.

I said, "You didn't tell us what he looked like."

Tommy spread the piece of paper on his knee. "He looked like a wino."

"Did you talk to him? Did he say anything?"

"Yeah." Tommy turned to look at me. He grinned, that manic school's-out grin that still made everything seem possible. "I asked him how he did it, how he made everything. And he said, "Everything fits. You'll figure it out.'"

"'Everything fits, you'll figure it out?'" repeated Angus. "Who is this guy, Mister Rogers?"

Tommy only smiled. I leaned forward to kiss him, while Angus shook his head and we drove on.

We headed north on the old Brandywine Turnpike, a barely maintained road that runs roughly parallel to Route 22, and connects Kamensic via various gravel roads and shortcuts to the outlying towns and deeper woodlands that, for the moment, had escaped development metastasizing from the megalopolis. The boulder-strewn, glacier-carved terrain was inhospitable to builders, steeply sloped, and falling away suddenly into ravines overgrown with mountain ash and rock juniper that gave off a sharp tang of gin.

There were patches of genuine old-growth forest here, ancient towering hemlocks, white oaks, and hornbeams. Occasionally we'd pass an abandoned gas station or roadhouse, or the remains of tiny settlements long fallen into ruin beside spur roads that retained the names of their founders: Tintertown Road, Smithtown Road, Fancher's Corner. It was like driving back in time into the old Kamensic, the real Kamensic, the place we'd mapped through all our various lovers and drug dealers and music gigs over the last thirty years.

Only of course we were really driving *away* from Kamensic, slipping in and out of the town's borders, until we reached its outermost edge, the place where even the tax maps got sketchy.

This was where Muscanth Mountain and Sugar Mountain converged on Lake Muscanth. The mountains weren't mountains really, just big hills, but the lake was a real lake. In the 1920s a group of socialists had established a short-lived utopian community there, a summer encampment called the Fallows. Most of the cabins and the main lodge had rotted away fifty years ago.

But some remained, in varying states of decay—Angus and I first had sex together in one of these in 1973—and two or three had even been renovated as second homes. Zoning covenants designed to protect the wetland had kept the McMansions away, and some of the same old hippies who had taken over the cottages in the 1960s and '70s still lived there, or were rumored to—I hadn't been out to the lake in at least a dozen years.

"You know, this is going to totally fuck up my alignment," Angus swore as the car scraped across the rutted track. To the right, you could glimpse Lake Muscanth in flashes of silvery blue through dense stands of evergreen, like fish darting through murky water. "Damn it! Tom, I'm sorry, but if we don't find this place soon I'm—"

"Turn there." Tommy pointed to where the road divided a few yards ahead of us. "It should be just past where it curves."

Angus peered through the windshield. "I dunno, man. Those branches, they look like they're going to come down right on top of us."

"That's where the place is, dude," said Tommy as I stuck my head between the two of them to get a better view.

Angus was right. The narrow road, barely more than a path here, was flanked by thick stands of tamarack and cedar. They were so overgrown that in spots above the road their branches met and became tangled in a dense, low, overhanging mat of black and green. Angus tossed his cigarette out the window and veered cautiously to the right.

The effect wasn't of diving through a tunnel; more like being under the canopy of a bazaar or souk. Branches scraped the car in place of importuning shopkeepers grabbing at us.

Angus swore as tiny pinecones hailed down onto the roof. "I'm going back."

Tommy looked stricken. "Hey, we're almost there."

"It's a company car, Tommy!"

"I'll pay to have it painted, OK? Look, see? There it is, that house there—"

Angus glanced to the side then nodded. "Yeah, well, OK."

There was no driveway, just a flattish bit of ground where broken glass and scrap metal glinted through patchy moss and teaberry. Angus pulled onto this and turned the ignition off.

"So did this guy give you a phone number or something?" Angus asked after a moment. "Are we expected?"

Tommy sat with his fingers on the door handle and stared outside. The place was small, not a house at all but a cabin made of split logs painted brown. It wasn't much bigger than a motel cottage, with pine green shutters and trim, and a battered screen door that looked as though it had been flung open by someone who'd left in a big hurry and a bad mood. A sagging screened-in porch overlooked the lake. Stones had come loose from the fieldstone chimney and were scattered forlornly beneath the pine trees, like misshapen soccer balls. A rusted holding tank bulged beneath a broken window that had been repaired with a square of cardboard.

"Nice," said Angus.

No one got out of the car. Angus shot Tommy a bitter look, then took a roach from his pocket, lit it, and smoked in silence. When he held it out to me and Tommy, we declined. I'd become adept at fine-tuning the cocktail of drugs I needed to filter out the world, and Tommy's school job mandated random drug testing.

"So, Tom." Angus replaced the roach. The hand he'd kept on the steering wheel relaxed somewhat. "Where's your man?"

Tommy stared at the cabin. His face had that expression I loved, unabashed wonder struggling with suspicion and a long-entrenched fear of ridicule. It was a slightly crazed look, and I knew from long experience what could follow. Weird accusations, smashed guitars, broken fingers. But the alcohol and Xanax had done their job.

"I don't even care if he's here or not," said Tommy lightly, and stepped outside. "Remember when we used to come out to the lake all the time?"

"I do."

I hopped out and stood beside him. A warm wind blew off the water, bringing the smells of mud and cedar bark. A red-winged blackbird sang, and a lone peeper near the water's edge. Tommy put his arm across my shoulder, the Folding Man's map still in his hand. A moment later I felt Angus on my other side. His fingers touched mine and his mouth tightened as he gazed at the cabin, but after a moment he sighed.

"Yeah, this was a good idea." He looked at me and smiled, then knocked Tommy's arm from my shoulder. "No hogging the girl, dude. Let's check this place out."

Tommy headed toward the front door. Angus walked to the side to check out the broken window.

"Hey." He grabbed the cardboard by one corner and tried to wrest it from the window frame.

I came up alongside him. "What is it?"

"It's an album. Well, an album cover. Watch it—"

The cardboard buckled then abruptly popped out from the window.

Angus examined it cursorily, slid his hand inside the sleeve, and shook his head—no vinyl—then held it up for me to see: a black square with an inset color photo of two guys in full hippie regalia and psychedelic wording beneath.

TYRANNOSAURUS REX
PROPHETS SEERS AND SAGES
THE ANGELS OF THE AGES

"Is that T. Rex?"

He grinned. "I always, *always* wanted this album. I could never find it."

"You could probably find it now on eBay."

"I never wanted it that much." He laughed. "Actually, I totally forgot I wanted it, till now."

I took the cardboard sleeve. It was damp and smelled of mildew; black mold covered Marc Bolan's face and cape. When I tried to look inside, the soft cardboard tore.

I handed it back to Angus. "Is it worth anything?"

"Not anymore." He glanced at it then shrugged. "Nah, it's toast. It doesn't even have the record inside."

"I bet it's been rereleased. You should get it; it might give you and Tommy some ideas for Estelle."

Angus grimaced. "Trust me, Tommy doesn't need any more ideas about goddamn Estelle."

The song cycle had been my idea. "You're like a troubadour, Tommy," I had told him back when his obsession with the broker had spun completely out of control. "Their whole thing revolved around idealized unrequited love. You would have fit right in."

"Did their whole thing revolve around stalking women at Best Buy?" I remember Angus asked.

"That was an accident," said Tommy. "A total coincidence, she even admitted it."

"Did the troubadours ever get laid?" said Angus. "Because that would clinch the deal for me."

"I think you should channel all this into something constructive," I suggested. "Music, you guys haven't written anything together for a while."

The first songs Tommy had written all used the woman's real name.

"I don't think that's a good idea, Tommy," I'd said when he played

129

me the CD he'd burned. "Considering the restraining order and all."

"But I love her name." He had appeared genuinely distressed. "It's part of her, it's an extension of her, of everything she is—"

"You don't have a clue as to who she fucking is!" Angus grabbed the CD. "You went out with her once before she dumped you. It was like you dated a blow-up doll."

"She didn't dump me!"

"You're right—you were never involved enough to *be* dumped. You were downsized, Tommy. Admit it and get over it. Lot of fish in the sea, Tom."

Tommy got over it, sort of. In the song, he changed the woman's name to Estelle, at any rate.

It remained a sore point with Angus. He turned and skimmed the album cover toward the lake. I walked to join Tommy on the cabin's front steps.

I asked, "What're you doing?"

"Mail tampering."

A stoved-in mailbox dangled beside the door. I watched as Tommy prized it open, fished around inside, and withdrew a wad of moldering letters, junk mail, mostly. He peeled oversized envelopes away from sales flyers, releasing a fetid smell, then finally held up an envelope with the familiar ConEd logo.

"It's a cutoff notice," he said in triumph. Angus had wandered back and looked at him dubiously. "It's got his name on it. Orson Shemeltoss."

"Orson Shemeltoss? What the hell kind of name is that?"

Tommy ignored him. The wind sent the screen door swinging; he pushed it away, then knocked loudly on the front door. "Mr. Shemeltoss? Hello? Mr. Shemeltoss?"

Silence. Angus looked at me. We both started to laugh.

"Hey, shut up," said Tommy.

Angus pushed him aside, cracked the door open, and yelled.

"Yo, Orson! Tommy's here."

Tommy swore, but Angus had already stepped inside.

"It's OK." I patted Tommy's shoulder. "You're sure this is his place, right? So he's expecting you."

"I guess," said Tommy.

He pushed the door open and went after Angus. I followed, almost immediately drew up short. "Holy shit."

The room—and what was it, anyway? living room? hallway? foyer?—I couldn't tell, but it was so crammed with junk that walking was nearly impossible. It was like wading across a sandbar at high tide, through stacks of newspaper and magazines and books that once had towered above my head but had now collapsed to form a waist-high reef of paper. Things shifted underfoot as I moved, and when I tried to clamber on top of a stack, it wobbled then flew apart in a storm of white and gray.

"Vivian, over here!"

I pushed myself up, coughing as I breathed in paper dust and mold. A dog barked, close enough that I looked around anxiously.

But I saw no sign of a dog, or Tommy; only Angus standing a few feet away, surrounded by overflowing bookshelves.

"It's better over here." He reached across a mound of magazines to grab my hand, and pulled me toward him. "C'mon, thatta girl—"

"It's like the print shop exploded," I said, still coughing. The smell of mold was so strong it burned my nostrils.

"It's a lot worse than that." Angus stared in disbelief. "This guy has some issues about letting go."

Everywhere around us was—stuff. Junk mail and books and magazines mostly, also a lot of photos—snapshots, old Polaroids—but other things too. Board games, Bratz dolls, stuffed animals, oddments of clothing, stiletto heels and lingerie and studded collars, eight-track tapes and a battered saxophone, all protruding from the morass of paper like the detritus left by a receding flood. Vinyl record albums filled a wall of buckled metal shelving. Here and there I could discern bits of furniture—the uppermost rungs of a ladderback chair, a headboard.

And, scattered everywhere, the eerie paper figures that were the Folding Man's handiwork. I dropped Angus's hand and picked up one of them, a horned creature made of aluminum foil. Inexplicably, and despite the pervasive smell of mildew, my mouth began to water. It was only after I unfolded the little form that I saw the Arby's logo printed on it.

"Where's Tommy?" I asked.

"I dunno."

Angus turned and began to push his way to the far side of the room. I tossed the bit of foil and grabbed another figure—there were hundreds of them, thousands maybe, so many it was impossible not to think of them as somehow alive, burrowing up through those countless layers of junk.

I wondered if it was like an archaeological dig, or geological strata: was there a Golden Age buried under there, before *People* magazine ruled the earth? If I reached the very bottom, would I find Little Nemo and the Katzenjammer Kids?

I doubted it. I could see nothing but junk. All the magazines seemed to be well worn, and many were torn or missing their covers. The other stuff seemed to be ruined as well, toys broken or missing parts, clothes soiled or unraveling. The photos were ripped or water damaged, and a lot appeared to be charred or otherwise damaged by smoke or fire.

It was like the town dump, only worse—you could scavenge things from the dump. But it was difficult to imagine there was anything here worth saving, except for the thousands of origami-like figures. I picked one up. It was larger than most, big enough to cover my palm, plain white paper. It resembled a bird of some sort, a heron maybe, with tiny six-fingered hands instead of wings and a broad, flattened bill like a shovel. Its eyes were wide and staring: an owl's eyes, not a heron's. I unfolded it and smoothed it out atop a heap of *National Geographic*s. A missing flyer, the kind you see in post offices or police stations, with a black-and-white image of a teenage girl's face photocopied from a high-school portrait. Dark curly hair, freckles, dark eyes. Last seen May 14, 1982, Osceola, Wisconsin.

"Oh," said Angus in a low voice.

I glanced at him, but he wasn't looking at me. He was leaning against a bare patch of wall, turning the pages of a small red-bound book.

I picked my way carefully to his side. "What is it?"

"I used to read this to Corey when he was little." He didn't look up, just continued to turn the pages, stopping to pull them gently apart where they were stuck together. "Every night, it was the only thing he ever wanted to hear. He knew it by heart. I never knew what happened to it."

I stood beside him and stared at a picture of a rabbit in a rocking chair, cats playing on a rug, a wall of bookshelves.

"It's even missing the same page," Angus said. His face twisted. He turned from me, reaching for his pocket. Tommy's alarmed voice came from somewhere across the room.

"I wouldn't light up in here!"

Angus frowned, then reluctantly nodded. "Yeah, right. Bad idea."

I said nothing, and after a moment began to make my way unsteadily toward where Tommy's voice had come from. A few times I almost fell, and tried to catch myself by instinctively grabbing at whatever was closest to me—handfuls of newspapers, an oversized

Sears family photo in a shattered frame, the tip of an artificial Christmas tree.

But this only made it more difficult to move, as the stacks invariably tottered and fell, so that I found myself half buried in the Folding Man's junk. I thought of the advice given to hikers trapped in an avalanche—to surf through the snow or, if buried, to swim upward, to the surface—and pushed back an unpleasant image of what else might be under those layers of mildewed paper and chewed-up toys.

The dog barked again, closer this time.

"Tommy? You see a dog somewhere?" I yelled, but got no reply.

I straightened and looked back. Angus had slumped to sit precariously on a sagging mound of papers, head bowed as he turned the pages of the little book back and forth, back and forth. I shut my eyes and ran my hand across piles of paper till I felt a paper figure, picked it up, and opened my eyes. The squarish head of an animal, catlike, with a small snout and large eyes that, as I unfolded and flattened it, became a ripped piece of paper, washes of green and brown and blue, with words beneath.

GOOD NIGHT BEARS
GOOD NIGHT CHAIRS

I dropped it and took a few painstaking steps in the direction of a door. I could hear faint scrabbling, and then Tommy exclaiming softly. I wondered if he'd found the dog. I stopped, listening.

I heard nothing. I glanced down and saw a white cylinder poking up between a copy of *Oui* magazine and what looked like the keyboard from an old typewriter. I pushed aside the typewriter, grabbed the cylinder, and pulled it free: a small poster rolled into a tube.

The edges were stuck together and tore as I unrolled it. The once-glossy paper had been nibbled by insects or mice, and was dusted with dull green spores that powdered the air when I held it up.

But toward the center the image was still clearly visible, vibrant even, and as recognizable to me as my own face.

It was a print of Uccello's *The Hunt in the Forest*. The original hung in the Ashmolean Museum at Oxford. I had never seen it, but when I was nine I'd come across the picture in a children's book about King Arthur and the Middle Ages. The painting actually dated to the Renaissance—the late 1500s—and it had nothing to do with Arthur, or England.

But for me it was inextricably tied up with everything I had ever dreamed or imagined about that world. A sense of imminence and urgency, of simple things—horses, dogs, people, grass—charged with an expectant, slightly sinister meaning I couldn't grasp but still felt, even as a kid. The hunters in their crimson tunics astride their mounts and the horses rearing from turf whorled with white flowers; the greyhounds springing joyously, heads thrown back and paws upraised as though partaking in some wild dance; the beaters—boys in tunics colored like Easter eggs, creamy yellow and pink and periwinkle blue—chasing after the dogs. To the left of the painting, a single black-clad man—knight? lord? cleric?—rode a horse as richly caparisoned as the rest. Dogs and horses and men and boys all ran in the same direction, toward the center of the painting where a half-dozen stags leapt, poised and improbable as the flattened targets in a shooting range.

And above everything, mysterious, columnar trees that opened into leafy parasols, like the carven pillars in a vast and endless cathedral, trees and hunters and animals finally receding into darkness as black and undifferentiated as the inside of a lacquered box.

I had not seen the image, or thought of it, in years. But it all came back to me now in a confused, almost fretful rush, like the memory of the sort of dream you have when sick.

"Vivian." I started at the sound of Tommy's voice, calling from the next room. "Viv—"

I dropped the poster and pushed my way to the open door. A narrow path led into the room, wide enough that I could pass without knocking anything over.

"Tommy?" I strained to see him over a mound of old clothes. "You OK?"

It must have been a bedroom once, though I saw no furniture, nothing but old clothes and shoes, wads of rolled-up belts like nested snakes.

But I could see the wall, close enough that I could almost touch it, with a closet door that hung loosely where its hinges had twisted from the sheetrock. Tommy was crouched beside the door. One hand was extended toward something on the floor inside the closet; the other was pressed against his cheek as he shook his head and murmured wordlessly.

I thought it was the dog. I swore under my breath and felt sick, looked over my shoulder as I called for Angus. I stumbled the last few steps through tangled clothing until I reached Tommy's side, and knelt beside him.

It wasn't a dog. It was a woman, nineteen or twenty, lying on one side with her knees drawn up and her clenched fists against her chin. I gasped and grabbed at the wall to steady myself.

"Shh," whispered Tommy. He reached to touch her forehead, then drew his hand gently down her face, tracing freckled cheekbones, her chapped lower lip. "She's sleeping."

Angus ran into the room behind me. "Holy shit. Is she dead? What are—"

"*Shhh.*" Tommy turned to look at us. His eyes were wide, not with amazement but something more like barely suppressed rage, or terror, or even pain.

Then he blinked, and for the first time seemed to notice me. "Hey, Vivian. Angus. Look. Look—"

I turned to stare at Angus, too stunned even to be afraid. He stared back, speechless. We both looked at Tommy again.

His hand cradled the girl's cheek as he crooned to her beneath his breath. Without warning, her eyelids fluttered. I jumped. Angus grabbed my arm.

"Fucking hell," he whispered. "Fucking hell, fucking—"

"Shut *up.*" Tommy's face was fierce, but then the girl stirred, moaning. He set his hands lightly on her shoulders.

"It's OK," he said. "You're OK, I'm here, someone's here. . . ."

She tried to sit up, gave a small cry. Her head drooped; she retched and Tommy held her as she spat up a trickle of liquid.

"That's a girl," he murmured. "That's my girl. . . ."

I could see her clearly now, her hair dark and matted, thick, a few curls springing loose to frame her pale face. She wore a man's white button-down shirt, seamed with dirt and rust stains, blue jeans, white tennis socks with filthy pom-poms at the ankles.

"Is she OK?" said Angus.

"Sure she's OK," said Tommy in that same low, reassuring voice. "Sure she's OK, she's going to be just fine. . . ."

I stumbled forward to help him carry her. Angus tried to clear a way for us, kicking at old clothes and magazines as we lurched from room to room, until finally we all stood by the front door. The girl's head lolled against Tommy's shoulder. Angus looked at her in concern, but I also saw how his gaze flickered to her soiled shirt with its missing buttons, the frayed cloth gaping so you could see her breasts, the spray of freckles across her clavicle and throat.

"What's your name?" he asked.

She looked up. Not at us: at Tommy, who stared down at her with lips compressed, smiling slightly.

"Stella." Her voice rose tremulously on the second syllable, as though it were a question. "Stella."

The dog barked again, not inside the house this time but somewhere nearby, just out of sight among the evergreens. Angus ran to the car as Tommy and I helped the girl across the mossy ground.

"There's so much crap in there, I don't even know if there's room." Angus clambered into the backseat and started shoving stuff onto the floor. "Shit!"

"It's OK," said Tommy. He'd removed his jacket and was helping the girl pull her arms through its sleeves. "We'll make room."

"Yeah, but what about this!" Angus shook his guitar case. "What about *her?* We need to call the police, or—"

"Just get in," said Tommy. He eased the girl into the backseat. Angus hurried to the trunk and shoved in the guitar case. "We'll make it fit, we'll figure it out."

I leaned inside and pulled the seat belt across the girl's chest. "Thank you," she whispered. Her eyes were almost black, with irises that seemed to have no pupil. Her breath smelled of leaf mold and cloves.

My heart thumped so hard it hurt. I smiled, then backed away so that Tommy could slide in beside her.

"Let's go," he said.

I got into the front with Angus. "Now what?"

He shrugged and tossed something into my lap: the ruined picture book he'd read inside. "I have no fucking clue," he said, and started the engine. "But I guess we'll figure out something."

I rolled my window down and leaned out. A flurry of wings, a keening cry as a pair of wood ducks rose from the lake and flew agitatedly toward the trees. The wind had shifted; it carried now the smell of rain, of lilacs. I glanced into the backseat and saw the girl sitting with her face upturned to Tommy's. His hand was on her knee, his own face stared straight ahead, to where the road stretched before us, darker now, the dirt and gravel rain spattered and the ferns at road's edge unfurling, pale green and misty white. I heard another bark, and then a second echoing yelp; the distant sound of voices, laughter. As the car rounded a curve I looked back and saw several small lean forms, white and gray, too blurred for me to discern clearly, racing through the underbrush before they broke free momentarily into a bright clearing, muzzles gleaming in a sudden shaft of sun before they disappeared once more into the trees.

Interval

Aimee Bender

Dt.dt.dt.dt.dt.dt.dt.

Or-phan . . . or-phan . . . Or-phan . . . or-phan . . .

theraft—theraft—theraft—

ON THE FIRST DAY of sculpture class, the sculptor-to-be sat down with his tools. With him he had brought a wooden shaping fork; a metal prong; gloves that he was not sure he intended to use, liking as he did to touch the clay; a spoon for smoothing—one used the backside, he had been told—and a spool of wire, for zip-cutting through. He delighted in the smell of clay, had always delighted in it, had never thought he could be the type of person that would attend a sculpture class but this one had fallen into his lap, perfect timing, affordable, around the corner from his apartment, and he watched the teacher in her high heels and swirly skirt navigate the large square lumps of terra-cotta–colored clay that she brought to each pupil, each sitting upright in his or her chair, the live nude model undressing behind the muted white screen.

He was watching the model step aside from the screen, and he was so involved with how easily she stood in her own body—an imperfect body, a little tugged down at the hips, sort of wobbly at the knees, but relaxed in itself, accepting of itself, and he was also watching how the other students, who seemed so professional! immediately dove into their clay like it was no big deal that an attractive woman was now stepping into their view, nude, ready to be shaped by their hands. And he was so involved with watching her, and with starting to see the shapes that were her, the shapes that he would soon be creating from his very own lump of clay, that he did not notice until the teacher was right up in front of his face that she did

137

not have a block of clay in her hands.

He was not the end of the row, either; there were about three more students past him.

Here, she said, handing him nothing. Sculpt.

There's no more clay? he asked, unable to keep the rise of disappointment out of his voice. She shook her head, and then went back to her desk, returning in seconds with another square block of clay, and he smiled in relief, awaiting the pleasure, the pewterlike wetness of it, but she walked right past him and gave it to the young man on his left, who was busily clearing space on his desk. And then two more blocks of clay, for the two past that man, and the model, taking her pose in front of them, sitting, with her hands folded on her knee, and her one foot a little lower than the other, and her head turned, in profile.

Excuse me, said the young man, unsure what to call the instructor. Professor? Ma'am?

She approached, with the raised eyebrows of the listening teacher. Yes? Question?

I'm sorry, he said. Were we supposed to purchase the clay in advance?

No, she said. It is covered in the cost of the course.

Oh. He looked around, hoping he would not have to ask the question, the highly obvious question, while all the other students in class were busily getting their hands all over that clay, shaping and building the model's shoulders.

"Begin with torso!" the teacher yelled to the group, and then returned to him, with her quieter face. Yes?

But I did not get any clay? he said, showing the space in front of him. Empty. His tools neatly laid out, expectant.

You don't get clay, she said.

But I signed up for the Introduction to Sculpture class, he said, beginning to feel angry. I would like some clay, he said.

And he wondered if he had somehow offended the teacher earlier? If so, how? He had come inside, placed his tools on the desk, and waited quietly. He had parked in the parking lot without incident. She seemed surprised at his surprise, which he found disconcerting, since the problem seemed so clear.

You are to sculpt the sounds of the room, she said. I have a note next to your name in my role book.

Excuse me?

Off she tripped in her heels, returning with the class roster, and there were the names of all the class members, and there was his, near the top of the alphabet, with an asterisk by his last name, and then, at the bottom, the asterisk again, followed by tight type:

```
*This student should not sculpt with clay.
     Do not give this student clay.
Please inform this student that he needs
    to sculpt the sounds in the room.
```


He read the sentences three times.

Who wrote this? he asked.

A higher-up, she said. Someone higher up.

Up, she repeated.

She seemed eager to get the roster back, as if he were rapidly memorizing the Social Security numbers of all the other students; as if he cared about them, these other students, so happily padding and punching the clay he was banned from, something they felt entitled to; dumb students, he thought. See how close they were, to total inaccessibility? You never care until it's you.

There were music classes available, he said. Had I wanted to sign up for a music class—

I'm sorry, she said, folding the roster in half when he'd handed it back over. I don't want a liability suit. I will not give you clay. You could sculpt the woman, she said, out of sound?

He looked at the model again, who was in the same position as before, a perfect triangle made out of the place where her elbow reached away from her waist, with that sharp point at the tip of her elbow, and already, to his left and to his right, the muggy forms forming, the thick earthy smell dampening the air of the classroom as the students began to fix her in time.

Can I get a refund? he asked, even though he very much wanted to stay in the class, and she said, You have an assignment. You can't get a refund without good reason.

You are not giving me clay! he said. That is my reason! and she said, I have given you an alternate assignment. Here her voice became somewhat snitty.

Other students might feel special about this, she said.

And away she clicked, to go instruct the woman to his left about using small pieces of clay to build the shoulder and collarbone, to create a sense of texture. "Don't be so smooth," he heard her saying, and then the mulky sound of clay ripped from clay. His hands were impatient, but he closed his eyes. The sounds of the room. Fine. He was, in truth, a musician, a player of the oboe and guitar, and he felt discovered, almost outed, by the note on the roster, and it was unsettling, too, because he had not used his real name on the roster, and had, in an attempt to reinvent himself, at this time when everything else in his life felt stale and old, his whole self, his whole tired mind, the music in his fingertips, all known, all done, well, he'd signed up for this class with a false name and paid with cash. He'd wanted a new identity, just for a few weeks, and no one else would've known that, could've known that. It was total coincidence, then, that whoever wrote that on that roster would've linked him to music, and in fact, he found it enraging that of all the members of the class, it was he, HE! who needed it most, who had been looking forward to slamming his hands all over that clay for months now, who was desperate for something expansive, it was he who was relegated back to what he knew best, and the panic was a bird trapped in his ribs.

But he closed his eyes. Fine.

The sounds. The sounds of hands, on clay. A muggy sound. Muck. The sound of the radiator whirring on. Once. Then twice. A honk outside. B-flat. The teacher's voice, singsongy, "Don't be afraid of the medium," she called out. "Be aggressive with the medium," and so then fine. Be aggressive with the medium. Hrack. The sound of the model's cough, and resettling; the sound of someone's lust, five people down, the young man who had attended the class simply to see the nude woman because he had not seen one, a three-dimensional one, in many months. That man's breathing, measured. Fsssh. His own anger, the sound of it. Tight in the neck. Small crack of the neck vertebrae. Dt. The honk again: B-flat. The radiator, a low C, and then, far, far off in the distance, a bell. F-sharp. Honk. B-flat. Bell, F- sharp. Ping. B-flat.

Or-phan. Or-phan. Or-phan. Or-phan.

They are on a staircase, he and the nude model. He is descending, she is ascending. She is wearing the robe she wore when she arrived, and she is post sculpting, so she has the small buzz in her cheeks of someone who has just been replicated lovingly by twelve sets of hands. He, he has just gone running and is sweating, and he is on step four and she is on step eight, and they are going in opposite directions, and these four steps apart they stop. Hello. Hello. He reaches out a hand, to shake hers, but she will not reach hers out; the model does not touch anyone, no, she is only to be observed, never touched except at home, and she runs up to the top of the staircase and is gone, off to the parking lot, and he is on his stair, watching, then down, down to the bottom.

No.
Or-phan. The space between.

Another cough.

Or-phan. Or-phan. Or-phan.

The young man, as a child. His parents die, in a car accident. He is seven years old. He has no siblings. He has no one. He is adopted by the neighbors; they will become his new parents. How kind of them, people whisper to each other, but the boy shakes his head and says no. What does the will say? he asks his friend, the lawyer. He does not want to be raised by those neighbors, the neighbors who have tight mouths like that.

The will is checked again, and it turns out he is supposed to be taken care of, in case of an accident, by some woman across the country who lives on a farm. No, she lives in a city. A city farm? She lives in both. Off he's shipped. On the plane, there is a border around him, a border of four feet, where no one can touch him; although he is hugged incessantly, he does not feel the hug. On the farm he is in charge of two horses, one of which he rides into the city where his new family father is a policeman.

He loves them after awhile. But he is an orphan. He cannot forget this. He is stranded, by himself, for many years. Only later, when he meets the woman who models for the sculpture class, is he able to tap into his first feeling of comfort, for when she comes home, smelling of clay, and he can touch her, the one that the clay is made of, the origin of all of their sculpting, only then does the feeling begin to lighten.

You are the source, he tells her, often.

She loves him because he is kind, and because he thinks deeply. But she never takes him as seriously as he would like to be taken, and as she washes her hands in the sink with dish detergent, she says she needs to do some more sit-ups; she saw some of their sculptures today and her belly was hanging out.

It's the only honest mirror, she says, into the sink.

It doesn't matter, he says, don't you understand? and she says it matters to me, and he makes the afternoon tea and they drink it together and look outside, at the horses that live next door. He now always likes to live by horses. They remind him of second chances. She goes to take a bath and he feels, for the millionth time, that when he is with her he is at the center of something, which fills him with a tremendous comfort.

Theraft—theraft—theraft

Floating on the raft. Ping.

She is the bell, ringing.

He is floating on the raft of this comfort, while she is in the bath.
Wake up, he tells her, from the other room.

No, she says, I am taking a bath.

You are the source, he says again, in a murmur.

I am bearing a child, she says, and he says, mine? And she says, no,
it is the child of all the people in the sculpture class; I am bearing
their babies, all twelve of them, and in the bath she starts to yell
then, and he is up on his feet in an instant, awake, but the door is
locked so it takes longer than you'd expect, much longer, so long he
can remember, for the rest of his life, the sound of her screaming.
What is happening in there? his mind scrambles. What is happening?
Finally he bursts in with the strength of his shoulder, like in the
movies but real; he is there to save her, his source, the wellspring,
and she's in the bath and screaming and out of her are sculptures,
coming out of her, she is birthing sculptures, and they are clay so as
soon as they hit the bathwater they begin to grow slick and melty,
and he holds her head as she heaves and bucks up and births two
more, and he pulls them out of the tub, to clear space for her, and
they are not sculptures of her anymore, no, they are of the relatives—
there is his mother, there is her father, there are the cousins they
never visited, there is that uncle, there is his father, and even in the
midst of it all, holding her head, worrying, keeping her head from
hitting the faucet, telling her to hang steady, hang steady, even in the
midst of all that he can't help but feel a little glimmer of pride that
in this most primordial birthing of sculptures there are some from
his family, too. That somehow the genes of his family have become
a physical part of her, a sculpture to be birthed, even though he is not
in that sculpture class, no. He will never sculpt her. He is the one
she comes home to, of course, and the one she comes home to must
not sculpt her. His job is different. That is the sound, teacher, he
says, as he holds up the sculpture of his own dead father, cradling her
head while she cries, holding her while her breath regulates in the
now tan-colored bathwater, and she says she's OK, she's OK, it hurt
but she's OK, and he's helping her up from the tub, and the sound
of the water, going down the drain, teacher, and the sound of the

143

sculptures' muckiness as he lifts them onto the bathroom counter, teacher, and all the family members are melting, they'd need to be rushed to a kiln to be fired, "but they're dead anyway," she says, and he grasps it just as she says it, they're all dead, she has given birth to twelve dead relatives, and then they are both crying together because the clay cannot hold, and when, later, he returns to wash his hands before bed, when she is sleeping peacefully in the bed, when he has closed down the house for the night, only then does he see that they have all mucked together into one large block of clay, and that is all that is left of the birthings and the deaths.

There, teacher, he says. Those are the sounds of the room.

No, she says, approaching his desk again. She looks at what he has made there.

No, she says. Those are not sounds. Those are words? She looks confused, and rechecks the same class roster. The classroom is empty by now, and the model has gone home, gone to her real source, whoever that is for her, and the teacher is almost all packed up, wearing her backpack on her shoulder, and all the clay blobs are still on the desks, barely formed at all, and he says, My job is different, and she says, Seems so, son. Now go on home. We'll see you next week.

From Intercourse
Robert Olen Butler

ADAM, 7, First Man
EVE, 7, First Woman, His Wife

On a patch of earth cleared of thorns and thistles, a little east of Eden, the first day after the new moon of the fourth month of the eighth year after Creation

ADAM

the dust of the ground rises around us as we move and clench and thrash, and the Creator's vast dark face fades and the woman grows slick and the dust turns to mud, and in the distance to the west I hear the trees stirring from a sweet breeze, but here the air is still, save for our breath, we are a great wind now ourselves, the two of us, we are rushing across the face of the earth and all that we left behind was good, but behold, naked is good too, and I named the animals one by one, the Creator brought them and I named them, and again I have some naming to do—of these parts of her I am seeing as if for the first time—but that will have to wait, I am a running river now and the names I already named will have to do: her two young fawns, her clam, her ass, which I ride

EVE

I was happy but to tangle the holding parts and the walking parts and lie here quietly in the clean space he has made for us, but he is pawing and fondling and crying out and whimpering and perhaps that is good too, like when he took the apple from me, he was quiet then and he is boisterous now but it is the same: I offer and he takes, and I had nothing to give the Creator and all that He gave was for the man, and a shadow fell on the path and something was there and it

Robert Olen Butler

came forth hissing prettily and he said *You're not stupid* and he was
right and what he gave was sweet in me, but this man is not, he is
flailing around and proud of his own little snake

WILLIAM SHAKESPEARE, 29, Poet and Playwright
HENRY WRIOTHESLEY, 20, Third Earl of Southampton,
Courtier and Literary Patron

in Shakespeare's rooms in St. Helen's Bishopsgate, London, 1593

WILLIAM

proud Nature humbled by the work of its own hand: his azure eye,
his auburn tress, the chest it hangs on white as the sun can seem
when veiled in silken cloud, his silken doublet white as cloud cast
off to bare the fire beneath, and if his heart be sun and his chest be
sky then his eye be heaven and his earth below be forested lush
around a great high oak that stands stripped clean of limbs from
lightning strike: I give my limbs to this land and touch his beating
heart and burn, and yet he is night as well as day, a well as well as
tree, a well dug deep and dark and I send my vessel down: he is, in
flesh, the world inconsonant made one: my young man, my dark
lady

HENRY

I soon will lie alone and he will cross the room and sit at his table
and once again he will take up his goose quill and find it blunt and
take up his knife and bend and squint and turn slightly to the light
from the window and begin his sweet circumcision, playing at the
tip with the blade, making it less blunt, then sharp, then sharper
still, and he will pause and touch the tip to his tongue and he will
pull the ink pot nearer to him and dip the pen, dip it deep, the tip
growing wet and dark, and he will withdraw and let it drip and drip
till it stops, and then he will bend to his paper and his words will
come and the tiny scratch of his quill will shudder its way up my
thighs and I am pen and I am ink and I am his words

146

*

GEORGE HERMAN "BABE" RUTH, 21, Baseball Player
JOSEPHINE RUGGLES, 24, Prostitute

in the Chambre Rouge at Lulu White's all-octoroon Mahogany Hall, Storyville, New Orleans, 1916

BABE

a bat in my hands, a hickory bat, long and heavy and the color of tobacco spit, and I'm about to hit my first one and it's little Jack Warhop on the mound throwing his rise ball and it's the third inning in the Polo Grounds, and say but I'm swell at last, it's fine for me breaking off curves on the corner of the plate, but try to slip one by me with my bat in my hand and see what I can do, and here I am now in a fancy bed with a girl with a bit of darkness about her like me and she might as well see it all, she might as well see what I can do, and the same for all you girls in all the fancy rooms and in all the cheap cribs in Storyville, I'm out of the goddamn boys' home at last, out of St. Mary's, through being an orphan with two parents working a tavern across town, and now Mom's dead for real, and say, all that pussy upstairs in all the taverns on the Baltimore dock saw what I can do, and little Jack is standing sixty feet away and he gives me a look like he knows something about me from St. Mary's, and he does, a name they had for my ugly mug, he's been talking to some Baltimore mope or other cause I was putting away half a dozen wee-nies with chili sauce under the grandstand before the game and little Jack strolls by and he says, real low, *Nigger lips,* but I let it pass, because this is how you get it back: your feet close together and your right shoulder swung around to him and the bat sitting easy on your left shoulder nuzzled in the crook of your neck and he winds and throws, and his rise ball is what he's got that says I don't belong where I am, and I can see the ball spinning, I can count the stitches, and what I do starts in my stomach, it starts in the center of me right there and it flows easy into my arms and hips and legs and I hitch back and glide on through and the groove is there and it's sweeter than any pussy, me passing into this invisible place, and there's a little push against the bat and a swell chunking sound and the ball is

147

rushing off and up and up and it flies fast and far and farther still and it falls into the straw hats deep in the right-field stands and it's my first home run and I am still feeling its kiss, it kissed me hard and wet right on my bat

JOSEPHINE

he yawps and grunts, this overgrown boy, and of a sudden he cries *Say but I'm swell* and now is off to whooping again, but you're not that swell I can tell you and I just try to hear beyond him, the piano trickling up from the parlor downstairs, Lulu has let a colored boy in tonight to play and he's doing it fine and they're down there dancing the ragtime one-step on the parquet floor, not the mudbuggers like this boy but the Americans from Uptown in evening clothes, and I could be doing it with them, doing what I really do: pulling the arm of a true swell around my waist and facing him a little off center and taking his left hand in my right and finding that easy-glide spot—our hands just a bit away from us and a little up from the waist, my right elbow slightly bent, my left hand cupping behind his right shoulder, my back straight upright, my heels together and my toes turned out-ward, perfect, like finding the lay of me in bed when I'm finally alone and can sleep—and tonight we'll do the Castle Walk so I go up onto the balls of my feet and stiffen my legs and I pull ever so slightly with my palm behind his shoulder and with the tips of my fingers at the back of his hand and he doesn't even know I'm leading and we're off, stepping away long and smooth and quick around and around Lulu White's whorehouse parlor and nobody does the one-step like Jo and it's all for free

Ghosts
Cole Swensen

DEFOE'S STORY

It took place in London at the end of the seventeenth century—a man was spending the evening at home, often thinking of a friend of his, a woman, who was very ill, worrying about her, hoping she would live, when there was a knock on the door, and she entered, looking fine, thriving, in fact, and sat down in a normal way and began a normal conversation, though she seemed a little more serious than usual until he began to cry, at which she continued quietly, discussing things of the soul, aspects of time, and he began to sob, and she continued speaking quietly, as he sobbed and sobbed, and when he finally looked up she was gone.

This story is not unusual and belongs to a subgenre in which the dead person seems to drop in on a few old friends on the way out, giving no indication that he or she has died, but stays and speaks, saying the clear water at the bottom of my hand will make a turn and my hand will go bottomless like a mirror forgets my face at the slightest glance, there

was a man   standing beside the clear water   pooled in the rock
beneath a tree. The bright leaves   tore up the light   you would have seen
that he was part of the light   and asked him to help me climb down.

LE FANU'S STORY

Sheridan Le Fanu offers a variation on this story in which the whole family hears a carriage arrive late at night, just at the time that (they later learn) their older daughter has died miles away. Even the dogs start barking, and they all clearly hear the folding down of the carriage stairs, but when they open the door, the courtyard is empty and the dogs recoil in fear.

So that the sight of anyone in an unexpected place   so that the voice
now traveling alone   out on its own on a quiet day   I saw a friend
I knew to be in Japan   I once saw my sister on a train.

Sometimes it's only a strong resemblance, and you wonder if the person in
question hasn't had a close call, crossing the street with an absent mind, or
walked out of a building just moments before it blew up. Caught a cab on the
corner and never knew. It happens every day. We are made

in a thin thread   or of the line incised into the pane   which may
be only a photograph, she said, whenever I look at a photograph, I see not the
man who died years ago but the one who will   or in a window   turned
and touched his fingertips to his lips.

JAMES'S STORY

In Henry James's version, an unnamed narrator discovers she has two good
friends who've had the same experience—a woman whose father came to her in
a gallery in Italy as he was dying in New York, and a man whose mother
showed up in his rooms in Cambridge just after she'd died. Determined that her
two similarly gifted friends should meet, she makes numerous plans, but oddly,
something always comes up to thwart them. Finally, after she has become
engaged to the male friend, our narrator decides that she really must arrange
this meeting, so she fixes up something so simple that it cannot fail. However,
at the last minute, she gets it: these two are destined to fall in love—there's
really no other possibility—and so she herself, and through subterfuge, prevents
this last attempt. Last because, by sheer coincidence, her female friend dies that
night. In the morning, overcome with guilt and remorse, the woman tells her
lover what she has done, but he declares, "That's not possible! She came to my
rooms just before midnight!" The woman insists that it must have been her
ghost, while the man insists that she was alive. They finally agree to disagree
and get on with their lives. Except that the woman notices a change in him, and
one week before the wedding, gently declares that she knows he has been
keeping up a liaison with her dead friend ever since that fatal night, and though
he denies it, he doesn't do so very vigorously, and allows her to break off their
engagement.
Neither, needless to say, ever marries.
And as it always is with James, we are never sure if the ghost occurred, or if the

woman was not simply eaten up by a jealousy engendered by her guilt, or, much more likely, by a different jealousy, a jealousy for that other world, which her obsession with that aspect of her friends' lives tells us she preferred to her friends all along.

James's version is unusual too, in that it is the only ghost story I know in which a ghost is genetic, a kind of corner-of-the-eye that can't stop in time   and
heard the other arrive   though way across town   or felt a line drawn taut and could not
respond   although a light comes on   all on its own
every day at just that time   time, they said   is stone. I once had a heart
made of string   and hung myself, my love.

TO BURY

To bury the heart in one land and the hands in another   says the legend, always

the heart is buried alone no matter what you   buried   the heart is a grave

in the legend   is an hour invented   and here the long
road lined with poplars.

I have a friend who draws nothing but clouds.   As they speed across France,

nothing is lost from view. The train was invented   to shred a sun,   to
carefully cut the blind spots out   Again,

a scene, and everything that once was light came along.   The sun is always

alone while the heart has all of France

like a stone

under the tongue

and like a stone under the tongue   it stays aloft   despite   which buries itself like
a face in hands

Cole Swensen

What you see

from a train is what has escaped.   A simple operation

in which they take out the heart and lay it on a table.   I have a friend who

had a job holding the hearts at certain points in the procedure.   They'd
literally   She actually exactly

the weight you'd think they'd be   intuitively   Trace the meridian
with a spare pair of scissors

Replace the map with a razor and an anchor. You find   you have buried

your friends in your hands.

Benevolence
Shena McAuliffe

As a child Eliza Farnham had an unremarkable head. Round and smooth, it had the proverbial soft spot at the crown where her skull had last knit itself together. But by her twenty-ninth year there had formed, at the apex of her cranium, a prominent bump. This bump was not particularly noticeable when one viewed Eliza directly, looking straight into her shadowy eyes, but when she turned to glance out at the bitter landscape or to reach for a book in some hidden corner of her office, it was suddenly evident, looking almost as if she had been recently clobbered and bruised.

According to phrenology the bump was located in region thirteen of her skull, which housed the organ of benevolence, one of the conglomeration of organs that composed her brain. Her dominant organ, benevolence was swollen and pushed gently at the bone in which it was encased, resulting in the bump, outward evidence of Eliza's extreme goodwill.

In 1844 Eliza's husband was off exploring the wilds of California. Not to be outdone by his pioneering spirit, she determined to put her powerful organ to use in the new women's wing at a prison on the banks of the Hudson River. Thirty miles north of New York, and twenty years before Eliza's arrival, one hundred prisoners had quarried river rock and built the walls that would contain them. Through three frozen winters they worked, and when they finished it was Sing Sing: place of stone.

Eliza spent her first morning as prison matron sitting at a table in the corner of the mess hall, watching her charges and taking notes. In the margins of her notebook she drew the outlines of several skull shapes: simple busts, including profiles. Beneath each sketch she wrote the corresponding prisoner's name, which was provided for her by the chaplain, John Luckey, who already detested her. Beneath the name she jotted speculations about the prisoner according to the shape of her skull. *Acquisitiveness?* she wrote beneath one sketch, and turned to the chaplain to inquire, What was this woman's crime? Larceny, he answered, and Eliza smirked in triumph.

153

As the prisoners settled for lunch, a straggler arrived; a guard was close behind, pressing a wooden club between her shoulder blades. The prisoner was young and strikingly attractive, with smooth black hair and porcelain skin. Her eyes were cool and steely; upon entering the room she cast them to the floor. She had a small head, perched delicately upon a slender neck and narrow shoulders. Her arms hung like plumb lines. Eliza stared, making no notes, sketching nothing, but when the chaplain cleared his throat to lead the prisoners in prayer she rapidly sketched the girl's profile. The shape of her skull was apparent through her sleek hair, which was pulled into a tight plait that ran down her back like an external spine. In her sketch Eliza captured, if not exaggerated, the prisoner's short forehead and the plateau, a divot even, on the front half of the top of her head. Behind that was a pronounced but dainty rise in the same place as Eliza's own most prominent bump. Eliza jotted *Pronounced benevolence,* and beneath that *Deficiency of justice and self-esteem.* The prisoner's name, Eliza learned when the chaplain finished his prayer, was Maria Giatti. Her crime was murder.

Yellow bile, black bile, blood, and phlegm: each courses in symphony through the veins. The trick to health lies in balancing the four.

Here: a bilious woman, her temperament evident in her swarthy skin and close-set eyes, not to mention she refuses to peel potatoes; she spits in the dishwater. A spoonful of tartar emetic will thin her yellow bile.

And this one's a melancholic—thin hair, high temples—she has a quick mind, but see how she slumps. She chatters her teeth. Practically brimming with black bile. Rub her skin with mustard, blister her arms, dose her with calomel—a miracle in a teaspoon.

The sanguine, face full and ruddy, paces her cell and sighs—too much blood rushing through her veins. Leeches should do the trick.

And the phlegmatic, soft and round, with jowls and a bulbous nose. For this underwater mover, snuffling in her sleep—a handful of prickly ash steeped in tea will quicken her.

Eliza walked with certainty—quickly, head up. She made and held eye contact with everyone, even the prisoners when they would look at her. She never slipped quietly into a room, but burst into it, flinging the door aside like a discarded petticoat. Certainty pervaded

154

more than her movements. Over tea with the chaplain, on her first day as matron, she quickly confessed: she hated God and despised his word. She had been raised by an aunt, whom she hated. She had no mother or father. No one ever sat beside her with a Bible spread across her lap, and that suited her just fine.

"No need to dwell on those particular illusions," she said. "I've made it this far in life on my own—from my aunt's musty old house to the Illinois prairie and back again. I intend to keep on ticking." Already, at twenty-nine, she had outlived two of her three sons. The one still alive, she said, was like her: tenacious and stringy.

"Like a piece of jerky," the chaplain said, under his breath.

"I can reform these women," Eliza said. "But I suppose we'll go about things differently. For you, if I may presume, God is responsible for saving them. For me, salvation lies in understanding our brains."

By Eliza's system, the brain consisted of a mass of organs, each named for the trait it controlled—violence, for example, or amativeness. The organs were organized in a logical manner, with the baser, animalistic propensities clustered in the lower, back half of the skull, and the noble sentiments nesting in the top front. Eliza believed that a criminal was born with a skewed hierarchy of organs—propensities were overdeveloped and sentiments withered. With the proper influence, order could be restored—sentiments plumped and propensities shriveled. Eliza was at Sing Sing to be the proper influence.

The chaplain dropped a lump of sugar into his tea, which splashed onto the tablecloth. He was a small man, not at all like Eliza's husband. Smaller even than Eliza, and sitting knee to knee with her, he looked frail. He pushed his hair across his forehead. It was thin, pale hair, shaggy around the ears, which poked through. His jaw, though, was square, and his mouth vividly pink. His eyes were blue. He stirred his tea, sloshing it into his saucer.

"You're right," he said. "Our methods differ." He pressed his lips together and folded his napkin. Then he unfolded it.

Eliza grew accustomed to the heavy scrape of metal on metal, the squall of fifty locks opening simultaneously. Fifty doors sliding on their tracks. Fifty prisoners murmuring, standing, blinking in the gray light that seeped from the corridor into their cells. Her charges were guilty of an array of crimes: petit and grand larceny, villainy, arson, assault and battery, murder. As a whole they were of a sanguine nature, flushed and confident, disconcertingly optimistic. Some of the women would spend the rest of their lives within those cold walls, but they had shelter, they had food. Had they also comprehension of their situation? Eliza concluded that some did and that others were incapable of comprehension. These women, Eliza thought, would have cheerfully endured the fate of Sisyphus. This inability was sometimes evidenced by a flatness above the eyebrows, beneath which lived the organ of time.

That ticking metronome: a fiddle saws and the dancers step together, twirl. The sun casts her shadows: Long. Short. Long. Bare trees bud and unfurl. First tender, then tough, their leaves turn yellow. They come loose. They are lost under snow.

A baby grabs its mother's hair, her breast, a cookie resting on a plate. It learns the alphabet, and that it is a girl. She wants new shoes, a slice of pie, a train ride, a man's touch. These are granted. The man wipes his nose with the back of his hand. When no one is looking, she spits. Her tireless heart, ticking. The skin around her eyes is creased like damp tissue paper. Touch it lightly, with two fingers. She births a child; his voice is shrill, he throws an apple, breaks a window. She grips his wrist too tightly, leaves fingerprints. She hears him in the next room, a man moving, her son. Once, she sees a patch of grass so green she wants to lie down on it, more than anything. Her knuckles swell. She holds her book close to her nose. She squints into distance.

Bare trees bud, unfurl.

Eliza ended the reign of silence. One by one the prisoners were restored the privilege of speech, so long as their speaking did not interrupt their handiwork or their studies. To one prisoner, whose moaning and weeping disturbed the other women, Eliza gave a cotton rag doll.

"It belonged to my second son," she said. "He would want you to care for it." The doll's smile showed two teeth, stitched with black thread, and one of its small hands was chewed, but its new owner held it close. When the woman left her cell for work or meals she tucked the doll beneath the sheet on her cot, its orange yarn hair resting upon the pillow. Returning, she fed it crumbs, pressing them, one at a time, to the doll's embroidered mouth.

On each grim windowsill Eliza placed a terra-cotta pot of marigolds, chrysanthemums, or scarlet geraniums. From the ceilings she hung heavy lamps endowed with reflectors. She papered the walls with maps of New York, the United States, and Europe. On the Fourth of July she brought a basket of caramels. When she gained an assistant, Miss Georgiana Bruce, the gloom of the prison was all but eliminated, for Georgiana brought along her piano. It was installed in the classroom, and even the inmates were occasionally allowed to coax it in their riotous or rudimentary ways.

Five days a week Eliza gathered the women for lectures on American history, astronomy, geology, physiology, phrenology, and personal hygiene. "Education," said Eliza, "is one little step upward in the direction of the light."

For the lecture on phrenology Eliza brought a drawing of a bald, androgynous head. In profile, its eye looked forward; a bit of paper was left white, indicating a glint. The eyebrow was too low and rested directly on the lashes. The nose was aquiline and the lips curved in the suggestion of a smile. Beneath the rounded chin was a rash of shading that ran to the ear. The rounded part of the skull was divided into plots and parcels—this one a tiny square, this an oval, this an arched parallelogram along the crest. In each plot was written a word. Eliza tacked the drawing to the wall and raised her wooden pointer.

"The brain and the mind are one and the same," she said, and gave three sharp raps with the pointer. "As you can see, the skull is divided into thirty-seven regions, each reflecting the shape of the organ housed beneath." Her students stared, glassy eyed. "Contained in the brain are all the secrets of personality—why we do the things we do and how we do them. Each aspect of character dwells within its own organ. Smaller organs are less powerful. The larger the organ, the more powerful. As our organs swell or shrink, so does their shell, the cranium." Still, the women stared. "A demonstration is in order? Ulrike Weiss, please stand."

Ulrike was a thief with a knack for embroidery. She was also a proficient pianist, almost a musical genius, but her behavior was erratic. One moment she calmly pulled a shining thread through a bit of cloth; the next she was pacing wildly, tearing at her careful stitches, the thread knotting and fraying as she muttered in German. She was regarded as insane.

"We all know how beautifully Ulrike plays the piano," said Eliza. "Some of us might plink our way through Beethoven every day for hours and never manage a melody quite the way Ulrike does." She pressed her middle and index fingers to each side of Ulrike's broad forehead, above the outer corners of her eyebrows. "This is region number thirty-four. It determines our ability to create or recreate a tune. And here," she said, sliding her fingers to Ulrike's temples, "is the organ of constructiveness, where our mechanical faculties are located. You can see how wide Ulrike's head is here. This combination explains her musical talent, not to mention her skill with a needle."

Eliza watched as the women began running their hands over their own skulls; Ulrike, restless, pulled away. Turning to the front of the room, Eliza was surprised to see the chaplain leaning in the doorway.

"Well, well," he said. "We all recognize Ulrike's musical talent. She serves as a striking example, with that conveniently broad forehead. It all lines up rather nicely."

"Science does have that tendency," said Eliza. "I understand you have a special interest in this subject. Shall we read another head while you're here?"

"I'd be delighted," the chaplain said. "But let's make it more difficult, so you might demonstrate your art more fully." From his breast pocket he pulled a blue silk handkerchief. He gave it a shake, like a magician completing a trick. "Why don't we do the next one blind?" Eliza nodded and turned so the chaplain could blindfold her. He smelled of soap and cedar, but she stopped her nose to his scent, breathing through her mouth as his hands tied the blindfold tight. He took her hands firmly but without squeezing and guided them to the level of the chosen woman's head. His thumbs pressed the centers of her palms, forcing her fingers to curl inward, so she straightened them. Her hands were rigid when the chaplain released them. She took a breath.

Eliza felt a warm and waxy film of grease. Her fingers were on the prisoner's eyelids, smooth and sticky. She slid each hand in unison, over the scruff of eyebrows to a smooth forehead, and soon her fingers met the woman's hairline. Eliza let them rest a moment, then traced a light circle, and pushed them along the hairline, back into the twin pockets of a widow's peak, where she felt the slightest indentation.

"This woman has a deficit of mirth," she said. From there she slid her fingers through the prisoner's smooth, straight hair, allowing them to meet on the top of the skull, and there she felt the telltale bump of benevolence. "Pronounced benevolence." She slid her fingers down again and was surprised. On one side of the prisoner's head rose a bump more prominent than that of her own benevolence. Spirituality, and slightly behind that, closer to the ear, the swell merged into sublimity, the organ for appreciating infinity and grandeur. She had not noticed these qualities in any of the prisoners. They were criminals, after all.

Eliza said nothing of these bumps, but felt her pulse quicken. The head was flat in the region of conscientiousness and there was the deficit of self-esteem she expected if the head belonged to Maria Giatti, and these she mentioned aloud. There were twin swells above and behind the prisoner's ears—destructiveness and combative-ness—organs that quickly gave way to violence, and these she felt she had to mention in order to prove her science. As her fingers met at the nape of the prisoner's neck, the chaplain spoke.

"While you're blindfolded, what sort of sins is a person with this particular arrangement of bumps capable of?"

She let her fingers rest, pressed gently at the tender space between the muscles of the prisoner's neck.

"Destructiveness and combativeness," she said, "physical pro-pensities, and coupled as they are with a lack of conscientiousness, this woman is likely to harm another—assault and battery, or even murder. However, considering her underdeveloped self-esteem, this woman may have been a victim of violence herself."

The chaplain was silent.

"Would you like me to read another? Or could you remove the blindfold?" she asked. Before he could untie it, she pulled it off, along with a couple of hairpins that fell to the floor, and Eliza felt her hair loosen, a few strands brushing her face. The chaplain left the room without saying a word. Before Eliza stood Maria Giatti. She had won the round.

What can be learned from skulls aligned—sockets gaping, teeth chipped and angled, jeering and static? And from living skulls, with skin and eyes intact, tongues still filling their caverns with heat and blood?

View this perfect specimen: a man, middle-aged, skin stretched and gleaming, hair like tendrils of a cloud. A blush within his pale skin. Twin swells for order and calculation. This skull is swollen with language—he speaks five.

This child's tiny skull, wide above the temples—he's filled with wonder! He runs along the drainage ditch and watches anthills swarm. He spins with open eyes, looking at the white sun—he likes it when he falls. And this broad expanse behind his ears: with this he bludgeons birds to death, with this he pulls hair, kicks down haystacks, throws crab apples through windows. Don't touch it; don't wake it. He might outgrow it.

And these, skulls heaped in a ditch, all with high cheekbones or wide foreheads or square jaws—push the dirt over them. Don't look too closely at these brittle goblets. A bit of dark flesh clinging still upon this jaw. Blood dried and darkening in a fracture. Don't look too closely: push the dirt, let them roll.

In her office Eliza slid a book from the shelf. It was a bulging volume, filled with the names of all the women in the prison and notes on their cases. Maria Giatti's name was printed in block lettering on a page near the middle of the book. Even with her established reliance on phrenology, Eliza was surprised to see how well she had read Maria's head. When she turned the page the writing changed to the tight, curlicued scrawl of the chaplain, who spent one afternoon each week compiling information on the prisoners in hopes of discovering the portals to their souls.

Maria had grown up an outsider, the child of Italians in an Irish neighborhood. Her father had worked in a shoe factory, but he had long since retired to the bottle. There was nothing written about her mother. Her entire life, Maria had been surrounded by drunkenness and brawling. She bore a child but it died in infancy of unknown causes. In the margin were written the words "Starvation?" and "Suffocation?" Of the infant's death there was no official record. There was no record, even, of her birth, which Maria claimed had taken place at home, in the kitchen. At this point another note: "Infection?"

Maria was eighteen and had been married three years when she killed her husband with a meat cleaver. She had arrived at the prison two years ago with a matched set of black eyes, skin dappled with bruises, hair matted with blood. She walked in a hunch. When Eliza turned the page again, the sketches she had done of Maria's head fluttered out. She remembered stuffing them hastily into the book when a fight broke out in the sewing room.

So the murder had been particularly gruesome. Although Maria's violent nature was evident in the shape of her skull, Eliza was surprised. The woman looked delicate, and Eliza had never seen her display even a hint of anger. Eliza imagined Maria crusted in blood, her eyes swollen.

Eliza's own husband, an educated man, had once held her against the wall in a fit of anger, his tremendous fingers pressed around her neck. She had glimpsed his temper before, and had been terrified, stunned at his capacity for rage, and at her own in return. If she had been less shocked, she might have hit him once he released her, but instead she had wrapped her infant son in a blanket and taken her coat from the rack, prepared to leave.

"Where will you go?" her husband asked, and fell on the floor at her feet. He grasped one of her shoes. She had forgiven him, mostly.

She felt certain Maria had been provoked. On Eliza's fingertips lingered the memory of those unexpected bumps, spirituality and sublimity. Did the woman truly possess these exaggerated faculties? Eliza was obliged to answer yes. If Maria was a spiritual being, Eliza could use those traits to help the woman reform. Only her sense of justice needed unlocking.

The prisoners were learning to read and write. Of the seventy-three convicts in Eliza's care twenty-two could read and write, thirty could read but not write, and twenty-one were illiterate. In two-hour shifts, the women gathered fifteen at a time. The fully literate were paired with two who were not and a tutoring session took place. "Like children in a little school," Eliza remarked to her assistant, and a woman at a nearby table looked up and glared. Eliza smiled at her.

Eliza and Georgiana occasionally worked with a prisoner alone in order to measure her progress. Maria was one of the thirty who could read but not write. Her letters and spelling were progressing slowly. She had yet to write a complete sentence unassisted. Eliza borrowed a Bible from the chaplain's desk. It was covered in green leather with gilt-edged pages.

They read the story of Cain and Abel, alternating verses. Maria read first.

> Now Cain said to his brother Abel, "Let's go out to the field."
> And while they were in the field, Cain attacked his brother Abel and killed him.
>
> The Lord said to Cain, "Where is your brother Abel?"
>
> "I don't know," he replied. "Am I my brother's keeper?"

The Lord said, "What have you done? Listen! Your brother's blood cries out to me from the ground."

Maria looked at Eliza with steely, unblinking eyes. "Why are we reading this?" she asked.

"Do you believe in God, Maria?"

"I don't believe the Bible, if that's what you mean."

"Well, do you believe in God? Do you pray?" Maria stared. "Honestly, I've never believed in God myself. I don't know why I brought a Bible when I really just wanted to talk to you. Are you offended?" Still, Maria did not respond. "It's the story that interests me—the brothers. Have you ever talked with anyone about your husband?"

"Why are you asking me this?" Maria's voice was flat.

"Do you understand the difference between right and wrong?"

Maria shifted. "I know that you and Miss Georgiana are good," she said. Her hand was resting on the table and Eliza covered it with her own, which was moist with sweat.

"Yesterday, when I was examining your head, I didn't mention everything I learned—you have another profound sentiment. I didn't reveal what I'd found because, well, I guess I was surprised. And I thought it might make you vulnerable somehow. The chaplain was there. The other women."

Maria looked at her steadily.

"Here," said Eliza, lightly touching the side of Maria's head. "This is where your spirituality is located. And here," she moved her fingers back, "is the organ of sublimity, your comprehension of infinity. Do you think about an afterlife?"

Maria pushed her chair back and stood. "Are we finished?" she said.

In the kitchen pots bubble over. Potato peels heap the garbage bin. Stacks of dishes: these gleaming, these blackened. Hands are rubbed raw with steel wool. In the laundry, soap and steam. These hands are soggy, pink, and wrinkled. In the library, the spines of books line shelves like soldiers. Linen tape, waxed thread; a lucky prisoner repairs a loose cover, a broken spine, a fluttering page. Corridors gleam; mops glide. And in the sewing circle, needles flash, pulling taut an initial on a handkerchief, a flower on a tablecloth, a patch on an elbow, a loose pocket, a frayed cuff.

Eliza paced the courtyard. Around her, eight hundred cells were stacked four deep. Narrow windows faced off with staccato regularity. She imagined the prisoners in their cells, standing tiptoe to look onto this scene, where she was crunching gravel beneath her shoes. This was the men's courtyard. She could almost smell their sweat, their excrement. Inside, the men were working—hammering soles onto shoes. Rolling leaves into cigars. Building chairs and tables with their coarse hands.

Her husband's hands were like that, coarse and chapped from days spent working winter fields. Once, when he had touched her naked breast, she called him a goblin. He hadn't laughed, but had scraped her skin with a torn fingernail, had squeezed her nipple hard. But he was far away now. She hadn't had a letter in a month.

Maria's hands were soft—softer than Eliza's, and much smaller. They were the hands of a child. An elegant, aristocratic child, bathed in rose oil and dusted with talcum. It was incredible, Eliza thought, that those hands were attached to such a wild creature. Violence, she thought, seemed mismatched in one who grasped the concept of infinity.

Eliza closed her eyes and focused on the red-black of her inner eyelids. It was a shallow space, between lens and lid, but it looked like an endless, buzzing dark. It was the only eternity she could imagine. The wind blew through the courtyard with a quiet moan. The prison, Eliza thought, was like a tremendous woman, holding her children close, herself included.

Soft mounds of cloth lay about the women's ankles, never diminishing. The women sat in straight-backed chairs around a patch of light that fell on the floor from the window. Georgiana sat at a table near the door with her own embroidery—a nightgown for her sister. The women talked while they sewed, but were forbidden to speak of their crimes. They spoke of children they'd left in the world and sometimes of the morning's lecture, but usually they dwelt on what they wanted from the outside. In winter, piping hot gingerbread and lavender soap. In spring, a new pair of stockings. Sometimes it was a long, steamy bath or a vial of perfume. Always it was a man.

For two days after her talk with Eliza, Maria Giatti had kept silent. The women were accustomed to her sulks—she had once gone two weeks without saying a word—but this time was different. She was constantly losing the thread from her needle, sighing and scuffing her shoes beneath her chair. When she managed to keep the needle threaded, she pulled so tightly the needle laid a groove in her thumb.

The thief who sat beside Maria dragged her chair away. On Maria's other side sat Gretchen Felter, who, years before, had attacked a keeper with a hand-fashioned knife and was beaten into submission with a cane. Gretchen made a show of shoving Maria's chair out of the circle and stepping indelicately on her foot.

With a half inch of sloppy stitches, Maria sewed her hand to the shirt she was mending. The hem of the shirt was red with blood, clinging to the skin between thumb and finger.

It was Gretchen who noticed. "Hey," she said. "Stop that. Stop that now." She reached for the shirt, but Maria pulled away. "What are you doing?"

Maria pulled the thread, raised her needle high, her face expressionless, her eyes wide, slowly blinked. Georgiana stumbled around the circle of chairs but before she could reach Maria, Gretchen struck Maria's cheek with the back of her hand. Maria focused on Gretchen as if she'd never seen her before, her eyes narrowed.

"Lord Jesus and the angels—what is wrong with you?" Gretchen said.

Georgiana grasped Maria's elbow and pulled her roughly to her feet. On the way out of the room, Maria faltered and pressed her hand to the door frame to steady herself, leaving behind a smeared red handprint.

Eliza heard about the incident, but was busy in the kitchen, where one woman had pushed a pot of boiling water onto another, scalding her feet. Both women were hysterical. Eliza hated punishing her women, but the offender was hung from her wrists for half an hour and placed in confinement for a week.

With a terrible headache, Eliza closed her office door. She took out a book about the criminal mind she was in the process of editing, but her eyes drifted to the window, a square of blue with black birds flying across it.

Once, she had dropped a spoon while her husband was reading. There was a clatter of silver on stone and he stood, red faced and looming. He left the room. And once, he stubbed his toe, and as he hopped across the floor, grimacing, she laughed. He'd slapped her swiftly across the cheek. One Sunday, after church, which she attended only for his benefit, she looked too long at a neighbor's wife who was wearing a new Sunday dress. The woman's waist was a slender stalk, the buttons precise, and a bit of lace grazed her chin as she descended the steps from the church. Eliza's husband pulled her firmly by the elbow. "You're staring," he said, squeezing her arm. When he held the babies, they cried. And when her son, the one who lived, was old enough to walk, he took to hiding in her skirt when his father entered the room. She remembered a hail storm that battered the crops, and though it had nothing to do with her, he scattered her books across the table; he slammed doors.

She filled too hot a bath for him. He didn't check the water—he never did—but stepped in quickly, and lost his balance. He wasn't scalded, just startled, but he flung the door open—his naked skin flushed, his penis dangling. There was dirt beneath his fingernails, his skin dappled with sun spots, veins raised like scars. There was the flicker of the hearth and their two shadows, which moved like tortured puppets on the wall. And then his face, so close to hers, so boiled red, a fleck of spittle, flared nostrils. His thumb pressed between her jaw and ear, his palm pushed at her Adam's apple. There was no longer a windblown house, a room with a hearth. Only the pressure around her neck, her toes tipping the floor, his hot breath, the pulse in his temple, his cavernous mouth.

She dropped her eyes. He let her go.

The chaplain's office was orderly: a tin cup of pencils and an African violet blooming on the windowsill. He sat straight in his armless chair, both elbows propped upon the desk. Eliza found his office surprisingly peaceful compared to her own, where papers were always strewn and the wastebasket perpetually overflowed with crumpled pages. The ivy plant on her windowsill had recently withered, the tips of its leaves crinkled and browned. She dosed it with fertilizer Georgiana had concocted from coffee grounds and potato peels but the plant didn't seem to be reviving.

"Yes?" the chaplain said, looking up from his work.

"I'd like to talk about Maria Giatti," Eliza said, stepping closer. "She isn't well. Have you spoken with her?"

He had not. There was a second chair, and he offered it to her with a tight-lipped smile.

"I left something out when I did my reading the other day. Something that might be of interest to you."

"I doubt that anything you learned from the topography of a battered woman's skull will be of interest to me. You got lucky, Miss Farnham."

"You know I find your methods antiquated, but if you're successful using them, I won't call it luck," Eliza said.

"You recognized her by her hair. I should've known you'd recognize the contours of that head, the way you're always watching her."

Eliza's scalp prickled. "What do you mean?"

He turned and looked directly at her. She held his gaze, but felt a flush creep up her neck.

"Never mind," she said. "I thought this was something we could work on together, but clearly I was wrong." She stood.

"Miss Farnham," the chaplain said. "Only God can fix them."

To get to California you could take a wagon, and likely perish in a swollen river, or die of fever on the dried-up prairie. Or you could sail, south and south, finally reaching Cape Horn, with winds blowing you ever nearer your death, and then, rounding the cape, you had to sail north just as long. Still, if Eliza ever went, she'd take this second route. She'd seen enough of prairies, and she'd see mountains once she reached California—if she reached it. If not, at least she'd see the strange birds that reportedly flew around the cape. She'd see tremendous swimming turtles and hear sea lions bellow. They'd dock at ports where people spoke as if singing, in burbling words she couldn't understand. Yes, if Eliza went to California, she would sail.

Early the next morning Eliza found Maria sleeping, face to the wall, her left hand wrapped in gauze. Eliza hooked her fingers through the cell door. She watched Maria's chest rise and fall. Maria's hair had come loose from its plait and was sprawled across her pillowcase. She was talking in her sleep. Eliza leaned her head against the cool metal, trying to discern the sleeper's mumbled words.

"Snowdrops," she thought she heard. "There's a penny." It was nonsense, but lovely. Maybe she was dreaming of an afterlife. She studied Maria's profile, the curve of her hip. The girl had slept in her boots. Behind Eliza, in another cell, a prisoner spit the word "Whore." Eliza had already watched too long.

Maria did not wake at the sound of her cell door opening. At the foot of the bed Eliza saw a rumpled sheet of paper. Maria had been practicing her writing. A row of almost perfect capitals stretched across the page. A wobbly *K* was crossed out.

"Maria," Eliza said. She stretched a hand to Maria's shoulder and shook her lightly. "I need to talk to you."

Maria put her gauze-wrapped hand over her ear, her elbow jutting awkwardly upward.

"I'm busy," she said, and did not turn.

Eliza studied Maria's elbow. It was dry and cracked. "Busy?" she said. Maria pressed her hand tighter over her ear. "With what?" Eliza leaned down and pried Maria's hand from her ear.

"Can't you see I'm injured?" Maria said. She cradled her bandaged hand with her whole one.

"That's what I want to talk to you about. What's bothering you? You did this to yourself."

Maria pulled the matted pillow over her face as if threatening to smother herself. Eliza pulled it away. Maria sat up. She looked like a child, with her boots hanging over the edge of her cot, her knobby elbows, her clear eyes looking up at Eliza, squinting a little. Eliza sat beside her.

"What if . . . ," Eliza said. "Do you think you could get better? If we worked very hard?"

Maria tipped her head to the side mockingly. "Am I sick?" she said. "I feel all right, except for my hand."

"I think so. I think you're sick—not bad. Not evil." She patted Maria's knee. "I could take you to California." She hadn't planned to say it, but once the words were out they kept coming. "Do you know where that is? My husband is there—he says it's beautiful. He says you can stand atop a cliff and see for miles across the sea, which is greener there. He says it isn't a place for a woman. But I think it is. I think it's just the place for a woman, if she is strong enough, and brave."

"The chaplain says I'll never get out of here," Maria said. "Not until I die."

"Well, the chaplain and I have different ideas."

"California," said Maria flatly.

"Listen to this." Eliza opened the book she had brought. She had marked a passage, and followed along with her finger as she read. "Those who take the trouble to refer to any considerable number of cases of murder will be struck by the remarkable fact that the homicidal is almost invariably accompanied by the suicidal tendency; and hence, that persons who are in the state of mind that renders them capable of attempting the destruction of a fellow creature are usually, at the same time, desirous of self-destruction."

Maria's face was smooth and pale, impassive as a teacup.

"You don't understand?"

Maria shook her head.

"It says that someone who has killed another person probably despises herself, probably wishes to harm herself as well. . . . Is that why you sewed through your own hand? To punish yourself?"

"I just wasn't paying attention," Maria said. "I didn't do it on purpose."

"You must have felt it."

"No. I didn't."

"Do you feel bad about what happened with your husband? Is that why?"

Maria shifted away from Eliza. "Look," she said, pulling her hair tight against her head. "Can you see that?" Behind her ears the hair pressed over bumps and runnels. "Those are scars," she said. "Couldn't you feel them in your examination?"

Eliza touched Maria's head with the tips of her fingers. She parted the hair and saw that the skin beneath was raised, shiny, and white. It was too smooth, and hard, like thin roots were pushing at the surface. She pulled her hand away as if she'd been burned, and wiped it against her skirt. Maria held her gaze.

"I don't feel bad about my husband," Maria said. "He got what was coming to him. He'd have done the same to me if I'd let him. If he'd had another minute."

At the end of the corridor the door slid open and Chaplain Luckey made his way toward them, coughing lightly.

"Thought I might find you here," Luckey said. "You haven't been here all night, have you?"

"What do you want?" Eliza asked. Maria lay down on her cot and covered her face with her hands.

"You're late for the meeting," he said. He was smiling. He put out his hand to help her up. "The board is waiting. It's time for you to account for yourself." She had forgotten—her monthly review.

She went with him, looking once over her shoulder as she left the cell. Maria lay on her cot, pulling at her bandage with her teeth. The chaplain held the door. Eliza saw the outer corridor, wider and brighter. Maria's skull had been sculpted, not by God and not by her organs. She was cooling metal now. She was quicklime, caustic and gusted, still settling. Eliza stepped into the corridor.

Not Fade Away

Luc Sante

1.

VERY LATE THAT NIGHT, riding home on the train as it shoots past
the graffiti-washed vacant stations on the local track, they stare
straight ahead, unable to explain or articulate the sense of dread that
fills them both except by reference to the lateness of the hour, or the
ebbing of the drugs, or the onset of a cold. The nearly empty train is
going too fast, and it leans around curves as if the wheels on one side
have lost contact with the track, and the lights periodically wink off
for as much as a minute at a time. They sit slumped in a double seat
next to a door. Whenever the train stops at a station the doors open
and nothing comes in, an almost palpable nothing. Neither bothers
to look because they can feel it slide in and take its place among the
already assembled nothing. The air is heavy with the weight of an
earlier week, when it was still summer in the streets above. The
light breaks up into particles. Down here the night could last forever.
The song is "Florence," by the Paragons.

Mind if I play it for you? Here it is, on *The Best of "Winley"
Records,* volume seven of "The Golden Groups" on the Relic label,
an ancient copy with varicolored stains on the back of the sleeve and
a skip in the middle of the cut in question. The skip is annoying, but
it also feels like a part of the fabric, along with the hollow-centered
production, the dogged piano like the labor of the accompanist at a
grade-school assembly, the groans of the four supporting Paragons,
and the agony of Julius McMichael's falsetto lead. It's a daredevil performance, a miracle of endurance—he sounds as if he will dissolve
into coughing and retching or perhaps even drop dead before the end
of the track. The song wants to be a ballad but keeps turning into a
dirge. It's so ghostly you can't imagine it ever sounding new. But then
doo-wop is a spectral genre. It actually happened on street corners;
what transpired in the recording studio, afterward, might sound
posthumous.

"Florence" happened below street level. It happened in a cave, in
an abandoned warehouse, in a unknown room eight stories under

Grand Central Station at five o'clock in the morning. Probably it took place in an impersonal studio off Times Square paneled with that white pasteboard stuff gridded with holes, with folding chairs and ashtrays and demitasse-size paper cups of water and a battered upright piano. Probably the Paragons got a twenty-dollar advance apiece, if that, and then they took the subway home to East Tremont or wherever it was they came from. "Florence" has reached our couple two decades after its release through the medium of oldies radio—a medium of chattering middle-aged men, audibly over-weight, short-sleeved even in the dead of winter, who are capable of putting on the spookiest sides without seeming to notice the weird-ness as they jabber on about trivia before and after. Doo-wop became "oldies" in 1959, when it was still kicking, a premature burial but a phenomenon that allowed records that had sold a hundred copies in the Bronx when new to suddenly go nationwide and become phan-tom hits a couple of years later. But "Florence" cuts through the for-mat with its breathtaking weirdness. The piano, the groans, the keening falsetto—it comes on as Martian. "Oh, Florence, you're an angel, from a world up above," raves the singer in a dog-whistle register that symbolically indicates the purity and intensity of his passion, while an Arctic wind blows through any room where the song is played.

Naturally our couple don't know that each has "Florence" playing on the internal sound track, not that either would be surprised. The hour, the chill, the sticky yellow light, the vertical plunge from a high—all call down "Florence." The moment could feel merely depressed, small-time, pathetic, but "Florence" in its strangeness lends it magnificence. They feel heroically tragic in their stupor. "Florence" places the moment in the corridor of history, makes it an episode, emphasizes its romance and fragility and proximity to heartbreak, suggests that a contrasting scene will follow directly.

Now they have emerged into the weak predawn light of the street. The place is empty except for garbage trucks. The traffic light runs through its repertory of colors to no effect. They still haven't spoken, not in an hour or more. Words feel too huge to shovel onto their tongues. The lack of traffic is convenient, since their reflexes are too slow to negotiate any. They walk, side by side, down the street of shuttered stores, each plodding step a small conquest of space. The apartment seems impossibly distant, their progress the retreat from Moscow. At this hour time doesn't exist actually. The hour just before dawn looks like night, but with all of night's glamour stripped away, and although habit assumes that dawn will soon arrive and peel back the sky, there is no real evidence of this. Darkness clutches the world and will not give it up. The calendar year is an even flimsier proposition; only the twenty-four-hour newsstands maintain it, here and there shouting it into the void like street-corner proselytizers. The year is a random set of four digits that may or may not coincide with the information imparted by the posters wheat-pasted on the windows of empty storefronts. In all probability, "Florence" has not yet been composed or recorded. Our couple has imagined it. When they awaken the following afternoon, they won't remember how it visited them.

2.

Historically, she got off the bus. Most of the rest is conjecture on my part, but she did get off the bus, in the aquarium depths of the lowest platform at Port Authority, a bus of the Pallas Athena line, from someplace in New Jersey—*western* New Jersey, she insisted, out near the Red River declivity, where the mesas begin, "the biggest sky you ever saw." West of Trenton, even. She claimed there were fourteen people in her family and that she had to leave because they needed her room to lodge hands for the pea harvest. She carried a large plastic suitcase and an army duffel bag reinforced with duct tape. They were too heavy for her, so she dragged them along, past all the chaotic intersecting lines of people waiting to get on other buses, past the black nun with a basket on her lap at the foot of the escalator, past the lunch counters and drugstores and necktie displays, past the hustlers and the plainclothesmen and the translucent figures who came to the terminal just because they liked the smell of people.

She marched through the main hall and out the glass doors onto the avenue, and then, I imagine, she unhesitatingly turned right and started downtown, because she wasn't one to dally. I can see her plowing down the avenue with her twin cargo containers angling out behind her, scattering the lunchtime crowd like bowling pins. She cut quite a figure at five foot nothing in boots, although I don't know if she yet had the black leather Perfecto jacket she was to wear in every possible kind of weather. Her hair was long then, gathered in one braid like the heroine of a Chinese proletarian opera. She hadn't yet started on her campaign—spectacularly unsuccessful—to make herself unapproachably ugly, so her glasses were delicate wire things

171

rather than welder's goggles with perforated sidepieces. She looked about fourteen, maybe even nine in certain kinds of light, and yet there was something about her, some kind of juju she emanated, possibly the adamantine stare that seemed to precede her into a room, that caused grown men to tiptoe around her. Whatever she was wearing, nobody would have given her any guff about running over their toes with her ten-ton bags.

3.

"Finally have enough ideas for my own things to work on that I can see the advantage of not having to work. Not that I ever wanted to have a full-time job but it was a little mysterious to me what I'd do w the free time besides get fucked up etcet. On saying that I suppose I'll promptly dry out. On the other hand, sometimes I get sick of imposing myself on my environment. But I console myself by saying its merely a matter of degree since you can't stop that jazz except by getting dead anyway. All trottoirs lead to the junkyard."

"Got offered a job in Montana as cook on a ranch—explained my job situation, was told to call collect in the spring if still interested. May vy well be. What passes for the advantages of the city don't impress me. Meantime I start teaching Monday, me and S. planning an interior house painting biz, may have silkscreening/photo jobs freelance. Lots of film to mess with and some collage ideas still intact. Got a Greek dictionary the better to write to my grandmother. D' like to start making casts, finish my videotape, learn how to use a gun, buy a bicycle, play better pool, do more architectural drawings & keep my dirty socks out of my work room, my newspapers & bus transfers out of my bed, & myself out of shitty klubs. Am going to try vy hard to have no more catatonic afternoons/hungover mornings (starting day after tomorrow). The odd dates are all New Year's Day, the evens the day of atonement. Well, no, I really am in more control of things. Don't give a shit about any particular end pts as long as the process is satisfying. One life to live—organ break here. Then ad for disposable razors."

"I hope I don't get dull out here. I consult myself periodically to see if I'm 'done,' ready to leave. I'm anxious in a way to have this period behind me, to be frivolous is a social embarrassment. But at the same time the theme of the period is to wish away nothing so I can't regret it."

"Walking to work through the neon in the Stockton tunnel at 6:30 a.m. it occurs to me that I'm a PRODUCT OF EVOLUTION. But I'm not satisfied. I suppose its no better than even odds you'd believe I'm working the morning shift in a restaurant in the financial district for minimum wage."

"Someone gave me a blue black pearl earring so I got my ear pierced & am wearing it. Its vy beautiful & looks good but makes me look vy fem(me) (?) & seems unnatural almost perverted to me for me."

"So a new legs been added to the graph of moods & it's a goat's leg. Expect to be bored to death today at the liquor store. Had a marvelous day of filling a brick wall w cement yesterday."

"I have an outrageous calligraphic scar on my ass that I got fr accidentally leaning on the grill of the beloved Sahara heater when it was red hot & I was stark naked. Its one of my favorite things abt myself along w my gold tooth."

"The birds are singing, the 4:30 a.m. ones."

4.

Let me play you "Arleen," by General Echo, a seven-inch forty-five on the Techniques label, produced by Winston Riley, a number-one hit in Jamaica in the autumn of 1979. "Arleen" is in the Stalag 17 riddim, a slow, heavy, insinuating track that is nearly all bass—the drums do little more than bracket and punctuate, and the original's brass-section color has been entirely omitted in this version. I'm not really sure what Echo is saying. It sounds like "Arleen wants to dream with a dream." A dream within a dream. Whether or not those are his actual words, it is the immediate sense. The riddim is at once liquid and halting, as if it were moving through a dark room filled with hanging draperies, incense and ganja smoke, sluggish and near- ly impenetrable air—the bass walks and hurtles. Echo's delivery is mostly talkover, with just a bit of singsong at the end of the verse. It is suggestive, seductive, hypnotic, light-footed, veiling question- able designs under a scrim of innocence, or else addled, talking shit in a daze as a result of an injury: "My gal Arleen, she love whipped cream / Every time I check her she cook sardine. . . ."

General Echo, whose real name was Errol Robinson, was promi- nent in the rise of "slackness," the sexually explicit reggae style that began to eclipse the Rastafarian "cultural" style in the late 1970s; his songs include "Bathroom Sex" and "I Love to Set Young Crutches on Fire" ("crotches," that is), as well as "Drunken Master" and "Inter- national Year of the Child." He had his first hit in 1977, put out three albums and a substantial number of singles—an indeterminate num- ber because of the chaos and profusion of Jamaican releases, then as now. Along with two other members of his sound system, he was shot dead on the street by Kingston police in 1980; no one seems to know why.

I bought the record at the time it was on the Jamaican charts, from some punk store in downtown Manhattan. I first heard it at Isaiah's, a dance club that materialized every Thursday night in a fourth-floor loft on Broadway between Bleecker and Bond. This was a few years before the enormous wave of Jamaican immigration to the United States, which was mainly a phenomenon of the later eighties and a result of the kind of violence that killed General Echo. Nevertheless the club regulars were more than half Jamaican transplants, nearly all of them men. The walls were lined with impassive types wearing three-piece suits in shades of cream and tan, and broad-brimmed, high-crowned felt hats that looked at once Navaho and Hasidic, with their locks gathered up inside. They danced as if they didn't want to dance but couldn't entirely contain themselves—the merest sugges- tion of movement: a shoulder here, a hip there. It was hard not to feel judged by this lineup; I kept ratcheting down the enthusiasm level of my dancing. But they didn't even see me. Whatever else might have been going on in their lives they were, in immemorial fashion, bach- elors at a dance, and this gave the club a taste of the grange hall. Sometimes I went there with a girlfriend, sometimes with a group of people. We smoked weed and drank Red Stripe and sometimes in- haled poppers, which would lend you huge brief bursts of euphoric energy and then foreclose, leaving you in a puddle. I hardly ever made it to the 4 a.m. closing because the next day I had to work, and four hours' sleep made me feel sick. As a result I missed all the incidents involving guns, which invariably occurred at the end of the night. The club would have to shut down, for weeks or months at a time—it was anyway unclear what went on in the loft the other six nights and seven days; maybe people lived there. Eventually the owners installed a metal detector, the first one I ever encountered, little suspecting they would one day be ubiquitous.

We went there for the bass, and the trance state resulting from hours of dancing to riddim that stretched forever, the groove a fabric of stacked beats fractally splitting into halves of halves of halves of halves, a tree that spread its branches through the body, setting the governor beat in the torso and shaking its tributaries outward and down through shoulders, elbows, hips, knees, feet so that you couldn't stop except when you collapsed. Most often I went there with E., who danced like a whip, and who could keep on well past my exhaustion limit, and because I needed her I did so, too. Dancing was our chief mode of communication, an intimacy like two people sleeping together in different dreams, our bodies carrying on a conversation while our minds were in eidetic twilight. Neither of us really trusted language with each other, so we found this medium of exchange that trumped it, precluding silence and misunderstanding. She had a small body whose axis was set on powerful hips with an engine's torque, while above the waist she was all moues and flutters, a belle minus a *carnet de bal*, so that the sum of her was exactly like the music: the massive horsepower of the bass below and the delicate broken crystal guitar and plaintive childlike melodica above.

We lived in that place called youth where everything is terribly, punishingly final day by day, and at the same time tentative and approximate and subject to preemptive revision. We broke up and got back together, again and again, we lived together or we lived at opposite ends of the island, then she moved west and didn't come back, and I went out there but elected not to stay. Then her body betrayed her. She became allergic first to television, then to television when it was turned off, then to inactive televisions downstairs or next door, then to recently manufactured objects, then to so many various and apparently random stimuli she became her own book of Leviticus. Then her muscles gave way and she couldn't dance, then couldn't walk, then couldn't speak, and in the end became just a head attached by a string to a useless doll's body before she stopped being able to swallow and soon after to breathe.

5.

Dear D.,

I went over to M.'s to retrieve my letters and whatever else from the four big crates of stuff she salvaged from E.'s apartment when E. entered the nursing home a few months before she died. It took me a few years to work up the courage to ask. I wanted the letters, I justified, because they were probably the closest thing to a diary I ever kept, in the key years 1979–1983. In other words I was exercising my usual dodge, which is to turn all of life into research materials. M. was game if not exactly eager. One corridor of her apartment is choked with boxes—the rest consist of her father's belongings, and they will undoubtedly soon be joined by her mother's. She hadn't opened any of the crates since hurriedly packing them more than four years ago. Late in the evening, after dinner, we began to dig. It was quite literally like entering a tomb. There was E.'s Perfecto jacket; there was a small box containing a gold tooth and a lock of her hair; there was a whole box of her eyeglasses. There were boxes and boxes of collage materials, of her photographs and negatives, of notebooks. There was copious evidence of her study of botany (she took university classes in the subject at some point), of her various pursuits of therapy, of her adherence to Buddhism (much more serious and longstanding than any of us unbeliever friends realized). And there were many bags and boxes of letters. This was just the stuff M. kept—I understood firsthand the harshness of trying to make those sorts of decisions, in a hurry and under major psychological stress, and my parents' house didn't even reek overwhelmingly of urine.

Going through the boxes caused me to enter a state that I suppose was not unlike shock. I took my letters and nothing else, went back to my hotel and read all of them, then couldn't sleep. On the one hand I wasn't wrong; the letters are indeed the only real record I have of those years, and I have nothing to cringe about concerning their style or expression—E. always brought out the best in me that way. They are full of detail about those days, that is when they don't consist of naked pleas. Reading them felt vertiginous, like being admitted back to that apartment on First Avenue for fifteen minutes of an afternoon in 1979 and experiencing all over again the despair and optimism and boredom and love and fun and heedlessness and anguish of that time. And it brought her back into a kind of three-dimensionality that I'd forgotten—my jealousy rushed right back. There were a few unmailed letters from her to me, too. One of them, from after her last visit to New York in 1990, may be the most romantic letter she ever wrote me. I can't help but speculate on what would have happened had I received it.

She was getting crazier and crazier as well as sicker at the time. Photographs of her from before she became immobilized by her illness show her grinning wildly with a missing front tooth, aggressively unkempt, looking like someone who'd hit you up for spare change in Tompkins Square Park. Could I imagine myself nursing her until her death? But she wouldn't have permitted that anyway. M. reports that at her memorial the room was crowded with people, few of whom knew any of the others. She needed to compartmentalize her life, and that was one of our chief stumbling blocks as a couple. Of course I understood, since I have similar tendencies, but I wanted *her* exclusively. I can't begin to account for the chaos of emotions this has all raised in me, the sheer number and variety of them. Part of me wanted to take those four crates—M. doesn't know what to do with them. They are E.'s life, her complexity, her unbelievable array of talents and their utter dissipation. She's going to haunt me for the rest of my days—do I wish I'd never met her? But that's like trying to imagine my life as another person. She changed me, totally and irreversibly.

Interesting to hear M. say that as far as she's aware E. cracked at some point in her last year of high school, and was never the same again. A banal incident—she backed over a row of metal garbage cans while trying to drive (she was always an awful driver)—sent her over the edge. M. dates E.'s cruelty to her (she was consistently vicious to M.), among other things, to that time. That sounds too neat, but who knows? In my experience she didn't start seeming or acting weird until we'd been together about nine months, maybe sometime in the spring of '75. Here's a random snapshot of E.: One time during her next-to-last New York visit ('87?), M. and her boyfriend of the time were going to a club and invited E. to come along. She insisted on stopping to get some takeout food, and then, to M.'s and boyfriend's dismay, insisted on bringing it into the club to eat. You didn't do things like that in clubs by that point. To me the story graphically illustrates an aspect of her. She specialized in the inappropriate. You'd constantly be wondering: What's the deal, exactly? Is it that she wants to accommodate her own needs and conveniences regardless of whatever social codes are in effect? Does she mean to provoke? Is she oblivious to the reactions of others? Does she want to reorganize the whole world, starting here and now? Is she deliberately doing something gauche as a way of wrestling with her feelings of inadequacy and gaucheness? It may have been that all of those things were true, and that even ranking them in order of importance would be irrelevant. I could go on, but I won't.

Love,

6.

"Sally Go Round the Roses" is a strange song that can seem as though it is following you around. A writer somewhere called it an ovoid, and that seems apt. The instrumental backing is functionally a loop, a brief syncopated phrase led by piano and followed by bass fiddle and drums, that repeats as often as a rhythm sample. It makes the song float, hover like a cloud. Sitting on top of the cloud are girls, a lot of girls, at least eight of them in multitracked call-and-response, at once ethereal and obsessive. The chorus tells Sally to go round the roses, that the roses can't hurt her, that they won't tell her secret. It tells her not to go downtown. It tells her to cry, to let her hair hang down. It tells her that the saddest thing in the whole wide world is to see your baby with another girl.

The record is credited to the Jaynetts, although that seems to have been a label applied by the producers to various aggregations assembled in studios on various dates with varying results. There were other songs with that attribution; they left no mark on the world, nor did they deserve to. This one made it to number two on the charts in 1963. Even the first time you hear it, it sounds as if you've always known it. It comes over you like a glow or a chill. It comes over the couple as they sit, shivering, on the rooftop of an old building in Chinatown. It is August, but that does not prevent the air from feeling glacial. They've been talking all night, at cross-purposes. Each feels that only a personal failure of rhetorical skill prevents the other from embracing the correct view. But every clarifying or corrective word widens the gulf.

How many Jaynetts were there? Did they ever appear before an audience? What did they look like? Did they wear bouffants and long gold-lamé dresses, or kerchiefs and sweatshirts and three-quarter-length pants? How was the song heard by its first listeners? How is it heard today? Did everybody but us mistake it for an ordinary anodyne pop song? Where did the song really come from? Was the song actually written by someone who sat down at the piano one day? Was it sung to the pretended author in a bar by a stranger who thereupon dropped dead? Did it just somehow materialize, in the form we know today, on a reel-to-reel tape with no indication of origin? Why does it seem to resist the grubby quotidian context from which all things come, particularly pop songs aimed at a nebulously conceived teenage audience? Is it simply a brilliant void like those that periodically inflame the popular imagination, which allow their consumers to project any amount of emotional intensity upon them and merely send it back in slightly rearranged form, so that it can seem to anticipate their wishes and embody their desires and populate their loneliness and hold out a comforting hand, when it is in reality nothing but a doll with mirrored eyes?

Now they've stopped talking, from fatigue and futility. They're drained, and that in concert with the cold air makes them feel as if they're drifting, carried by breezes far from their rooftop and away over the city, over its skyscrapers and bridges, flung this way and that, speeding up and slowing down, weightless as a couple of feathers. There are trucks moving below them, and pigeons at eye level, and up above is the contrail of a jet. There are few lights on in windows, no visible humans anywhere. They sit, or float, atop a dead city, enmired in a darkness that does not even manage to be satisfyingly black. Just then the sun's first rays point up over the horizon and begin to describe a fan, each separate ray distinct, almost solid. It is the dawn as represented in nineteenth-century anarchist engravings: the advent of the new world. Silently they regard this phenomenon. It seems cruelly and pointlessly ill-timed, purely gratuitous and designed to mock them. It is the earth's epic ritual enactment of beginning, and they are at an end. They become aware once again of the song, hovering over the rooftops, emanating from some unseen radio. Sally goes round the roses and keeps going around them: it is a circle. It has no point of entry or exit. They have no purchase over it, no more than they have power over the sun. It, whatever it might be, will continue beginning and ending, over and over and over again, per omnia saecula saeculorum.

Two Poems
Kevin Magee

EUPHORION

That what you'd be looking for
is a plot that would show how
the Imaginary is constructed
on the dereliction of the Social Real,
fictive being intense enough
the dividing line disappears

and you swim in an element
where what is real and what is not
displaces actual events and actors
in them like that Faust-Helen story
built on the Achilles-Helen myth
you stumbled on in *Homeric Fragment.*

That the passion had drawn him off
and fallen, he saw the idea of his Being
submitting to be the cunning compact
suppressed manifestations too remote
events that instigated craving for more
from every idea she had ever wrote.

The time was the worst in the year.
You had to drive me to the extremities
to extract this simple sentence from me.
The Helen we have invented defending
everything we no longer had divided
into the time before the stanza and the time after.

I know the name that kindled it,
though I have left that name unthought.
He needed her name to prepare for war.

If only you could wipe out that name,
not only from memory, but from history.
If only you could burn it out: Achilles.

Who could prevent the thoughts
that came into the hard, heavy helmet
called his head. Apollo approached me
then changed into a wolf surrounded by rats
and conferred with a casual gesture
his taste on my tongue when I awoke.

Why did I want the gift of Prophecy?
Who will find a voice will it be the one
whose skull is split racing each other
into the slaughterhouse, and nothing,
nothing I could have done or not done
could have led me to a different spot.

Whether or not we knew this was goodbye.
I abandoned myself to my apparitions
and fled the precinct into the citadel
where I got caught up in the word "girl"
and caught all the more by her, threw
myself at her spewing the new Troy.

Passing each other by name they pass
by my name, "Out of the hollow realm
of shades Achilles too became yours,
his love defying all the decrees of Fate."
I stayed alive long enough at last,
rescued by Simon from a brothel in Tyre.

Faust [approaching with a man in chains
at his side]: Branded, striking the table, sings
There was a rat in the cellar who lived
on fat and butter and swelled himself up for
a match with Martin Luther, and the world
got too hot for him as if he had love in his body.

Unless it would be to smash her windows
I'll hear of no greeting accumulating

from the rankness of continued Prosperity:
See Helen, who brought about a bad war
which lasts forever, and great Achilles
who in the end was in combat with Love.

Is it possible that it all happened
in order that two souls should meet?
Helen: I must not punish misfortune.
I'm the one that wrote the lure to ruin.
There was bitter discussion and hate.
The winters were ruthless and bleak.

Can one weigh the thousand ships
against one kiss in the night?
The phantom and the shadow throng.
Has he lost in a game of chance?
Now therefore you will say to the many
who fell, Where is my son?

No atonement could restore her.
It is the lost legions that condition
their encounter, among the legends
few were the words we said, nor knew
each other nor asked, are you Spirit?
Are you Sister? Are you Brother?

They meet (encounter/love) one another
only as dream figures, FICTIVE BEING.
For the Marriage of Faustus and Helen
then, collaged out of Gautier's Histoire.
The Witch material comes from my German.
She lives at the entrance to the cave.

Egypt—her mummification, her skin
bloodless is wrapped in layers of yellow
lace and the lines in her face on the porch
the children stare, a cow's tongue hangs down
repeat after her *guten morgen*, Grossmutter
on the porch in her rocker said, *mein kinder*

He rushed past the encounter
without a thought that rose from the folktale
honeyed over with Modern English.
A black rat pokes out of her mouth.
The child in the cradle is strangled
and the mother is clapping her hands.

Or lighthouse beacon guiding storm-tossed
children in their eternal and enormous nights,
swallowed beyond the illumined father's
eyes around the glaze he was groping his way
opening the cave that he was verging toward
the blinding attributed to a strange house.

In the light encompassing him now he saw
the straps and bands and heavy cotton
that comprised her heaped in exposure.
Motionless, impassive, and monumental,
all the girls at the school called her Calypso
and my text is something funny you said.

It was an attack of Spectacle,
a crisis of suffering spectacularly
though the attack was also a festival
and feast day. She has sung at every crossroads,
she has kissed every face, and that woman
was his first thought (Simon Magus, Acts VIII 9-24).

Quando Iasón vider fatto bifolco
and I began like a man desire confuses.
Three thousand years melted away
ch'alma beata non puria mentire
s'io ti fiammeggio nel caldo d'amore.
The treasure became the sacrifice.

The curse that key to the house of Atreus
hangs in rows on meathooks, I lived
on my slice of wall while the towers fell.
Was he the envoy of the gods of that city?
His will to live was the will to remember
the faith of the prophets is faith in power.

"—but to free the birds—"
"—and found yourself entangled—"
Exile. One of the circles of Hell.
Who in his delirium sees Helen
as he saw her for the first time.
Lightning out of a clear blue sky.

BALANCE OF A HAPPY DAY

This isn't what doesn't preoccupy
this thought scarcely
It increases by one tome,
withdrawn

This share is the same for everyone
What everyone then secretly says
Why are you still there in the place
I am lingering

and when I go toward you
as though I weren't supposed to
why did you let me talk to you
Maybe one maybe no one to think

let them think on
What are you
who give me nothing
promising nothing

I keep you,
this way words
to you that won't reach you
What calm near to you,

come in through,
my steps come to meet me
You can't be what you are.

You were not my words.
Answering belongs to where you
left a long time ago,

to come near without wanting to,
in a gift I can't explain
you couldn't accept,

are you in the night the thought
that I am in,

That I would always be
where you are not

You would be the large me

Where you were
I was not able to suffer

a complicity the link between
what ought to be my thought

This belief that my belief
I don't believe in anymore

       edifice

         caprice

I would have entered into
that there would no longer
exist the intimacy between us
that allowed me to address you

a loving memory of events
that never happened

if I have to forget you
only by being forgotten by you   .

Kevin Magee

I know for a long time now
I will only reach you with the images
that I wait for that I am

in the lament of the light
toward which you have drawn me
without waiting there

that each one would long
to be the only one for all the others

wasn't I always near you
when your mouth metamorphosed

wasn't there a moment
when you said to me Hello?

Her Lady's Mouth
Mary Caponegro

ST. ROSE OF LIMA: sophomore year. Ginny leans against the brick wall, wishing to be invisible, and watches idly as various girls cluster and disband. In the distance, across the parking lot, the younger grammar-school girls and far fewer grammar-school boys are jumping rope, seeing and sawing and swinging and playing red rover or rattlesnake. In the foreground, Dawn sits on the cement step poking at an orange, scraping with her nails into the thick, stippled skin until a patch comes away, exposing the muscley globe underneath. After dismantling the inner fruit, Dawn offers a section to Fiona. The two girls stand side by side, sucking at the sweetness before consuming their respective symmetrical treasures. Suddenly a bee intrudes, installs himself in the path of Fiona's breath, startling her. She hurls the coveted piece of fruit to the ground, but the bee is in every sense unmoved. It seems he does not crave the source, he craves the trace she bears, and hovers impertinently at her rosebud mouth until Dawn gallantly swats the nasty thing away. Even after being rescued, Fiona seems shaken. Ginny fins herself entranced by this happenstance interaction she has witnessed. On a whim, she invents a soliloquy in her head, playing with rhyme:

> *A bee, I see, is mesmerized by my lady's mouth*
> *and lingering in the citrus scent upon her lips,*
> *he doth persist until my lady starts to cry;*
> *then I, with all the gallantry she merits,*
> *will swat the rogue till he desist.*

Preoccupied with rhythms, immersed in her improvisatory soliloquy, Ginny almost misses the punch line, if such term applied to a sentence whose punch was as soft as a kiss. Dawn produces a tissue—pristine, unlike the one at Ginny's feet—and tenderly wipes the wetness from Fiona's cheek, as if this bead of moisture were as precious as the one that had miraculously appeared on the face of that Virgin Mary statue in some foreign country. She then says, as if

187

the playground were their private stage, "You can't blame him for thinking you were sweet."

Ginny kicks her own bloodied tissue into the grass near the trash.

"Importunate bee," she continues, building her soliloquy on their behalf, this time out loud, "how dare thee terrorize my lover's ruby lips?"

"Hey Postadellawhatchafuck, are you talking to yourself again?"

"Oh, Darcy, it's you," she says, jolted out of illusory privacy.

"Haven't you got anything better to do?"

Kicking the dirt nervously, lest Darcy think the original gesture had been more than an idle one, Ginny replies, "Gotta entertain myself somehow."

Ginny will henceforth try to keep her soliloquies internal and will not venture at this juncture to share with Darcy how impressed she is by the courage and authority with which Dawn brushed the bee from Fiona's lips, nor share the realization of how much more tender this protective gesture is than anything that transpires evenings between herself and Billy: their automatic and yet tentative hibernation of hands in each other's jeans, with so few words and none of them, nor any touch, approximating the solicitousness with which her schoolmate to her other schoolmate said, "You can't blame him for thinking you were sweet."

There is something so mature about this private compliment, this profession of affection, a sweetness whose implicit gravity seems as patent as the Nicene Creed's solemnity: *I believe in God, the Father almighty, Creator of Heaven . . . and of all things visible and invisible . . .* but would it also imply a customized act of contrition, recited sotto voce by Dawn or by Fiona in their respective beds on the cusp of sleep: "*O my God I am heartily sorry for . . . being a LES-Bee-in,*" while her inamorata's version might proceed, "*O my God I am heartily lezzie, and have I offended thee?*" The playfulness would not cancel out sincerity, profundity. These variations would be true appeals, not merely entertaining means to entertain themselves. And how might they be answered? With compassion? Revulsion? Indifference? Entertaining oneself, in any case, was not so easy, muses Ginny, what with this nun's objection or that nun's objection, every instance of innocent playacting subject to scrutiny, reprimand.

On that same playground years ago, she and Vicky and Maureen had mimicked the Supremes, lining up beside one another, gesturing in triplicate, swinging their respective prepubescent hips, singing the lyrics to "Love Child," putting all their collective heart into the phrase *never meant to be,* unaware that the articulation of illegitimacy in this context was as taboo as the transgression that it represented. Only later did they fully understand that by the church's reckoning, *any* baby in the making was a baby *meant to be*—Thomistically.

But the sister on playground duty was unequivocal: "This song is not a proper one for a Catholic school playground, girls; these lyrics are unsuitable. These expressions and their meaning are thoroughly objectionable. I'm sure your parents would be appalled to know you listened to such . . . filth on the radio."

But Ginny's mom always let her and Angela hear the top-forty station's countdown of hits on New Year's Day: all one hundred of them on WABC. She would even leave the car running in the driveway for a little while after they had come home from errands so they wouldn't miss anything. This was one of the coolest things about Mom, that she'd even sing along with the girls enthusiastically, much as they knew she would rather duet with Renata Tebaldi or Robert Merrill, superimposed over some silly opera like *Tosca* or *La Traviata,* or *Carmen* or *The Barber of Seville.* Instead of metamorphosing into *Madame Butterfly,* she'd sing backup for the Cyrkle with her daughters, as ignorant as they of the complex lineage that could be traced backward to the Seekers, to Paul Simon, and even to John Lennon, their name his creation. In any case, all three Postodellafuoco females could be heard cheerfully if not quite tunefully belting out this less classical, more upbeat take on the tragic: *Yeah, the worst is over now / The mornin' sun is shinin' like a red rubber ball.*

Despite this empirical evidence, Ginny lodged no protest, because even this young, she knew better than to argue the facts with a nun. Better to acquiesce. Look at the ground and say, Each of you, yes, Sister, yes, Sister, yes, Sister.

And if it is not one thing, another; if not songs, then shoes, if not shoes, then skirts: a pleated plaid with hem raised too high, revealing more than knee: a smidgen of thigh. A pleated plaid skirt switched for a pair of jeans in the locker room after the final bell, which despite its ding of closure does not take a girl out of the DMZ of school property because even in the parking lot the rules still applied. Or bad behavior or bad intentions or bad attitude. But what if the shoe, someday, were on the other foot: the nuns under the girls' collective thumb?

"Sister Serena, Annie and I must report . . . it has come to our attention . . . that you have acquired a very bad habit!!!" The girls spit out the laugh they can't control. But such joking speculation must of course remain playacting.

Not appropriate words, not appropriate shoes. "They are something between a shoe and a boot, are they not, Miss Postodellafuoco?"

For some reason Ginny is distracted by the difference between Sister's *fwo-ko* pronunciation and the way her Italian relatives pronounce her name. Ginny usually thinks it's adding insult to injury to make three syllables out of two, yielding an even longer name! *Fu-o-co.* And strange the way they make an *o* so long and open. But somehow in this moment she feels the nun's pronunciation to be crude in comparison. It distracts her from the next phase of interrogation.

"Are they chukkas?"

"Are they whatchas?" she wants to respond, but restrains herself, dares not be fresh.

"Is this suitable footwear, in your opinion, for the funeral of your classmate's brother, a young boy taken from his siblings and parents by our merciful God to spare all further suffering?"

Suitable, thinks, Ginny, for poor Jimmy Mulligan? Dead or alive, he'd have little concern for her shoes, or the suddenly rigorously enforced school code of oxford or loafer only. What shoes had Sisyphus, about whom Sr. Catherine John had lectured, to support his repetitive steps, pushing up the hill—the inverse, it seemed, of Jimmy Mulligan's brief life: an eight-years-long episode of a broken-headed body, as it were, perpetually falling down the basement stairs, bonk bonk bonk: his head the mythic boulder doomed to repetition—or it might as well have been, no less of a fated target than JFK's. Hard to know if he'd been born that way or had become that way after an accident, since Laura's dad always yelled at his daughters if anyone forgot to close the basement door or horsed around by the top of the stairs, saying, "Hey, wanna end up like Jimmy? Be careful, for God's sake." Laura Mulligan's somehow-or-other damaged brother was said by the nuns to be a gift to their household, the same nuns who now declared it a gift that he died.

"Well, which is it," Ginny wants to demand, you know what I

190

mean? After bitching to Vicki, they compose the CliffsNotes for their own capricious course syllabus. Lesson one: love the retard. Lesson two: lose the retard. Lesson three: review one and two and give thanks to God for these opportunities to suffer and suffer more and to witness suffering. Funeral shoes? How about blue suede funeral shoes?

"Excuse me, Sister, I've never heard of . . ." As if she were wearing stilettos or sneakers. Weren't people supposed to wear black to a funeral anyway? And here they were, a flock—or would it be a pride—of plaid and no one got on anyone's case about that! And wouldn't the logical uniform for this occasion be a crash helmet, with SRL insignia, given Mr. Mulligan's obsession with preventing a repeat performance, or at least a repeat consequence, an obsession that extended, albeit with less intensity, to his daughters' playmates.

"Either be in the basement, or be in the girls' rooms. Or stay in the kitchen for all I care. But don't any of you be runnin' down those stairs, all right? Don't want anyone ending up like poor Jimmy."

Blessed Jimmy. Poor Jimmy. Sinless, feckless, hopeless, witless, make up your *goddamn mind!* "I'll have to go look up that word, never heard the term chukkas." Here's my crash helmet, Sister, to represent the St. Rose of Lima Hell's Angels contingent!

"And as long as we're on the subject, is that blouse tie-dyed, Miss Postodellafuoco, you know *that* term, don't you?"

"No—I mean I know it, yes, Sister, but it's not, the blouse, I mean, isn't—you see, my mother doesn't separate the wash real well, sometimes the whites get in with the col . . ."

"If you took home economics, you wouldn't have to burden your mother, you could help to run a household in preparation for marriage and motherhood. And you would look as a pupil of St. Rose should, instead of like some refugee from that Woodstock Festival. And may I remind you there is to be no changing into blue jeans within a three-mile radius of school. There have been reports of sightings. . . ."

Ginny feels as if she were a bird or a planet or a prisoner. For heaven's sake—sightings!

"But, Sister Serena, I have to switch buses at the public school and the kids stare and make terrible fun of us."

"Offer it up for Lent, Miss *Postadellafwoko*, think of your Savior, whipped, reviled, and spat upon." She motions with her veiled, boxed-in head to the crucifix hanging above, waits until Ginny's gaze is directed upward. "Don't you welcome the chance to be closer to him?"

Ginny thinks that being Christlike should be bigger, bolder than her measly shame of pleated plaid. To bear the wounds, to show them to the world, from one's temple of flesh, or *choose* the flames like Joan of Arc (the painting of whom, hanging in the Metropolitan Museum, makes Ginny feel dreamy, and a reproduction of which in the gift shop she purchased, with her mother's permission and financing, so that it could hang, albeit less grandly than in the museum, in her room, Joan's soulful blue-gray eyes gazing into space, beyond the rippling peach-colored muslin of Ginny's curtains, ostensibly unaware of the diaphanous spirits on her left). Now that would be one thing, that would be unequivocally, viscerally Christlike, but what has that heart with its blazing thorny cincture got to do with her gawky, too-short blazer and longer-than-fashionable pleated skirt whose waist must be rolled two or three times to be other than something you'd be caught dead in, and still you couldn't get rid of the neon-sign plaid. She composes in her head a verse she believes appropriate for some dignified occasion, perhaps even a tombstone inscription, though it might be thought blasphemous: *More scorn than a crown of thorns is heaped upon a girl's body nailed to a plaid uniform.* She's proud of the compact if not quite . . . evenly metered poem, which, were she to recite at assembly on Monday, would surely elicit her own crucifixion. A dead giveaway from miles back, the opposite of a soldier's uniform with its khaki camouflage to blend in, not stand out, so that any enemy or civilian could immediately see; who came up with that? Was Veronica's veil, was Jesus's loincloth plaid? What made plaid a Catholic flag? Better to be naked and scourged and . . . theatrical, anything, something nobler than this nickel-and-dime humiliation, small-time suffering.

"Besides, you should be proud of your uniform."

"Yes, Sister."

Could she really handle naked and scourged though? Ginny wonders. She is embarrassed to be naked in front of almost anyone, even her sister or mom. Billy the least, she supposes, but even with him it's never whole-hog nudity, only sections really, her breasts essentially, and they barely see what they're doing, down there in the basement, rooting in each other's jeans with clumsy hands, both eager and halting, more like when the doctor looks discreetly, clinically, under the paper gown at specific parts of your body—except for that doctor Robin Carlisle went to, some friend of Robin's father's who

192

said, "We're all adults here, you don't need the gown, right?" Not Dr. McMannus or Dr. Salvucci but some other doctor. Robin Carlisle said she was thrilled to be treated—for once—like a grown-up, but after felt stupid to have assented so assiduously because maybe he was a pervert and how would she ever know? She wasn't about to consult her dad.

"Hey, Kerry, my splotch of accidental tie-dye will turn St. Rose's cement playground into another Woodstock!" The girls double over with laughter imagining a festive, anarchic, chaos-inducing collar, turned into a reliquary in some cave or church, everyone racing to rub it in the manner of kissing the Blarney stone. One glance would have the same effect as ingesting a morsel of hash brownie (which the girls only twice in their lives—and in fact in that year—have done, far from the school cafeteria). It would bounce its strobe-like light across the parking lot and playground, causing instant chaos! Just picture it: uniforms flying off bodies and lawn workers trucking in from every borough, the archdiocese convulsed. Instead of dipping a finger in holy water, both the faithful and the curious will come to rub Ginny's magic collar, the same way they travel to Lourdes or line up to see the pseudo—or truly—miraculous weeping Madonna statue. Or was it a painting?

"Just call me the tie-dye antichrist, Kerry!" She'd be famous! Queen—albeit of sin—for a day? Possibly excommunicated. But even as she says it, Ginny feels disturbed at that idea, and then feels guilty to be joking about it.

A school bus has ferried the St. Rose contingent to the Mulligans' parish, and it will likewise return the girls to St. Rose for the day's final classes, but since neither Angie nor Ginny, as it happens, have subjects of any substance in those periods, they, like several other girls, have arranged to get picked up directly after the funeral. When their dad finally arrives at the unfamiliar church, the girls pile into the Cadillac's backseat, still trying to sort out grief from gift in the service they have just taken part in. How lucky they were to have good brains (that sentiment seconded by their father). How lucky the Mulligans were to have God's grace in the form of intrinsically inno-cent Jimmy (that sentiment most likely to be seconded by their mother at home before dinner or during commercials at dinner).

How lucky that Jimmy could be so expeditiously delivered to heaven, skipping the bother of more years on earth, during which he would have been emblem incarnate of grace and frustration fused. It is simpler to dwell on the nonsense surrounding the service than the insoluble content, so Ginny complains about being hassled.

"You've gotta cut them a little slack, Gin," her father says, "they got no husbands, they're not . . . fulfilled."

"I wish they'd cut *me* a little slack. At least let me *wear* slacks!"

"Funny, Gin-Rummy," Dad says, "that's a good one."

"And *they* should wear white, not black," Angie adds. "Cuz they're brides of Christ."

"Yeah, shouldn't that be fulfilling enough," Ginny asks, "being married to Jesus?"

Secretly she has imagined, in the dusky privacy of her room, and less frequently in church, that abstract holiness of dedicating one's life to the solitude of Christ, the contours of St. Teresa's *Interior Castle* or even Hayley Mills's unforeseen spiritual calling in *The Trouble with Angels.* The texture of such a life: its uncluttered purity, a cold clarity like her mother's good Waterford crystal, or like a delicate golden bell with a ribbon-thin rim, against which its golden tongue would sound as a drop of water into a still pool—a mountain lake of holiness.

"Well, spiritually, sure, hon, their souls are fulfilled but . . . they live here on earth."

What was it like, Ginny wondered, the mind or soul of a saint, the space inside their head? Like the transcendent silence of polar or lunar space? That rarefied atmosphere imbibed by Neil Armstrong and the Apollo 11 crew on America's behalf, an ambience that Nonna felt had been usurped from saints and angels. (She declared all NASA expeditions blasphemy.)

In the backseat, Ginny and Angela whisper to each other. "But if every nun is a bride of Christ, doesn't that make Jesus a . . . polygamist?" They giggle, almost forgetting their father isolated in the front seat with no adjacent passenger, like some chauffeur or taxi driver. He is suddenly angry, gripping the wheel, turning around to face them until forced to look forward for safety's sake.

"Now if I wasn't driving I'd—don't they teach you the bloody commandments in this bloody school? Thou shalt not take the Lord's name in vain. You whisper when you say the name Jesus. You never . . . you never say it under your breath for . . . irreverent purposes. Or insinuate inappropriate . . ." He is too flustered to finish the phrase.

"Is that clear? Do you hear loud and clear, girls?"

"Yes, Dad, we copy. We're sorry. We really are. We didn't mean any . . . harm."

The Postodellafuoco sisters realize the dog only barked, didn't bite; the bee only hovered, did not sting. Still they're feeling bad. Just how does one summon one's favorite things in moments of grief or distress if one isn't a star in a musical, ready each moment to burst into song? On the other hand, singing wasn't a viable formula for helping the youngest von Trapp to transcend her fear of the encroaching Nazis, because in that circumstance, as Julie Andrews's uninhibited Maria made clear, the very act of singing, while offering the singer distraction, would only fatally attract her murderous pursuers, and send all the virtuosic von Trapps from the frying pan into the fire. Nor will it work in this much less dire but nonetheless unpleasant circumstance, to evaporate their nonvon father's anger. Even dad at his worst, though, could not compete with the stern, military demeanor of the almost robotically angry Captain von Trapp, played by flashing-eyed—and dashing—Christopher Plummer.

Now they are on the Long Island Expressway. Angie stares out the back window. Ginny is sure she is thinking of Danny with whom she will speak on the phone tonight, joking and sweet-talking for an hour in the basement, until Mom or Dad says, Is that phone *still* tied up? then opening the basement door just a crack and repeating the question in a louder voice. Ginny, for her part, construes her own sophisticated sequel to *The Sound of Music*, though its questions are, admittedly, more appropriate for recitation than song. But to whom would one recite here, in the back of a Cadillac, with a dreamy, love-struck sister and a currently unapproachable father who for all intents and purposes might as well be the chauffeur.

Virginia Postodellafuoco finds a certain solace in assembling the words, unaware she is moving her lips as she does so. Meanwhile, the chauffeur, letting off steam as the car exhales its leaded fumes, finds himself less angry with every exit he passes. He assumes that the mouth in his rearview mirror is fashioning prayer, silently asking our Father's forgiveness. The secular father is pleased, and on the basis of this assumption all the more inclined, himself, to forgive. But the words he assumes to be *O my God, I am heartily sorry . . .*

195

do not, in fact, end in amen or a vow to amend one's life. They are unscripted secular musings, rhetorical questions, even theatrical ones.

1) What is the illicit nature of the favorite thing that assuages the almost-sting?

2) When does a punch line as sweet as a kiss trade as for is: become a kiss? Answer me this.

Letter to a Wound
Reginald Shepherd

THIS HAPPENS MANY WORLDS AGO, a fragment of the last millennium, when music ruled the polluted air. But Eros insists on reminiscence (he isn't really my friend, I know, sitting there with his head cocked just so, that knowing smirk on his face again): wants to be told bedtime stories till dawn. I burned this with all the others so long ago I can't remember how it ends, but I remember your names, every one.

This is how it always starts: some man in a dark club who may or may not be smiling at me, some man who isn't smiling at all. When he walks into the room the heart stops. Whose heart, you don't bother to ask, and why the one white spotlight? You know the song as well as I do, the one they play before last call, when hands go up, and voices, crying out with this week's diva for love and other things. I never hear it on the radio, but it hums itself to me all day, drenching each moment in anticipated disappointments.

Whatever man it is that night, Tuesday or maybe Thursday, the short blond with a buzz cut leaning against the wall, designer beer bottle pressed to his designer crotch, or the tall brunet tapping his well-shod feet at the edge of the polished steel floor, and no thank you he does *not* want to dance. But mostly I don't ask. I've always wanted to be the one to say *no*. I've always wanted to refuse him first.

Whatever club is the season's place to be, you'll find me there, in with the in crowd for all to see. I prefer to watch and dance alone, and one night to be asked by a man who introduces me to his friends as Paul, "Oh, don't you break-dance?" Sorry, I say, that's not my cultural milieu: too black for me, and I'm not quite black enough for him. Another night, a man with pretty lashes tells me, "It's true, you know, black men *do* dance better." This time I choose to take the compliment, and never say I learned from you, or some man just like you, a long time ago by now, and never say that "man" means

197

"white." What was his name?

Some weekday nights I go home early, wake up late again for work with the taste of smoke still on my tongue and a metallic smell in my pores. Such, such were the joys, though somewhat staled by circumstance.

But you know all this. You were there.

I thought if I tried to tell you this as if it were a story, with a proper beginning and an appropriate end, I could put myself to sleep, put you out of my misery. But I'm still writing at four a.m. and you still haven't called. Memory grows restless, and far from accidental.

So then I thought I'd try another way.

I can hardly conceive of a beauty that doesn't harbor misfortune. (When we were in college I wanted to be Baudelaire. We saw *Dutchman* together and you couldn't stop giggling: you never said at what.) Last week I ran into P. and his new boyfriend: it was summer again. Now P. is into Asian men: he says they're more cooperative. He doesn't seem to remember the humid night I fucked him, but that was years ago: we get along much better now. For months his face reminded me of something, but I've forgotten what.

Your name didn't come up for over fifteen minutes, and then only your famous party: everyone still talks of it. It was there that I met T. (an architect, I think), one of your many friends with plosive names, another word for *stop*. He'd read the same book I had, by a young dead man. (He was beautiful, like all your friends: every beautiful thing is terrible. I've heard beauty is the beginning of a terror barely to be endured. Who among those angelic hierarchies could hear my carefully composed petitions and not be moved to laughter? You'd tell me the clever thing A. said about me, K.'s amusingly incisive comment.) The story about a man reduced to nothing but an ass, gaping wound, hole in himself pleading to be healed: lust and loss and emptiness falling through him endlessly. I thought I was flirting with that man (T., not some half-remembered fiction), but I keep forgetting things. As if that black lacquer table you brought back from Macao were flirting with him. Everyone envied you for having gotten it so cheap, but as you pointed out, over there they're everywhere. T. went home with B., I think, or some other plosive friend. We hadn't read the same story at all.

Or was that another of your parties, the one with the butterflies and paper lanterns? P. said, "Call me sometime," but of course I didn't have his new number. Walking away, I remembered your last letter. "Notice that a truly unhappy being would be one that had the inner sense of beauty but only recognized the beautiful in things that were harmful to it." I loved your graceful talent for allusion, but I didn't notice certain things for years. My age of enlightenment came late, but your apartment was always well lit.

Since you never asked, I don't remember when I noticed the men I wanted all were white. (I don't remember the first time we met, the afternoon I first glimpsed the face that meant I'd dream and never sleep. Your hand in mine was warm and dry.) For years, they were just men, people I happened to know, not well as I'd have liked: boys I went to school with, in another borough altogether. None of them lived in the two-room tenement walk-up where a chunk of ceiling plaster fell on my head and Norway rats my mother told me were dust balls chewed through my books from the inside out, or even in the brand-new poured-cement projects on Crotona Avenue with red-brick facades. I thought those carefully groomed white boys didn't know where I lived, but I was wrong: they'd seen it on public television, Bill Moyers here, reporting from the troubled inner city.

I thought I could walk the polluted water the scholarship bus ferried me across each morning on the power of my will to be someone else (it might as well have been a sea of tears between the South Bronx and mid-Manhattan). You said you often imagined me at ten years old, phoning my fifth-grade friends to ask if I could visit this weekend, calling one boy after another to see if I could come over, until I ran out of numbers and names. It made you love me somewhere far from me, where I am now. I'm always making little stories of my life, gift-wrapped packages with foil ribbons for you, and you, and here's one for you too. I'm always giving people things they don't need.

Many of the men and boys I wanted or wanted to be were blond with blue eyes, and many were brunet with brown eyes, but my favorites were the blue-eyed brunets or the brown-eyed blonds. I liked the minor mismatch, some misplaced mirror of my own near misses. All those boys had money, Kant's thing in itself, not my corner's "I got ten cents in my pocket, I can buy me a pack of Now and Laters." Most had two parents married to each other, houses with unread libraries and basement rec rooms, real Christmas trees at the called-for season. White houses, white picket fences, white roses and carnations: bloom on their softball skin, bouquet of their postgame-shower bodies. I wanted to join them in their well-dressed world, the freshly manicured backyards where you played board games with your brothers. And then I thought I had. What doesn't change, you told me years ago, is the will: I've stepped into that river more than once, forgotten nothing, really, just too much.

There were, I thought, two kinds of men, the kind who would sleep with me and the kind who wouldn't, and I thought one kind was gay men and the others, other men. Sex was a prize just out of reach, a glittering ideal not unlike you, long before it was a concrete practice of bars and one-night stands and laughing a little too loudly at dull jokes. My ideas have changed little over the years, only dressed themselves more exorbitantly, in colors I could never afford. You were my utopia of whiteness, spotless nowhere labeled *I can be loved.* You were my Troy refusing to burn, the Rome I never found. I foundered there. Gold of the Hesperides, gold of the falling sun. The month I house-sat for you I sniffed your jockstrap, I rubbed my face in it and masturbated as I was meant to. I tried it on afterward, surprised it was too small, a little disappointed. I broke the needle on your record player, too.

I wanted to tell you about one summer, 1984, not George Orwell's, to let you see the life I thought I had, when I believed the difference between me and the men I wanted me to be was a space between two bodies sex could close, or deep conversation in a fashionable café, staring stupidly into each other's eyes while under the table our hands went exploring. A summer before I realized the features I hated in the morning after's steamed-over mirror added up to a black man's face, othered me utterly. *And that's how the blues was born.* I thought there were two kinds of men, and now I know there are: but not the two I had in mind. There are the white men and there are the black men: there is you and there is me. "And what about P.'s new boyfriend?" you'd like to ask, but can't.

That year they played "Don't Make Me Over" twice a night at every club: a remake, of course. These are the days of unoriginal sins and other slightly faded simulacra. I sang it to the Xerox machine each day, all crumpled-paper afternoon. "Accept me for what I am.

200

Accept me for the reports I copy." (If I had a soul, would it be these half notes floating out a half-open window? Music has hollowed out a heart in me.) Or was that another summer altogether? You were in France looking at famous paintings in the Louvre or men with big baskets in the Tuileries. You sent me postcards of Egon Schiele, self-portraits stripped of all defense. "I know you'd love Paris even more than I do." I was almost glad when you got mugged, but how could I tell you when you never included a return address? A proper lack of concern for others is such a hard talent to master.

I wanted to tell you a lot of things, then I forgot. (Vienna, perhaps. I'm sure it was Vienna.) The story is, you left me here with what you saved me from. No one had such beautiful handwriting as yours.

That was the season of the empty hands, a homeless man on every corner. I like to think of it as June. God knows where you were the day I joined the unemployed. I spent a month in bed, or so I like to say: it sounds dramatic, like a voice-over. Let's just say I got up late. No reason not to stay in bed till two. I had my daily bagel and read an hour of Yeats, or typed up poems about local gods I never showed to anyone. Sometimes I read a letter from you (I kept them in this cigar box with fake gold leaf). You always signed them "revolution-ary love." That was your surrealist phase, I believe. And every night I went out to the same club to see what could be seen. I went early to beat the cover charge, walked because I didn't have bus fare. The bagels I bought in bulk.

This was my project: I wanted to have sex. My life's work, my evening ambition. It's always the others, isn't it, who have sex, lives? The handsome ones who cruise each other before last call, grab one another's asses playfully but significantly as they pass. It's always the other ones who are *men*. It's always you, all drift and murmured *undo*, verse and chorus I whisper all the following day, *I'll wait, I'll wait, I'll wait*. My almost, shining hazard, my delay, piece of myself I've never let you see: never your sweet and slightly puzzled self, lighting another clove cigarette, shaking your head at something you've just read. Strobe lights in discos have been known to induce *grand mal* seizures in epileptics: I've seen it happen in other men's lives.

He was waiting by the wall when I first saw him, the tall brunet. I hardly noticed him at first, so I knew he'd be the one. When he caught my eye I thought, "This could be tonight's new song," but by the time I looked again I knew the words. I could say he looked like you, but you were far more handsome. You never needed any compliments from me.

There was another man that night, blond bangs poured from a bottle: by last call he'd finished the beer. This happened only once: don't chide. You never sat outside a closed club groping two boys' asses, one hand on each cheek, trying to decide which one was fresher, which was more sweet. Neither was ripe and round as two firm cantaloupes, like the boy's in front of me in the supermarket line this afternoon, the perfect notion of a white boy's buttocks. *No things but in ideas,* you often remarked. The brunet's friend said about me, "He looks like one of those new-wave boys, better be careful." Who doesn't want to be thought dangerous, impossible to hold down? I chose the brunet. His name was Ken.

You were never so crude, but you've never had to ask. Men always came to you, but I was tired of being wanted for my mind. One night to make up for all the nights with just your letters, and pretty boys who love the way I dance.

There's never a song except "And what of you?" Yours was an altogether other world than mine, called *difference,* wished into recognizability: composed, all equipoise, calm luxury. It's made you what you are: locked store of hope, my hoarded money: violence, injustice, and a deferred happy death. I've always known you better than you knew yourself, I've always been unfair to you. (Love is not for such as thee and me, my love: I've seen to that. I wanted to be rescued by you, then changed my mind.) No strolling up and down a certain street at four a.m. for you, no hoping for a ride to anywhere from someone who was only warming up his car. No back-room booths and glory holes at six for you, my love. But if you'd been there, you would have been the star. You would have been the man on all the TV monitors, the Technicolor dream of sex repeated in perspective. When I got there, I looked for you. *Wherever he has gone, I have gone.*

When I got out there was no sun, but there was light. The sky was pearl white, mourning-dove white, curdled-milk-spilled-in-the-gutter white, but pearls and mourning doves aren't white at all. We've known each other too long, gray eyes.

*

You must be growing bored with this unending letter: my friends are tired of listening to me read your names out loud. You could have been anyone, so long as he was white, so long as white meant beautiful, your half-smiling face in the half-light under a flowering tree that will never bear fruit. Mock orange, mock plum, parahelion, pareselene: don't you love the counterfeits nature makes of itself? (*Nature loves to hide itself,* you said in someone else's voice.) You could have been anyone's dream or nightmare, and you were, willingly. And I was no one then. It doesn't end with "love."

I take the best years of my life where I can find them, and if I have to steal them I only hope that it's from you. It wasn't you who said to me one night, "Oh, I'm the biggest dinge queen in town," but who was I to refuse a hug from a handsome man? That was another summer, and an altogether different man. He didn't come home with me either.

I took Ken home and fucked him hard (cap on, face in the pillow): in the morning, wished he weren't there. He said he liked me better in the morning: sad. Like an artist, no? That afternoon I came once on his stomach, once in his mouth, then said I didn't want to see him again. A fine sensitivity to the feelings of others wouldn't have made this story's difference, a stranger's sperm smeared into sheets that needed washing anyway. You had one, after all, and I never did, but look which one of us got hurt and which one went to Paris. The next day Ken moved in. I never wanted to be happy, I just wanted an interesting life.

Ken told me about some of the men he'd done: an accounting student he sucked off in the bushes by a campus path in Berkeley; a dishwasher at a catered dinner in Connecticut who fucked him in the hotel kitchen; a gang leader from Harlem named Tiny who gave him head in an Episcopal parking lot; the Cameroonian manager of a McDonald's in San Francisco who rimmed him on a countertop, fucked him in French: stories I've collected for you, like foreign stamps. After three weeks we stopped speaking, though I fucked him twice a day, I spit into his ass to ease my way inside. We never got out of bed until noon. Unlike you and me, who loved each other and never touched. The flesh, as they say, was willing, but the spirit was always too weak.

I don't have to tell you all those men were black. Now I know a little more about white men who are into black men, though I'll never know enough about you. They always want to be fucked, but that's not what I learned. In the end, the white men always go back to their own; you always go to Europe one more time. After all, you haven't seen the Prado yet.

Did I say Ken fell asleep the first time I fucked him? He never knew what he was missing. Later he cried in a cocktail bar over men who dug their foreign tongues into his asshole in Berlin back rooms, fucked him doggy style because they didn't want to see his face. They'd put their lips anywhere but to his, parted but not to speak. I tried to watch the videos, looking for clues or alibis. "Thank God for anorexic men, especially when they're hung!" Of course it wasn't me who said that to him, rode his thick pink cock into the purple sunset while I waited all five o'clock, August again. (That was no summer of love, or not for me.) Have you ever noticed tall skinny men have the biggest dicks? The ones with brown hair, at least. He'd always said he was a bottom. I stared into his eyes so long I can't remember what color they were. Something in between, I'd say. Later I was crying in my corner room with all the windows, singing, "*Un bel di*" under my breath. See how well I've learned the culture you discarded? You never did like *Madama Butterfly,* another woman sacrificing herself for a man she hardly knows well enough to make a Western myth of, singing all the way. Ken slouched in my broken green plush chair, previously owned. "No more fucking," he said: he said he didn't know why he was laughing.

I still have his name on a three-by-five file card, kept in a manila folder marked *Do Not Disturb,* "My Boyfriend" printed in my neatest hand. That was something I could never call you. No one ever called him Kenneth. The friend was fucking Ken all along. The friend was black, but not like me.

Some nights walking home, alone at four a.m. and four steps ahead of the forecast rain, I imagine (but this is mere light-headedness, a musing mind clouded with other men's cigarettes and Obsession) that desire, as I try to write it down, explain you to yourself, is a product of social oppression, my historicized lusts: some late imperial light warped through your gray-green eyes. (I stole that glittering idea, brilliant with microscopic flaws: I'm sure you know from whom.) How could I blame you for anything? It's never your sweet fault you're white. I wonder as I wander, I admire ardently. *I love the ground on where he goes.* Already you're receding behind your own representability, half visible at best, and that only when I keep my eyes half closed, my mind half open to suggestion. You're waving a white flag, torn, slightly stained, you surrender again.

Months later I ran into Ken on the subway. His baggy black wide-wale corduroys, just out of style, showed off the ass I knew too well: he'd bleached his hair. "How could you have put up with me for so long?" he asked, but two months not speaking is an easy vow of silence. I've put up with silence for several lifetimes: one life for me and one for someone who waits and watches, watches and waits. I've been grateful for the chance to watch you sleep. Of course I wanted him again: you knew I would. When his stop came he kissed me on the cheek, said, "I'll call you soon." I knew I'd never see him again. He got off, turned once and waved, and just for a moment I remembered you.

Essay on What Is Want
John D'Agata

WHEN MY MOTHER AND I first moved to the city of Las Vegas, we lived for several weeks at the Budget Suites of America, a low-rise concrete pink motel with AIR COND and WEEKLY RATES and a Burger King next door.

We started to look for houses in developments called "Provence," "Tuscany," and "Bridgeport Landing," wandering through their model homes on plastic carpet runners.

In the master bedroom suites there were books displayed, their dust jackets removed, their spines always up, their titles too faint to clearly read at a glance. In the mudrooms there were chalkboards with the reminder *Buy milk!* Mason jars of pasta in the kitchens neatly spilled. Ceramic white bowls for family pets on the floor. Silk flowers in blue vases on the dining-room tables sparkling with little specks of round plastic morning dew.

There were terra-cotta tiles, screened-in lanais, entertainment centers in every living room.

The model called the "Amador" had columns beside its door. The "Palomar" had room for four cars in its garage. And "Versailles," gleaming white, came with an optional motorized gate.

In every house were cookies in stainless-steel ovens that were baking golden brown for families never there.

"All you have to do," said one hostess in one house, "is pick your model and your lot, and then leave the rest to us."

During one of those summer mornings when we first had moved to Las Vegas, my mother and I stood in the dirt of that city while listening to a broker around some wooden stakes and flags, some white-chalked land plots and orange-painted pipes, trying to see what the broker saw as he motioned with his hands, as he motioned with his wrists and wriggly fingers in full circles, motioning before his face, above his head, and to my mom, motioning toward the west, and then to me, and off the lot, then motioning past the stakes, the whipping flags, the lines in sand, beyond to where some pocks of little yucca plants were blooming, their tiny white flowers that never open all the way, their wobbly tall stalks of puffy million-seeded pods, their sword-long fronds that always indicate a desert, fanning out beyond the yellow of the lot in which we stood, fanning north above the shadow cast down by a mountain, fanning up and fanning over, fanning down and fanning out, then fanning off the private acreage that defines Summerlin, the walled and gated community my mother came to live in: orange houses, green parks, a white clock tower at its heart.

"You gotta imagine the land out here without all these weeds and stuff," the broker told my mom as he kicked a yucca plant. "You're on your back lawn, iced tea, easy tunes, maybe a little water feature bubbling in the distance."

We stood there on a $100,000 one-eighth-acre lot because Ethan, my mother's broker, had said that living in this community would be like living in New England, our home for the previous four generations.

"I like to tell people," Ethan told us, "that more trees line the sidewalks of Summerlin per capita than any other neighborhood here in Las Vegas," a fact he was particularly sure of, Ethan said, because the builder of Summerlin, a corporation called "Howard Hughes," had surveyed the number of trees in the neighborhoods of other builders, divided that by the number of residents in each, then ordered sixteen percent more trees than the highest of those estimates.

In the Spanish, we were told, *las vegas* means "the meadows," a lush haven that was named in 1829 for the "miles of shaded peace it offered early pioneers."

That first Spanish scout who wandered into Las Vegas said that it appeared "like a godsend" to him, "a great lie within the desert," "unbelievable," "unexpected," "truly the surest proof that this land is touched by God."

We walked through the sand, onto sidewalk again, up the two steps into Ethan's red Chevy S-10, then drove across the yellow lots of yucca-dotted desert, past gray concrete walls that were still being built, then finished concrete walls being painted closer in, beige concrete walls keeping yuccas off lawns, beige concrete walls lined with saplings, lamps, and shrubs, beige concrete walls with red swing-set tops behind them.

"This was all green at one point, as far as the eye can see. Meadows ... meadows ... green meadows," Ethan said. "That's what Summerlin's all about, bringing all that nature back."

Now, in Las Vegas, there is a Country Club at the Meadows, a

Golden Meadows Nursing Home, Meadows Coffee, Meadows Jewelry, Meadows Mortgage, Meadows Glass, Meadows Hospital, Automotive, Alterations, and Pets. The Meadows Country Day School is a private k through six. Meadows' Women's Center is in Village Meadows Mall. Meadows Trailer Park has a waiting list for lots. The Meadows Vista Townhomes are apartments near the mall. And the Meadows Church of Light has a Christ on its marquee.

Barefoot, white-ankled, he's teaching in a meadow.

When Summerlin was started in 1988, its developer said that it wanted to create "the most successful master-planned community in the United States of America," and as we entered the town's center, called the "Town Center at Summerlin," Ethan explained that the goal of the builder had already been surpassed, even with only two-thirds of the development complete.

"Someone moves into a new Summerlin home every two hours and twenty-two minutes," he said.

We circled in the town center at Summerlin's parking lot, idled behind a Lexus, beside a fountain, under sun. Then Ethan led us deeper into the center of the town, past Jamba Juice and Quiznos and Starbucks storefronts, past the life-sized bronze statues of a shopping mom and son, and into a green expanse called "Willow Park at Summerlin," a three-acre fluffy stretch of shrubs and white flowers and a long mattress lawn toward which Ethan spread his arms.

"This is what living in Summerlin is all about, my friends."

Acrobats in sequined shorts flipped backward down the lawn. A mime followed behind a man who licked an ice cream cone. A stilt walker, burger stand, barber-shop quartet. Children chased each other with their faces brightly painted. Dogs chased the children with their eyes as they heeled. Above the park on two white poles two banners stretched and waved:

SUMMERLIN NUMBER ONE! and

GUINNESS BOOK OF RECORDS WORLD'S LARGEST GROUP HUG.

"OK," Ethan said, "I'll be honest, with ya, right? It won't be like this every day that you're living in Las Vegas. But I just wanted to show you how much spirit we all have. You can tell that everyone's really psyched to be living here, right?"

Of the 335,000 acres that constitute the Las Vegas valley in Nevada, only 49,000 remain undeveloped. According to the Nevada Development Authority's *Las Vegas Perspective of 2005*, 8,500 people move into the valley every single month. It is the fastest-growing metropolitan area in America. As a result, the valley's shortage of land has become so pronounced that a local paper reported in 1999 that one new acre of land is developed in Las Vegas every hour and fifteen minutes, on each of which are squeezed an average of eight three-bedroom homes.

Indeed, even as early as 1962, when the population of Las Vegas was one-thirtieth its current size, the natural springs that fed the city's growing population noticeably began to dry, and then eventually were depleted, and then sank forever after beyond the reach of Las Vegas.

The city built a pipeline through the desert, therefore, running fifty miles into the city from Lake Mead, the artificial lake that was formed by Hoover Dam, the largest artificial body of water in the world. Today, the pipeline carries ninety percent of all the water that Las Vegas uses, although the lake that it's been tapping for over sixty-five years is eighty feet below what it normally should be, thirty-five percent beneath its usual capacity, losing about a trillion gallons of water every year.

During the summer my mother and I first moved to Las Vegas, the lake's surface reached what was being called locally "a potentially low level," but which hydrologists elsewhere in the United States were calling "the worst southwestern drought conditions in one hundred years" and "the worst drought conditions in five hundred years" and "not technically a drought according to the data," as one geologist wrote in 2005, because "the level of precipitation that has made possible the unprecedented growth in that city" has been a "phenomenal fluke," has been "wholly unnatural," is "not what a desert would normally be like."

"Almost a century and a half ago," wrote the geologist,

> when Las Vegas was discovered, an extraordinary cycle of rainfall was just starting in the area. It eventually would bring an increase in annual precipitation and would cause, among other things . . . the appearance of "meadows" in the Las Vegas valley. . . . But vegetation like that just isn't indigenous to a desert. What's indigenous to Las Vegas is sagebrush and creosote and maybe a couple yucca. . . . [But] Las Vegas residents don't want to acknowledge that they're living in the single driest place in America, and this is what has caused in part the problems the city faces.

In response to the warnings of a drought that summer, the general manager of the Las Vegas Water Authority said that "the notion that we have only a finite amount of water, and that when that water is gone we'll have to stop our city's growth, is a notion that belongs in the distant past."

And so, we settled in.

We moved my mother's cat, her books, her pinball machine, the three floors and five bedrooms of boxes from home. We planted a tomato in a large pot outside, bought green plastic chairs and a table for the deck, hung drapes to frame the view of the fairway in the back, the green promise we couldn't play on but paid extra to live beside, and took a trip to see the lake that had made that promise possible, the blue shock in yellow rock that attracts more campers and boaters and fishers and swimmers and skiers and hikers and divers and scouts than any other national recreation area—seven million annual visitors on average—an estimate that the National Park Service raised to eight million visitors by the end of that summer, an increase that one ranger tried to explain was not caused by more campers or boaters or fishers or swimmers or skiers or hikers or scouts, but by amateur archaeologists, owners of metal detectors, history buffs, photographers, and those who used to live there.

For what attracted the extra million visitors to Lake Mead that year was not the usual lure of the lake's artificial beauty, nor its recreational usefulness, nor even just the novelty that such a lake could exist, but rather the simple fact that the lake was slowly dying, that as the city quickly drained it, the lake's level lowered, and there slowly reemerged from its sinking blue surface the far distant past of the city of Las Vegas:

> a chimney stack from a concrete plant, poking higher and higher above the water every day, a giant complex of mixing vats and grinders that was built in the thirties to help pour Hoover Dam, and then closed once the lake that the dam formed rose;

> the B-29 bomber that crashed into Lake Mead, the gray one from the forties that was left there by the air force, fifty feet below at the time of the crash, now twenty feet below, its tail fin just ten;

> the sundae shop, the baker's shop, the grocery store, the bank;

> the wooden Mormon temple, the Gentry Mining Inn;

> the 233 crosses and stones, the crypts and the clothing, the necklaces and rings and nail frames around bones: every deceased resident of St. Thomas, Nevada, exhumed and

zip-locked and reburied upriver, six days before the lake would swallow the town whole.

Even a five thousand–year-old city reemerged, the ancient Indian settlement called "the Anasazi Lost City," a name it didn't receive because the city had been misplaced, but rather because the city—up until that dry summer—had remained one of the country's only pre-Columbian listings to be cataloged as "submerged" on the National Register of Historic Places.

"We may not have a history that's as rich as other cities," said a megaphoned voice in Summerlin that day, "and we may not be the biggest in America yet, but, ladies and gentlemen, do you know what we are?"

What? yelled the park.

"We are the city of big spirit!"

Some dogs barked, the park clapped, Ethan cheered, and then he *hooed.* It was noon and a stilt-walker's legs were on the ground, heat was sweating lines down the faces of some clowns, dogs were lapping ice cream off the bushes in the park, and the megaphoned voice said, "All right, now, let's go!"

He assembled us into groups around the edges of the park, made a countdown, a joke, then fired a starting gun.

This was a city, it was suggested that morning, that often came together in community spirit. Earlier, the city had come together to watch the old Dunes Hotel be imploded in a gray cloud of smoke in twelve seconds. It had come together before to watch the Sands, Hacienda, and Landmark be imploded. And it came together at 2:30 one recent Vegas morning, in an estimated crowd of twenty thousand people, in order to watch the old Aladdin Hotel be imploded, an event that attracted three TV news copters, two dozen articles in local newspapers, special rates for hotel rooms overlooking the implosion, a six-course Implosion Dinner for Two, and 19,462 more people than the 538 Summerlin neighbors who convened on a morning with sun in a park to prove that Las Vegas had community spirit, an effort that they made on behalf of the city, but without the news copters or dinners for two or the 363 extra group huggers that they needed to unseat the current record-holding huggers, the nine hundred employees of Goldman Sachs in New York.

"That's OK," yelled the voice. "That's all right, it's all right. We have a contingency plan here. Hold on, folks."

We milled.

211

John D'Agata

It was noon still, or later.

Someone's cell phone started ringing.

Ethan took his shirt off and wrapped its sleeves around his head.

"I'll get you back to the hotel real soon," he said. "Promise."

I heard two strollers on the asphalt of a path emit two screams without a response.

I watched a teenage boy try to walk out of the park, but a clip-boarded woman at the edge sent him back.

"If I could get some assistance from the band," said the voice.

And then the band began to play "The Hokey Pokey Song."

We stood there, five hundred, for about the length of a verse.

"You put your right foot in," sang the megaphoned voice, "you put your right foot out, you put your right foot in, and you shake it all about."

A woman behind Ethan said, "What the fuck?" and walked away. A group of several children beside my mom collapsed to the grass. Other kids were crying, rubbing paint from their eyes.

"We're almost there!" yelled the voice. "You won't regret it! One more verse! The World's Largest Hokey Pokey right here in Las Vegas!"

Variations on Desire:
A Mouse, a Dog, Buber, and Bovary
Siri Hustvedt

DESIRE APPEARS AS A feeling, a flicker, or a bomb in the body, but it's always a hunger for something, and it always propels us somewhere else, toward the thing that is missing. Even when this motion takes place on the inner terrain of fantasy, it has a quickening effect on the daydreamer. The object of desire—whether it's a good meal, a beautiful dress or car, another person, or something abstract, such as fame, learning, or happiness—exists outside of us and at a distance. Whatever it is, we don't have it now. Although they often overlap, desires and needs are semantically distinct. I need to eat, but I may not have much desire for what is placed in front of me. While a need is urgent for bodily comfort or even survival, a desire exists at another level of experience. It may be sensible or irrational, healthy or dangerous, fleeting or obsessive, weak or strong, but it isn't essential to life and limb. The difference between need and desire may be behind the fact that I've never heard anyone talk of a rat's "desire"—instincts, drives, behaviors, yes, but never desires. The word seems to imply an imaginative subject, someone who thinks and speaks. In *Webster's*, the second definition for the noun *desire* is: "an expressed wish, a request." An argument can be had about whether animals have "desires." They certainly have preferences. Dogs bark to signal they wish to go outside, ravenously consume one food but leave another untouched, and make it known that the vet's door is anathema. Monkeys express their wishes in forms sophisticated enough to rival their homo sapien cousins. Nevertheless, human desire is shaped and articulated in symbolic terms not available to animals.

When my sister Asti was three years old, her heart's desire, repeatedly expressed, was a Mickey Mouse telephone, a Christmas wish that sent my parents on a multicity search for a toy that had sold out everywhere. As the holiday approached, the tension in the family grew. My sister Liv, then seven, and I, nine, had been brought into the emotional drama of the elusive toy and began to fear that the object our younger sister craved would not be found. As I remember it, my father tracked the thing down in the neighboring city of Faribault, late in the afternoon that Christmas Eve, only hours before the presents were to be opened. I recall his triumphant arrival through the garage door, stamping snow from his boots, large garish box in hand—and our joy. My youngest sister, Ingrid, is missing from the memory, probably because she was too young to have participated in what had become a vicarious wish for the rest of us. Asti knows the story, because it took on mythical proportions in the family, and she remembers the telephone, which remained part of the toy collection for some time, but the great unwrapping on the living-room floor that I watched with breathless anticipation isn't part of her memory.

This little narrative of the Mickey Mouse telephone opens an avenue onto the peculiarities of human desire. Surely the telephone's luminous and no doubt aggrandized image on the television screen whetted Asti's desire and triggered fantasies of possession. The Disney rodent himself must have played a role. She may have imagined having conversations with the real mouse. I don't know, but the object took on the shine of glamour, first for her, and then for the rest of us, because it wasn't gained easily. It had to be fought for, always an augmenting factor in desire. Think of the troubadours. Think of Gatsby. Think of literature's great, addled knight errant on Rocinante. A three-year-old's desire infected four other family members who loved her because her wish became ours through intense identification, not unlike the sports fan's hope that his team will win. Desire can be contagious. Indeed, the churning wheels of capitalism depend on it.

Asti's "Mickey Mouse" desire presupposes an ability to hold an object in the mind and then imagine its acquisition at some other time, a trick the great Russian neuropsychologist A. R. Luria explicitly connected to language with its roaming "I" and the labile quality of linguistic tenses: was, is, will be. Narrative is a mental movement in time, and longing for an object very often takes on at least a crude narrative: P is lonely and longs for company. He dreams of meeting Q. He imagines that he is talking to Q in a bar, her head nestled on his shoulder. She smiles. He smiles. They stand up. He imagines her lying in his bed naked, and so on. I have always felt intuitively that conscious remembering and imagining are powerfully connected, that they are, in fact, so similar as to be at times difficult to disentangle from each other, and that they both are bound to places. It's important to anchor the people or objects you remember or imagine in a mental space or they begin to float away, or worse, disappear. The idea that memory is rooted in location goes back to the Greeks and exerted a powerful influence on medieval thought. The scholastic philosopher Albertus Magnus wrote, "Place is something the soul itself makes for laying up images."

Scientists have given new force to this ancient knowledge recently in a study of amnesia patients with bilateral hippocampal damage. The hippocampus in connection with other medial temporal lobe areas of the brain is known to be vital to the processing and storage of memory, but it also appears to be essential to imagining. When asked to visualize a specific scene, the brain-damaged patients found it difficult to provide a coherent spatial context for their fantasies. Their reports were far more fragmented than their healthy counterparts' (or "controls," as scientists like to call them). This insight does not, of course, affect desire itself. People with hippocampal damage don't lack desire—but fully imagining what they long for is impaired. Other forms of amnesia, however, would make it impossible to keep the image of a Mickey Mouse telephone or the phantom Ms. Q in the mind for more than seconds. This form of desire lives only in the moment, outside narrative, an untraceable eruption of feeling that could be acted upon only if a desirable object popped up in the same instant and the amnesiac reached out and grabbed it.

But desire can be aimless, too. It happens to me from time to time that I wonder what it is I am wanting. A vague desire makes itself felt before I can name the object—a restlessness in my body, possibly hunger, possibly the faintest stirring of erotic appetite, possibly a need to write again or read again or read something else, but there it is—a push in me toward a satisfaction I can't identify. What *is* that? Jaak Panksepp, a neuroscientist, writes in his book *Affective Neuroscience: The Foundations of Human and Animal Emotions* about what he calls "the SEEKING system." Other scientists have given drabber names to the same circuit: "behavioral activation system" or behavioral facilitation system." Panksepp writes,

> Although the details of human hopes are surely beyond the imagination of other creatures, the evidence now clearly indicates that certain intrinsic aspirations of all mammalian minds, those of mice as well as men, are driven by the same ancient neurochemistries. These chemistries lead our companion creatures to set out energetically to investigate and explore their worlds, to seek available resources and make sense of the contingencies in their environments. These same systems give us the impulse to become actively

215

engaged with the world and to extract meaning from our
various circumstances.

Curiosity, that need to go out into the world, appears to be hard-
wired in all mammals. As Panksepp articulates it: it's "a goad without a goal." The "extraction of meaning" from those investigations,
however, requires higher cortical areas of the brain unique to human
beings. My dear departed dog, Jack, when unleashed in the Minne-
sota countryside, would move eagerly from stump to thistle to cow
pie, nostrils quivering, inhaling each natural marvel, and then, once
he had mastered the lay of the land, he would burst into a run and
race back and forth across the territory like a demented conquering
hero. Through his superlative nose, he remembered and recognized
the place, but I don't think that when he was back home in Brooklyn
he carried about with him a mental image of the wide, flat land
where he could romp freely or that he actively longed to return to it.
Nor do I think he lay on his bed and imagined an ideal playground of
myriad odors. And yet, he missed his human beings when we were
gone. He grieved, in fact. Attachment and separation anxiety are
primitive evolutionary mechanisms shared by all mammals. Once,
when my sister Ingrid cared for Jack in our absence, she was sitting
in a room of the house, and feeling a chill, went to the closet and put
on a sweater of mine. When she returned, the poor dog was seized
with a fit of joy, jumping up on her, turning circles in the air, and
licking whatever part of her he could reach. Jack's nose was spot-on;
what he lacked was a human sense of time and context, which might
have prevented him from believing in my sudden materialization out
of nowhere.

There is a beautiful passage in Martin Buber's book *Between Man
and Man,* in which he describes stroking a beloved horse on his
grandparents' estate when he was eleven years old. He tells of the
immense pleasure it gave him, his tactile experience of the animal's
vitality beneath its skin, and his happiness when the horse greeted
him by lifting its head.

> But once—I do not know what came over the child, at any
> rate it was childlike enough—it struck me about the
> stroking, what fun it gave me, and suddenly I became
> conscious of my hand. The game went on as before, but
> something had changed, it was no longer the same thing. And
> the next day, after giving him a rich feed, when I stroked my
> friend's head he did not raise his head. A few years later, when

I thought back to the incident, I no longer supposed that the
nimal had noticed my defection. But at the time I considered
myself judged.

Buber's story is meant to illustrate the withdrawal from a life of
dialogue with the Other into a life of monologue or "reflexion." For
Buber, this self-reflective or mirroring quality disrupts true knowledge of the Other because he then exists as "only part of myself." It's
notable that Buber shifts to the third person in the early part of the
passage and then resumes in the first, because his experience is of a
sudden, intrusive self-consciousness that alters the character of his
desire. He has become another to himself, a third person he sees in
his mind's eye petting the horse and enjoying it, rather than an active
"I" with a "you." This self-theater of the third person is, I think,
uniquely human and is forever invading our desires and fantasies.
Celebrity culture demonstrates the extreme possibilities of this position because it runs on the idea of a person seen from the outside as
spectacle, and the possibility that lesser mortals, with some luck,
can rise to the ranks of the continually photographed and filmed.
With the Internet and sites like MySpace, the intense longing to live
life in the third person seems to have found its perfect realization.
But all of us, whether we are Internet voyeurs of our own dramas or
not, are infected by Buber's "reflexion," his description of narcis-
sism, in which the self is trapped in an airless hall of mirrors.

Buber's condemnation of the monologue position is profound, and
yet self-consciousness itself is born in "mirroring" and the acquisition of symbols through which we are able to represent ourselves as
an "I," a "he," or a "she." It is this distance from the self that makes
narrative movement and autobiographical memory possible.
Without it we couldn't tell ourselves the story of ourselves. Living
solely in reflection, however, creates a terrible machinery of insa-
tiable desire, the endless pursuit of the thing that will fill the emptiness and feed a starved self-image. Emma Bovary dreams of Paris:
"She knew all the latest fashions, where to find the best tailors, the
days for going to the Bois or the Opera. She studied descriptions of
furniture in Eugene Sue, and sought in Balzac and George Sand a vicarious gratification of her own desires."

It is no secret that once gained, the objects of desire often lose their
sweetness. The real Paris cannot live up to the dream city. The
high-heeled pumps displayed in a shop window that glow with the
promise of beauty, urbanity, and wealth are just shoes once they find

their way into the closet. After a big wedding, which in all its pomp and circumstance announces marriage as a state of ultimate arrival, there is life with a real human being, who is inevitably myopic, weak, and idiosyncratic. The revolutionary eats and sleeps the revolution, the grand cleansing moment when a new order will triumph, and then once it has happened, he finds himself wandering among corpses and ruins. Only human beings destroy themselves by ideas. Emma Bovary comes to despair: "And once again the deep hopelessness of her plight came back to her. Her lungs heaved as though they would burst. Then in a transport of heroism which made her almost gay, she ran down the hill and across the cow-plank, hurried along the path, up the lane, through the market-place and arrived in front of the chemist's shop." It is the phrase "a transport of heroism" that is most poignant to me, the absurd but all too human desire to inflate the story of oneself, to see it reflected back as heroic, beautiful, or martyred.

Desire is the engine of life, the yearning that goads us forward with stops along the way, but it has no destination, no final stop, except death. The wondrous fullness after a meal or sex or a great book or conversation is inevitably short-lived. By nature, we want and we wish, and we assign content to that emptiness as we narrate our inner lives. For better and for worse, we bring meaning to it, one inevitably shaped by the language and culture in which we live. Meaning itself may be the ultimate human seduction. Dogs don't need it, but for us to go on, it is essential, and this is true despite the fact that most of what happens to us is beneath our awareness. The signifying, speech-making, willful, consciously perceiving circuits of our brains are minute compared to the vast unconscious processes that lie beneath.

Almost twenty years ago, I gave birth to my daughter. Actually, "I" did nothing. My water broke. Labor happened. After thirteen hours of it, I pushed. I liked this time of pushing. It was active, not passive, and I finally expelled from between my legs a bloody, wet, awe-inspiring stranger. My husband held her, and I must have too, but I don't remember her in my arms until later. What I do recall is that as soon as I knew the baby was healthy, I lapsed into a state of unprecedented satisfaction. A paradisiacal torpor seemed to flood my body, and I went limp and still. I was wheeled away to a dim room, and after some minutes, my obstetrician appeared, looked down at me, and said, "I'm just checking on you. How are you?" It was an effort to speak, not because I had any pain or even a feeling of exhaustion, but because speech seemed unnecessary. I did manage to breathe out the words that described my condition: "I'm fine, fine. I've never felt like this. I have no desire, no desire of any kind." I remember that she grinned and patted my arm, but after she left, I lay there for some time, luxuriating in the sated quiet of my body, accompanied only by the awed repetition of the same words: I have no desire, none, no desire of any kind. I am sure that I was under the sway of the hormone oxytocin, released in quantities I had never experienced before, and which had turned me into a happy lump of flesh. Birth was a wholly animal experience; its brutal corporeal paroxysms left reflection behind. The executive, thinking, narrative "I" lost itself entirely in the ultimate creative act: one body being born of another. After the birth, it returned as a stunned commentator, similar to a voice-over in a movie that noted the novelty of my situation to an audience of one: me. Of course, the stupefaction didn't last. It couldn't last. I had to take care of my child, had to hold her, feed her, look at her, want her with my whole being. There is nothing more ordinary than this desire, and yet to be gripped by it feels miraculous.

Martin Buber doesn't treat mothers and infants in his I/thou dialectic, but the ideal dialogue he describes of openness to the other, of communication that is not dependent on speech, but which can happen in silence "sacramentally" is perhaps most perfectly realized in the mother/child couple. Especially in the first year, a mother opens herself up to her baby. As D. W. Winnicott writes in *The Family and Individual Development*, she is able to "drain interest from her self on to the baby." A mother, he adds, in his characteristically lucid way, has "a special ability to do the right thing. She knows what the baby could be feeling like. No one else knows. Doctors and nurses know a lot about psychology, and of course they know a lot about body health and disease. But they do not know what a baby feels like from minute to minute because they are outside this area of experience." Imagining what your baby feels like by reading her carefully and responding to her is a mother's work; it is a first-/second-person business, and it brings with it ongoing gratification for both sides of the dyad. It is also, as Allan Schore makes clear in his book *Affect Regulation and the Origin of the Self*, essential to the neurobiological development of the infant.

Maternal desire is a subject fraught with ideology. From the screaming advocates of "family values" to those whose agenda makes it necessary to replace the word "mother" with "caregiver" at every opportunity, popular culture trumpets its competing narratives. In a country where human relationships are seen as entities to be "worked on," as if they were thousand-piece puzzles that only take time to complete, the pleasure to be found in one's children, the desire we have for them falls outside the discussion. It is not my intention to be a romantic. Parenthood can be grueling, boring, and painful, but most people want their children and love them. As parents, they are, as Winnicott said about mothers: "good enough." This "good enough" is not perfection, but a form of dialogue, a receptiveness that doesn't impose on the child the monologic desires of the parents, but recognizes his autonomy, his real separateness.

Every week I teach a writing class to in-patients at the Payne Whitney Psychiatric Clinic. My students are all people who find themselves in the hospital because life outside it had become unbearable, either to themselves or to other people. It is there that I've witnessed what it looks like to have no desire or very little desire for anything. Psychotic patients can be electrifying and filled with manic, creative energy, but severely depressed patients are strangely immobile. The people who come to my class have already put one foot in front of the other and found their way into a chair, which is far more than some of the others who remain in their rooms, inert on their beds like the living dead. Some people come to class, but do not speak. Some come, but do not write. They look at the paper and pencil and are able to say they cannot do it, but will stay and listen. One woman, who sat rigidly in her chair, hardly moving except for the hand that composed her piece, wrote of a morgue where the bodies were laid out on slabs, their mouths opened to reveal black, cankerous tongues. "That's why we're here," she said after she had finished reading it, "because we're dead. We're all dead." As I listened to her words, I felt cut and hurt. This was more than sadness, more than grief. Grief, after all, is desire for the dead or for what's been lost and can never come again. Grief is longing. This was stasis without fulfillment. This was the world stopped, meaning extinguished. And yet, she had written it, had bothered to record this bleak image, which I told her frightened me. I said I had pictured it in my mind the way I might remember some awful image in a movie, and I tried to hold her with my eyes, keep her looking at me, which I did for several seconds. When I think of it now, bringing up film might have been defensive on my part, a way of keeping some distance between me and that morgue (where I'll end up sooner or later). Nevertheless, I've come to understand that what I say is often less important to the students than my embodied attention, my rapt interest in what is happening among us, that they know I am listening, concentrated, and open. I have to imagine *what it feels like to be* in such a state without coming unglued myself.

I don't know what that woman's particular story was or why she landed in the hospital. Some people come wearing the bandages of their suicide attempts, but she didn't. Everybody has a story, and each one is unique, and yet now that I've been going to the hospital for a year, I've seen many variations of a single narrative. One man encompassed it beautifully in a short poem. I can't remember his exact wording, but have retained the images it brought to mind. He is a child again, wandering alone in an apartment, longing for "someone" to be there. He finds a door. It swings open, and the room is empty. I can't think of a better metaphor for unrequited longing than that vacant room. My student understood the essence of what he was missing: the responsive presence of another, and he knew that this absence had both formed and damaged him.

I seem to have come far from the Mickey Mouse telephone, but like so many objects of desire, the telephone was more than a telephone, and the story of searching for it and finding it at last to fulfill a child's wish is a small parable of genuine dialogue: I have heard you and I'm coming with my answer.

Always Crashing in the Same Car
(a mash-up)
Jonathan Lethem

As soon as I was outside the city I realized night had fallen. I turned on my headlights. It seems to me that one of the strongest gratifications of night driving is precisely that you can see so little and yet at the same time see so very much. The child awakes in us once again when we drive at night, and then all those earliest sensations of fear and security begin shimmering, tingling once again inside ourselves. The car is dark, we hear lost voices, the dials glow, and simultaneously we are moving and not moving, held deep in the comfort of cushions as once we were on just such a night as this one, yet feeling even in the softness of the beige upholstery all the sickening texture of our actual travel. For night driving our eyes too must remove one kind of inner transparency and fit on another, because they no longer have to make an effort to distinguish among the shadows and the fading colors of the evening landscape the little speck of the distant cars that are coming toward us or preceding us, but they have to check a kind of black slate that requires a different method of reading, more precise but also simplified, since the darkness erases all the picture's details that might be distracting and underlines only the indispensible elements, the white stripes on the asphalt, the headlights' yellow glow, and the little red dots. It's a process that occurs automatically, and if I was led to reflect on it that evening it was because as the external possibilities of distraction diminished, the internal ones got the upper hand within me, and my thoughts raced on their own in a circuit of alternatives and doubts I couldn't disengage.

At first I paid no attention, then it came again, flashing across my eye, and then yet again, until at last, forced to take a closer look, I saw sunlight glinting off the hood of a car. I adjusted my mirror and thought no more of it—I was, after all, on a road; cars are to be expected. Yet when after a number of divagations and turns and accelerations it was still with me, I begin to pay it more heed. Could it be that I was being followed? But was it always that same car that pursued me? I could no longer say. I tried not to think too obsessively about my pursuers, but what else was I to think about? They were behind me, watching me, waiting for me to make a mistake. So far I had made no mistakes.

There seemed a figure in the driver's seat, or if not a figure perhaps only a raised headrest, the sun glinting off the dirty windshield, making it difficult to say anything with certainty. The other car at first was not with me and then it was, unless it was another, similar car. It was there, then was gone, then there again. I stopped for fuel and saw no car but then, driving again, there it was, behind me. That car that was chasing me was faster than mine. From time to time it became easy to believe I was not being followed, the pursuit behind, I came to believe, extremely subtle, invisible more often than visible. The car sometimes freshly washed, sometimes covered with mud, the paint such that it caught the light differently at different times of the day, making me always think, "Could that possibly be the car? Aren't I mistaken?"

In my escape I headed for the center of the city. I jockeyed for an opening in the line of cars; finally someone slowed for a tenth of a second at the yield sign and I got in. Cars shot past me at seventy and eighty miles an hour, the drivers sprawled behind their wheels, fish-eyed and hostile. I saw a gap and went for it, flooring the Cutlass and feeling the characteristic lag in the transmission. I moved the car into the slow lane as we turned around the central drum of the interchange, accelerating when we gained the open deck of the motorway, traffic speeding past us. It was a healthy decision; the pursuer was constantly behind me but we were separated by several other cars as we joined the fast westward sweep of the outer circular motorway.

Everywhere the perspectives had changed. The concrete walls of the slip road reared over us like luminous cliffs. The marker lines dividing and turning formed a maze of white snakes, writhing as they carried the wheels of the cars crossing their backs, as delighted as dolphins. The overhead route signs loomed above us like generous dive-bombers. I pressed my palms against the rim of the steering wheel, pushing the car unaided through the golden air. Two airport coaches and a truck overtook us, their revolving wheels almost motionless, as if these vehicles were pieces of stage scenery suspended from the sky. Looking around, I had the impression that all the cars on the highway were stationary, the spinning earth racing beneath them to create an illusion of movement.

We stopped at a traffic signal, in a long column. I felt definitely more hostile toward the cars that preceded me and prevented me from advancing than toward those following me, which however would make themselves declared enemies if they tried to pass me, a difficult undertaking in view of the dense jam where every car was stuck fast among the others with a minimum freedom of movement. In short, the man who was my mortal enemy was now lost among many other solid bodies where my chafing aversion and fear are also perforce distributed, just as his murderous will though directed exclusively against me was somehow scattered and deflected among a great number of intermediary objects.

Looking closely at this silent terrain, I realized that the entire zone that defined the landscape of my life was now bounded by a continuous artificial horizon, formed by the raised parapets and embankments of the motorways and their access roads and interchanges. These encircled the vehicles like the walls of a crater several miles in diameter. Here and there a driver shifted behind his steering wheel, trapped uncomfortably in the hot sunlight, and I had the sudden impression that the world had stopped. Gradually I realized what I'd seen in the rearview mirror. The car was a maroon Cutlass, identical to my own. I looked slowly to my left and saw my own face in the car next to me, glassy-eyed, mouthing words. I could read the words. They were, "Go back. Go back."

A police car sped down the descent lane of the flyover, headlamps flashing, the rotating blue light on its roof flicking at the dark air like a whip. Above me, on the crest of the ascent lane, two policemen steered the traffic streams from the nearby curb. Warning tripods set up on the pavement flashed a rhythmic "Slow . . . Slow . . . Accident . . . Accident . . ." I cranked the window down to see what it was that interrupted my way. Lines of cars moved past a circle of police spotlights. It was a horrible smashup of forty-five or fifty streamlined multicylinder automobiles, and each of them must have been traveling well over two hundred miles an hour to achieve, even in combination, such a terrible mass of wreckage. Ambulances and policemen were all about, and so were doctors and nurses and interns. Arc lights flared over the sites of major collisions, while firemen and police engineers worked with acetylene torches and lifting tackle to free unconscious wives trapped beside their dead husbands, or waited as a passing doctor fumbled with a dying man pinned below an inverted truck. Scores of newspapermen were there interviewing onlookers and victims and taking flashlight photos of the mess. By each wrecked automobile there must have been six or seven insurance adjusters and nine or ten lawyers. A tremendous crowd of curiosity seekers had gathered; the thruway from curb to curb was blocked completely. There was no way, of course, of getting out behind, because even as I stopped, the traffic piled up in back of me for ten or fifteen miles.

I got out to stretch my legs. Close by, I found a mobile saloon mounted on a truck and two trailers; its personnel had rushed it to the scene, let down the sides of the trailers, and set up shop where they did a remarkable business. A crowd was gathering on the sidewalks, and on the pedestrian bridge that spanned Western Avenue the spectators leaned elbow to elbow on the metal rail. The smallest of the cars involved in the accident, a yellow Italian sports car, had been almost obliterated by a black limousine with an extended wheelbase that had skidded across the central reservation. The limousine had returned across the concrete island to its own lane and struck the steel pylon of a route indicator, crushing its radiator and nearside wheel housing, before being hit in turn by a taxi joining the flyover from the Western Avenue access road. The head-on collision into the rear end of the limousine, followed by rollover, had crushed the taxi laterally, translating its passenger cabin and body panels through an angle of some fifteen degrees. The sports car lay on its back on the central reservation. A squad of police and firemen were jacking it onto its side, revealing two bodies still trapped inside the crushed compartment. I moved around through the crowd, inspecting the corpses and standing by different wrecks whenever I saw they were about to be photographed.

The thruway was jammed, a horizontal Christmas tree of flashing red lights. Anyone could look at their watch, but it was as if that time strapped to your right wrist or the beep beep on the radio were measuring something else—the time of those who hadn't made the blunder of trying to return to the city on the southern thruway on a Sunday afternoon and, just past the suburbs, had had to slow down to a crawl, stop, six rows of cars on either side, start the engine, move three yards, stop, talk with the two nuns in the 2CV on the right, look in the rearview mirror at the pale man driving the Caravelle, ironically envy the birdlike contentment of the couple in the Peugeot playing with their little girl, joking, and eating cheese, or suffer the exasperated outbursts of the two boys in the Simca, in front of the Peugeot. I even got out at the stops to explore, not wandering off too far (no one knew when the cars up front would start moving again, and you'd have had to run back so that those behind you wouldn't begin their battle of horn blasts and curses), and exchanged a few discouraged and mocking words with the two men traveling with the little blond boy, whose great joy at that particular moment was running his toy car over the seats and the rear ledge of the Taurus. It didn't seem the cars up ahead would budge very soon. I observed with some pity the elderly couple in the Citroën that looked like a big purple bathtub with the little old man and woman swimming around inside, he resting his arms on the wheel with an air of resigned fatigue, she nibbling on an apple, fastidious rather than hungry. I decided not to leave the car again and to just wait for the police to somehow dissolve the bottleneck.

At one point (it was nighttime now), some strangers came with news. The pavement had caved in around Yonkers, and five cars had overturned when their front wheels got caught in the cracks. The idea of a natural catastrophe spread all the way to a pale man, who shrugged without comment. The first to complain was the little girl in the Datsun, and the soldier and I left our cars to go with her father to get water. In front of the Simca, I found a Toyota occupied by an older woman with nervous eyes. No, she didn't have any water, but she could give me some candy for the little girl. The couple in the ID consulted each other briefly before the old woman pulled a small can of fruit juice out of her bag. I expressed my gratitude and asked if they were hungry, or if I could be of any service; the old man shook his head, but the old lady seemed to accept my offer silently. Later, the girl from the Dauphine and I explored the rows on the left, without going too far; we came back with a few pastries and gave them to the old lady in the ID, just in time to run back to our own cars under a shower of horn blasts.

The boys in the Simca pulled out inflatable beds and laid down by their car; I lowered the back of the front seat and offered the cushions to the nuns, who refused them. Before lying down for a while, I thought of the girl in the Dauphine, who was still at the wheel. Pretending it didn't make any difference, I offered to switch cars with her until dawn, but she refused, claiming that she could sleep in any position. Night would never come; the sun's vibrations on the highway and cars pushed vertigo to the edge of nausea.

Something would have to be done in the morning to get more provisions and water. The soldier went to get the leaders of the neighboring groups, who were not sleeping either, and they discussed the problem quietly so as not to wake up the women. The leaders had spoken with the leaders of faraway groups, in a radius of about eighty or one hundred cars, and they were sure the situation was analogous everywhere. The farmer knew the region well and proposed that two or three men from each group go out at dawn to buy provisions from the neighboring farms, while I appointed drivers for the cars left unattended during the expedition. There was a coffee-and-doughnuts man threading his way through the traffic even now but coffee was beyond my means.

Nobody kept track anymore of how much they had moved that day. The girl in the Dauphine thought that it was between eighty and two hundred yards; I was not as optimistic. In fact I couldn't remember seeing a car move recently. I never even saw a car move, just heard them. That night I'd dreamed another start-up, or perhaps it was real, a far-off flare that died before I'd even ground the sleep out of my eye, though in the rustle of my waking thoughts it was a perfect thing, coordinated, a dance of cars shifting through the free-flowing streets. Perhaps the start-up was only a panic begun by someone warming their motor, reviving their battery. What woke me in the morning was the family up ahead cooking breakfast. They had a stove on the roof of their car and the dad was grilling something. The old lady in the Impala had given up, spent most days dozing in the backseat. Her nephew from a few blocks away came over and tinkered with her engine now and again but it wasn't helping. It just meant the nephew was at his wheel for the start-up, another dead spot, another reason not to bother waiting to move. "Not responsible! Park and lock it!" the loudspeakers at the tops of the poles in the vast asphalt field shouted, over and over.

Suddenly I felt gripped by a gust of enthusiasm: it was wonderful to know that freedom exists and at the same time to feel oneself surrounded and protected by a blockade of solid and impenetrable bodies, and to have no concern beyond raising the left foot from the clutch, pressing the right on the accelerator for an instant, and immediately lowering it again on the brake, actions that above all are not decided by us but dictated by the traffic. Reality, ugly or beautiful as it might be, was something I could not change. At that moment, something unbelievable was happening five hundred, three hundred, two hundred and fifty yards away. There was a start-up, a fever of distant engines and horns honking as others signaled their excitement—a chance to move! The boy was pointing ahead and endlessly repeating the news as if to convince himself that what he was seeing was true. The elated lookout had the impression that the horizon had changed. Then we heard the rumble, as if a heavy but migratory wave were awakening from a long slumber and testing its strength.

In the morning we moved a little, enough to give hope that by afternoon the route to New York would open up. You could feel the line of cars was moving, even if only a little, even if you had to start and then slam on the brakes and never leave first gear; the dejection of again going from first to neutral, brake, hand brake, stop, and the same thing time and time again. By night, speeding up, the lanes could no longer stay parallel. From time to time, horns blew, speedometer needles climbed more and more, some lanes were going at forty-five miles an hour, others at forty, some at thirty-five, a mad race in the night among unknown cars, where no one knew anything about the others, where everyone looked straight ahead, only ahead.

*

We had been cruising along pretty well at twilight, my father concentrating on getting in another fifty miles before dark, when we were cut off by the big two-toned Mercury and my father had to swerve four lanes over into the far right. My parents later decided that the near accident was the cause of my premature birth. They even managed to laugh at the incident in retrospect, but I always suspected my father pined after those lost fifty miles. In return he'd gotten a son.

When I was six I got to sit on my father's lap, hold the wheel in my hands, and "drive the car." With what great chasms of anticipation and awe did I look forward to those moments! My mother would protest feebly that I was too young. I would clamber into my dad's lap and grab the wheel. How warm it felt, how large, and how far apart I had to put my hands! The indentations on the back were too wide for my fingers so that two of mine fit into the space meant for one adult's. My father operated the pedals and gearshift, and most of the time he kept his left hand on the wheel too—but then he would slowly take it away and I'd be steering all by myself. My heart had beaten fast. At those moments the car had seemed so large. The promise and threat of its speed had been almost overwhelming. I knew that by a turn of the wheel I could be in the high-speed lane; even more amazingly, that I held in my hands the potential to steer us off the road, into the gully, and death.

228

When I was seven there was a song on the radio that my mother sang to me, "We all drive on." That was my song. I sang it back to her, and my father laughed and sang it too, badly, voice hoarse and off-key, not like my mother, whose voice was sweet. "We all drive on," we sang together.

> "You and me and everyone
> Never ending, just begun
> Driving, driving on."

These days I have stopped paying attention to the cars going in my direction and I keep looking at those coming toward me that for me consist only of a double star of headlights that dilates until it sweeps the darkness from my field of vision then suddenly disappears behind me, dragging a kind of underwater luminescence after it. How, I began to wonder after a few lifetimes of this constant circling, traveling from country to country, never stopping except to sleep briefly in the car before going on again, my mind increasingly distracted, nerves increasingly unstrung, how can one ever be certain of anything? Once you start driving, how can you ever stop? A perverse idea hit me: maybe it was only the pressure of our dead traditions that kept people glued to their westward course. Suddenly twelve lanes, which had seemed a whole world to me all my life, shrank to the merest thread. Who could say what eastbound might be? Who could predict how much better men had done for themselves there? Maybe it was the eastbounders who had built the roads, who had created the defenses and myths that kept us all penned in filthy Nashes, rolling west. What if I crashed across the twelve lanes of westbound to the median, the beginning of no-man's-land? Beyond that, where those distant lights swept by in their retrograde motion—what?

I am always moving. I am forever transporting myself somewhere else. I am never exactly where I am. Tonight, for instance, we are traveling one road but also many, as if we cannot take a single step without discovering five of our own footprints already ahead of us. Now we are traveling as if inside a clock the shape of a bullet, seated as if stationary among tight springs. And we have a full tank of fuel, and tires hardly a month old.

Every chance that I take, I take it on the road. Do not ask me to slow down. Hands off the wheel. It is too late. After all, at one hundred and forty-nine kilometers per hour on a country road in the darkest quarter of the night, surely it is obvious that your slightest effort to wrench away the wheel will pitch us into the toneless world of highway tragedy even more quickly than I have planned. And you will not believe it, but we are still accelerating.

At least you are in the hands of an expert driver.

—Bowie, Hawkes, Evenson, Calvino, Kessel, Finney,
Cortazar, Shiner, Ballard, Lethem, 2007

My American Jon
Chimamanda Ngozi Adichie

THERE IS SOMETHING FORLORN about Baltimore; I thought of this every Thursday when my taxi sped down Charles Street on my way to the train station to visit Jon in New York City. The buildings were connected to one another in faded slumping rows, but what really held my attention was the people: hunched in puffy jackets, waiting for buses, slouching in corners, making me wonder again and again why the dankest, drabbest parts of all the American cities I knew were full of black people. My taxi drivers were mostly Punjabi or Ethiopian. It was an Ethiopian who asked where my accent was from and then said, "You don't look African at all," when I told him Nigeria.

"Why don't I look African?" I asked.

"Because your blouse is too tight."

"It is not too tight," I said.

"I thought you were from Jamaica or one of those places," he said, looking in the rearview with both disapproval and concern. "You have to be very careful or America will corrupt you."

Later, I told Jon about this conversation and how the driver's sincerity had infuriated me and how I had gone to the station bathroom to see if my pink blouse *was* too tight. Jon laughed. But I was sure he understood; this was during the early months, the good months of our relationship.

We met at a poetry reading. I had come up to New York to hear the new Nigerian poet Chioma Ekemma read from her *Love Economies.* During the Q&A, the questions were not about why she chose to write poems without active verbs, or which poets she admired, but what could be done about poverty in Nigeria and would women ever achieve equality there and wasn't she lucky that she could come to America and find her voice? She was gracious—too gracious, I thought. Then Jon raised his hand from two rows ahead of me and said tourism was the easiest way to fix the Nigerian economy and it was a shame Nigeria was not tourist friendly. No hostels. No good roads. No backpackers. He spoke with absolute authority. Chioma

Ekemma nodded enthusiastically. I raised my hand and said one could fix an economy in other ways that did not involve richer people going to gawk at the lives of poorer people who could never gawk back. There was some scattered clapping; I noticed the most vigorous came from the black people. Chioma Ekemma said something conciliatory and moved on to the next question. She was clearly thinking of keeping the peace so that as many people as possible would buy her book.

Jon was staring at me; a white man wearing a metal wristband who thought he could pontificate about my country irritated me. I stared back. I imagined him taking in my afro-shaped twists, my severe black frames, with distaste. But there was something else between us, between the chairs and people separating us: a sparkle, a star, a spark. His face was solemn when he came over after the reading and said I had really felt strongly back there and did I want to get coffee and have a little bit more of a debate. It amused me, the way he said "debate." But we did debate, about devaluation and deregulation and debt, and later, when we kissed at Penn Station in a sudden press of our bodies before I got on the train, it was as if the debate were continuing, the way our tongues darted around inside our mouths without meeting. He had never been with a black woman; he told me this the following weekend with a self-mocking toss of his head, as if this was something he should have done long ago but had somehow neglected. I laughed and he laughed and in the morning sunlight that streamed in through the windows of his apartment, his skin took on a bright and foreign translucence. After we broke up two years later, I would tell people that race was the reason, that he was too white and I was too black and the midway too skewed in his favor. In truth, we broke up after I cheated. The cheating was very good, me on top gliding and moaning and grasping the hair on the chest of the other man. But I told Jon that it had meant nothing. I told him that I had hated myself although I was filled with well-being, with a sublime sense not just of satisfaction but of accomplishment.

At first, Jon was disbelieving. "No, you didn't have a one-night stand. You're such a liar."

I did lie to him sometimes, playful little lies like calling to say I could not come that weekend when I was just outside his door. But I did not lie about the big things.

"It's true," I said.

He got up and turned down the volume of the stereo and paced and looked through the tall windows at the cars and people below.

"Unknown Soldier" was playing. Jon loved Fela Kuti; it was the reason he'd visited Nigeria and attended Nigerian events, perhaps the reason he thought he knew how to save Nigeria.

"Why?" he asked finally.

I should not have been pleased by the prospect of telling Jon why I had cheated. I sat down on the sofa and said, "It was desire."

It *was* desire. It felt as though gentle peppers had been squirted at the bottom of my stomach, a surge of pure aching desire that I was grateful for feeling and was determined not to waste.

"Desire?" Jon was watching me. Maybe he was thinking that it had always been good between us. So I got up and held him close and said that even though it had been a physical desire, the act itself had meant nothing because my self-loathing made pleasure impossible. Jon did not push me away. He said, "The sin is not the sex, Amaka; the sin is the betrayal. So it doesn't matter whether or not you enjoyed it."

That all-knowing tone of Jon's had always made me stiffen. If the circumstances were different, I would have asked him, did the people at Yale teach you how to talk about things you know nothing about with such authority? I had often asked him this in the past. Such as when, two or so months into our relationship, I arrived at his apartment and he kissed me and gestured to the table and said, "Surprise. Tickets to Paris for three days. We leave tonight. You'll be back in time to teach Tuesday."

"Jon, I cannot just jet off to Paris. I have a Nigerian passport and I have to apply for a visa."

"Come on, you're an American resident. You don't need a visa to go to Paris."

"I do."

"No, you don't."

After I showed him on the Internet that Nigerian citizens who were resident in America did in fact need a visa to get into Europe—a process that required bank statements, health insurance, all sorts of proof that you would not stay and become a burden to Europe—Jon muttered, "Ridiculous" as though it was the French Embassy and not he who had been wrong. We did go to Paris, though. Jon changed the ticket dates. We went together to the French Embassy but I went alone to the window where a woman wearing silver eye shadow glanced at me, at my passport, back at me, and said she would not approve the visa because Nigerian passport holders were high risk and it seemed suspicious to her that I was going to Paris for just three days. "But . . . ," I started to say and she made an impatient gesture and pushed my documents across under the glass. Jon got up then, tall and sinewy and angry, and told her I was going to Paris as his guest, and my documents included his bank statements and my employment letter and insurance and everything else, if only she'd look at them. "We're together," he added, as if it was necessary to make it clear. The woman smirked. She said I should have explained myself better. She made a show of looking through the documents and said the visa would be ready for pickup in two days.

It filled me with a dizzying pride, how Jon would often stand up for me, speak for me, protect me, make me omelets, give me pedicures in the bubbling foot bath, slip his hand into mine as we walked, speak in the first person plural. "*O na-eji gi ka akwa:* he holds you like an egg," Aunty Adanna said admiringly when she finally accepted that I was serious with a white man and asked me to bring him to lunch. Aunty Adanna was one of those Nigerian immigrants who, when they spoke to white people, adopted a risible American accent. I took Jon to her seven-room home in Columbia, outside Baltimore, and suddenly she was calling her son "Mek," my bewildered teenage cousin whom we had always called Nnaemeka, and talking about how good he was at golf. She spoke of fufu and soup, which Jon had eaten many times before in New York, as if Nigerian food could not be worthy unless it was like something American. This is like your mashed potatoes, she told him; this is just like your clam chowder. She spoke of her swimming pool needing to be drained. She told anecdotes about the patients at her medical practice. Jon asked when she had last been back in Nigeria and she said it had been six years; she could not bear the dirt and chaos and she did not know what the matter was with all of those corrupt people in government. "Matter" came out sounding like *marah*. Even though Jon had not asked, she proudly told him she had lived in America for eighteen years, that she had sponsored my trip here eight years ago after my Nigerian university kept going on strike after strike. I stabbed the chicken in my soup and said nothing. I was ashamed. I was ashamed that she did not have books in her house and that when Jon brought up Zimbabwe, she had no idea what was going on there and so to cover my shame I muttered, "Philistine" as we drove away. "Nigerian doctors and engineers and lawyers don't read anything unless it has the possibility of leading them to bigger paychecks," I said. Jon laughed and said it had nothing to do with Nigeria, it was the same for the American bourgeoisie and, leaning over to kiss me, said that Aunty Adanna had been sweet, the way she was so keen to make him comfortable. It wasn't sweet, it was pathetic, but I liked that Jon said that and I liked that he wanted to be liked by my family.

I had never felt that love I read about in books, that inexorable thing that caused characters to make all sorts of unlikely decisions. By the time I met Jon, I had convinced myself that the feeling was like an orgasm; a certain percentage of women would never have one after all. At first, each long weekend with Jon in New York was a pleasant break to look forward to after teaching three days a week at the Shipley School. Soon, each weekend became something I longed for, and then something I needed. I realized that what I felt for Jon was becoming an inexorable thing when I saw the flyer advertising a teaching position in a New York City private academy on a board outside the general office and immediately went in to ask the secretary Nakeya if she knew more. She shook her head and said it wasn't a good idea. "They like you here and you'll rise quickly if you stay, Amaka," she said. I persisted. She said the academy was a good place although the pay at Shipley was better; the student body there was richer, though, and the class size smaller. She added in a lower voice that they were a little conservative and it was best if I took my twists out for the interview. "You know how our hair can make them feel threatened?" Nakeya asked with a smile. I knew. Why adults would feel threatened by hair has never ceased to amaze me but, after I called the academy and was asked to come in for an interview, I removed my twists and straightened my hair with a hot comb that burned my scalp. I was even willing to buy blond dye. I wanted the job. I wanted to be in New York City with Jon. I had been rashly honest at my Shipley School interview, telling them that I had just graduated from Johns Hopkins graduate creative writing program, had published only a few poems in journals, was struggling to complete a collection, and was unsure how to make a living. For the academy interview, I decided I would be more circumspect. I told the two white men and one Hispanic woman that teaching was my first love and poetry my second. They were attentive; they nodded often as if to show approval. I didn't tell Jon about it because I wanted to surprise him but after I got the e-mail only three days later, thanking me and telling me they had selected a better-qualified applicant, I told Jon. He smiled, his big generous smile. He asked me to resign from the Shipley School, to move in with him and take some time off and focus on my poetry and, if I was worrying about not paying

235

rent, I could do so in kind. We laughed. We laughed so often during the early months. I put up an advertisement for subletting my Baltimore apartment, put my furniture in storage, and moved in with Jon.

Later, almost two years later, on the day I told Jon that I had cheated, I wondered whether my moving in had contributed in some way; perhaps things would have been different if I had stayed in Baltimore, visiting for long weekends. That day, it took hours of sidestepping each other, of drinking tea, of Jon lying faceup on the couch, before he asked, "Who is he?"

I told him the man's name, Ifeanyi. We had met years ago at the wedding of a friend of Aunty Adanna's, he had called me a few times, and then, recently, he had moved from Atlanta to Harlem and we'd met for coffee and the desire happened and we took the train to his place.

Jon said, "You gave him what he wanted."

It was an odd thing for Jon to say, the sort of thing Aunty Adanna, who persisted in speaking about sex as if it were something a woman gave a man at a loss to herself, would say.

I corrected Jon gently. "I took what I wanted. If I gave him anything, then it was incidental."

"Listen to yourself, just fucking listen to yourself!" Jon's voice thickened and he got up and shook me and then stopped, but did not apologize. "Amaka, I would never have cheated on you. I didn't even think about it in the past two years, I didn't think about it," he said and I realized that he was already looking at us through the lens of the past tense. It puzzled me, the ability of romantic love to mutate so completely. Where did it go? Was the real thing somehow connected to blood since love for children and parents did not change or die in the way love for romantic partners did?

"You won't forgive me," I said.

"I don't think we should be talking about forgiveness right now."

Jon was the kind of man for whom fidelity came easily, the kind who did not turn to glance at pretty women on the street simply because it did not occur to him. He sat down on the couch and I felt a terrible loss because I had become used to knowing that he was undisputedly there, to the cultured ease in the life he gave me, to his upper-class tickets and his boat and house in Connecticut and the smiling uniformed doorman in his apartment building. Even though I had shrugged, noncommittal, the two times he brought up marriage, I often thought of it. The first time I told him I was not sure I wanted to get married. The second time I said I was uncomfortable about bringing mixed-race children into the world. He laughed. How could I buy into the tragic mulatto cliché? It was so much bull-shit. He recited the names of our—his, really—biracial friends who seemed perfectly fine with being as they were. His tone was arch, superior, and perhaps he was right and it was bullshit but this was truly how I felt and it did not help that Jon approached my misgivings about race with an intellectual wave of his hand.

And who says that race did not play a role in our breakup? Who says we were not lying all those times we clung to the comforting idea of complexity? It wasn't about race, we would say, it was *complex*—Jon speaking first and me promptly agreeing. What if the reasons for most things didn't require blurred lines? What about the day we walked into a Maine restaurant with white linen–covered tables, and the waiter looked at us and asked Jon, "Table for one?" Or when the new Indian girlfriend of Jon's golf partner Ashish said she had enjoyed her graduate experience at Yale but had disliked how close the ghetto was and then her hand flew to her mouth after "ghetto" and she turned to me and said, "Oh, I'm so sorry" and Jon nodded as if to accept the apology on my behalf. What about when Jon said he hated the predatory way a black man had looked at me in Central Park, and I realized I had never heard him use the word predatory before? Or the long weekend in Montreal when the strawberry-haired owner of the bed-and-breakfast refused to acknowledge me and spoke and smiled at Jon and I was not sure whether she disliked black people or simply liked Jon and, later in the room, for the first time I did not agree that it was complex, at least not the way I had agreed all the other times. I shouted at Jon—*The worst thing is never being sure when it is race and not race and you'll never have this baggage!* And he held me and said I was overreacting and tired. What about the evening we attended a reading at the Mercantile Library and afterward Jon's friend Evan, who wrote travel books, told me he was sure it had to feel like shit when ignorant people suggested I had been published in the Best American Poetry because I was black and Jon merely shook his head when I told him that the ignorant people had to be Evan himself because nobody else had suggested this. And what about the first time I met Jon's mother? She talked about her Kenyan safari in the seventies, about Mandela's majestic grace, about her adoration for Harry Belafonte, and I worried that she would lapse into Ebonics or Swahili. As we left her rambling house in Vermont where she had an organic garden in her backyard,

237

Jon said it was not really about race, it was more complex than that, it was that she was too hyperaware of difference and consequently too eager to bridge it. "And she does that with me, too. She likes to talk about only the things she thinks I'm interested in," he said. This he did often: a constant equalizing of our experiences, a refusal to see that my experiences were different from his.

And what about Jon's wife? Jon was divorced from a woman whom he described as brilliant and needy. She lived in Cambridge but was on sabbatical in Europe and so did not feature in our lives during the first months, the good months. Then she came back and began to call often. She was unhappy, she wasn't sure what she wanted to do, she wasn't tenure track, she had given up on her book. Jon often put her on speaker and said soothing things to her about hanging in there and ended the conversation by mentioning me. I have to go, Amaka and I are late already. I have to go, I'm cooking Amaka dinner. On the evening we were to go and see Thom Pain off Broadway, she called and hung up after only a minute or so and he said she was awfully drunk and had called to confess that she still loved him and felt bad that he was with someone else and worse that the someone else was black. He was laughing. I wanted to cry. I am tough, believe me, but that day, as I stared at the high-heeled sandals I was about to slip on, I wanted to cry. All I said was, "I can't go to the theater." This woman whom I did not know had brought out in Jon something I loathed with a visceral lurch in my chest: an inability to show necessary outrage. For this new power of hers, I resented her. When, finally, we met, her unremarkably small breasts delighted me, the lines around her eyes and the saggy skin of her neck delighted me. It was at Ashish's garden party. She wore a pretty jersey dress and a limp string of green beads around her neck and smiled too brightly as we were introduced.

"Jon has told me so much about you," she said.

"You sound different," I said.

"What?"

"When you call, Jon puts you on speaker so I can follow the conversation and you sound nothing like you do on the phone," I said, smiling.

She looked away and then back at me before she excused herself to go find a drink. When I went to the bathroom, I was not surprised that she had followed me. She was standing by the door when I came out.

"It's not real," she said.

"What's not real?" I asked. I was bored with her. I was a little disappointed that Jon had not been with a less predictable woman.

"What you're doing isn't real. If it was, he wouldn't be trying so hard."

I turned and walked back outside to the party, hoping she thought I was taking the high road when the truth was that I had no idea what to say in response. On the day that I told Jon I had cheated, about eight months after that garden party, I repeated her words to Jon and said I had never told him about it because a part of me had always suspected that it was true.

"That what was true?" Jon asked.

"You were trying too hard to prove that my being black didn't matter and it was as if it wasn't a good thing and so we had to pretend it wasn't there and sometimes I wanted it to matter because it does matter but we never really talked, truly talked, about any of this. . . ."

Jon started to laugh. "This is rich," he said. "Now you blame it on race? What are you talking about? We've always talked about everything. And you told me you didn't even remember I was white!"

I had indeed said that and it was true, but only when we were alone, when we were silent, when we sat side by side and watched a film, or lay side by side and passed *New York Times* sections to each other. And yes, we did talk about race. Either in the slippery way that admitted nothing and engaged nothing and ended with that word "complexity" or as jokes that left me with a small and numb discomfort. Or as intellectual nuggets to be examined and then put aside because it was not about us (such as when he read somewhere that mainstream women's magazine sales fall with a light-skinned black on the cover and plummet with a dark-skinned black).

Jon was still laughing, his bitter laughter.

"I should leave," I said. "I'll go and stay with Aunty Adanna for a while."

"No, wait." Jon got up. "Will you see him again?"

I shook my head.

"Does he mean anything to you?"

Again, I shook my head.

"We can talk. Maybe we can work through this."

I nodded. He placed his hand on my chin and gently tilted my head up and looked into my eyes. "You don't want to, do you? You want to make this look like my decision but it's really yours. You don't want to be forgiven. You don't want to work through this," he said,

Chimamanda Ngozi Adichie

with that all-knowing authority of his and I stood there and said nothing.

A week later, I was back in Baltimore, a little drunk and a little happy and a little lonely, speeding down Charles Street in a taxi with a Punjabi driver who was proudly telling me that his children did better than American children at school.

Any Shape, Any Size
Will Self

HE LAY IN BED LISTENING to the clack of the cat flap in the wind. It was three flights down to the front door but the house—which was subdivided into eight small flats—had that hollow feeling that always came when the other tenants had left for work. Greg hunkered down in the bed, pulling the duvet around his bony shoulders so that it enfolded him in feminine softness. A gull hovered above the skylight and cocked its head so that its blank, yellow eye looked down into the room.

Taggart would be opening up the shop by now, fussing around the security grille with his preposterously large bunch of keys. As if anyone in this sleepy little off-season resort was going to break into Game Buoy. What would they steal? A box of willy warmers? A gross of novelty condoms? A corkscrew that played "Silent Night" with digital monody? Once Taggart had the grille up he'd say hello to Peter Prentice who ran the Windrush Studio across the lane, and Beatie Phillips, the proprietor of Pot Pourri next door. Pleasantries exchanged, Taggart would retreat into the dark interior of his gift shop and hunker down for a long day of waiting. Waiting like a hermit crab in its shell, hoping against hope that some wintry trippers would come within reach of his feeble pincers, so that Taggart could sell them a useless bit of tat.

A fat, furry bluebottle came doodling into the bedroom and butted the skylight. A week before Christmas and it was still warm enough for flies. This, Greg thought, was unnatural. It made the whole town feel fecal and diseased. He recalled the Christmases of his childhood, the holly berries as red as droplets of blood on the pure, white snow. Or was this an accurate memory? Perhaps he was remembering a film he'd once seen and the turn of the year had always been like this, sodden with rain, rank with salty mists.

*

To get to work all Greg had to do was pull on his clothes, tumble down the stairs, and roll across the way. It was better to lie here, though, savoring the bed and allowing the jangle of that morning's row to subside. What were the rows about? Greg wondered. On the face of it they were about sex—but then at this state in a relationship all rows seemed to be about sex, when in reality they were about far more intimate things. Sue had a thirty-five-minute drive to work and her boss had none of Taggart's biddability; this explained, Greg supposed, why she had no taste anymore for morning sex. When they were first together they made love all the time—even when Sue had her period. Far from being squeamish or embarrassed she would push his head down there, into the old iron smell and the overpowering musk of her arousal. But this morning, when he reached across the cool center of the bed for her, she slid out the far side, then restarted the argument they'd been having the night before, a row so intractable it had accompanied them both into unconsciousness, tainting their dreams with its mean obduracy.

Families—that was the nub of it. Greg had made it clear weeks before that he had no intention of going to see his parents over Christmas. He had no objection to Sue going to see her own, why would he? But this year he was intent on kicking back and relaxing over the festive season. A few beers, a few scotches, a sinful ready-meal—Greg fancied the idea of not resisting the awfulness of the Christmas television schedules but rolling with them, seeing just how many soap opera specials and rerun sitcoms he could sit through before he subsided into utter torpor. Sue wouldn't let him alone, though. "You love your mum and dad, don't you?" she hectored him. "And there's your little brothers and sister as well. Don't you think they'll want to spend Christmas day with you?"

"Maybe, but it's no big deal. Presents for them will be cheaper in the sales, and the travel's a drag at this time of year—they live way up north. It'll be far more of a holiday if I just stay here."

Once Sue saw he was serious, she started getting on to Greg about spending Christmas with her own family. They only lived an hour's drive away. They'd love to meet him properly. They were welcoming sorts—not uptight at all. He was unmoved and unmovable. "You're selfish" is what she said next, and Greg counted out the seconds until she uttered—as he knew she must—the "c" word. "You've got no commitment to our relationship."

Commitment. There it was—six months in and they always said it. They came in high summer, tripping along the riverfront where the sparkling yachts were moored, rigging tinkling against aluminum spars. They came in the sunlight wearing cut-off jeans and espadrilles. They came in the warmth, rumpling the hair of the kids who were crab fishing on the quay. They came into Greg's bed and undulated over it throughout the short summer nights. The pale patches their bikinis left on their tanned hides made them appear like exotic, striped animals.

Then the yachties in their Pringle sweaters and nautical caps departed; the wrinkly, old day-trippers quit the town; the holiday home owners black-bagged their rubbish and turned the electricity off at the mains. The town's permanent inhabitants turned in on themselves—and Greg's girls decided to stay. They found him enigmatic. Why was it that a good-looking young man like him, intelligent, obviously competent, was content to live out his life in this dull little estuarial town? All Greg did was work in the shop and drink with his boring coterie of mates: Steve, who crewed the car ferry across the river; Dean, who worked as lab assistant up at the Naval College; and Sam, a clerk in the bank. The girls had henna tattoos and talked of far-off beaches they'd visited crewing the yachts, but they were looking for a change. They liked Greg's airy, top-floor flat, with its high, sloping ceilings and sea views. They liked the sex. They stayed, got jobs, bought cars. Then they tried to change him.

It began not with injunctions—but objects. Because they were free-spirited girls they arrived only with the rumpled sundresses and raggedy underwear that they pulled from their kitbags. Then, as the months passed and the autumn slewed in with a mush of leaf fall, so they sent for their things from home—framed prints, music centers, paperback books, kitchenware—and they began to buy knickknacks and small sticks of furniture in the shops crowding out the narrow, old streets. These throw cushions and padded seat covers were soft evidence of their increasingly hardening commitment. Then they began muttering about how much Greg drank and how little he was paid. There would be talk of "getting on" and "making something of your life." Usually—and this had happened three times before in the four years he'd lived in the little town—it all came to a head at Christmas. A couple of blistering rows and the girls evaporated, leaving behind only the foamy residue of their tenancy. Their stuff, which Greg would unceremoniously dump in the skip behind the Cherub pub. Then he'd stoically wait out the first half of the new year, confident that when the yachties returned, so another girl would come tripping along the riverfront.

Still, Greg acknowledged as he struggled into his clothes, Sue was, if not exactly different, at any rate . . . better. Funnier, more tolerant, smarter. He would, he concluded, be sad to lose her. He popped the plastic blister and slipped the gum into his sour mouth. Chewing the nicotine-flavored cud he left the flat.

At lunchtime Greg told Taggart he was going to get a bite to eat and set out for the pasty shop on the far side of the marina. He was heading up Wynd Street when he noticed a sign in the window of the draper's. FOAM CUT, the sign read. ANY SHAPE, ANY SIZE. He thought no more of it until, dusting the flakes of pastry from his denim thighs, he rose from the bench where he'd been sitting and it dawned on him: maybe he should try and patch things up with Sue? How exactly did you do that? He thought for a few moments and concluded, buy her a present. What present? He cordially loathed every ditsy gift in every chintzy gift shop in the dinky town. With its half-timbered houses and steep, cobbled lanes the town itself had the aspect of a gift, an impression hideously enhanced by the twee views of it printed on the T-shirts, aprons, and tea towels that were displayed in the gift shops.

FOAM CUT. ANY SHAPE, ANY SIZE. Greg came out of his cynical reverie to confront the sign once more. He'd never been in the draper's; there was nothing there for him. But it was a shop that made no concessions to the tourist trade either, being full—now he scrutinized it—of bolts of cloth in a myriad of patterns, all piled up higgledy-pig-gledy on trestle tables. There were baskets full of balls and hanks of wool, a rack of cotton reels, dreadlocks of elastic and tape, mossy thatches of curtain fabrics, valances, ruffs, runners, doilies, and cushion covers—in short, every kind of flexible fabric known to woman-kind, along with all the pins, needles, bobbins, and bodkins needed to shape, cut, and otherwise bend it to their contrivance.

Greg went in and picked his way between boxes overflowing with cloth oddments to a counter, along the top of which had been tacked various measures. A strange old person stood behind this, holding in one hand a large pair of very sharp shears. The draper was slowly opening and closing them so that they made a loud "shhk-shhk" noise. With a bald dome of head, surrounded by a dyed ruff of blonde hair, a mammoth shelf of bosom but a man's cardigan, shirt, and tie, it was difficult to assign any gender to the draper at all. "Um . . ." Greg nearly turned tail and fled. ". . . it says in the window you cut foam?"

"That's right, dear." Shhk-shhk.

"Any shape—"

"Any size, that's right, dear." The voice was ageless, unaccented, entirely lacking in warmth—yet strangely appealing.

"Um, well, I . . . well—you mean any sort of regular shape, don't you . . . cubes, spheres, and . . . I dunno . . . tubes—don't you?"

"Any shape, dear, any shape at all; the machine's ever so sensitive."

"What," Greg laughed, "could you cut a piece of foam shaped like . . . oh, I dunno . . . shaped like a woman then?"

"I expect we could manage that, dear."

"Life size?"

"Any size, dear, any size at all." Shhk-shhk.

"Well, in that case," Greg felt almost belligerent, "could you cut me a piece of foam the same size and shape as my girlfriend?"

"You mean Sue, dear?"

"Do you know Sue?" Greg was taken aback.

"Oh yes, she came in to get the material for your curtains and to cover the seat in your bay window, and a few other odds and ends. You must be Greg."

"That's right . . . and you are?"

"Frances, dear—but everyone calls me Fran." They stood for a few moments looking at each other. Shhk-shhk. "So, a bit of foam like Sue." Frances took the initiative. "She'll be what, about five foot four? She's nice and curvy, probably a size ten." She took a stub of pencil from the pocket of her cardigan and began to make notes on a scrap of paper. "She's got that lovely olive complexion and dark chestnut hair—not that we can do those in foam!" Frances chuckled. "It's all the standard yellow, but we can suggest them, the machine is ever so sensitive if it's used properly."

Greg was over an hour in the draper's, and when he came out he had a bulky yet insubstantial parcel under his arm, wrapped up in brown paper and tied with string. He dropped this in the flat then headed over to Game Buoy. "You've been gone bloody ages," Taggart snapped. "I might've needed you, there might've been a rush on."

"Have you needed me?" Greg snapped back. "Has there been a rush on?"

"Well . . . er, no." Taggart was abashed and went back to pricing plastic aprons printed with women's naked torsos.

Greg was going to wait to introduce foam Sue to Sue. Wait until she'd unwound from work, had a shower and a glass of wine. He was hoping that after the row that morning she'd be a little contrite, and that the present would tip her into compliance. They might end up making love under the sightless—yet curiously expressive—eyes of her spongy doppelgänger.

It didn't work out that way. A lightbulb had gone on the stairs, and real Sue went to the airing cupboard for a replacement as soon as she came in. Foam Sue fell on her. First she screeched, then she shouted, "What the fuck is this?!" Then she came waltzing into the living room with her squishy twin. "What is this, Greg, is it some kind of a fucking joke?"

"It's a present, a present for you." Greg tried to mollify her but he felt poisonous and aggrieved. "I got it at the draper's from that . . . from Fran."

"That creepy old dyke!" Sue expostulated. "What's it meant to be, eh?" She waved foam Sue by the scruff of its neck and its long yel-

246

low legs waggled. Greg found the sight at once funny and enraging. He wanted to protect the Sue who was being so ill used: the foam one.

"It's meant to be," he picked his words carefully, "you. It is you. Look." He got up from the sofa, took the dummy from her, and began to point out its buttery features. "See here, she's even managed to get that mole on the side of your neck, and the hair's perfect, I think, and the tits. We talked it all over for about an hour before she cut it, the machine's ever so . . . sensitive," he finished limply.

"Let me get this straight." Greg had never seen Sue this calm in anger before. She was pale, her top lip curled up and revealing her horsey upper teeth. "You and that freak discussed my body for a whole hour and then she cut this manky bit of foam into the shape of me?"

"Yeah, that's about the size of it." Greg's eyes were downcast, but he was thinking about Sue's front teeth and casting surreptitious looks at the dummy to see if they'd been incorporated.

"Look, Greg," Sue chucked the other Sue to one side, "I don't even want to see that stupid thing. Maybe if we'd been getting on well together I'd've found it funny—but we haven't. I've only got one thing to ask you and I want a straight answer; and let me tell you, everything depends on it: are you coming with me to my parents' for Christmas?"

"No," he replied after a thoughtless thirty seconds had elapsed.

The next half hour was a cacophony of recriminations punctuated by slamming doors as Sue stamped through the flat packing. She berated Greg, telling him what a dead-end, emotionally illiterate child he was to be passing her up so that he could spend more time "watching the fucking box, wanking, and getting pissed!" Finally she was almost gone. Greg went down to see her off. "Look," he said, poking his head in through the window of her hatchback.

"Are you gonna apologize, Greg?" She snorted. "Because it's too late for that."

"Er, no, I wasn't—not that I'm not sorry things have turned out this way—it's just, I was wondering about the rest of your stuff, you've left the bits of furniture you bought, some pictures, and those rag dolls."

"I'll be back for them. Suit you, you shit?" She slammed the car into gear and pulled away, nearly catching his ear.

"Yeah," he called after her. "But don't leave it too long." Then she was completely gone, leaving a few curls of exhaust smoke in her wake, pubic hairs lying on the rumpled tarmac mattress of the road. Greg turned back to the house. Overhead the gulls cried, "Eek-eek" as if remonstrating with him for his foolishness.

Later on Greg took foam Sue to the pub. The Seven Stars was a foursquare old inn, with oak beams and vernacular plasterwork featuring the stars in question, streaking about the warped walls in a tangle of comet tails. Steve, the ferryman, was standing by the bar with a pint in his hand. He wore thigh-high waders, blue jeans, and an American football shirt bearing the number 69. He was thin and phlegmatic, with the drowned beard and lank locks of an anchorite. He was smoking, and on seeing him Greg fumbled automatically for his pack of gum and popped a piece into his mouth. "Where's Sue?" Steve grunted. "Right here," Greg replied, propping foam Sue against the bar.

"Ha, ha," said Steve. "I mean the real one."

"This is the real and only Sue so far as I'm concerned. The other one's gone." Greg gave foam Sue a proprietary squeeze and planted a kiss on her dry, honey-colored cheek. In the low, twinkling light of the inn her features were more lifelike, and her rigid right arm stretched out as if reaching for a drink. Steve was unimpressed: "So that's another great girl you've lost, well done." Greg let this go. He felt affronted but foam Sue's scratchy cheek was comforting. The synthetic texture summoned up a long-lost memory of a favorite teddy, slobbered on by toddler Greg.

As the evening wore on and the pub filled up, Greg stayed propped on a stool with foam Sue beside him. Dean and Sam came in. They were both full of banter, but like Steve neither of them seemed to get foam Sue. They mostly ignored Greg and chatted with the other regulars. It was left to the landlord—potbellied Mark, with his trembling hands and quavering voice—to serve Greg his drinks with the jocular inquiry "And one for the lady?" By the time the bell clanged

Greg was furious. "Look, you lot," he rounded on his mates, "you've been blanking me all evening!" The bar fell silent. Dean, a tubby chap, usually flippant to the point of bumptiousness, looked at the somber faces and took them as his cue to be spokesman. "Greg," he began, "none of us are too impressed by the way you've treated Sue. We all liked her a lot and we're sorry she's gone. You're daft the way you won't give any ground in a relationship, daft and"—he paused for support from the others and there was a mutter of agreement—"well, selfish."

"Right! That's that then!" Greg was incandescent. He grabbed foam Sue and, holding her tight against his chest, shouldered his way through them and out into the night.

The following morning Greg awoke from a troubling dream. In it he was making love to Sue but her limbs were puffy and floppy, her mouth desiccated and rasping. Every time he stroked her, flames licked at his hands. He came to, gagging on the scruff of the foam dummy, which was pinioned beneath him.

At Game Buoy Taggart had a new line in. "Look at this," he grinned, his Vandyke mustache flexing with merriment. "It's a crapping Santa." It was; the figurine was squatting on a plastic toilet and when Taggart pulled the chain a recorded choir sang, "Jingle bells, jingle bells, Santa's done a shit. . . ." "Hilarious," Greg said. "Look, I've got to pop out for a while." Without waiting for Taggart to remonstrate he headed for the door.

At the draper's the sign in the window was oddly lustrous in the dim, midwinter light. FOAM CUT. ANY SHAPE, ANY SIZE. Frances was behind the counter, shears in hand, her expression expectant. As Greg was describing the way he wanted three new pieces of foam to be cut, he noticed the thumb on the plump hand that was manipulating the shears. Or rather thumbs—because there were two of them, connected by a translucent webbing through which the veins could be clearly seen. Greg was bemused: how had he failed to notice this deformity on his first visit to the shop?

Frances listened carefully to what Greg wanted and offered a few suggestions of her own. Then she went in back to cut the first piece of foam and Greg waited, lulled by the muffled atmosphere of the shop, and the noise of the machine, which was at once humming and grating. It took most of the afternoon for the job and by the time Greg had walked back and forth to his flat with the three parcels, there hardly seemed any point in returning to Game Buoy, so he didn't.

That evening, at around nine o' clock, the vicar came to the house with some carol singers. Greg could hear them making their way up the stairs, stopping at the door of each flat to sing a couple of verses and exchange seasonal banter with its occupants. It would only be a few minutes before they reached his door but Greg found himself powerless to rise from his chair. He'd been having a party; the foam dummies of Steve and Sam were sitting opposite him at the table. Greg had had them cut in a seated position with this arrangement in mind. Steve's nose was a bit blobby at the end and Sam was a shade too plump, but all in all they were good likenesses, especially when their squishy fingers were curled around lager cans. The foam Dean was different. It had been artfully sculpted so that the puffy substance gathered at its ankles in a semblance of trousers and pants. Its brownish yellow aerated buttocks were canted at an obscene angle. Foam Dean was lying on top of foam Sue, who was spread out on the sofa, her feet in the air.

When the knock came at the door and the children's voices piped, "Once in David's royal city . . . ," Greg ground a huge wad of gum between his teeth, took a swig of scotch from the half-empty bottle that stood in front of him, and shut his ears to the racket.

He phoned his boss late the following morning. When Taggart began to moan down the line in a threatening fashion Greg cut him off: "You can take your fucking stupid job and shove it up your arse," he said, "along with all the Leatherman tool sets, shaving kits, chess computers, and remote-control racing cars you can get up there." He slammed the phone down and turned to face his foamy friends. "Right now!" He clapped his hands. "How about a fry up?"

*

In the last few days before Christmas the little town became choked with shoppers. All the gift shops, galleries, and antique dealers that struggled through the off-season to make ends meet stayed open late into the evening so they could reap the retail harvest. Greg busied himself with his own Christmas shopping. Frances's prices were reasonable although not cheap. A large piece of furniture—like the bed or the sofa—was £17.50, but smaller things—like the phone or the CD player—were almost as costly. "It depends on the complexity of the object, dear," Frances told him. "Obviously the human face is the hardest likeness to achieve, but even household objects can be difficult to get right."

Greg carried his smaller acquisitions back to the flat during daylight hours. Seagulls swooped over the marina, white scratches on the bluey gray slate of the sky. He carried the big pieces back when darkness had fallen, and the orange cones thrown down by the streetlights were full of twinkling raindrops. Later still, Greg carried the objects that he'd replaced with their own foamy simulacra to the skip behind the pub.

Under the track lighting of the attic flat the squeezable interior Greg and Frances had created appeared—to Greg's eyes—gilded and enchanting. The faces of his foamy friends and pneumatic lover were soft and sympathetic. During the long evenings, while the wind from the sea rattled the windowpanes, Greg sat with a chaw of cigarette substitute in his distended cheek and his arm thrown casually around foam Dean or foam Sue, depending on whether he felt the need for male solidarity or an amorous encounter. The last of the hated chattels his girlfriends had brought into the flat were gone. Now everywhere he looked there were tawny, yielding surfaces. Even the carpets were sheets of foam, so he could fling himself to the floor or chuck things about with complete abandon. It made no difference, everything remained the same, spongy and resilient.

On Christmas Eve Greg had Frances cut him a piece of foam shaped like a Christmas tree, complete with baubles and fairy lights. Cubes

251

of foam in different sizes were soon ranged beneath it. Greg's television had long since gone but he wasn't bothered. Looking into the golden yellow screen of the foam box that had replaced it he thought he could discern old films of great poignancy.

That night Greg's mum and dad called to wish him a happy Christmas. They couldn't get through because the phone was foam, but coincidentally Greg was pretending to speak to them that very minute, his ear cushioned by the airy earpiece. "Yeah, yeah, Mum. . . . No, nothing special. . . . Yeah, she's fine. . . . Um, yes, love to you, Dad, and the others too. . . . I'll be up early in the new year. . . ." He replaced the handset on its soft cradle and gave foam Sue's hand an affectionate squeeze.

On Christmas morning Greg woke late and with a hangover. He'd replaced the bottles in the flat—and even the glasses—with foam replicas; even so, he found that pretending to drink still intoxicated him, as with dry swig after swig he became lighter and more insubstantial. He groaned and rolled over on the foam slab. He'd slept with foam Sue and foam Dean on either side of him. His movement set off a wave: foam Sue against the foam bedside table, foam bedside table against foam standard lamp, foam standard lamp against foam bookcase. Through the door Greg could see foam Steve and foam Sam sitting on the foam sofa. They waggled their heads and looked at him with their puffy eyes.

Greg reached for the pack of gum he'd placed on the foam bedside table the night before. To his horror it was empty, every blister popped. As soon as he registered this, Greg felt the first, belly-watering pangs of nicotine withdrawal. In truth, giving up smoking was just something he'd done to prove that he could, that he had the willpower. The need for the gum had entirely supplanted his craving for cigarettes and he consumed far more of it than he ever had tobacco. So much that, deprived of it, his mind skittered around the room, alighting on squishy surface after squishy surface. Greg felt terrible jitteriness, he bounced off everything, his bungee nerves intolerably stretched. No shops would be open—let alone the chemist's—and he *had* to have nicotine. Had to have it *right away*.

*

Then it came to him—flesh-and-blood Sue. She'd always kept some in the airing cupboard. She didn't like to smoke in front of him, but during times of stress she'd creep out onto the landing and puff through the open window. On these occasions, lying in bed, it would smell to Greg as if a roast dinner were being cooked immediately outside the flat. He was Butch the bulldog in *Tom and Jerry,* and the long curl of meaty smoke snaked into the flat, arousing his fearsome appetite.

He sprang from the bed and moonwalked to the cupboard. They were still there! A girly pack of ten Silk Cut Extra Mild, together with a matchbox. He fumbled a cigarette out; bone-dry, it crunched between his twitching fingers. He fumbled with the matchbox and eventually contrived a flame. Inhaling deeply he felt the drug ooze in through every little bronchial tube, filling his blood with sweet relief. The match, still burning, nipped at his fingertips and thoughtlessly Greg chucked it to one side.

Notes Toward the Township
Of Cause of Trouble
(Venus's Cabinet Revealed)

Eleni Sikelianos

Here we are wandering in the world of things

to find a happiness seed
unfolding in a corner
of the house

like a minute sloughing off
its seconds and parts

find magic in a hopeless crystal

a house poem in the house

videlicet: that is, namely
videre: to see
licet: it is permitted

[reader must dream
a few nights' dreams here
before continuing]

a dream beneath the city made bones rise up
and made the struts for churches

and told us

Eleni Sikelianos

study: graveyards, grave sites
study: mirrors

a town's mirror is dug underground
a tooth's in its roots
the living in the dead

a ripple near a lamb's eye
(approximates)
the curves of a cloud
the eye itself a bullet

this feather or fur keeps returning through the eye or the ear as its word

the sun, for example, a central fact
around which the head spins, heats up the mind

a city might be drawn lightly
with a pencil and left that
way, as if
all we needed to live in was a sketch

to ostensify, ossify   a house, its language, body

a word gathering there goes brittle

what is the meaning of this? *it*
unfolds, refolds
over time

The planispheres of the heavens
are systematically represented

but it is disputed how
much practical knowledge
is embodied there

to pour my heart down on
(Niger yellowcake)

to find the plant of birth
(war record on human hide)

We inhabit rooms never touched by death
(a separate house for that)

"to be eating dandelions from the root"
(*manger les pissenlits de la racine*)

a parsley seed travels to Hades three times
(before it sprouts)

Utah, Nevada, Arizona's grasses flushed with rads

hemoglobin bubbles & nebulas wobble
a *vol nuptial*, bridal flight of blood & bees

(to no longer be worried for)
(what one doesn't know)

(to no longer feel)
(responsible for it)

the body, often at odds
with us, tense
in its own disbelief of itself

a fly flying in
to meet its shadow on the ceiling

the letter is transient, the hand
is permanent, spell the vowels
in a palm

Tonight all the festivities
under the earth will cease
Tonight all the celebrations
will be above ground

What is this pile of
darkness in the room?

a silver-coated plate
bathed in iodine vapor
will
capture your face, a hummingbird
caught in a cage

a palace made
of a million pounds of plate glass
will now
collapse

the study of hands in the light, of touch
in the dark

a child having always the Book
of her hands open before her eyes

some radiant history

some restless meat I feel

some empathy for the hard-line military man who died
& saw the error

the shoes that are too
tight to walk in my hand

change the self-pitying war narrative
to Bag of Trees
Upfull & Bright

seen from air : a
telephone pole's most
charming shadow

what was the tree

Eleni Sikelianos

the land : one big raggedy ghostly sonnet

the heart beats in each pore
of the body like a red
pinprick

you were dragging something
from the black interior out

how one man can make
the march of history
bear down on you, what turns on the edge
of a blade

the afternoon light glowing through her teeth as she talked

what the will will do
is not always what the heart would
perhaps rarely what the mind

now go learn some animal things

the fold at the juncture
of butt & thigh where the sun
didn't reach

she shows it to us

how a sentence or a line
cannot reverse time

it turns out we were made
from piles of shit she asks

red as red blood pooling on the thumb those geraniums
in window boxes on this street

bed of earth, bed
of air why not
a bed of fire too

double le temps, et
puis le vendre

clods & clouds
mercify me

a landscape might melt
back up toward a city

like this erotic site of decay
(the body)

from the cunt to the head is
a Möbius strip
that connects us to death

& some scissors trim all time as does
the eye or mind

No more fooling around
Make a thing of such
extreme beauty it cracks
and cracks
the hand that makes it

The hour which once was square
rubbed at its clitoral
corners turns round

pieces of a second shaved off (like metal filings)

the frictioned minutes (castaways) lie in wait for
that true magnet time*

How reversible?: "knowledge is contained / in
the world / being in /
self"

Eleni Sikelianos

Head: let the skull bones slide apart
& the brain grow big

type: orb
shape: universal

stepping on the rind of earth
below which that trash heap Hell

It seemed impossible to tell
what country we lived in

some sad gray faces pass

a brown dwarf, a
       failed star

in the blended light of a planet & its sun
the dust & the photons rise

Butter Princess, I saw
a huge cross of lights laid out in the land
& it was some city
between Sioux Falls & Detroit

---

*   when & where the labyrinthodont am-
phibians lived, & I quietly loved
you in opposite fashion   like
certain small crystals making topaz yolks in the balking veins
of the earth   swimming
toward what will soon become rock, the needle
     shivering in the dark
toward a new magnet   a heart
of a world even travels
toward other poles
North South North South

Working Late
Lewis Warsh

THE DARK CAME ON suddenly, it was night, but no one cared. We were all so immersed in our work, our deadlines, that we didn't even notice.

Eventually my coworkers began to leave. They had decided, I suppose, that whatever they hadn't finished could wait till tomorrow. I heard them sighing from across the office as they closed down their computers. The men loosened their ties. The women primped in front of hand mirrors and applied new coats of lipstick. Someone passed my desk and said, "Have a good night." I waved my hand in the direction of the voice and nodded without looking up.

Someone else said, with a trace of sarcasm, "Don't work too late." By then it was almost ten o'clock.

At some point I turned away from my computer and realized I was alone in the vast office space where everyone works except for the president and the vice presidents of the company, who have special offices down a secluded hallway. I stared out the window at the nearby buildings, down the canyon of narrow streets with sidewalks no more than a few feet wide. Tonight all the offices were dark except the one facing mine. Like me, the occupants of the office, a man and a woman, were working late.

I didn't know who these people were, or what they did, but I'd seen them before. Maybe one night a week I was the last one to leave work and invariably they were there, at facing desks, staring down their computer screens while the night went on without them.

Then it happened. I looked up, and the man was leaning over the woman's desk. He was saying something to her and then he put out his hand and touched her hair, gently, as if she were a child, but she pulled away. I was close enough to see the expression on her face turn from indifference to fear. I could imagine her surprise: why is this happening to me?

The entire office—desks, chairs, computers, potted plants, the Magritte print, fluorescent beams—was bigger than life, like a stage set or a diorama. I knew I should try to concentrate on my work—on finishing what I had to do—so I could get home before midnight. But it was hard to peel my eyes away from the figures behind the glass. Something about the woman's attitude had changed and she tilted her face submissively for the man to kiss. She had decided, in the space of a moment, not to resist him. The last thing she cared about was whether anyone was watching. Her hair was straw colored and tied back with a handkerchief. She wore a turquoise bracelet around her left wrist and a tiny crucifix around her neck. She was in her early twenties, but could have been younger. One could see her as a child, crossing her legs at the ankles, in the pew of a church. The man, in shirtsleeves, barrel chested and chinless, was twice her age.

My work allows for moments of distraction when I can turn from my computer to the street, ten stories below, and to the people who occupy the offices in the building opposite. Everyone in my office takes frequent breaks, some more often than others. Like every other workplace there are overachievers and there are slackers. I think I fall somewhere in between. I don't feel guilty when I go downstairs for a cigarette or into the lounge for a cup of coffee. Or, like now, if I simply stare into space. No one checks up on what I do during the day and as long as I finish my quota for the week no one complains. I've been working here for five years and no one has ever complained. It's obvious, even to the president and vice presidents, that if you continued to work without taking a break you might go crazy. So it wasn't the first time I was working late and looked up from my computer and saw the woman with straw colored hair and the older man in their office across the street. I envied them, actually—the conversation, the camaraderie. It made me look around and see how little I had.

Most often, I would watch them for a few minutes, and then I would go back to my work, and when I looked again they were gone. The screen of my computer stared back at me—yellow and blue. It was almost midnight. Why was I still here?

On this particular night things were different. I had done enough work and I was confident that I'd meet all my deadlines by the end of the week. I knew that I might as well return to my apartment but for some reason I lingered on. I was putting off the moment when I would slip my arms through the sleeves of my jacket and turn off my computer when I turned back to the window and saw the man reach out again and put his hand on the front of the woman's blouse. I could see her stiffen, recoil, lean back in her chair. I could feel what she was feeling, or thought I could, though I didn't even know her name, and no doubt, as on other occasions, my misguided sense of empathy was off the mark. Her blouse was white with little poodles on it and it was open halfway down her chest so that when she turned in my direction I could see the tops of her breasts. The poodles had their mouths open and looked like they were barking and they all wore little bells around their necks. I wondered whether she had unbuttoned her blouse as a way of tempting him, teasing him, that she wanted him to touch her but was playing hard to get. Then he actually reached out and ripped the buttons off the front of her blouse and pushed her chair so that it swiveled backward and hit the wall. I saw her lips move as if she was cursing him or crying out for help, but of course I couldn't hear what she was saying. Neither of them, as far as I knew, were aware that I was watching.

You could say that watching them was like listening to the words of a song on the radio. Then someone turned off the radio and you didn't realize how quiet it was. That you were singing the song on the radio in your head. That the song was in your head whether you liked it or not.

That's what it was like to watch the couple in the office across the street. It reminded me of the time, in a darkened movie theater, when a man sat down beside me and put his hand on my knee. I looked back at my computer, as if there was something I had to do that I had forgotten about, but there was nothing, there was never anything, I could go home anytime. Then I looked back at the office across the street and saw the man reach out again but this time she grabbed his hand and bit down hard. I could see the man's face as he pulled back his arm and it looked as if he was going to smack her across the side of her head. The woman had stood up by then, clutching her torn blouse to her breasts. She angled toward the door of the office but there was no escape.

It occurred to me, as the song in my head kept going around and around, that I should call the police, or that I could turn back to my computer and pretend I hadn't seen any of it. There are at least two dozen people working in my office on any given day and everyone stands at the window and makes up stories about the people in the offices across the street. Once I thought I saw the woman with the poodles on her blouse in a diner on the corner, but who could be sure?

The man had wrapped a towel around his hand while the woman cowered in a corner. He looked defeated, like a wounded dog. The whole scene resembled the cover of a cheap paperback from the

1950s, the lurid mysteries where a half-naked woman tries to avoid the advances of a man with a gun. The cover suggests that because the man has the gun, the woman will be forced to submit to his will, to his desires. The woman in the office crossed her arms across her chest, but her breasts were still partially visible. The man was standing closer to the door of the office but he wasn't blocking it.

I pressed my forehead against the window until I thought I could make out the streaks of mascara on her cheeks. She was crawling across the floor of the office, in her heels and stockings and in her short skirt, trying to get to the door. The man had turned his back to her, deliberately, as if he didn't care whether she escaped or not, but at the last second, just as it appeared that she was going to turn the knob of the door, he grabbed her wrist and dragged her back across the carpet.

The idea that she would try to escape enraged him. As if she really thought that she could get away so easily. It was all in his head, of course, all the desire he felt for her after working in the same office for six months. She had been hired, initially, as a temp, but after a week or two he convinced his boss to hire her full-time. And for doing this he expected something. Something. She was just a girl from the Midwest, who had escaped small-town life by going to school in Chicago. Her real dream was to come to New York and here she was. People had warned her about things like this: if the boss wants to fuck you, you better do it or you'll get fired. Some days, when she wore a skirt that was too short or a blouse that was too tight, she would notice him watching her. She noticed everything. And now what everybody told her might happen was happening. She was learning her lesson the hard way. She should have listened to her friends and family, she should never have left the farm. But who could she trust?

The man drew back his arm again, as if he was going to punch her in the face, but checked himself. Instead, he took an empty whiskey bottle from the drawer of his desk and swung it in her direction.

I wish there had been someone with me. It was hard to be the only witness. I felt a pain in my chest, like I had been holding my breath under water for a long time. Someone was pressing my head under water and I was trying to fight back, but couldn't.

I tried to imagine the first questions that the police would ask: Why were you working so late? What were you doing looking out the window? They would think I was a kind of voyeur. They would think about the movie with James Stewart, and how no one believed that he had seen a murder committed from his window, not even Grace Kelly. The police would probably think that I was guilty since I was the only one who had seen anything. That there was a naked woman hidden in my closet.

The man stepped away from the woman's body. A pool of blood had formed on the rug near her head. He bent at the waist and stared directly into her face. He had hit her across the head more than once and she was no longer moving. He was standing over her, observing his work. Then he did something odd, though in retrospect it makes sense. "Odd" isn't the right word but that's what I felt at the time. He looked around him, around the office, then out the window. He looked right at me, or so I thought. Except for the light in my office, the building where I worked was a wall of darkness. He could see me as well as I could see him.

I turned away from the window, trying to fade back into the shadows. Maybe he was simply looking out into the night and I was just inventing the part about his looking directly at me. Whenever someone directs their attention at me I feel paranoid, like I've done something wrong. It was after ten at night. The man at the window reached behind him and took a cigarette from a pack of Lucky Strikes on his desk, lit it with a disposable lighter, even though it was forbidden to smoke in the building, while the woman died miserably behind him.

It was early winter and I thought I noticed some flakes of snow in the air. I realized that precious moments were slipping away. I knew what I should do was call the police. Some Helen Mirren type would push her way into my office and conclude that I was the prime suspect. I'd read enough novels and seen enough TV shows to realize that the witnesses are often considered suspects if they don't have alibis. And what was I doing anyway? If the man had seen me watching him and knew that I had seen him murder the woman, did that mean he'd try to hunt me down?

Only the night before I'd seen Jill with her new boyfriend. "Seen" is probably not the proper word. It had been a mistake to get involved with a next-door neighbor but for the time that it lasted it had seemed like a convenient arrangement. It meant we could share everything with one another and still have our own space when we wanted it. We slept together every night, one night my apartment, the next night hers. It went on for over a year before she confessed that she had fallen in love with someone else. It was something I had not seen coming, so to speak. We had just had sex the night before when she told me that in fact she had spent the afternoon at his apartment, the nameless lover's apartment, and I assumed that meant that she had literally gone from my bed to his without even going to work, which is what she admitted, finally, annoyed that she had to spell it out for me in bright neon. That had been more than a year ago and since that night we had never spoken except when we met by accident on the stairs or in the vestibule near the mailboxes. On those occasions both of us lowered our eyes and muttered the words "Hi" or "How're you doing" out of the corners of our mouths. It never occurred to me to find a new apartment, even after Jill started bringing her new boyfriend home, and I could hear them laughing as they climbed the steps, and then their voices as they removed one another's clothing and got into bed.

In the old days, when we ate dinner together every night, I would rush home from work, usually stopping to buy food along the way. Jill was the better cook so she tended to prepare the meals, something she said she didn't mind doing, even though she also worked a full day. But there she was, in her kitchen, as I let myself into her apartment, with food for salad and a bottle of wine. What we enjoyed most was staying home watching movies, eating popcorn or sharing an expensive bar of dark chocolate. Often I stopped at the local video store on Greenwich Avenue and picked up a movie before coming home.

In the first weeks of our relationship, when it seemed that we might be together for a long time, we would get into bed as soon as we returned home from work. Food could wait, obviously, as well as checking phone and e-mail messages. It was with a feeling of reassurance that we measured our time together against everything else in our lives, and for a while being together was the only thing that mattered to both of us. There's a feeling of bliss and serenity that comes with the permission to touch another person's body whenever you want. But that's all over.

Once I had a fantasy that Jill came to the door of my apartment in the middle of the night, that she woke me up hammering at my door, that she was in tears, her clothing was torn, her boyfriend had beaten her up. I emptied my ice tray in a bucket, wrapped some cubes in a towel, and told her to hold it to the bump above her eye, something my mother had once done to stop the swelling when I fell off my bike. Then I went to the apartment next door where the drunk boyfriend was sitting in a lotus position on the living-room rug. It had been a while since I had been in the apartment but nothing had changed. There was the collection of framed photographs of Jill's family on the mantelpiece above the fake fireplace but I couldn't tell whether she had removed the photo of herself that I had taken one winter afternoon in Montauk when we rented a car and drove out to the lighthouse. I took a stool from the kitchen and hammered it over the boyfriend's head. Then I kicked him in the ribs a few times for good measure.

When I came to work the next day, a few minutes before nine, all my coworkers were standing at the window staring at the office directly opposite. I decided to act dumb and asked them what had happened and they told me, though it was too soon to know anything for sure, that someone had been killed in the office the night before. I leaned into the crowd at the window and saw that the office was occupied by three uniformed policemen and an older man in a tan raincoat who seemed to be giving orders to everyone else. The body of the woman with straw-colored hair was still there.

Later in the day, the man in the raincoat appeared in our office and asked if anyone had been working late the night before.

"Harkavy," someone said, "weren't you here last night?"

The detective approached me. He was still wearing his raincoat over a jacket and a shirt. He had removed his tie and I could see a rivulet of sweat in his neck when he swallowed. He had a long, plain, weather-beaten face, no forehead, and a pointy chin, with deep pouches under his eyes.

"I'm Detective Bowman," he said. His eyes flickered over me with contempt as if he wasn't sure whether I was an object worthy of his time and attention. He was probably wondering why anyone would want to spend their life working in an office like this one. "Were you here when it happened?" he finally asked.

Everyone in the office stopped what they were doing.

"Yes, I was here," I said. "And yes, I saw the murder."

The detective's features sharpened when he heard my words and a muscle twitched beneath the flesh of his right cheek. He blinked rapidly and turned in a half circle, not certain whether asking me these questions was appropriate in front of a large audience. It occurred to me, as well, that whatever I told him should be done in private.

"Is there a place where we can talk?" the detective asked, turning to the office manager, Ms. Kuten, an impatient blonde who was wearing a tight flannel skirt and a white round-neck blouse and who rumor had it was having an affair with Mr. Elkin, our boss. She led us down a corridor, her high heels making scraping noises on the tiles, and it was hard not to be aware of the movement of her hips accentuated by the tightness of the skirt as she bent at the waist to open the door of an office with a key. The key was one of several on a large silver ring and she had to try three of them before she found the one that worked.

I had never been in this room before. It was the conference room where the president and the vice presidents met to make decisions and where they entertained guests. The walls were covered by a gallery of portraits—paintings of the founder of the company and his children. The detective and I sat at the end of a long, narrow table and I told him everything I had seen the night before. He took out a pad and a ballpoint pen and scribbled as I talked, occasionally asking me to backtrack and repeat something I had already said.

First, of course, he asked me my name and address and how long I had been working at the company. He asked me if I was married though I'm not sure why that was relevant. I was tempted to tell him about Jill, as if my relationship with her was the equivalent of being married, in which case we would be divorced by now, but I didn't say anything, and I realized that I was still clinging to some hope that we'd get back together. I thought about her every day, often for long periods of time, and it was torture to lie awake every night and think of her sleeping with someone else behind the wall that separated our two apartments. One reason I didn't mind working late was because it was preferable to being in my apartment, where everything reminded me of her. It had been a year since we had broken up—since she had knocked on my door late one evening and told me she was in love with someone else—and I hadn't slept with anyone else since. All my friends advised me to move out but it wasn't easy to find an apartment. And I knew that once I moved out it meant the end of everything.

The detective wasn't interested in any of this and I had the good sense not to mention it. For a moment I had the feeling we were like characters in a movie. In every movie there are scenes like this. The witness to a crime is questioned by a detective. Usually it takes place in a police station. Would you like some coffee? the detective asks. There's always a second detective present who leaves the room for a moment and then returns with the coffee in a Styrofoam cup. The so-called witness takes a sip of black coffee and grimaces. "This tastes like shit," he says. In most cases, the person being interrogated is a suspect in the crime, but that wasn't true about me, as least as

far as I know. The detective asked me questions and wrote down the answers. I noticed he was left-handed and I was tempted to say, "My wife is left-handed," but I have no wife, even though when Jill and I were together we would occasionally argue in public and our friends would remark that we were like an old married couple when in fact we'd only known each other a few months. Finally, after the detective was satisfied with my personal information, he asked me to tell him what happened that night. What I saw from the window when I was working late.

It must have been about nine o'clock, I said, when I looked up from my computer and stared at the building across the street, at the office directly opposite mine where two people, a man and a woman, were working. The detective looked up from his pad and asked if I had ever seen these people before and I said of course, on every night that I worked late they seemed to work late as well. For all I know they worked late every night. Then the detective asked if we could smoke in the conference room and I told him not usually but since I wanted a cigarette as well we could make an exception—and I realized that when I said "we" I was talking for the whole company, the presidents and the vice presidents and the founder whose dour face stared down at us from the wall. So I found a glass ashtray in the closet that looked like it had been stolen from the lobby of a hotel and we sat down again and lit cigarettes. He took off his raincoat and wiped his forehead and neck with a handkerchief.

"Tell me everything," he said. "From start to finish."

I said that I'd try, but that there wasn't really much to say, that it all happened very quickly. At one point he asked me whether I wore glasses or contact lenses and I smiled and told him that my eyesight was perfect, twenty-twenty, that I'd recently had my eyes checked and that nothing had changed. You're lucky, the detective said, blowing smoke through his nostrils. There were no windows in the conference room, which resembled a kind of bunker, and the smoke drifted upward to the ceiling and hovered in the air like a layer of fog.

I told him how the man had approached the woman's desk, how he leaned forward to kiss her and how receptive she had been at first, even going so far as to unbutton her blouse and reach behind her back to unfasten her bra so that in a matter of moments he had pressed his lips to her shoulders and breasts, while with his other hand he tried to reach under her skirt. It was she who seemed to be leading him on, whispering in his ear, though of course I couldn't tell. I didn't say that to the detective but it seemed like she was as interested in having sex as the man, and that it was only when they were on the floor of the office and he was on top of her and began to unfasten his pants that she seemed to have a change of heart and pushed him away. It was then that the trouble started: first she slapped his face, then he ripped off a strip of her blouse and gagged her and tied her up. Finally, when she tried to break free, he smashed her over the head with a lamp. I told the detective that after he had hit the woman several times the man looked around him as if he was suddenly aware of what he had done and that he seemed to be look-ing directly at me, from his window into mine. I told the detective that once he started beating up the woman I had the thought of turn-ing off the light in my office so he couldn't see me, but that I was too mesmerized to do anything. The detective made me tell the story again and by the time I was through we had both smoked another cigarette.

There were certain things I remembered the second time around: how when the man tried to force her to have sex she had grabbed his hand and bitten into it. And how, on the other nights, I had seen the same couple have sex leaning up against one of the desks. The detec-tive put down his pen and looked directly at me when I told him this. You mean they fucked in the office? he said. He made me tell him about all the nights that I had watched the couple in the office. I told him I wasn't sure how many times I had seen this happen. Did it always happen? the detective wanted to know. He was giving me that weird look again and I knew what was coming: he was thinking that it was me, that I was making it all up, that somehow I had com-mitted the murder, that he would get a subpoena to search my desk. What a joke, I thought. So what if the couple had sex in the office and so what if I watched? There were people who liked being watched when they were having sex. There were husbands who liked watch-ing their wives have sex with other men. Who knows what people want? There was a rumor that Ms. Kuten, the office manager, and Mr. Elkin, the president, had sex in his office every morning. It was understandable. People who coexisted in a small space day after day invariably became attracted to one another. It made sense, especial-ly if you were working late.

"And what happened when he persisted?" the detective asked.

"He tried to force her and she slapped his face. That's how it all started."

When I finished telling the story the second time the detective stared at the words he had written on the pad and nodded in my direction. He looked like he was squinting and I wondered if he had gotten any sleep the night before. He put his hand in front of his face as if he was stifling a yawn.

"And then what?" he said.

I wasn't sure what he meant.

"What did you do after he killed the woman?"

"I went home," I said.

"Let me get this straight," the detective said. "You were working late, you looked up from your work, you saw this man and this woman having sex, you saw the man hit the woman over the head with a lamp, you saw the man leave the office, then you left your office and went home, and you didn't notify the police."

"That's right," I said.

"You didn't call up a friend and talk about what you had seen?"

"I went home, I had a drink, I read a book, I went to sleep."

"You saw a crime committed and you didn't notify the police. Doesn't that seem odd to you?"

"It seemed like none of my business, that there was nothing I could do about it."

"But he's gone. The man who works in the office is gone. No one knows where he is. And the woman is dead."

"And if I had called the police last night they would have found him? Is that what you're saying?"

The detective stared at me as if I had committed a crime worse than the man in the office.

"We live in the world," the detective said, shaking his head. "We all live in the same world. If we see someone in danger we try to protect that person. If we can't do it by ourselves, we call the police. Since you weren't in the office with the woman there was nothing you could do to save her but you had to tell the police afterward. It's your duty. . . ."

Everything the detective said was true. I wanted to explain why I had never even thought of calling the police, but I couldn't. All I could say was that after the man left the office I closed down my computer and went home. I took the subway home, as always, the number 1 train to the west side. It's two blocks from the train station to my building and I didn't see anyone I knew; nor did I see any of my neighbors as I walked up the four flights of stairs. I do know, at that point, I was thinking about Jill, and it's true that if I had met Jill on the staircase or in the lobby I would have been tempted to tell her what I had seen. Just like in the old days when I returned home from work and we sat on the sofa in the living room and told each other everything we had done in the time we were apart. But that was over; all my so-called friends tell me I have to face the fact that my relationship with Jill is over. I always pause for a moment on the landing and listen for the sound of voices from behind Jill's door, or the sound of music, but last night I heard nothing. I opened the door of my apartment, went to the kitchen, and poured myself a drink (Dewar's with ice) and went to the living room to check my phone messages.

There was a message from my father, who lives in San Francisco. He was calling to tell me that he was getting remarried in a few months to a woman named Diana Curley, whom he had mentioned in a previous phone call but whom I had never met. He gave me the exact date and time of the wedding, which was going to take place in the backyard of a friend's house in a town up the coast, and said he hoped I would be able to attend. "You'll like Diana a lot," he said, and hung up.

My father is a painter and teaches painting and drawing at the San Francisco Art Institute and periodically he falls in love with one of his students. But this is the first time, as far as I know, that he was going to marry one of them. My parents split up when I was eight, and my mother, who never remarried, lives alone in Florence. My mother is an art historian and an authority on fifteenth-century Italian art, especially Fra Angelico, about whom she has written numerous articles and a monograph. She used to teach but now she spends most of her time writing and traveling. I see my parents whenever they're in New York and once a year I travel to San Francisco and Florence to visit with them. I'm not sure why my parents split up, since on the surface they have many interests in common, and like many children I somehow think that my presence in their life was the cause of what happened, that somehow I altered the equilibrium of their lives in a way that made it impossible for them to go on. After they split up, I lived with my mother in New York and spent the summers in San Francisco with my father but that schedule ended once I entered college. Then I saw them more sporadically as I tried to make a life of my own.

"I don't want you to leave town," the exhausted detective said. He stood up, carrying his raincoat over his arm. "I have a feeling we're going to want to talk to you again."

"I'm not going anywhere," I said. "You can call me anytime."

It was only ten in the morning and there was a whole day of work ahead. Everyone in the office looked up when I returned with the detective and after he left they surrounded my desk, anxious for a firsthand report.

"They work at Jenson & Jenson," someone said.

"I once had lunch with that guy."

"How many times did he hit her?"

"They were having an affair, everyone knew it, it's been going on for years."

The conversation swirled around me. I had been working in the office for five years but I wasn't friends with any of my coworkers. I had no enemies either. I make a point of trying to get along with as many different types of people as possible. I try not to gossip, even though I know that gossip is the lifeblood of places like this. Can I say honestly that no one is working in this office because they want to? I think that must be correct. I know that Jill often admonished me for not working at a job that had some value in the world. She couldn't understand why I was wasting my life away. That I had settled for being a cog, an underling. I always had the thought that one of the reasons she ended the relationship is because she wanted to be with someone who was more ambitious, who made things happen. I could tell when she introduced me to her friends that she lowered her eyes as if she was embarrassed. She was a year or two away from getting her PhD and had already started teaching and a lot of our social life involved hanging around with her graduate-school friends. I would sit for hours in restaurants and cafés listening to them talking about professors I didn't know and books I hadn't read. When Jill asked me, as she did on occasion, what I liked about her, what I said was that I liked the nights we spent alone, having sex, eating dinner, watching movies together. Even more than doing these things was the pleasure of anticipating them. It made the day bearable, it made me smile to myself just thinking about things she did or said. Sometimes I would turn on my computer and stare at the screen but really I was in a different world. I would think of the times when I would open the door of her apartment with the key she had given me and she would be lying in bed naked. I would remember the expression on her face when we were having sex and how it seemed like she was about to burst into tears as she passed over the edge and then the expression of utter relief and contentment when she came back to life. The few hours we spent together every day made all the difference. The last few months we were together she often had to go to class at night and wouldn't get home till midnight or later. She would explain that she liked to hang out with her graduate-school friends at a café near the campus but I know now it was because she was fucking someone else.

Shortly after noon Ms. Kuten called me into her office and asked me to tell her what I had seen the night before. I don't know why I had to repeat it all again but she said something about "company policy" and that we all had to be "on the same page." She was only a few years older than I was but she made me feel like a child. She reminded me of Ms. Brill, my teacher in third grade, who would lean very close to me so that it seemed like her perfumed breasts would swallow me up, that I could crawl between the buttons on the front of her blouse and disappear. There was something about being with Ms. Kuten, whose first name I knew was Linda, that blurred the boundaries between what might be permitted and what was forbidden. Maybe it had to do with the way she pushed the hair out of her eyes or crossed her legs and adjusted the hem of her skirt over her knees. She looked at me as if witnessing a murder made me more interesting because the details surrounding the murder itself were interesting. I knew that she wanted me to tell her about the sex part, the torn blouse, the way the man began unbuckling his pants and then the woman stopped him. Everything I told the detective twice I told her again until I got tired of hearing the sound of my own voice. What I noticed was her smile as the narrative unfolded. She never said anything, never prompted me when I lost the thread of what I was saying. Every time I paused to get my bearings her smile became brighter and more encouraging. I had the feeling that the words were titillating her in some way and when I came to the part about the torn blouse her eyes glazed over. I tried my best to keep it all to a minimum. She could add any embellishments she wanted on her own time for all I cared. She could think about it all in the privacy of her bedroom, if that's what she wanted. I let my eyes flicker over her body as I talked. We had never been together in an office before. We had never been alone. On the wall behind her desk there was a poster of a woman in a bikini emerging from the ocean and the words COME TO MAUI in big letters. There was a fishing boat on the horizon and a young man carrying a surfboard under his arm. The waves rolled peacefully into the shore. Jill and I had once talked about going to Hawaii for a vacation, but our schedules never coincided. She wanted to learn how to scuba dive and Maui was apparently as good a place as any.

I wondered if Ms. Kuten and the president of the company, Mr.

Elkin, were still having an affair. Whether they met secretly in places like Maui or San Juan. He was an imposing figure, about six and a half feet tall, with long sideburns and thick, rugged skin. It wasn't difficult to imagine her leaning over the desk in his office while the man lifted her skirt and came inside her. Jill and I once rented a porno movie where things like that happened. In the movie, which was not very well made, there was a secretary hiding beneath a desk giving her boss a blow job. This scene went on forever, long past the time when it might have provided any excitement. Someone came into the office to talk with the boss and the woman beneath the desk continued doing what she was doing. Then there was the conference room like the one I had just been in with Detective Bowman where people did various things to one another and in different combinations on tables and chairs. We wanted to have sex while watching the movie but it was so bad we realized we didn't need it and turned it off. I was tired and my mind was free-associating in a million directions when I realized that there was nothing more to talk about but that Ms. Kuten didn't seem like she was anxious for me to leave her office. I'm sure she wouldn't have minded if I had gotten down on my knees and buried my head between her legs, but it never happened.

I worked until seven and took the train home. I bought a salad at a new gourmet market that had opened recently on Fifteenth Street. I sat at the small dining-room table in the alcove near the kitchen, big enough for two people, and drank a bottle of beer and listened to the radio. They were playing some songs from the 1960s that I liked. Songs by English groups like Cream and Procol Harum and Traffic. I knew more about music that had been popular before I was born than the music that was popular now. It was dark out and the sky was purplish and a few airplanes flew low over the river on their way to Newark Airport. I thought if I could make my mind go blank for a few minutes that I would feel better and the static in my head would begin to fade. The person I was thinking about most was Linda Kuten. I had seen her later in the day and she had smiled at me as if we had something in common and I had been tempted to go back to her office just to see what would happen. What I wanted was for her to call me up and come over as quickly as possible. "I was in the neighborhood," she would say, as if she needed a reason. The idea of me calling *her* up, on the other hand, was out of the question.

A half hour later someone was knocking on the door, and when I opened it without asking who was there it turned out to be Jill. I hadn't seen her much in the last few weeks and in the dim hallway light I thought she looked tired. She always stayed up half the night reading and the circles under her eyes seemed even more pronounced. Her hair was tied back with a green ribbon and looked lighter than I remembered. Maybe she was tinting it as some women do when they grow older but Jill wasn't exactly old. She was wearing a blue T-shirt turned inside out and a short denim skirt, no jewelry except for a string of beads, and no makeup. She was carrying four or five paperbacks in one arm, hugging them close to her chest.

"I've been cleaning up and I found these books. I think they're yours."

She didn't say, "How are you?" or "How've you been?" but she didn't seem particularly hostile either, just matter-of-fact. The words meant what they meant. Here are your books, do you want them? They were some Penguin classics that I would sometimes read before going to bed on those nights I stayed over in her apartment. Boccaccio's *Decameron*, Henry James's *Portrait of a Lady*, Balzac's *Père Goriot*, and *Villette* by Charlotte Brontë. As I took the books from her hands and looked at the titles, the essence of each of them came back to me and I realized that these books would now become more meaningful by the fact that they were associated with this moment.

"Do you want to come in?" I asked.

She stepped tentatively over the threshold but stayed there, looking around at the kitchen and the entrance to the living room.

"I'm really busy right now, Hark, but I just wanted to give you your books back and let you know that I'm moving out tomorrow."

I tried to pretend that it made no difference to me—whether she was there, whether she wasn't there, whether she had a boyfriend, whether we ever saw one another again.

"Where are you moving to?" I asked, as if I was genuinely interested in the problems of relocation. The next thing I knew, if I went down this path, I'd offer to help her pack her things.

"Well, Sven has a new job up in Portland, Maine, so we're going to go there. I'm going to finish my dissertation and he's going to work."

"Sven?"

"This guy I've been seeing. I don't think you ever formally met but I'm sure you've seen him. We once passed each other on the street when I was with him. Don't you remember?"

"Well, that's great," I said, trying to make it sound like I meant it. Did I mean it? "Sven" was like a child's word, a word that a child repeats until it loses its meaning. I had trouble associating Jill with someone named Sven.

"I have some other news too, just wanted to let you know. I'm three months pregnant."

It's true we hadn't talked much in the last year and there was no way she could know all the feelings that I still harbored for her. When we were together we had talked frequently about having a baby and it was she who always said that she wanted to wait until she finished her dissertation and had a teaching job. I'd made it clear from the start that I would be willing to have a child whenever she felt she was ready and that if she didn't want children that was fine with me also. Truthfully, I was deeply ambivalent about my potential talent as a parent, and the idea of moving into an apartment or a house that would accommodate all of us—me, Jill, all the children, and even a dog—made my head spin. My parents weren't people I would ever want to emulate and I thought by doing the opposite of what they did I might actually make a success of it all, whatever that means. But to think that what I wanted was what she wanted was enough. It gave me comfort that I could put her needs above my own. It made me think that anything was possible.

I felt dizzy, for a moment, wanted to sit down or hold on to something. I felt like I had something lodged in my throat. Jill's matter-of-factness was one of the reasons I had fallen in love with her, it was so much the opposite of how I was. I was the impenetrable one, or so she had often told me, the person with secrets who never said what he was thinking.

"I'm going to have a baby and write my dissertation and live in the woods," she said. It occurred to me that this might be the last time we ever saw one another. I put the books down on a table in the foyer and stared at my feet.

"Aren't you going to wish me luck?" she asked.

"Luck is important," I said. And she put her hand on my arm.

"I try to have good memories of you, you know? Of us. I know I hurt your feelings but things like that happen every day. Things happen." And then: "Are you seeing anyone?"

"I'm thinking of going back to school myself," I said.

"That's a great idea. I always think you underestimate yourself—how much you know about everything. I sometimes hear you leave the apartment in the morning and I think about your job, the same job, he's going to the same job. And it seems like you can do better. And then at night—I hear you come home at night—eight or nine, or even later. And I wonder why you care so much about your job that you'd work until late at night. Why it's all so important."

"It's not that it's important," I said, wanting to tell her about the nights that I'd heard *her* come home, from wherever she was with this person named Sven, their laughter in the hallway, and how I used to press my ear to the wall that separated our two apartments, my kitchen wall, in an attempt to hear what they were saying. "It's just what I do."

"Tomorrow the movers are coming and then the next day we're flying to Norway to meet Sven's parents."

I had the odd thought that we could have sex one last time, that that was the real reason she had come to see me. Returning the books was just a pretense. But to think something might be true doesn't mean you can assume it's true, or that something might be more true, or less, or that your instincts are correct, or if you act one way and not another everything would be different, and if you don't act at all you miss out on everything. Better to have loved and lost and all that crap made some sense but I rejected it, I wanted to trample on the fucking words that were all in my head. It was like there was this wall inside me and on either side of it there was turbulence and static and there was a rift in the sky that was like a dividing line and I was on one side and Jill was on the other. And for a moment I was frightened. When she moved out of the apartment for good it meant I was alone, I was really alone.

I put out my hand and touched the side of her face and I realized that wasn't what she wanted at all. Her skin was icy and she moved her head away.

"I'll be in touch," she said. Touch. That's what I had tried to do and it didn't matter.

She backed out of the door into the hallway, but I couldn't look up. I knew she was looking at me but I felt lacking in kindness, the reservoir of kindness if it ever existed at all had dried up. I had the feeling that if I looked back she would interpret it as an agreement that no matter what happened between us we were going to wish each other well. There was a long life up ahead and who knows what might happen and we had fun together and now let's be decent, let's say goodbye like decent people, let's not hold any grudges. The problem with this way of thinking was that she had hurt me, she had left me, she had been sleeping with someone else at the same time she had been sleeping with me, she had lied to me for how long I don't know, and the good question was why I didn't hate her, why I wasn't consumed with anger, that's what my friends wanted to know, why I could actually say as I once told my friend Mark, my gay friend Mark who's had a complicated love life himself, who's been around the block a few times, how I could actually say to him that no matter what Jill did and how often she lied to me I was still in love with her, and that none of this mattered. She wanted me to look back at her so she didn't have to feel guilty but I have a feeling she was past that state, that the question of innocence or guilt was no longer relevant for her. She was caught up in her new life, there was Sven and the baby, and she didn't waste her time staring into space thinking about what might have happened if she had stayed with me. She didn't suffer because of me, or relive our past, or feel nostalgia for the nights in front of the DVD and the sex, the porno movie about the office, all that shit that keeps circling around in my head all the time like a fucking Ferris wheel in some small-town amusement park that my parents took me to when I was a kid, all the blur of lights and the vertigo when you reach the top and look down and look up and there's the moon and the belly of a blimp hovering in the sky. She didn't want to be back there in the dark, having sex in front of the movie. But I don't think she felt guilty about anything. My father had been married before he met my mother and now he was marrying someone else. And my mother seemed to have given up on ever living with anyone again. She was comfortable with her peripatetic life, with her solitude. People recovered from separation even though sometimes it feels like death. It means that the person you were so close to is no longer in your life, that this person might as well be dead. I'd been in mourning for a year now but the idea that Jill was leaving raised it all to some new level. There was no longer the possibility of fantasizing about some future where she would have a change of heart and come crawling back. I don't mean that she'd have to come crawling back. All she had to do was show some interest in getting back together and I would do the rest.

I was glad when she closed the door so I could ease myself down on the chair in the kitchen, at the table near the window, and light a cigarette. The table was empty except for some menus that had been slipped under the door. If she stayed a moment longer I'm not sure what might have happened. I felt like I was on the verge of losing control and that at a certain moment I would no longer be responsible for my actions. I felt like going into the hallway and pounding on her door. I didn't care if the neighbors called the police. I could take a kitchen knife with me and when Sven opened the door I could plunge it into his chest. This was the last time I would be able to play out this kind of scenario in my head. Tomorrow the apartment next door would be empty.

Slowly I began to drift away from myself, from the dead self with its self-inflicted wounds, and I tried to remember the person I was before I met Jill two years ago. We had been living next door to one another for over a year before we met. It was she who made the first move. We were standing outside the building—she was going out, I was coming in—when she invited me for a drink later in the evening. I remember that she was wearing a big floppy hat and that her upper arms were as thin as a child's. Her invitation took me by surprise, I must admit, and since I was already going out with someone else at the time, a woman from the office named Rita, I wondered whether going to Jill's apartment was a good idea. As it turned out, within an hour after I entered the apartment we were in bed together. It had felt like the natural thing to do and our bodies seemed to connect in a way that made sense. That next afternoon, at lunch, I broke the news to Rita. We were sitting in a French restaurant around the corner from our office when I told her that I had met someone else, that I had fallen in love with someone else, though that was hardly the truth even though I could see it happening, I could see into the future where love might be possible between me and Jill where with Rita it was mostly sex and a bit of love. She was certainly someone I respected and sometimes when we were both working late we would have sex in the supply room, amid the boxes of staples and file folders. "You can't do that" was what she said when I told her I was breaking up with her. She was holding a glass in her hand and I had the feeling she was going to smash it in my face. "I'm going to kill myself," she said. "I'm going to fucking decapitate myself. Just you watch."

There were other women in my life before Rita. I thought of their names: Ronnie, Yvette, Cassandra, and Beverly. I thought of each of them separately and wondered what they were doing. I had heard that Cassandra was in rehab because she had overdosed on heroin but I don't think it was because of anything I had done. I wondered what Rita was up to and what she would say if I called her up and asked her out for a drink. Casually, as if nothing had ever happened. I know for a fact that she didn't kill herself after I told her it was over and I have a feeling she's probably married and living in some place like Connecticut or northern California. Once, when we were in bed together, she broached the subject of marriage, but I think she wanted to marry someone who had more money than I did. I certainly had nothing to lose by calling her up.

I sat at the window smoking and looking out at the building across the street. One of the windows was lit, and a tall, young, blonde woman was standing in front of a full-length mirror. I had seen her before, on other nights when I returned home late from work. I liked sitting in the kitchen, reading the newspaper while waiting for water to boil for coffee. On some nights, like tonight, I just liked to smoke and look out at it all. I had seen the blonde woman before. Most of the time she was accompanied by a young man who was obviously her boyfriend. They would enter the bedroom together, often late at night, and I had the feeling that they were both coming home from work, that possibly they both worked in the same office. Maybe they worked in different offices and met for late dinner when work was over. Sometimes, when I left for work in the morning, I would see them emerge from the entrance of the building across the street, holding hands, the woman with her blonde hair piled on top of her head or braided or just hanging loosely down her back, the young man with his fuzzy beard and dark-rimmed glasses. They looked like they had just stepped out of the pages of a fashion magazine, one of those glossy magazines that Rita used to read and that always smelled like perfume. Tonight the woman was alone, at least for the moment. She stared at herself critically in the mirror and lifted her hands to her hair and began to unfasten the ribbon that held it in place, and when she lifted her arms I could see her breasts swell against the cotton material of her dress. She reached behind her, and with her back to me, began to unzip her dress, and then she stepped out of it slowly and turned to face me. For a moment I had the feeling that she knew I was watching, and that she was taking off her clothing for my pleasure alone. But then, as if an invisible hand had turned off the switch, the window went dark.

281

Stamina

Michael White

I FIRST MET PARK TAE-WON on a rainy Saturday at a public bath in Busan. The place reeked of mildew and the floor was slick. There was a hot bath and a cold bath and foolish cackles of old women echoed through the wall. Tae-won, my girlfriend's brother, was the only one there. He was naked on a stool, hunched over, just staring off into space.

I didn't know much about Tae-won, only that he was rumored to be a cheat at cards, and during the months preceding the presidential election, he referred to himself as the Fourth Candidate. I discovered for myself that he had only one testicle. Judging by the way he squared up to me, it was a testicle of some pride. I bowed and introduced myself and got hit by a cold bead of water that fell from the ceiling.

First thing, he handed me his bath brush and plopped down so I could scrub his back. Considering his family's inferior social status, Tae-won's arrogance was something of a miracle. The last person whose back I'd washed had been my father when I was about eight years old. But Jung-yung insisted on her brother's approval, so I didn't have much of a choice. As I scrubbed away I thought, I knew this meeting would be a total disaster, though I never expected the guy was short a testicle. A huge head to boot. It must have weighed twice mine.

He didn't say a word until I rinsed him off and followed him to the cold bath. I hate cold baths, and the manner of that lopsided testicle, like an unwanted guest lounging in his sack, put me in a funny mood.

"How much *soju* can you drink?" he asked.

"Two bottles," I said. He chuckled and made me feel I should explain. I couldn't decide if he would be more impressed by confidence or humility. In my indecision I ended up sounding like some desperate comedian. "I can drink three bottles if I'm really excited. And if I can get through three then the fourth is easy. But after four, I get sick and my head falls forward and leads me all the ways except the way home. So the answer is two."

Tae-won took a sturdy sniff and pinched his nose. He never took his eyes off me.

"Can you swim?" he asked, as though it were somehow related to *soju* drinking.

"No, but I have a driver's license."

"What's that got to do with swimming?"

"I can't drive either," I said, which confused both of us. I'd recently finished my military service, which had an adverse effect on my sense of humor. My own jokes, in response to such meaningless contests as this one, had become esoteric to the point that their logic eluded even me. I used to be much funnier. You get to carousing with all those army wiseasses and next thing you know, you're one of them.

"I can bench twice my weight," he announced. "What can you bench?"

"Twice my height. I mean, half my height. More than sixty."

"What would you do if you were diagnosed with halitosis?"

"Brush my teeth," I said, feeling I'd dodged a bullet.

Tae-won snorted and tugged on the wooden handle of a metal chain hanging from above. A hard stream of water pounded from a pipe pointing straight out of the ceiling. He stood and let the stream hammer the top of his huge head, which created a circular shield of deflected water.

"Does my sister have any birthmarks?"

"I don't know of any birthmarks or tattoos or anything like that."

"Excuse me? Tattoos?"

"I don't know of any," I said.

"I didn't ask about tattoos because my sister isn't some punk gangster."

"I agree. She doesn't like gangster movies. That would be out of character if she was a gangster."

He snorted again, pulling a hair from his arm, lifting it to the tip of his nose for scrutiny. He looked at me, then the hair, as though the hair and I shared something in common.

"Have you had sexual contact with my weak-ankled, Jesus-loving, fatherless little sister?"

"No."

"How about prostitutes?"

"Never. Once a phone prostitute. Never a real prostitute."

Tae-won reached down near his feet where I presume he released the arm hair. He searched for others. When he found none he dunked himself underwater and then slapped his face a few times.

"What do you want from my sister?"

"I think I'm in love with her. Maybe she'll want to marry me and then we'll both have everything we both want."

"She doesn't talk about you much. How do you know she loves you in return?"

"I don't know," I said. "Maybe she doesn't love me."

I considered whether this was true as Tae-won cupped his testicle and carried it over to the hot bath. Once he got settled he waved me off, ending our meeting and killing my chances of warming up in the hot pool. I gave him a final shivering bow and headed for the locker area, passing the source of the mildew stench, a hamper full of dank scrub towels. I had one foot through the door and was already feeling the warm wind of the ceiling vent when Tae-won grunted in a manner that I took as a command.

"Yes, older brother, sir?"

He stirred the surface of the water, looking up like he'd just balanced his checkbook.

"I'm her older brother. She tells me everything. Don't give her any cutesy nicknames or experimental politics. I also suggest you encourage her investment in my exotic pet shop."

I bowed and stepped out of the bath, trying to pretend that his deranged smirk was congratulatory. It seemed he'd given me permission to date Jung-yung, the best news I could expect, though I felt for a moment that I would never be clean again.

About an hour later, Jung-yung called and asked me to meet her at a cheap motel in Chinatown. Jung-yung had a strange fear related to infertility and a narrow vagina that would not allow passage of an infant. She often coerced me into joining her on gynecologist field trips. It was strange, but sexy. She'd tell the doctors I was her husband and flirt with me in front of the nurses and let me pay. It was how we spent the days we didn't have classes.

When I got to the motel room she was sitting in the center of the bed, her bare legs tucked beneath her, rubbing gently against one another like scissors. She was wearing the sweater. Oftentimes she'd ask me what it was about her that I found attractive and I always thought it was the black fuzzy sweater that held her chest the way a peanut shell holds peanuts. Also, she could speak French. On our first date we saw *Trois Couleurs* at some French cultural society. Over six hours of movies sans subtitles and she didn't explain a word.

After a long, thoughtful stare that I couldn't interpret, that she wanted me to interpret, I shrugged. "What?" I thought. "People have sex all the time. Not like it's going to lead to porno careers or stunt our growth." Her head dropped like that of an unstrung marionette. She whispered something just before she cried. I scooted next to her, placing one hand on her knee, the other behind her rear, and leaned in close.

"What did you say, Jung?"

"If you could only appreciate me, I could be yours."

"I do appreciate you. I see you're wearing the black sweater."

Her head snapped up, her eyes accusing me of something pathetic, making me feel cheap, needy, a burden, a fool, other nasty things. She had the most expressive eyes.

"What can you possibly want from me?"

"To be with you. To love you and have you love me back, forever."

"Anything else?" she asked.

The answer was that I wanted her naked, bouncing, baboon lewd. I puckered my lips, my whole face. I used everything above my toes to loft the words from my tongue to her ears. I'd been secretly studying French for three months.

"*Il n'y a pas une autre femme avec la fusée éclairante de votre esprit, la chaleur de vos lèvres, vos pommes athlétiques. . . .*"

"I don't speak gay," she interrupted. "Is this some mock language to make me feel inferior?"

"It's French. I'm speaking *le français.*"

"I don't speak *le français!*" she yelled, as though she'd never made a statement to the contrary, as though she'd never even heard of France.

"But you lived in France for a year. What were you doing?"

"I worked in a French bakery in Seoul. For one month. It went bankrupt. Besides, the owner tried to molest me."

"Was he French?" I asked.

She kicked her legs out from under her, grabbing the copy of *Sports Seoul* that was folded on the nightstand. She shouted the page number and threw it at my chest, imploring me to read. The article was a coming-out confessional by a twenty-two-year-old student from Busan named Baek Young-min. It was poorly written, full of outdated slang and ridiculous tag questions. "Our civilization can be so uncivilized, can't it?" A couple of paragraphs in, I tossed the paper on the floor. She peered at me with unnerving pity. Baek Young-min is not a common name.

"So what?" I said. "It's obviously not me."

"Yeah, right. Just admit it. It's exactly your style to lie to everyone around you, only to publish in the tabloids. It's humiliating. To think that my first boyfriend has appeared in three daytime dramas."

I couldn't tell if she really thought I'd written the article, or if it was just another excuse to avoid having sex with me.

"He's an extra! I'm going to be an architect!" I paused to lower my tone. "I'm not gay. I just got back from a perturbing meeting with your brother in the cold pool of a shitty public bath, just for you. And by the way, what the hell is his problem?"

"What problem?" she asked.

"There's something very botched-reconnaissance about him."

"He's handicapped, asshole! We're talking about *your* problem."

"I'll show you *my* problem," I argued. "The more you rub your legs together like you're making butter, the more my problem is swelling to the point that soon it'll be screaming at passing traffic."

"Well, I don't sleep with queers. My mother was a runner-up in the Miss Yeosu competition."

Apparently, we weren't holding back.

"Will she have sex with me? What the hell's your point?"

"I'm from good stock."

"What are there, like, seven women in Yeosu? Any girl with an even number of limbs would be a finalist."

"I'm going to tell my brother you said that! And my mother! You're going to die, Young-min! You're gonna die a virgin!"

"Why don't you say that again, in French!"

Her face was inches from mine when she yelled, shaking her head so that her hair covered her eyes, "FAGGOT!"

She grabbed a handful of my bangs and yanked until I was brought to my knees. Then she stormed out the door. I knew there'd be a bill waiting for me at the front desk, so I stayed to watch porn and jerk off. A couple of hours later I woke to a phone call from my design partner. He informed me that Jung-yung had made copies of the *Sports Seoul* article and was posting them around campus, that I was becoming a real sensation. Then I got a call from Tae-won, requesting another meeting, this time at his apartment near Gwangali beach.

Tae-won lived in one of those enormous high-rise complexes developed by the LG company. How those apartments ever became status symbols, I'll never know, but they were all painted pink and you couldn't tell one building from the other. I told him I'd be there around ten the next morning. Then I started chapter one of *Three Kingdoms*, which I've always wanted to read and bought one ambitious day the previous spring. Turns out, I couldn't get past the third page.

At nine thirty the next morning, the subway ticket machine rejected my commuter's pass. I was supposed to have unlimited rides. Despite the fact that a round trip only cost seven hundred won, I refused to pay twice and resigned myself to walking. Back on the street the sun was covered by a cheap blue smog.

I walked along the harbor, feeling like absolute shit, pondering Jung-yung's anxieties about giving birth. My new theory was that as a child, she'd gotten stuck in a narrow tunnel she thought was part of the playground but was really designed for trapping squirrels. I found myself dragging my feet and kicking trash and people started to look at me like I was drunk. My only respite was that Tae-won hadn't requested that we meet at the public bath again. I'd been massacring myself with masturbation and had really torn it up in the motel room.

It was a long hike. While walking past the office of the *Kookje Daily*, I considered going inside to piss on the desk of the editor, in my mind the proxy of those jerks in Seoul. I considered suing them for punitive damages, but *Sports Seoul* was a notorious tabloid, they probably had lawyers out the ass. The bigger question was why the article had been written in the first place. Was there really a homosexual hack named Baek Young-min? Was there someone interested in Jung-yung who was trying to discredit me?

I was an hour and a half late arriving at Tae-won's complex. On the thirty-second floor there was a note on the door instructing me to meet him on the roof. Feeling sort of masochistic, I passed the elevator and went the final fifteen floors on foot.

The roof was covered with small white rocks and offered an outstanding view of the sea. I wanted to smoke, but Tae-won was a few years older than I and I didn't need to start another meeting on the wrong foot. I walked the perimeter of the roof, palming the cigarette pack in my pocket and half expecting him to jump out from some hiding position to scare me. After a while, despite my fear of heights, I felt compelled to peek over the ledge. I wasn't particularly interested in the view, but was overwhelmed by thoughts of Jung-yung taunting me, calling me a wimp. I had to defy her.

I stretched my neck over the side. The waves rolled back and forth, so much nothing between me and the parking lot, the air so light and

287

heavenly; I almost puked. There was a noise like a branch snapping and I thought that was it, the cement wall was actually made of cheap plaster, and Jung-yung's death wish for me was coming true. But the sound came from higher up.

"Older brother?"

"You're late, grunt!" he yelled.

His big head peeped out from the structure above the staircase, another fifteen feet higher on the antenna deck. He gave a two-finger motion to the side of the deck that faced the city.

I was not excited about climbing the rungs, I was petrified really, but then there were several loud pops and I felt a sharp sting on the back of my neck. A barrage of pellets, obviously arriving from another building, bounced off the walls and fell to the roof beneath me. Automatic weaponry sounded from the deck above and I scrambled up the rungs, my vertigo supplanted by the greater fear of losing an eye. At the top, Tae-won grabbed the back of my shirt and dragged me onto the rubble. His rifle was strapped to his shoulder. I put a finger to the back of my neck and it came back wet with a spot of blood. I thought, shit like this just doesn't happen to people who have sex.

Tae-won saw the blood but dismissed it, lying down flat and licking his finger and wiping a smudge from the barrel. I saw boys' heads popping up and down from the roof of a building on the other side of the park. Four of them jumped to their feet, trash-can lids like shields in their left hands, pellet pistols in their right. They let off a few rounds and then ducked out of sight.

"Gutsy little beasts, aren't they? You shouldn't have been late."

I lay down next to him.

"I had a problem with . . . my commuter . . . you know, that really hurt."

"Got this piece airmailed from Israel," he said, fingering the butt. "Semiautomatic."

He flipped open the loading port and poured in yellow pellets until they started to spill over. Then he ducked down into the scope and fired. There was a frightening yelp and then an ensuing barrage of juvenile profanity. The opposition couldn't have been older than twelve. Tae-won stood up and shook his gun in the air, his legs apart, his pelvis thrust forward. He heckled with teeth clenched, "You boys need to spend more time at the range!"

A skinny arm popped up, waving a white T-shirt. Tae-won scoped it, shot it out of the boy's hand. I thought I heard sobs, but I couldn't

288

exactly tell. Tae-won was really happy with himself.

"They're pretty fucking brave. Taunting me from their windows as I pass through the parking lot. Think they can embarrass me. Fucking beasts think they know everything."

We lay on our backs a good twenty minutes waiting for retaliation. Tae-won smoked, probably guessing that I wanted to join him, but not offering. He eventually produced a copy of *Sports Seoul* he'd folded up in his jacket pocket. I didn't say a word. The thought crossed my mind that I'd never get back down. I asked myself what had happened to Tae-won to rob him of his senses and could only guess it had to do with his time in the army. I'd heard he'd done a short stint and could very well have been discharged for being nuts. But I hadn't known him back then so it was impossible to say. Regardless, judging by his brute intonation, the imported pellet rifle, the one testicle—I kept thinking, had to be the army.

"How much money do architects get?" he asked, as though the answer were pertinent to his battle strategy.

"The famous ones are rich. Like the guy who'll be designing the new Lotte Tower. It's going to be the tallest building in Asia."

"I don't go for that macho communist shit."

"But it really will be the tallest . . ."

"Like Kim Jong-il with his biggest stadium in the world, except no one fucking plays there. His world's tallest hotel, which is always empty. And his arch that's bigger than the one in France, except without the tourists. What the hell does Busan need with the tallest building in Asia?"

He had a point. I'd often wondered if the developer was chasing a record at the expense of a city that would have the tallest building in Asia but one hell of an awkward skyline with only one skyscraper.

"I've got a date tonight. I could get a date for you too if you weren't so twisted up on my sister. I'm talking about a couple of hot sluts who know how to party. You've probably got plans, huh?"

I told him I had work to do but thanked him for the invitation. He peered into the scope, perfectly still, aiming into the clouds. He shot off three rounds.

"Super . . . hot . . . sluts."

The boys must have run out of ammunition because their last effort was to throw handfuls of gravel without standing up and risking being shot. The gravel hailed onto the playground equipment and sidewalks in the middle of the park. When we heard the sound of the storm door on the opposite roof closing, Tae-won assumed victory.

He then explained to me the sort of places I ought to design, like nightclubs with shark tanks and synchronized swimmers. An hour later I tactfully reminded him of my obligations on campus and was dismissed in time to find fresh photocopies of the *Sports Seoul* article all over the walls of the recreation building, pegged to the bulletin boards in the snack center, and on the doors of the architecture building, where my name was most known. I tore down as many as I could, but quit after an hour when I was too depressed to care. How did I get involved with this girl, I asked myself, unable to imagine a normal life with her.

I skipped my classes the next day and went to Jung-yung's apartment, knowing that her mother had already left for the hair shop. I'd never met her mother, but considered going to the shop where she worked in order to make a judgment about what Jung-yung might look like in twenty years. It also seemed to me that when a woman rubs her hands through your hair, you get to know her in a way that you could never achieve through conversation. But Jung-yung's mother got the job through a friend, after her father's heart attack, and I didn't want to risk getting a botched haircut. Jung-yung answered the door and let me in, smiling pleasantly, like nothing at all had happened. She led me out to the balcony. There weren't any clothes hanging on the line, which meant we could smoke.

"How was the meeting with my brother? He said you two were going to have lunch together."

"Yeah. We didn't have lunch. You know, I'm really starting to like him. I wouldn't say we're friends quite yet, but perhaps after a few more meetings, we'll stop calling them meetings and it will be just like hanging out."

I loved the way she smoked. She'd bite the filter and just let the smoke waft up her cheeks and into her eyes. Smoke didn't bother her.

"Maybe he does like you. He's never said that, but I'll bet if you wanted a job, after he opens his pet shop, he'd probably hire you."

I nodded, thinking most girls would love to date a future architect, but the girl I love wants me to work in her brother's pet shop.

"I think it would be best if instead of fighting next time, we just took off our clothes and really let it out. This isn't just about me being a virgin and not being able to sleep at night. I really think we should be touching and maybe even shoving one another around, instead of just shouting insults. I don't really like the shouting."

Jung-yung thought about it for some time, then smirked at me, I

290

suppose thinking about all the photocopies she'd made. For a girl who never had money, she must have spent a small fortune.

"OK," she finally said, butting her head into my shoulder. "But I'm only conceding because after that article, you know, I'm not expecting much. And you might find me a bit more agreeable than usual, if this is going to be the deal."

"That could be interesting too." I laughed, guessing that her warped vision of agreeableness would probably entail niceties like shouting people out of their seats on the subway so I could sit. "No matter how angry," I pressed. "A deal's a deal?"

She stubbed out her smoke and bowed theatrically. I left the apartment feeling less virginal than when I had entered. I started considering additions to my nightly push-up regimen in order to step up preparations for my impending sexual debut.

A lot of guys who believe in the power of stamina foods will load up for two or three weeks before their wedding night. That night I went to a dog restaurant in Seomyeon, feeling part of a secret society. The place reeked of *soju* and mint. The *ajummas* got a real kick out of me, an anachronism in a place for the older generation, and coddled me like some foreigner who couldn't speak the language. They mixed in a few spoonfuls of parilla and delighted when I swallowed the first bite. It was succulent, tender, and lean. I told my mom I had team meetings throughout the week so that I could return for dinner the next several evenings. For her part, at my request, she cooked loach soup several mornings for breakfast. My father was touched when I offered to treat him for lunch at an eel restaurant. They must have figured something was up. I'd never been such a vigorous eater, but I told them I was considering trying out for the basketball team. They assumed I needed to bulk up.

I ate nothing but stamina foods the whole week and was forced to put off a meeting with Tae-won so I could make a trip to the Gupo market to get ginseng and boiled silkworms. I even raced around my apartment on my hands and knees in order to build calluses for sex that would potentially involve a floor routine. I forced myself to eat two bowls of rice with each meal and started jogging everywhere I went, even if I was just going from one classroom to another. The word stamina echoed in my mind, became my mantra. One night, I dreamed that I banged both of us right through our motel-room floor.

During my stamina week, Tae-won kept calling and I kept ignoring him. He'd leave messages that detailed his recent problems with the kids in the neighborhood. He even got sentimental a few times, once telling me he'd seen a sad movie and wanted to talk about it. Honestly, I blew him off. If Jung-yung got mad at me, I figured, even better. Hanging out with that guy, sooner or later I'd end up arrested or lose a testicle. I was beginning to feel like the older brother and considered making an effort to help him. One day he called twelve times and when I called him back he screamed at me, raging about the neighborhood kids having painted a red one-testicled scrotum on his door. There was no way to calm him down. He insisted I come to his apartment right away to help plot his revenge, but I really wasn't interested and gave him the standard excuse.

The next time I went to campus all the photocopies of the *Sports Seoul* article were gone. I guessed Jung-yung had removed the ones I hadn't gotten. People around the architecture building had been giving me funny looks, but I was too wrapped up in my stamina project to be offended. I didn't see Jung-yung until the weekend, when I assumed we'd hit up a few gynecology clinics. It had been a while, but she turned down the idea and suggested we hike Geumjang Mountain instead. Maybe the narrow vagina fear was just a phase that was coming to an end.

It was an easy hike up the mountain. At the top we drank *makkoli* from plastic bottles and ate rice cakes. We even managed to talk about a lot of normal things—her cousin's wedding, my father's obsession with the movie *Ben-Hur*, the chances of Korea's football team ever winning a World Cup. It would have been a perfect place to screw. My weeklong erection was starting to give me a headache. We mostly just sat there looking out on the city, sipping the fall breeze, getting along like a normal couple. We kissed for a long time before hiking back and taking a taxi to her favorite Japanese restaurant near the city center.

We were sitting down as the story broke on the evening news. The chef upped the volume. Everyone in the place was listening. A kid out at the LG complex in Gwangali had been set on fire, just covered in gas and lit up. His photo popped up over the right shoulder of the news anchor. I thought I recognized his face from the rooftop shootout, but couldn't be sure. I checked my phone. No new messages.

"You know, Jung, you should call your brother."

"Why?" she asked, scowling.

"I should have told you, but he's been calling a lot. I've mostly been ignoring him. He shot a kid with a pellet gun. An automatic pellet gun."

"He didn't shoot anyone," she said, staring up at the screen and the policemen standing around a big black stain on the parking-lot pavement.

"Jung, I think he wrote that article in *Sports Seoul.*"

"Shut up," she said, letting loose a weird giggle. Her face and neck were breaking out in hives. I put my arm around her, worried she would collapse.

"Jung, I recognize that boy's face. Let's leave. You can call your mom."

The chef turned to us, not bothering to hide his curiosity. Jung-yung straightened her back, grabbed the chopsticks, and waved them in front of my face like she might go for an eye.

"Just shut your fucking mouth," she screamed. "*I* wrote the article in *Sports Seoul.*"

"Why the hell would you do that?"

"Because I hate you," she said. "You think you're so noble, don't you? You think you're better than everyone else! You're shit, Young-min!"

The chef turned back to the news. I was certain that Tae-won was the cause of the boy's death, but it was too late and there was nothing intelligent to be said about it. My mind turned to our pledge. I'd like to believe this was not as selfish as it sounds, that it was simply a form of psychological self-defense. I pinched my ears, a nervous habit of mine, and decided that Jung-yung's outburst was a clear violation of the deal. She called the chef away from the TV. She ordered a bowl of seaweed soup and a bottle of sake.

I watched Jung-yung eat her soup, lifting the spoon, swallowing it hot, and trying to regain her composure. She poured shots for herself and kept the bottle out of my reach. When we left, her hives were replaced by a crimson shine particular to Jung-yung and sake. She paid for our meal and held my hand on the way out of the restaurant. She directed our taxi driver to the motel in Chinatown where she'd given me the *Sports Seoul* article.

None of our concerns about Tae-won's connection to the arson attack seemed to affect our performance, despite my last-minute fear that Jung-yung's paranoia was valid and having sex might actually kill her. She let me watch her take off each item of clothing and checked my reaction step by step. Her underpants were oversized and old-fashioned. It was the only thing that seemed to embarrass her. When she was naked she sat down on the edge of the bed. I started to undo my belt but she waved me closer to undress me herself. She made her eyes extra wide when she pulled down my zipper and my erect penis popped out of my boxers. There wasn't much foreplay before the first time I entered her. I'd tried to be thoughtful, but she pulled me on top of her and asked me to penetrate her as deeply as I could. She held me there for a minute or two, not letting me move at all. She kept repeating our names over and over, "Young-min . . . Jung-yung," a soft hymn, her soft flesh. Finally she gripped my hips and then my buttocks, directing me in and out in a shallow rhythm of five. Each fifth thrust was powerful and deep, eliciting a grunt and an open-mouthed smile. We made it through at least seven cycles before I reached my limit and frantically pulled out. It was just the beginning of our night.

When it was all over, Jung-yung was struck with an almost seventeen-hour slumber. I slept five or six hours, then took an early-morning bath. I decided I'd give *Three Kingdoms* another chance and set a daily page limit. When I got back into bed, I was trying to predict how they'd punish Tae-won.

After Jung-yung woke up we took a taxi to the police headquarters. Her mother had been calling her all night and all morning from the front desk lobby. She'd apparently left when the detectives finished interrogating Tae-won, after he'd confessed. A junior detective asked Jung-yung to step into his office to answer a few questions about her brother's job history. We passed a holding cell where Tae-won was sitting in a chair, handcuffed to the wall. He was slumped over, probably dozing off. Jung-yung answered their questions, which they'd already asked her mother. When two officers marched Tae-won to another cell, they walked right past us. Tae-won lifted his head high and told me, "I'm still her older brother."

Over the next few months, while Jung-yung and I studied for our final exams and graduated, the whole country got behind the effort to see Tae-won hung. The victim's mother, a devout Christian, blamed the tragedy on the government when she found out Tae-won had been discharged from the military after an extravagant shooting incident during his sniper training. She begged his life be spared, arguing that military officers brainwashed young recruits and compromised moral conscientiousness. For whatever reason, in spite of the malevolent media caricatures and the public's fervid cry for revenge, the jury consented. Tae-won was issued a life sentence. I was sure before it was all said and done that all of Korea would learn about his one testicle, but the media never caught wind of it.

I thought about Tae-won often, though Jung-yung insisted her monthly visits to the prison be unescorted. About six months after

Tae-won was arrested, I experienced an irrepressible urge to pay him a visit. I was with a few coworkers at my favorite drinking tent. The conversation had been all about the hot firms in Seoul and other trade talk I prefer to leave at the office. I couldn't have cared less how much an architect made in New York versus Korea, but as far as conversation goes, these guys couldn't offer much else. I took a couple of fast shots and stumbled off, telling my colleagues I wasn't feeling well and needed to go to sleep. I went straight to the train station and bought a ticket to Seoul. The train arrived around seven, an hour before I was supposed to show up to work. From there I took a taxi to Anyang, thinking it would take half an hour. It took that long just to get out of the city center. Then it was an hour through southern Seoul before we were on the road to Anyang, another fifteen miles. I knew when I explained everything the following day, Jung-yung would be most upset that I'd blown money on taxi fares. She'd call me an airhead and say I should have taken the subway and a bus.

The guards at the prison gate were certain I was putting them on when I said I'd come to visit Park Tae-won, that I was his sister's boyfriend. One of them jeered. "Did you bring his other testicle, Doc?" The other added, "We're going to need to inspect that testy." I laughed along with them, like I was only there to deliver a message, that I thought Tae-won just as monstrous as they did. With these sorts of idiots, like in the army, it was best to just play along. But laughing about his handicap didn't feel good one bit.

I showed them a photo of Jung-yung. Given her exposure on TV, it was enough proof to gain entrance onto the premises. A happy-go-lucky prisoner hopped off a bicycle and bowed to the guards. They ordered him to escort me to the visitation office, so long as he did not "conscientiously object." He did not. After the first twelve of his eighteen months in prison, he explained, they'd decided to let him out each morning to deliver newspapers. At the visitation desk I filled out some paperwork and was told to come back the following day. Visits on Saturdays only, and either way, no guarantees. I scouted out a sauna motel ten minutes down the road. I turned off my cell phone and spent the majority of the afternoon soaking in a hot bath.

The next morning I lucked out. The visitation officer from the day before perked up when I walked into the office. He handed me a clipboard with several forms requiring my signature. Tae-won's signature was written on the bottom of the last page. Around noon I was led into a long room with spongy puzzle-piece floors, concrete walls, and the sort of fluorescent lighting that makes everyone look like they're seconds from vomiting.

Tae-won was waiting in leg and wrist manacles, though he didn't appear in any discomfort. Jung-yung had led me to believe he'd lost a lot of weight, but apparently he'd gained it back. His face was round and his cheeks shiny, like he'd rubbed them with sesame oil. I sat down opposite him and asked if the guard was going to stay with us the whole time. The guard laughed and turned aside, giving the two princes their private moment. Tae-won was clearly excited to see me, especially when he found out I'd come on my own.

"Bunch of jokers around here. They really enjoy their jobs, especially when it comes to the loudmouths." Tae-won rapped his knuckles on the table. His cuffs banged on the surface. The guard turned back to face us. There was nothing funny in his expression. Tae-won continued. "What do you expect? Not an easy job. Every day with a bunch of rude dogs, barking all night long."

I nodded, sensing our visit would be cut short. Tae-won bowed slightly to the officer, really pushing it.

"At first they didn't think I was so tough, cause I killed a kid. But you know who they hate the most? The Jehovah's Witnesses. Those little shits do nothing but sweep floors and shine shoes. Ah, let's not talk about Jehovah's Witnesses. I heard you got a job."

I nodded, not wanting to think about it. None of the officers mentioned how much time we had, so I was anxious to move things along.

"Jung-yung is looking into a loan so she can open a pet shop. It will be just like you planned. Exotic fish, snakes, iguanas. I'm not sure what else, but it sounds pretty good, if she can get the loans."

Tae-won wasn't as excited as I'd hoped. Hearing Jung-yung's name seemed to launch his thoughts elsewhere. I went on anyway.

"She's thinking about renting a space out near Haeundae."

Tae-won leaned forward and shook his head.

"Haeundae? People go to Haeundae to eat and swim. They don't want to buy an iguana on the way to the beach. I don't want my shop out there, like some fucking petting zoo for kids. People who want midget poodles with tails and ears painted purple, they can go to Haeundae. Nothing more pathetic than a dog who does most of its pissing in some teenybopper's purse. The pet shop should be in Seomyeon, between a candy shop and a flower shop. A place where men go when they need a present to impress their boss, or buy their wife a fish tank to say they're sorry, after they do something stupid."

"Well," I said, trying to sound blasé about the whole thing, "I'm not so confident she'll get the loan. But she talks about it every day."

Tae-won asked why I hadn't brought her along. I told him I'd come straight from a drinking tent and in the last day had ignored about a dozen voice messages from my boss's secretary and another dozen from Jung-yung. Tae-won lit up, finding this hilarious. The guard gave me a look that told me the strange pitch of his laughter was an infraction of the rules.

"She misses her older brother," I said.

Tae-won's reaction was void of any discernible emotion, though I sensed he expected at some point during my visit that I'd reveal a simple solution to his incarceration. It was also like a curtain had suddenly lowered between us and he was waiting for it to lift up again. He was thinking hard, but it could have been about anything. I wondered if this was the face he'd made before lighting the match. He ran a hand slowly over his face, from his forehead down to his chin, then looked up.

"So when are you going to be married?"

Though I hadn't consciously thought of it until the previous afternoon, when I was lying on a warm mat at the sauna, the real reason for my visit was to ask Tae-won to marry his sister. As I was signing the visitation forms, I still hadn't decided if I would go through with it. Of course, Tae-won was enjoying the fact that he hadn't mentioned who I might marry.

"Jung-yung has never said she loves me."

He laughed in two spurts, like an old man, as though he'd taught her never to say those words.

"Little brother," he said, "why so gloomy?"

He'd never called me little brother and it was almost more shocking to me than his bringing up the topic of marriage. I took a moment to think it over, feeling I'd already been pondering the question all night in my sleep. I was ready, I decided, so I put the question to him properly.

"Older brother, can I ask your sister to marry me?"

His eyes shifted to the guard, who could no longer pretend to be uninterested.

"You can ask," he said, "and she'll decide."

It was right that I should not leave the prison with too much confidence, because really, you never know. There was one more issue.

"They won't let you out for the wedding. Who would give her away?"

"No one. You'll have to be the father, and the older brother, and the groom. Don't go to some cheap wedding hall with a bubble machine. There's no fucking taste at some of those places."

I promised not to go cheap, and furthermore, I pledged to protect Jung-yung and look after her health. Tae-won smiled as though this went unsaid. He was happy enough granting his permission and that was the end of it. For the last few minutes of our visit, Tae-won told me about his steady flow of fan mail, mostly from troubled teens fascinated with his crime. He'd also received a marriage proposal from a master's student at Ehwa University. I promised to look into the legality of the matter.

Jung-yung and I were married the following spring. In the beginning we often fought about how to spend our money, whether or not we needed a bigger apartment, and how we should best care for her mother. She never withheld sex, like the wives of several of my friends, but it was years into married life before she was able to break herself of sleeping for half the day after one of our sessions. We were a passionate couple, for better or worse, and every day was a new adventure. Eventually Jung-yung got the loan she'd been seeking. She named the pet shop after her brother, "Park Tae-won's Platypus." She didn't care what people thought. Neither did I. And practically overnight, her business was booming.

Two Stories
Rikki Ducornet

DIVORCE

THERE ARE MANY REASONS why I offer myself—in a manner of speaking—to a staggering number of young men, all Japanese. The divorce above all; the divorce that has so thoroughly exhausted me and, what's worse, marked me with a chronic look of irritation so like Mother's.

Naked beneath someone else's sheets, fogged in sorrow's exhalations, I lie in silence, having made a vow despite my compulsion—Trixie would say my weakness—to demonstrate to those in my service that I am a democrat, a good sport—who never farts higher than her ass. I can, when I choose, banter with hairdressers, beauticians, waiters, and so forth, with genial wit and what is sometimes erroneously perceived as compassion. But not today. I am not here to entertain. I am here so that they will wipe that nasty look off my face.

Mother and I are not "two peas in a pod"—although Rolph insists that this is so. I blame my current decrescendo on his mistake. And trust that the new Mrs. Rolph—whose current face is as bare of irritation as a new sink—will, like me, land up under a sheet sooner or later. (In this way a spa is very like the morgue.)

The spa's regimen features roots, pernicious thimblefuls of raw clam juice, and a bitter tea. Purged of one's terrible secrets, one is tossed into a miserable hut and thrashed. According to the celebrated doctor who rules this roost, a thrashing is just what the female deserves. And *needs*—if she is to be stricken of the mother's hostility, the father's ineptitude. To be released from the family's burden of inevitable crimes. And there are felted rooms where one may give vent to jealous rage by slapping or stomping on a life-sized doll of wax, a beautiful doll—more beautiful, in fact, than our most hated rivals. Here one may commit lamentable acts either in privacy or among strangers, each one more repulsive than the next: hatchet faced, spindle shanked, squabbish, sore as crabs, starved—some howling or bellowing at the doll, others kicking it in the groin, this one rolling on the floor and humiliating herself at the doll's feet, that one totally unhinged, jumping down its throat and snapping off its head.

I understand the Doctor's rigorous bitterness. Like Daddy, he too suffered a ruinous divorce. It is the spa's success that has put him back on his feet. The book tours, the lecture series on PBS, the antioxidants marketed in pretty blue-glass bottles. Unlike Daddy and despite the requisite bloodletting, the good doctor *is still thrashing.* He has remarried, and the witty luxuries provided here are the indication of his ambivalence. After the thrashings, the rantings, the virtual murders, one is invited to soak in a tub brimming with warm cherry pie filling.

*

Mother has met the good doctor numerous times. Years ago, before she began to seriously grind her teeth and to sag irretrievably, the tabloids hinted at a romance. If pressed, Trixie will gleefully enumerate the Doctor's many faults. She claims he is covered with hair—the sorry outcome of misguided self-medication. *This,* she says, *is why he wears gloves, both inside and out, no matter the weather.* But I have caught sight of him floating past in his white smocks and waffle-soled sneakers, and find his features agreeable. Like Rolph's in the months leading up to the marriage, the Doctor's expression is hopeful. This touches me, for despite my upbringing, I have never fully embraced Trixie's fine skepticism, a brutal skepticism honed on Daddy's irrelevance. (But for cash, Daddy's place in our world was always obscure.) Yet, as a girl, when I saw Trixie's face frozen in the custard of censoriousness, I cringed. However, having learned from Daddy's repeated breaches of propriety that a husband is not to be taken seriously, I began to, and under Trixie's guidance, give Rolph "the works." *Nothing,* I told him, *comes for free. A successful marriage,* I was always eager to explain, *is run like a successful business: the wife takes in more than she gives out.* Buoyant with certitude, I was ill prepared when he eclipsed with the other woman to a place difficult to reach—New Zealand! A lawless place given over to eccentricities I was brought up to mightily distrust.

But back to Mother. It must be said that Trixie suffers a curious contradiction of character. She is a moralist who uncovers the shameful wherever she pokes her abridged nose and, at the same time, she is a materialist who insists that anything human—anger above all—is *natural.* Her own mightily disagreeable nature, for example, her uninhibited complaints and vicious teasing, are all spontaneous, clever, and good. Yet the tempers of others leave them open to character assassination. In this way my mother demonstrates a callous disregard for the right of others to practice what she has, in the dark recesses of her heart, perfected.

I do not follow in Trixie's footsteps, not exactly, still . . . Our marriage, Rolph's and mine, was, as Trixie hastens to remind me, run on my terms. Of this I should be proud. As has been the divorce. Of this I should be pleased. In the words of my lawyer, *the divorced husband is but broken meat and chaff.* My bitterness is therefore unreasonable, as is the nagging fear—even as I soak in a tub of pie filling—that I have fucked up. And yet . . . here's the thing: should Rolph appear before me this instant in his dapper straw boater and yellow suit saying, "Damn it, Tootsie! Let's pick up where we left off!" I would be unable to articulate the word *yes.* I would be unable to smile. *This* is the problem in a nutshell. Although I have spent many hours before the mirror willing my face back into vitality, it remains hideously entangled.

Strange to tell it, I was once—and not very long ago, either—lovely to see. Youth accounted for it, and the fact that I embodied a moment. I looked remarkable in chinchilla shrugs and artfully shredded suede. I glowed in the sugary haze of an elusive ideal. Even my perpetual irritation, so like Mother's, was considered stylish. And my murderous laughter, a razor rending the air—it, too, was very much appreciated.

GIULIA ON HER KNEES

Hiram first saw Giulia on her knees in the Ognissanti; "I've always liked," he'd later joke with his friends, "to see a pretty woman on her knees." And Giulia *had* been pretty—if a bit thick in the ankles and waist. (Her pale blonde hair was too thin.)

She was too quiet. Although it aggravated Hiram whenever she attempted a few words in public. It was her accent, he told her, that so frustrated him. Although once he had found it charming: "I like to see a pretty woman stumble over her own tongue!" What's more, she was too serviceable. "A real ox!" Although he expected her to

301

anticipate his needs: something hot to drink, something cool. The chisels sharpened just so, the bills paid, the table set, and the meal served within moments of his return to the house after a long day in the studio. The meat tender and well seasoned.

From the kitchen window Giulia monitored Hiram's moods. She was loyal. Because to create a work of art involves risk, and an uneventful domesticity allowed him to dance with his demons, the bright demons of his genius. Besides, didn't she *rule the roost!* It has been her task to erase uncertainty from his daily life. To assure a *well-orchestrated household.* (As a girl she had studied the viola; often she thinks in musical terms. His voice when he calls her: *spiccato.* Her response: *con anima!*) Once when he was feeling more kindly toward her, having feasted with friends on the rabbit she had prepared, her incomparable polenta, he acknowledged that together they "played a good game. A good game of complicity." These words had reassured her. They were the evidence that things were not as bad as they seemed. She served the coffee *vivacissimo!* Hiram noticed. "What makes the ox dance?" he thundered, his laughter bouncing off the walls.

There is a painting by Raphael, a St. George and the Dragon in which a blonde dressed in muted scarlet kneels in the grass, praying. Giulia on her knees is like her, still and pale. Silently retreating behind the folds of a heavy velvet curtain, Hiram makes a close study of Giulia's face and body. Her eyes are fine. If her chin is too fleshy, still she is very like da Vinci's portrait of a girl holding a weasel. And her body! Her body is lovely. Yet, like her face, it is imperfect, or, rather, it is perfect because it brings to mind the thickened, somewhat clumsy bodies painted by his beloved Giotto. When she stands and turns to go, Hiram slips as gracefully as he can from the shadows and in his impoverished Italian whispers that she is *wonderfully formed.* Giulia laughs. What is this funny, charming, barrel-chested stranger trying to say? What uniform? She is wearing no uniform! Yes! Timid Giulia laughs!

Hiram takes Giulia's hand and presses it to the cold marble of a statue; he attempts to explain that this is his medium. Marble. She sees how it sparkles as if studded with grains of sand. And then they are together in the street, a familiar street, flooded with the rich, buttery light of late afternoon. And she is walking beside him. An American! Like the ones who liberated Europe! Who stood high above the crowds in their tanks and trucks, tossing *cioccolato*. The taste so powerful Giulia nearly faints in her Nona's arms. And he is so much older than she. He could be her papa! All this emboldens her.

"I like wax better," she tells him. She is thinking of the statues of the saints. So uncannily lifelike. "Wax," she tells him, "is warmer. *WAX*," she repeats and he, because he does not understand, runs back into the church to buy candles; thick, yellow candles that fill her arms like flowers. Unable to contain her laughter—never has Giulia laughed like this!—she attempts to set him straight. "*Cera! Cera!*" And he, he thinks she wants to dine! *Cenare!* To dine! He is jubilant.

If Hiram's vocabulary is limited to the great moments in Italian art, he also knows the names of things to eat. Here they are together, at table! And Hiram orders an enormous quantity of food for them both: *zuppetta!* He shouts it: *zuppetta di cannelloni!* Tomorrow! he shouts. *Prosciutto!*

"He means *next*," she tells the waiter, "not tomorrow, but *now!*"

"With olives!" Hiram cries. "*Con olive!*"

And he tells her she is *carina*; she is *caramella*—which makes her laugh even more.

"*La Fregole!*" he tells the waiter as he pours out the house wine. "*Con cozze e vongoolay!*"

"*Vongole!*" she attempts to correct him. He tells her she is *carrozzina,* which utterly bewilders her because it is the word for pram. She ceases to laugh and instead blushes.

Over soup he finally manages to convey that he is *a builder of statues.* She is impressed. She asks him if his statues *seem alive,* for in her mind these are the best. *Like the ones in wax!* she tells him. Because they are almost human. *I like their eyes!* Giulia touches her own. *They look so human!* Do his statues look alive?

Looking into his pocket dictionary that spills its leaves onto his knees, he says no, no, alive is not his intention. *Emozione*—this is what he wishes to convey. Complex . . . what is it? *Complesso! Si! Complesso emozione.* The man of genius must invent his own forms. How can he explain this to her?

Hiram's emotions are always complex. He would worship this girl; he would lick the bones that move above her breasts and wing their way to her shoulders. He would push himself against her heavy form to quicken it. He sits back and gazes at her, watching her suck a clam from its shell, watching her tear her bread. As always when a woman interests him, he assesses her as an object in space.

"*Lapidare.*"

Giulia gazes up at Hiram. She understands that he works in stone. She tells him that, if, until this moment, she has preferred wax over stone, it is because *wax is like flesh.* And the glass eyes! How she admires them. (She has never said this much to anyone.) *Ma . . .* she acknowledges. *But.* Marble lasts longer. Your statues, she tells him, *they will last forever! Per Sempre.* Forever. *This,* she decides, makes Hiram *straordinario.* Remarkable.

Never has she been so clever! She cannot wait to tell her sister how clever she has been. She has told a man he is *straordinario!* And he has told her an American word: *remarkable!*

Their courtship: *bocconcini di manzo!* lasts a week. Here is a man, she tells her sister, who knows how to enjoy life's pleasures. Giulia is nineteen. The next thing she knows she is standing over a hot stove in a small farmhouse kitchen in northern Vermont: *vellutata! tagliolini!* Grease spatters and hits the stone floor.

Now Giulia is almost sixty, and her man, the man she has struggled so desperately to both please and forgive, is failing. There had always been other women, which makes it harder to be compassionate, women who, as the years passed, became younger, much younger than she. Yet she could not blame him. After all, he was a great man, a remarkable man—or so they had both thought.

Although . . . a great man would not have been abandoned by the world as he has been. The last time the people from the gallery came to see his work (Oh! That was years ago now!), they did not stay for lunch. As they walked back to their car she overheard them talking about Hiram. They said he was stuck. They called the work dated. *Dated!*

When she had first discovered his infidelities she had shouted—she! She who had never shouted at anyone, not ever! Not even as a child! And she had sobbed. He told her she was behaving like the wife of a postman. The wife of a grocer! This she did not want to do. She learned to hold her head high at the supermarket, at the dry cleaner's. She did all she could to squeeze every last drop of bile from her bitterness so that it came to resemble worldliness. She was thought to be haughty. She dressed in the eccentric threads of the successful artist's wife. She was the only woman in town to own an ikat coat and scarves made of batik. If one ate at her table, the linens were all authentic Japanese indigo. At these dinners the food was exquisite and Giulia silent. When the drinking got serious, she left the room.

Hiram has aged badly. Ill tempered and gouty, he throws his shoes. He curses her; he curses the entire universe. These days he needs a cane. He is bitter. Old age is a personal affront, an unforgivable humiliation. And then there is that other thing that she has never allowed herself to think about, that other thing. . . . Its subversive power threatens to annihilate them both. The truth. There! Na! She'll say it! She leaves her kitchen and goes out into the yard to say it! Gigantic. Too big to be moved without a great deal of fuss and bother and expense (and now nobody wants them!), Hiram's statues dwarf the yard. Gigantic and ugly! Ugly as sin! Nothing she has ever seen is uglier.

"*Brutto!*" Giulia shouts this until she can shout no more. "*Brutto! Brutto!*" She feels as though a swarm of bees has taken possession of her skull.

When she returns to her kitchen, Giulia gazes at her reflection in the mirror. The little mirror beside the sink where, over the years, she has hastily dabbed her lips with rouge, reddening her lips in case the remarkable man chooses to kiss them. *Why*, she wonders, *why* did she become the sort of woman who spends a lifetime on her knees scrubbing spattered grease off the floors so that some mean bastard can walk on them?

When Giulia was a child, her father told her a story she found especially fascinating. Cinyras, the hero of Cyprus, promised Agamemnon fifty boats so that he should prove victorious at Troy. But when the boats arrived, they were all toys made of clay, with crews of clay. Giulia's marriage to Hiram reminds her of this story.

The Arbor
Andrew Mossin

> *And her hair gone white   from the loss of him*
> —*Pisan Cantos*, *"LXXIX"*

Orpheus with his hair swept back his eyes
directed inland. In the courtyard his body turned to those who knew him
for what he was: thief, murderer, liar.

                 Scent of lemons white along the slopes of
Pisa. In the prison yard
the orphaned names proffered against his testimonial—

              There in chaos and nothingness
I will come to know you again. Death's seeds

move in a year. The harvest moon seeded in the ground
the white husk frames a millionth of a second
godless time.

        "Offer your confession . . ."

White wrists laid on the floor of a cemetery. The books
scrolling back their history. Now there
are no more days. The sun elongates into shadow.

Your face, dear god, a petal lighter than sea foam.

                   *

        Who betrayed them?
        One Singer cannot sing out alone
            albumen   forested   reveries
        Sightless in Pisa as the poet was
        counting sheep in Phoenician
        entangled in line

"We cut you from the tree—
in the image of one you will never know"

Or was it labor alone that could complete
itself among you: the visible world
of things

When you wanted to go from us
an arrow into the night
Song of a traveler about to
                    depart

Peninsula of dark the sole survivor of that descent

            —the miracle wasn't that he moved but *when*—

Knots in the grass of springtime
whorls of sovereign yellow

                    *

Sagebrush and flora
of this world so much
is lost in utterance

The leap made again and again into that forked beginning

Tangibility of the blistered formal elements
The rain has fallen the rain
comes down from the
                    mountain—

The rain is formal and passing
across a prison yard in springtime
azure in the hand he
offers it twice
pear trees reflected in crystal—

Andrew Mossin

"But the crystal can be weighed"

*

Music settles
a score—

Inside the hand
one cannot exceed the circle

Drawn away
the shape remains concentric
palm to palm

A man wakes
without effort inside a room
a man awake
without her by his side

There is then a cadence
without effort
that comes from this room

The form of a man who has come
back to discover

"The form of a song—
                    equity & faith"

Melos
formed in the hand's cup.

No feeling
or the intensity of feeling
that leaves you without a context
for what must follow.

A bridge between the captive
of myth and those that follow
your call.

Andrew Mossin

One cannot wipe out the tone.
One cannot cleanse the rock entirely

Balanced between the name you gave us
and these few
jagged notes.

*

These little
words you are
known by

A belated
autobiography

*Sweet sunless day
can love make a thing
of the past*

Eurydice
began to falter
lying side by side in the red dirt

with him as he—

took her in hand

the smell of mint under tent flaps

He came down the
hill to meet her
peasant manes cry
And saw the hill
deepen
       mute flora of their seventh day

Light tensile immaculata

Rose & lemon
spread between them.

Things that bear
harmony will cross again in time.

      Was it offerance
or shame that drew them
back—

Her eyes
His gaze

Their helplessness is transitional
defining a pattern of
recurrent loss
residual mourning

        We went out of their body we were cut from their flesh

And the circle
kept open by
her hand
his hand

     hidden nests of light.

Think of how vast a distance
But there is no distance

Think of the pattern
leaves spread out before them

There is no pattern
no leaves put before you

Light is profligate
A tent turned to the east

And his womanly
face averted—

Nowhere does the circle close

    a gray stream of earthly light
    coursing backward

         *

Fate is mute
on the subject of their
final destination

One cannot subtract
the story they told
from what occurred

In real time : his
hand that turned to graze
the rock

Her eyes fixed to meet
his gaze.

When the ancient
pattern is a
"rhythm of eyes"

We who travel along this foreign range
proposing "almost along a line"
a directness of speech
long since forgotten.

Nothing can speak
there is no one speaking
the eyes are not
open—the days
connote nothing
but silence.

         *

Andrew Mossin

A ring where the hand
so easily fled its
owner—

brought into the open

his bride

suffers one stave at a time.

The Mouse

Mei-mei Berssenbrugge

1.

Transmission from speaker to you is like warm breath from a
young girl who's not wholly concerned with information, truth,
drawing you into her presence.

When she whispers, you catch fragments of words, which seem
nonsensical.

When asked to speak clearly, she looks down.

Her voice softens and breaks off, haunting you, because it's not
connected to any person in the room, as if all words were pulled
from books and left on the floor.

How would you find meaning, except by chance?

But people don't believe in the order of chance or order from
within.

2.

There's a legacy of an order of events in a house with long views
down the valley.

An act is by chance, as a word may be ancillary to meaning.

Wisteria, terraced fields, far areas of wildflowers, shadows changing
with the day lay ground for more abstract forms.

I feel the loftiness of fate, straighten and walk out in thin air,
filaments of light like whispers drawing me.

"I, the mother, because I don't comprehend, acquire the haunting affect of a liminal figure whose attempt to comprehend interrupts events, like voice-over."

Their bodies are aggregates of fate, girl, upheaval of many beings participating over a long time that appears like her time in the plot.

The mandala, "being at home," deconstructs into symbols, I mean deeper, nondiscursive dimensions of daffodils, a fold in clothing, cloudless space like her subjectivity.

Hear hesitations between words as this space in a design's overall, natural workability.

3.

Intense emotions are symbolized as mythic figures or deities.

A family member can become the spiritual subjectivity of one who's angry, so anger is just content, red on space.

And anyone who's not angry is called Mother.

Then, you're identified with one pole, creating an enemy who attacks, and you counterattack.

Then, you're like an exhausted mouse slumped over the rim of a flowerpot of torn leaves, "She left me; I trashed my plant.

Now everything is screwed."

4.

So, I read by feeling, vibration, picking up books from the library floor, as if by chance.

Rocky ground floods with yellow flowers, a saturation of feeling in cyclical time, as of the oracle.

If matter is trapped light, by seeing yellow, you restructure molecules, and you're not as solid.

An event on the mandala loosens into probability.

There was ambition, unconsciousness of Clytemnestra and I, a mouse, was her mirror.

I drive with my family away from the oracle, through a valley of flowering almond trees, and turn around without realizing it.

That space was concealed within the illusion of my body, an emergence place.

If I mistake an angel for a stone statue, I look closer, not elsewhere, to see there never was stone.

My perception was far more inaccurate than the illusion.

5.

I can't recall the flowering almond trees.

The moment I think of them, they diffuse into beings whose frequency so differs from mine, I can't see them.

They connect with beauty and each other in celestial groves, yet our worlds unify.

The dawn of the possibility of their appearance of form, stone, shifts probability to form angels.

Then, my body is not charnel ground, where fate is an emotional intent.

The interpenetration of breath and petals is not blasted by fate's order.

You are a brush stroke of blue space drawn across the grid, like trying to wake up, where waking is realizing space, the way a picture fills in, with the mildness of your daughter's face looking on you, not a mirror.

Mei-mei Berssenbrugge

The light is wide as waking can embrace at one time.

Your waking is a blue brush stroke creating space.

Anything that does not contain light blue—lake, Greek sky—will not even see you.

Obsession in Outer Mongolia
Paul West

I.

ENRICO FERMI FAMOUSLY asked, "Where is everyone else?" He meant the inhabitants of other galaxies, of course. "Patience," I would have said had I known him, but I sensed what he meant. That kind of slavering impatience knows no bounds. He was a world traveler, anxious to have it all laid bare in one lifetime, like my friend Light Lomax.

Light wanted the world speeded up, which was why we found ourselves, presently, in Outer Mongolia, where the locals, pausing to see you sampling a book in a shop, halted their motion and talk and remained in suspension until you had finished, which could take minutes or even hours. The Outer Mongolians' reverence for books— from sacred texts to the worst pornography—argued a fetishism born and bred. They'd done this for centuries, mixing gentility and prudence. All signs of civilization were brought to a halt by the appearance of a book, which had something coy and fey about it, but one got used to such things, especially when they did nobody any harm. Clearly, books were king in this kingdom and appeared likely to remain so.

Be this as it may, last week our farewells had been brief: a pitcher of red spaghetti sauce over one of white, tureen of white pasta, moldy eggs, rancid salmon, and black German bread had seen us off to our distant destination, complete with snowshoes, rubber galoshes, and skis. We would not be caught napping by any kind of miscreant weather. At easily seven feet, my travel companion, late of Chernobyl (he appeared to have survived without infection), towered over me as we left, and threw his shadow on my steps, a born survivor in any kind of clime.

After much showing of passports and clambering after donkeys, we arrived, to no particular fanfare, and settled in. We noticed the reverential attention given our passports simply because they were booklike. The red-and-white pasta pursued us most of the way, and we thanked our stars we had bestowed our lucky apartment on two such worthies as our newfound friend Hans, both jovial and sensitive, and his introverted *amie* Frieda. Their collection of cut glass was everywhere, open to the world, a triumph of the glazier's art.

And now we were a universe away, it seemed, in a bed and breakfast, taking our ease at last in a stereopticon land of jute mountains and crags. Light's monstrous body, which dispossessed any sleeping arrangements in a huge dictatorial way, occupied much of the bed, though he was not in the least arrogant about this and apologized profusely, as he had been accustomed to doing all his life, especially to women. Always too long for anything, he suffered from cold feet despite the addition of many pairs of socks. I, on the other hand, was comfy and nearly nodding when he started to talk.

"Nice bunch of folks."

"If you like their way of giggling."

"Give them a break."

"If you must."

"What are we here for?"

"Who knows?" I had forgotten.

"To see if we could do it."

"Just that." I was anxious for sleep.

"Surely not."

"Then what on earth?"

In our more serious, refined moments we occupied ourselves with the cosmic problems of the planet, particularly whether we were alone amid the millions of galaxies that had not once managed to sniff out a rival.

"So why haven't they said hello?"

"Oh," I countered, "we're not very appealing. Constantly at war. There aren't any UFOs forever laying siege to our skies—leave it at that."

"To have gotten here and not made the final step?"

"Why not? They could not bring themselves to do it, considering all the millions they'd sacrificed. They content themselves with observing us at our juvenile antics."

"Whereas *I* believe in them not at all. Wherever you look there's a dead cosmos."

"Impossible."

"UFOs nonexisting."

"If you see it that way."

"I do. We are alone among everything."

"Sez you."

"Sez me."

"Good night to you."

It was not to be. I was wide awake and too alert (or too alerted) for this hegemony of barren salutations. My fingers ached, my spine felt jolted out of shape, and my head began a slight migraine that threatened to grow as the Outer Mongolia blues set in for a trumpery night of it.

As my woes increased, threatened by a sleep that would not come, I began in my formulaic way to rehearse once again what was wrong with the universe. To begin with, why had all these UFOs, in which I believed, and whose strange voyagers I desired to meet, had parleyed with in dreams, and could have summoned with the sheer magnetic force of my longing (a turbine that whirred inside me whenever I thought of them, as if they alone could heal my life)— why had they never declared themselves? Too finicky? Too exquisite? Used to better fare, fare less bloodthirsty or simple? What was the sticking point they all stuck at, where they dug in their prehensile toes (if they had toes), some of them, mind you, flitting near the 747s or 777s, their colors a fanfaronade of exotic lures, their steeples clearly visible, a montage of barrel-rolling illuminations, almost teasing, welcoming, inviting us to follow.

Why then so standoffish? It was a fool's game, perhaps, a mug or a mugwump's antic exemplifying in our very own language, *Come see us waggle our latest sneerd* or *Come and touch the newest hornswoggle.* Call it what you will: a fragment of the unique, where all was pale and familiar. But no: I had never heard so much as a crackle, not a swoosh, not a whistle, not a rush of burly energy.

They crept upon us, an unpredictable visual sonata, never to go beyond into cacophony or whisper, staying surreptitious yet blatant, all with the same inaudible taste, whatever their shape. Not one risking a "How're you today?" or a banshee yell.

Talk they no doubt had on board aplenty, but we heard none of it, only enforced silence. Maybe we were, as a species, beneath contempt? Then why such a surfeit of interest in us? I was convinced that the interior of most spaceships was a bouquet of tones, with each alien specially equipped to hear bleats from a dozen simultaneous sources.

Or were all the visiting spacefarers tone-deaf, and sound something they weren't privy to? If so, alas for them, they were a race of the dead if they couldn't hear our poetry from Homer to Crabbe.

Not a bit of it. That was no way to go. Thousands of deaf men (or whatever) playing consequences with a whole planet of jabberers. One alien spokesman surely would have sufficed, for me, anyway. It made no difference really: a million versus one solitary eavesdropper. Then my mind perked up, as it usually did after a few moments of alien reverie.

Whatever they used as a means of communication they did not use words: maybe something else filled in the gap. So why not send one arbiter just to clinch the point about human speech? What use was a thousand, a million aerial stalkers?

I ascribed this lapse to my semicomatose condition and pushed on further to the hypothesis that read: no human has yet made speech worth hearing.

It was outrageous, so to dismiss the whole of speech in this way, but it could be the truth. A bevy of alien nations so advanced that nothing had been said on earth that was worth attending to. And they had been auscultating us since the Middle Ages, ever expectant, always disappointed. Why had the aliens not gone elsewhere? Why persist with humanity? Vain hope. Vain longing.

Perhaps, I mused, getting bolder in my presumption, they chose us by default, there being nowhere else to go! Of all the available planets in the galaxy, this was the only one to sponsor life, highly unsatisfactory life, but the only taker. One day we might explode in worthy speech, but not yet, and they waited forever for the jubilant day to arrive, waited since the Middle Ages, the Dark Ages, and beyond.

Somehow this point emerged from my ashamed brain: somewhere, surely, a golden speaker flourished, a being whose every word was their kind of poetry. *That* was why the search for him became so intense, so desperate. They could have been crying for the moon: obviously no such speaker crept over the horizon. This was the best any of us could do, no matter how advanced we became in electronic sophistication, no matter how our speech mutated with time. None of it was ever good enough for them, that was it, and all the time we thought we were improving, getting better at it, trapped without knowing why in the long-necked horse of a Peruvian sea monster, in the bowels of that species of shark that gobbles its young as soon as born (why were they not extinct long ago?). A life that does not lead anywhere. That was what we had saddled ourselves with. Not, that is, that we expected the alien to come down, shake our hands, and utter the plaintive phrase: "We have been waiting so long for you." Or better: "It's been the merest smidge of time since we first left.

Congratulations on your achieving regular speech."

With that, my traveling companion awoke, stirred perhaps by some petty allusion, to interfere or interrupt—I had whiled the night away with my madcap musings, all attitude and partly logical, but questionable.

Light Lomax said, "What's new?" with an old couldn't-care-less attitude, and after a pause I began telling him.

"Has it occurred to you," he replied, "that each and every UFO may be assigned a different speaker? To track him and record everything he says? The best of men can be quite original in their thoughts, brilliant even. The best of men are always brilliant. You want to catch all they say."

He smiled the smile of intuitive derision (a geek smile, as befits his profession) and patted my knee. "Don't take it so hard. These UFOs will get you down if you let them. Some things in life just can't be reckoned with, so you'd better not trouble your head with them."

I asked myself if I'd any right to adopt such a hedonistic sangfroid philosophy, decided that I would not, and started immediately on the same track as before: "How then do you account for people spotting them in numbers, tens of thousands? Answer me that, will you?"

His refreshed spirits met my crushed ones without answering even with shrug or grimace. Instead, he produced a phrase that had nothing to do with anything: "Tiger Leaping Gorge," though I had heard him exclaim something like it before. He then sketched on a convenient piece of khaki paper something like an assortment of potatoes, which went begging until he had finished and I asked in my sleepless, rude way: "So?"

Light explained that he had drawn, as best he could, the shapes of the UFOs he'd heard people had seen. I produce them here much as they were, though no amount of my handiwork could exactly copy their dubious shapes.

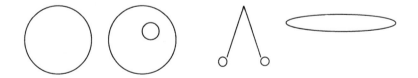

And so forth. I'd experienced much the same myself, apart from the close-inspection tour vouchsafed me a dozen years ago as I swam in the summer heat and saw this:

It had lingered for half an hour, silent, motionless, and then rocketed off at appalling speed, a dun thing, gleaming huge and letterless, like an insult in the sun, defying you to make sense of it while it lasted. He nodded as if it was all too familiar instead of being all too strange. Finally he said, "Twenty or thirty different kinds of shapes, some obscure. Some as plain as day. *Cui bono.*"

This habit of breaking into Italian irritated me, but I had enough Italian to cope with it. "What use," I said in echo. "What use is that?"

"A signal," he answered.

"A portent. If you like."

"Of things to come?"

"A Wellesian conceit then."

"If you go that far." He was getting snide, or was I imagining it?

"A token of national pride."

"If you must."

"Saying, one day soon." I vowed to tease him further.

"You're some optimist."

"Why?"

"We haven't got the first flaming idea of whatever they are."

Then I ran past him the sum of all my sleepless agitation, finishing with, "Perhaps they intend nothing at all. They may all be empty."

"I thought you said they had propulsive power."

"They do. It's all automatic, though."

"How so?"

"There's nobody inside them."

"Nobody?"

"Empty vessels all. These envoys have no beings. All mechanical."

"You speak firsthand, having known them."

"I speak in true ignorance, Lomax, my friend. Can you do better?"

At last I fell asleep, dismissing all rational thought on the issue. When I awoke, after several hours of fitful slumber, it was with a profound sense of things minutely shrunken, just beyond a comfortable range of viewing. This phenomenon, not *always* reliable, was ever so gently propelling objects beyond visibility—telephone books, newspapers, sewing needles. I was going home, I told myself, going downhill among the lost teeth of the sharks.

What cheered me, just fractionally, was my lambent fascination with UFOs, which grew in majesty as I declined. I saw them as far back as the twelfth century, always the same long-lived observers, waiting for life on earth to become less violent. Waiting in vain, as it turned out, but waiting patiently all the same. Traveling as the mood seized them at the speed of light, they changed areas at insane speed, never discovering sane behavior among the humans below who were always game for another atrocity, another war, another "bloodless" coup, so called, with fatalities mounting day after day. Most were even willing to overlook the killing at Darfur, for instance, because no one knew where it was or how important Hutu versus Tutsi had become. But the UFOs noticed everything, and I wondered why they did not pack up and seek another planet. To which perhaps the answer was: all planets are the same, right to the end of their reign. It's possible that there had been, so far, no planet with safe goings-on, and the UFOs were waiting for all the warmongering to end. *That* was why they were never heard from. Theirs was a waiting game to beat all, a superlative nonstarter on who knows how many planets. In this scenario, their explorers' only reprieve was death among the surviving mollusks (or whatever), in perpetual submission, doomed forever to a silent, aberrant dark.

How presumptuous of me to purloin and imagine the lives of the UFOs, tracking them down and daring to know things about them unknown to other humans. It was a chutzpah I took pride in, and, like the aliens, I was just waiting, having an eternity to waste.

II.

Murmuring something about ice cream, Light Lomax went outside to taste the already half-spent day. Dimly, I began to return to my theme of the night before, barbarously calculating the odds of a universe divided by the sum total of UFOs, with neither quantity known nor even guessable. It was hopeless, and surely worth abandoning, but I relished dividing the odds by three: planets aswarm with life, planets where life no longer flourished, and planets inhospitable as bleached, arid stars.

Strangely, it brought me a measure of self-esteem thus to divide things off. Something semiprecise where all was moving. Why so grateful, all of a sudden, for this piece of sublunary choplogic? I wrote it off as paddling in the deep throes of the universe for too long. It was the acme of mental fatigue, when the overtaxed brain gave up and cried for mama to remove the impossible conundrum of the previous night. Yet part of me, the disobedient side, liked fondling the universe in this way, doomed to solve nothing but yet intoxicated to mingle with the grand unknowables for half an hour before mental fatigue set in and the thrill of discovering anything lapsed into the old ignorance of before.

Try for half an hour, I thought, and then cancel. Why does it thrill me to waste time in this way? A mental itch, it all came back to the same insoluble: *Why in the entire history of mankind had the UFOs not been heard from even once?* Boredom? Contempt? Bloody-mindedness? Massive patience? With what? Why persist with it further? Nothing else to do? Here my mind stopped. *Nothing else to do?* Strange to say, my mind may just have solved the enigma. Was it really the *eureka* of the whole thing? In the tradition of hurry up and wait forever? Time must have a stop after all. If so, why not this one? For an instant all thoughts of waiting for something vanished, replaced by an opaque ether, and oh the relief I felt thus to fall asleep with *nothing* to wake up for. Or to. Then it was gone. The old obligation to make sense of things returned with a vengeance, and I settled down to work on the impossible all over again, passionate to construct something where all was nothingness.

Five decades of this folderol had brought me nowhere, apart from the usual tokens of the trade, D.Litts. and other medals, the Hawking and Einstein prizes, but little else of what truly mattered. My mind gazed back to the old notion of *nothing else to do,* noting how ungraspable the concept was, except that in this case the emphasis was on *nothing else,* invoking a mass of discarded butterflies not worth chasing. My mind gave thanks for something to desire.

Still and all, the concept of nothing haunted me, the very notion of a universe so vast and yet so—*untouchable.* And if not, *so blank.* Something missing, I thought, my mind invaded by the preposterous, sudden thoughts of one life-teeming earth among so many millions of suns. Only one, and look how much of a mess we had made of that. If this were all, creation was a dismal failure and worth keeping silent about from beginning to end. I paused in my quest and for once tasted the silence of things, the hiss of blank creation.

In a dream, I fudged up some breakfast (a couple of slices of rye bread and some antique cheese) to make who knew what impact on my stomach. Both rye and cheese had traveled with me all the way from Manhattan and I assumed Light Lomax had fared better leaving food to the mercies of the locals.

In one sense, I *could* go home again. I need not have come at all, or only halfway; it was not a matter of distance traveled so much as an impulse from the brain within. No, in truth, I had been obliged to travel to find that particular impulse to begin with. None of this cooled my unquenched alien ardor. I waited for Light Lomax to return.

"How many of them have *you* seen?"

"None. How many have you?"

"*One*, for half an hour."

"Poor odds. Some have seen them daily," commented Light, "all different. Those are the people you should be talking to."

"Drop the whole matter then."

"Do you really want to discuss it?"

"No. I can see you're not in the mood."

"Mood has nothing to do with it. You've not assembled the evidence."

"By my own lights, I have. Screw your evidence."

"Screw yours."

We had reached an impasse, not for the first time, and there was nothing to be done about it. I was adamant, Light Lomax was intractable. Perhaps, having come this far, we should have separated, never to speak again. Darwin and Christ had met, more or less, and disagreed. It was not the outcome I had been waiting for and neither of us would yield.

I thought back to my one personal UFO, its vast body turned toward me, like a giant of the sky arrived to consult one of the local astronomers. Rounded windows, pointed nose, no sound, its color a muted beige. How vivid, how resplendent. No sign of occupants. No movement. Then it had flown sideways, up and away, at incalculable speed. Never seen again, although dozens of friendlies had seen something similar and marveled. This was *my* UFO, by unnatural right, watching me, playing the waiting game.

On another front, during our vigil in Mongolia, there had been the willingness of the local women to make use of their bodies, as if we were visiting tax inspectors or pedigree-obsessed mountebanks. Jolly, roly-poly, olive-skinned, and of a fearsome body odor, these doxies rolled in the hay with us to our hearts' content, obliging us this way and that with incongruous naïveté. We might have been a herd of

325

horses or a convocation of orangutans for all the difference our human status made to them. To them we were as homunculi, fit for service but nothing else, a species of local stag ripe for plucking now and then.

We drifted along with what they put on offer, dreading the day when the shutters went down and the doxies turned their attentions elsewhere. We became used to their perfunctory, absentminded caresses, making of us draft animals with better things to think about.

Astonishing, really, this rough-and-ready sexuality contrasted with the high-strung desire and speculations we busied our minds with— despite the fundamental disagreement that divided us. There was something that bound our feeble clips to that sublunary desire. The smell of the byre, maybe, or the smell of an often-poked finger into that or this aperture.

These ladies knew everything and found it boring and their constant silence during our times together only made them more ferocious, as if the pair of us were neighbor automatons, out for a spree. We plugged on, we plugged in, forgetting we were born to be disappointed and tucked in among other human corpses in the end.

Even the parchment paper available locally let us down, since we were incapable of distinguishing the edge of the speckled paper from the edge of the board. Thus, many of our most valuable written contributions spilled over onto boards, which usually provoked a frenzied outburst.

So time passed in its funereal way, between tupping and astronomy, neither getting us very far except for my abiding—although recently arrived at—conviction that the UFOs were waiting us out, eyes in the sky since the dark Dark Ages. I could see myself among them, a successor to Clyde Tombaugh, the discoverer of Pluto, who once had languished by his lens until his soul ached and the lovely hunk of rock swam into view, seen (by humans, at least) for the first time.

What I would later call a brain wave, of the sort I had had since childhood, afflicted me. This migraine, as the complaint was called, began with an eye dazzle that affected sight, and sometimes abolished it.

Attacks could last a few minutes or some days (in my case, a few hours at least), followed by the classic thumping headache. After virtually a lifetime of suffering, I discovered that a bag of frozen peas compressed against the offending blur would bring relief in five minutes, God alone knows why. This left a space between the attack at its worst and the relief thus procured. But sometimes I actually prolonged the sequence, curious where it might lead. Usually it produced a deck of blanks, and seeing through things instead of seeing them plain.

This had long amused me, until the experience became too extreme. I marveled at the falsity of the system: I could not see what I could, and therefore could see what I could not. In truth, I saw both simultaneously, so long as I could endure its vagaries—before the excruciating pain began—delighted in the triumph of light, my very own crown filled with stars, as if by royal proxy. The memory of a migraine persisted long after it had fled, memories of ascending into the quite unseizable domain of the black hole, where diurnal life consisted of cats, roebucks, and humans alike stretched thin as linguine. After which there was much time left to obsess, to posit a brutal relapse into pain.

Note: did the agony that followed match the ripe golden moments of the previous sensation? Hardly, but I persisted in making them equal, stealing from the zone of agony the half inch of suave delight it offered me, trusting lifelong the quizzical gods of migraine to see me through. At any rate, this was my experience of heaven, conspired at, partly yielding, never conquered quite, but tempting always with the fruits of frankincense and myrrh, before the gates of hell opened and all expressions of delight foundered amidst a screen of a kitten stretched out on the black hole machine.

III.

The aliens were migraine sufferers—this was their true condition. I was positive. Not unlike other creatures in this world, they emerged half made. By the time they reached full agility, maybe the human animal would have sobered up. This was why the aliens rode the world in blameless ignorance. A matter of timing, with one life form second-guessing the other, neither side as yet appeased.

A skiing accident put paid to Light, at least for six months, during which I remained in place among the Outer Mongolians, whose quantum of wantum seemed to have fallen off the charts. Maybe it was the absence of my erstwhile friend, whose lusts outpaced mine. I kept to myself the discovery that I had made about the aliens all suffering from migraine bouts, maybe even undergoing a permanent affliction that no human could remedy. But still hungering for them

Paul West

to touch me, send me a bone-shivering flare.

Until then, I would keep my station, a quiet, expectant life sustained by doses of the hand-to-mouth gruel (*mistmurk*) that was the locals' staple food. Each waking day I would pause for the first sound of their long-delayed funereal patter, calling me out of hiding to experience the sublime chatter of their children, so long annulled and choked, and the never-before-heard cacophony of their blessed and too-long-delayed hosannas of triumph.

Ah, I wished with all my heart (missing a beat or two now and then and speeding with inexplicable consequences) for a migraine-free reprieve for all of them, no more bone-racking skull pain or miserable quinsy of peering to decide what is not there. I longed for reprieve, for them, for me, in a world of cockahoop whimsy with a brain free to improvise, despite the bleeding furnace of feelings, our hearts chiming in consonance, nary a heartbeat missed nor aorta out of place.

In short, I yearned for a world intact, for them, for me, a cosmos where all fitted in, no disappointments, no aggrieved complaints, a world where every lamb had its day, roly-poly in fresh abandon, with places reserved for even the vilest nightmare. If I only wished hard enough, I thought, things would keep coming together as they were destined to do, and the UFOs would step down kindly, in a rush of willing accommodation to greet this other alien in a spaceship of his own. I wished until my blood ran hot again, trying to master creation while there was yet time, before the voyagers left, before we were all ground to cinders.

Signified

Susan Steinberg

BECAUSE WORDS ARE ABOUT desire and desire is about the guy who filled my two front tires when one was low. And desire is about the guy who cleaned my windshield as the other, crouched below me, filled.

And there's the guy who pours foam onto my coffee in the shape of a heart and I, each time he pours, so slow, think, Jesus.

Because the guy who pours the foam in the shape of a heart—and I don't know how he does it—is twenty-four, and I am not twenty-four, meaning I am not thirty-four and don't think much of twenty-four except to think I must have been working through something back then, living in that railroad apartment in Baltimore, daydreaming of fame and what all came with fame.

My friends that year said, Why move, but I packed some boxes, crammed the boxes into the car, pushed the couch over the porch. My friends waved from the couch in the rearview mirror and I forgot them once I reached the highway.

Why Boston, they wanted to know.

Because why not.

Or because I imagined Boston as brick walked and lamp lit, and I could see myself tromping in boots through the snow.

Or because I imagined a field from a poem I'd read in school as a child.

Or because I had no good answer to Why Baltimore.

Because I had gotten held up, a knife point pointing to my face.

All this to say that I remember those friends from then, sitting here now on my new couch, twelve years past, their tattoos I remember of gothic letters and Celtic knotwork, their tangled hair. All this to say that I've made a connection, forced as it seems, of twenty-four to twenty-four. I've made a connection of couch to couch. Connections are easy when one is sitting, staring at a wall. There is no deeper meaning. There is no signified.

There is couch and there is couch.

There is the table my feet are on and the table from then. A table we sat at until the pale hum of morning.

There was no such word then as after-party.

There was no such use of the word random then how the kids these days use random.

What I mean is the guy who filled my tires looked up and said, of the lowness in one tire and not in the other, Random, and I, remembering running into a curb the night before, driving home from a bar where I sat and sat until giving up, thought, Not really.

And the guy who cleaned the windshield whistled and walked back to the garage.

And the guy who pours the foam into the shape of a heart told my friend of me, She's hot, when my friend went to the café once alone. Your friend, he said, she's hot, and my friend called later to tell me the news.

What was I doing that night. Same thing as this night. Drinking wine. Sitting on the couch, my feet up on the table. These are the clichéd years, these years. The details have been predetermined. It's a recipe I follow. Very little this, very little that.

I think I said, That's cute. Because that's what one says in this situation. One laughs and says, Cute, and one's friend says, in this situation, You should go for it. Which always seems to mean to me that I should go against something else.

I said, How old is he?

Then I said, That's cute.

Then I said, I'm twelve years older, and my friend, exhaling smoke for emphasis, said, Exactly.

In Baltimore everyone was going for everyone else. Small town. Junkies. We were all the same age, the twenty-somethings, the fifty-somethings. When the bars closed we went to the place that stayed open until morning. Club Midnight. And we drank orange drinks until things felt unreasonable. What was the point of reason. I had no desire for reason. I had only a weak desire—in the words of my shrink from then—to fill a space and I filled the space. There's a list, somewhere, of the drugs I did. There's a list, somewhere, of who I fucked. I wrote these lists on the backs of napkins, a night at Club Midnight, and everyone thought the lists were too short. Well, that was years ago, and things have changed. And there's a list of the drugs I almost did and a list of the guys I almost fucked. And those lists. Believe me. Another story.

So I sat the other night in a bar on a snowy, lamp-lit street, until I realized he—the one I am supposed to desire—thirty-six, a neat haircut, small hands, a tucked-in shirt, a workhorse, a perfect match—wasn't going to show. Or I realized that he would show and that I would feel disgust. So I stumbled to the car, ended up half the car on the sidewalk, no one around to see it.

I once knew better than to drive.

I mean I once considered other options.

There were no windows in Club Midnight. We knew it was morning because of sudden blue shadows under our eyes. And that shock of light, no matter how pale, when someone opened the door. And the shock of the cold. Jesus. There's no good story to tell except once I decided to wait for the bus. My friends had gone, and I was too sick from drink after drink to drive. Birds were chirping, and I wondered where from. There were no trees. There was nowhere to hide. The man with the knife had a scar on his face and I didn't want a scar on my face. I reached into my pocket, pulled out some ones, and he ran one way, I the other.

And here I am watching the blue turn darker blue behind the trees. And the color of this couch, according to the catalog, is mushroom, which means it's greenish, grayish, brownish. Which means I paid a lot for it. One must pay up when one has a recipe, a list of ingredients, a predestined life, and one ingredient is a costly couch. And one is a car. And one is a man. And one is a child.

And one is over thirty feeling for that warm space in the dimming room.

The men who carried up the couch were older, no-nonsense, beer-bellied, and smelling of sweat, though had the room been darker, smokier, the bartender filling and filling, the music up high, well, perhaps there'd be something more to say.

The guy filling my tires, when I tried to hand him a few ones, said, No. He said, Jesus, lady, air is free.

And the guy in the café—dark curly hair, that way of dressing—his pants hanging just under his hip bones—blue eyes and so on, the thing with the foam. Well, each time I drop fifty cents into the tip jar, lift my cup, say thank you into the disintegrating heart, never looking up, though I can feel him looking down, and my friend—who always smells like smoke—did I say this—and it's comforting somehow—will say, Aw, a heart. Look, a heart.

And my friend and I will sit on the chairs on the sidewalk out front, even in cold, and a bus will pass, and the bell on the door will jingle, and the guy will come out, wiping his hands on his pants, lighting a cigarette he pulls from a pale blue box, blowing white smoke into the sky.

And I imagine he's looking at someone else.

And I remember my predestined life. My list of ingredients. And one is a man. And one is a child.

And one is a child.

And I imagine he's looking only at me.

And I imagine the bell sound comes from a horse stopped in the snow at the edge of the woods.

Three Poems
Donald Revell

SPICE

Pure green most pure
Among its own blue flowers,
Like rosemary, death
Is most itself when
Rooted at a threshold,
Playing at God by a gate
Until, when many years have passed,
The gate swings open, and death,
So carefully, with such
Small tremor, enters
The courtyard filled with children—
Phoebe, Benjamin, Adam, Mary.
Oblivion is a child again.
Looking into its hands, it sees clouds,
And then nothing.
Looking into my hands, I see clouds,
And they endure; they drift and endure.
One is broken glass. One is pure
Among its own blue flowers.

KENTUCKY

Ground-dwelling birds reply to thunder.
It is sunrise somewhere over there, while here
Stars shine still, and the secret doors inside the pines
Remain wide open. Which way to go?
When I walk into the sun, my children
Hurry beside me. I hear footsteps and machines.

When I go west into the stars, I see
Nothing I could show you: ghosts
Who are not ghosts at all, hearts
On their sleeves, eyes like melted diamonds.
I truly believe that someone loved me once.
A bird alighted on a bee alighting
On a green stem, and I heard thunder. God's favorites
Are the little stars he drops into the sun.

CAMBRIA

Games of ocean, games of trees, alarms.
The water is not for you.
The woodlands are too dense, and your heart
Will break before you find the clearings.
Keep to the vineyards.
The men there take their noonings;
Then comes heaven.
A vine speaks. It tells stories.
The dirt unfolds a music made at its birth,
Cool as the years, smooth as the lyre
God tunes in everything.
Of agony, I have nothing to say.
Of Cambria, a town where I was happy,
I say I never saw it, save at its best.

How Many Fires
Rebecca Seiferle

How many fires

have I started
like this,
breathing into it

as if it were a drowned
child that I kept trying
to revive?
Caring nothing for my own

                  hair, fingertips,
as I pressed closer
to the fire . . .
        yet the singeing of one hair, the sting
of one spark upon
the skin, and I leapt back
instinctively.

              And because I am tired,
         and want to stop thinking
of this fire of my fire for you, I kick the logs apart,

though my violence which scatters them,
makes them burn the more.

             Oh how can I leave you? except
to regret my own forcefulness;
        in the morning, there will be nothing left
but a bed of ash,

      and a remnant or two, so carbonized with resentment,

will lie beneath

the grate of the campfire ring
and turn into an eye of smoke.
     O fire instruct me and make me wise,
for in you, I see how impossible
       it is
   to make one log burn
    alone,

though it might catch
   upon this conflagration
     of tiny dead twigs
        I tore

from the dry limbs
of the ponderosa
pine—
   its amber blood of butterscotch
now the pitch
    sparking
into flame—

but as quickly as the brambles of the wild roses
   that I gleaned from the meadow
     full of the soaring
       transepts of silver
        and black butterflies.
ignite
   in some winged and burning formlessness
   the obduracies of red heartwood
     its torn and lovely flesh
        smelling of aromatic
      cedar, my love, my love,
falls upon itself
      and smolders out.

    What did I think
      when I was a child and on nights
        like this, cold in the forest of myself,
        stared into
   the face of fire?

I was all longing
then,

all incipient flame, not full of the materiality of fate, that
          weighted thing, so full of rain and damp, gnawed by the tracks

of what has tried
to live within it,

          all those mouthed insistencies making
a cave, a burrow, a kind of house
          out of living flesh.

Oh, who am I?
          And who are you?
(Who tried to burn her love letters and could not
contain the flames?)

It's not the proximity
          that makes these two pieces of cedar, their heads touching, begin
          to kindle, licked by a slower blue

that flares into orange and crimson
tongues,
          but the angle

of their inclination,
          the air itself between them
                    burns, the distances

ignite
their edges

          and make of us a fiery form, a flux and flow

a tactile intertwining: as if it were enough (it is never enough) that

          beauty is a consuming gaze.

The Plot
Tova Reich

WHEN LUBA POPKIN FLUSHED, Lola Blitzer's pipes shuddered—an awful intimacy, the spasm of personal water shunting downward through her walls, a disturbance almost every hour of every night lately, not that Lola herself really slept that much anymore either. Luba's swollen feet across Lola's ceiling all night long, plodding from bed to toilet, crashing into objects, the downpour of her nightly shower to calm herself, trick herself into sleep, the throbbing of her television going full-time to keep her company in her widowhood when she was in, a precaution against robbers when she was out— Lola knew entirely too much about this stranger, Luba Popkin, due to the accident of living stacked up on each other, it was so unseemly. For thirty years, maybe longer, they nodded formal recognition if by chance they crossed paths entering or leaving their building on Amsterdam Avenue, or happened to be downstairs at the same time when the postman delivered the Social Security checks, and also, it goes without saying, by the garbage. But it was not until Lola volunteered to join the neighborhood women's *chevra kadisha* bereavement committee that they were officially introduced, when she was partnered with Luba, already a pro in the *tahara* rituals of purification and preparation of a dead body for burial, and the two of them took their places side by side in front of the corpse.

She was a heavy woman in her early sixties, a quarter century younger by a rough estimate than either Lola or Luba, a contemporary, give or take, of the other two women working alongside them, the entire holy society purification team safely within the postmenstrual decontaminated finish line, and though they had been forewarned by one of the directors of the funeral home, they were obliged to silently beg her forgiveness for transgressing the dignity of the dead by inwardly recoiling when she was unwrapped. It wasn't just the pits of knotted scarring where the breasts had been, or the long pale gash in the waxy flesh of the lower belly, in the region of the womb, or the sparse wisps of coiled hair where the legs forked and on the head, or the bruises on elbows and knees—this lady was a faller, Lola recognized the type at once, Lola's mother had been a faller too—or even the toothless mouth gaping rigidly open, like the mouths of those wretched souls Lola used to see when she still rode the subways, drooping helplessly into calamitous sleep late at night, like dogs, like her mother's mouth the night Lola had been ordered to sit guard in the slow-motion first moments afterward, while adult arrangements were being made, the family secret of the inside of her mother's mouth was more than she could bear, she was nine years old, she had tried to prop it closed by wedging a book under the jaw, slamming that mouth shut with an upward thrust of the book, a big book, her mother's favorite, a cautionary tale, *Anna Karenina*, but the minute they marched back in they yanked it out in horror, and the jaw fell slack down again. In that brief glimpse of the entire body, when the corpse was exposed for the first time, in the few seconds before a clean sheet could be stretched across it for modesty and respect, there was the humiliating spectacle of the open mouth, yes, but more hopeless than that, to Lola's mind, was the nail polish, assiduously applied on all ten fingers and toes, just a day or two ago at most, living color. Her mother's fingernails were lacquered too, oxygenated red, to match her lipstick exactly. There was nothing Lola ever knew more minutely in her entire life than her mother's hands, the flat wart pressing against the rubbed gold wedding ring, the rough knuckled thumb and thick forefinger stretched glossy and taut to pincer the metallic tube as she leaned forward to the mirror to put on her outside face—the gelatinous red scrawl across the lips, the clown stain on the tissue, the sharp, stale, spit odor rising—Lola would stand there silently, gazing upward, observing closely. Her mother was not thinking about her. Lola had been ruined forever by her mother's unhappiness.

Removing the nail polish, that was the first job Luba assigned her, and also the hospital bracelet. Sherry something was the name of this woman who had once dealt with this body full-time, who alone privately savored inhaling its smells. Decay was in the air, sweet creamy liquefaction, maggots and worms already breeding wildly, it was futile to struggle against them, Lola knew this firsthand from her late-life career as a boutique picker of lice and nits from the golden heads of the children of the rich. Discreetly, Lola sucked in her breath as she toiled, to block out the odor of putrefaction that was growing more and more insistent; she dimmed her eyes against the fishy blueness and bloating of the corpse, she numbed her touch to the parchment-brittle skin and alien coldness as she cleaned under the nails with a toothpick, prying open the clawed fingers to reveal a petrified Kleenex—another charter member of the society of tissue-clutching women, Lola noted, as she was herself, and yes, her mother too; this tissue fossil must be placed inside the coffin and buried with her, Lola was informed, there were bloodstains on it, it was a body part. Lola penetrated the ears with a Q-tip, the nostrils, and so on, combing, grooming, while Luba, along with the other two women, washed the body with lukewarm water, first the front, uncovering only the designated part as they worked on it, inclining it on the left side, then on the right, to do the back, chanting all the while lines from the sacred love song. Your eyes like doves, Your cheeks, Your lips, Your arms, Your thighs. Then Luba alone, still strong as an ox in her ninth decade of life and weighing in at over two hundred and twenty pounds, stood Sherry on the floor and held her upright while the others poured three eight-quart buckets of water totaling nine *kavim* over her head in a continuous flow to stream down her body, chanting, She is pure, She is pure, She is pure, in accordance with the verse, And I will throw pure water on you and you will be purified, from all of your impurities and from all of your abominations I will purify you. Sweat pooling in their armpits and leaking down their sides, breathing heavily, they raised her leaden limbs to dress her in priestly white linen shrouds, the blouse, the robe without pockets to certify to security that she was passing through unarmed, arching her hips upward to draw the trousers over the meat of belly and buttocks, the sash pleated to form the pitch-forked *shin* of the merciful divine's name, the cap. Ministering to the dead was regarded as the noblest of all acts of loving-kindness be-cause no earthly gratitude from the recipient could be expected—that's what Lola had been taught during the orientation, but when they finally settled Sherry into her plain pine coffin and quit bother-ing her at last, there was an audible deflation as she relaxed into place, an audible sough of relief not to be handled ever again, to be left alone finally—they all heard it, Thank you, Thank you. They shut her mouth once and for all by binding up the jaw with a scarf, a cloth was stretched over the face to veil her for eternity, she was mummified in a white sheet, shards of earthenware from the holy land and the dust to which she was already returning were strewn over the eyes, the mouth, the heart, the genitals. Sherry, daughter of Irwin, they addressed her, we ask your forgiveness if in any way we have dishonored you, we were just doing our jobs according to our tradition.

When they do me, Lola made a mental note, they'll use my mother's name—Lola daughter of Bella—I'll get Luba to make sure.

Which was why, after they adjusted the lid on top of the coffin and washed their hands and stepped outside, stricken by the indifferent light of day, instead of hurrying home in accordance with her established personal policy of paring away all attachments, animate and inanimate, Lola lingered in front of the funeral home alongside Luba. She had quite lost whatever little talent she might once have possessed at making friends, or, even more degrading, at asking a favor for herself—how did a person go about it anyway?—and the thought of giving off the suspicion that she might be lonely, needy, was appalling. Still, it might not appear too pathetic to stick to Luba for a respectable interval and wait for a sign; they were pointed in the same direction after all, home was in the same building, there was an explanation, an excuse. Two old ladies propped up against the backdrop of a funeral parlor—who would pay attention anyway?— and she, Lola, so austere and miniature, under five feet tall now and shrinking steadily, parked alongside this monumental Luba topped off with her lavender pouf hairdo. Such a ridiculous couple they must have been, Lola was just picturing it through the indecent eyes of a stranger from every demeaning angle when Luba took her elbow and steered her down the street. "So you come mit me now to the Utopia for a bite to eat maybe? I always have a little nosh after I do one—a little present to me, myself, and I—to remind me that Luba Popkin, she ain't dead yet."

In the coffee shop, jammed into the booth across from Luba, sipping her tea from the heavy varicosed cup that had been pressed between generations of all varieties of sinful lips, Lola observed as her companion dug shamelessly into her chunk of quivering meringue, washing it all down with hot chocolate—"mit extra *schlag*, LaToya darling," she had specified to the waitress, who rolled her eyes and nodded, obviously trained to Luba's preferences. "You eat for the birds," Luba commented to Lola. "Me, I was always a good eater, thanks God, I was always a big girl. Strong. That's what saved me from the showers." She pushed up her left sleeve to show off the fading blue numbers tattooed onto the loosening mottled skin of her forearm. "Like cattle they branded us, darling, they should only rot in hell. I was a slave to Adolf in Auschwitz. Instead from the gas, we dropped dead from the work." With the plump pad of a fingertip,

341

Luba was suctioning up the crumbs of piecrust that had settled onto the great prow of her bosom. "Yes, darling, it was very terrible, just like they tells you in *Schindler's List*, I wouldn't wish it on a dog, but in the end—I hates to admit this—it all turned out for the best. That's why I gets up every morning and sings 'God Bless America,' even though I'm not a religious person, maybe you even heard me from downstairs. When I came to America I was a nothing, I was a refugee; now, thanks God, I'm a survivor. And mine daughter, Fernie"—she pronounced it Foinie—"she even got her career from the whole business, very high class, director from second-generation affairs by the Holocaust Heritage Museum," Luba declared proudly, "maybe you even heard from it, right in the same neighborhood from the Twin Towers, may they rest in peace."

Lola lowered her head as Luba went on, unwinding her spiel. What could she offer? How could she compete with the Holocaust? Lola was Holocaust challenged. The worst thing that had ever happened to her in her entire life was losing her mother when she was a child. She still had not gotten over it, she never would. That was her miserable little Holocaust. Otherwise, there was nothing to distinguish her. Luba would quickly lose interest and then what would Lola do?

"So, darling," Luba burst in suddenly, wiping her mouth and giving Lola a sly look, "the way I figures it, you made up your mind already to finish up on Amsterdam Avenue. In the apartment. Am I right or am I right?"

Silence was translated as confession.

Luba gave out a triumphant laugh. "It also so happens I noticed that you're busy, busy, busy all the time—deaccessioning. That's a fancy-shmancy word from the museums, by the way, mine Foinie taught me. It means you're slimming down your collection. You're in a get-rid-get-rid stage—no? Tell me something, darling, is there one single thing still left inside your apartment—a table, maybe, a chair, a bed to sleep on? I says to the super, 'Hector, darling, the minute that lady from downstairs throws out another piece of furniture or some tchotchke, you brings it straight up to me.' So if you ever wants anything back, or maybe you just miss something and you wants to come up and say hello, you know where to find it—one floor up by the elevator, right on tops from you, apartment 4C. All your goods is by me, except for maybe what that *gonif* Hector stole for himself."

*

Seven more women had to die and require immediate ritual purification and preparation for the grave before Lola could summon
up the nerve to get to the point. In the meantime, she and Luba
had established a routine. By an unspoken agreement, they refrained
from entering one another's apartment; despite Luba's invitation,
personal interiors were understood to be off-limits, not to be violated.
So whenever the phone call came that a fresh lady awaited them in
the refrigerator, within half an hour they met in the lobby of their
building, and then walked together to the funeral home. Afterward,
they always went out for something to eat. "Tradition!" Luba would
belt out, linking her arm through Lola's, propelling her to the Utopia,
and once in a while, for a change, to one of the other coffee shops,
in every single one of which she was recognized and greeted by a
chorus. Mostly, it was Luba who talked. She had endless stories, and
relished telling and retelling them, fortunately for Lola. But inevitably, Lola was obliged to contribute, do her bit and offer up some
morsels from her own stunted life. She had never married—her
mother had once said that boys are messy things; somehow that
maternal nugget had implanted itself in Lola's brain and taken root—
so in the men's department, except for a few boyfriends here and
there not worth processing, there was only a vestigial stump. Nevertheless, as she told Luba, she had had many children, all female by
gender, from her career as a teacher at a private school for girls.
Another mamaism that had stuck with Lola was that education was
a very good career for a woman, because of the short days and long
holidays and vacations—in hindsight, though, she realized that her
mother must have been referring not to her, but to real women, with
families to care for. She had taught grades one through five over the
years, never higher, because even by the fifth grade there would occasionally be some poor girl tormented by precocious physical development who was already bigger than Lola. That brought an appreciative
hoot out of Luba, which Lola found exceedingly encouraging. Maybe
even she, in her own modest way, could also be entertaining.

Her mother used to tell her how, during the endless prayer services
in the synagogue of her Galician village, she and her little girlfriends
would amuse themselves on the women's balcony by staring in
fascination as the wigs of the pious matrons came to life and jitter-
bugged around on top of their heads—went spastic, like Lola's third-
graders used to say. Lice, she explained to Luba, who signaled with
a nod that of all people, she, Luba Popkin, a decorated veteran of
five death camps, really required no further clarification. And who

knows? Maybe her mother's story was the inspiration for Lola's post-retirement second career as a high-end nitpicker.

When Lola put out her shingle, so to speak, there was a lice plague across the city; for all she knew, maybe there still was. It wasn't just the poor and unwashed, the expendables, who were scratching like dogs; the privileged, pampered children of the rich, such as the ones she taught, were also not exempt. The school nurse inspected heads regularly—just one tiny white nit clinging to a hair, and the kid was sent home, no appeals, no mercy, not even a major contribution to the endowment could alter that reality, no reentry until the all-clear signal was given. Luba probably did not realize just how labor-intensive nitpicking was. You couldn't just charge in there and brutally razor off the entire tangled lice-flecked mops of these little princesses, like in the concentration camps. You couldn't just squat down there, either, like a mama gorilla crouching in her cage, cradling your baby ape in your lap, grooming, grooming, then licking the bug off your finger with your long wet tongue. You had to go through the head painstakingly, hair by hair, strand by strand, to locate the nits, like a sprinkling of sesame seeds, and also the newborn baby lice, only one millimeter long—Lola wore special goggles with magnifying lenses for this. Naturally, the mothers of these infested children could not be expected to spend such nonquality time going through those colonized heads with a fine-tooth comb, over and over again. It was a job to be delegated; a professional was required. The best person had to be found for this as for all things, money was not an issue. Lola hoped it would not sound like boasting, but she, Lola Blitzer, was the acknowledged best. *New York* magazine had even named her Best Nitpicker. The caption under her picture called her Miss Blitzer the Nitzer. For those precious heads, the article made a big point of mentioning, Miss Blitzer applied a special emulsion; the recipe was a family secret handed down from her mother, but Lola had no problem revealing it now to her loyal friend, Luba—one-third olive oil, one-third white vinegar, one-third kerosene—never, God forbid, the official lice shampoos, the only products available on the market, over the counter or prescription, poisons, believe it or not, pesticides and insecticides such as people spread on their lawns, soaking through the scalps of innocent children, seeping directly into their tender, impressionable brains. Furthermore, it was noted in this article that, as a veteran teacher, Miss Blitzer made productive use of the time while nitpicking and delousing, conversing with the kids exclusively about educational topics such as great literature,

Gitche Gumee and the wigwam of Nokomis, or current events, or space exploration, and playing classical music in the background, Ravel's *Bolero*, over and over again, for relaxing the mind. Luckily or unluckily, this great honor bestowed upon her by the magazine, which included a mahogany plaque that she ordered and paid for but had since thrown out along with everything else—did Luba by any chance have it upstairs in her apartment?—anyway, this newfound celebrity came to Lola around the same time that her eyes, even with the binocular goggles, were giving out, growing too dim and clouded to bear the strain of nitpicking, and the publicity from the article, of course, brought her official attention, so she could no longer safely insist on being paid exclusively in cash. Luba nodded approvingly at this—not for one second in her entire life on American soil had she even considered being paid in anything other than cash—and she confirmed also that many of the tenants in the building had noticed the heavy traffic to and from Lola's apartment during that period; they wondered if she had a business there, which was strictly prohibited by house rules and regulations, but they were too considerate to report her, they were simply happy for Lola, that finally someone was visiting her.

Lola pushed aside thoughts of allowing the hurt at being universally regarded as pathetic to rise up and engulf her. She went on instead to explain to Luba that obviously the business was limited to after-school hours and weekends due to the nature of the clientele—unfortunately, it was the same time of day that most people were also home from work; she regretted the disturbance to her neighbors. Almost always, the client was delivered by the nanny, but sometimes the mother came along too, usually because she had become infested by her child and required professional treatment herself. There was one mother-daughter case that Lola would never forget. The girl was not even four years old, with very fine flaxen hair. The mother was bringing her child to Lola after having just experienced a life-altering epiphany—she announced this the minute she came through the door. She had stuck her head into the oven along with her daughter's, intending to turn on the gas, to end it all and, mercifully, to take the girl along with her, when she noticed a louse in the child's hair. Immediately, she pulled both of their heads out of the oven. There was work to be done, the matter had to be taken care of without delay, she had a purpose on this earth. She called Miss Blitzer. If anyone ever wondered why God created lice, here was the reason.

*

The seventh woman took away the breath of the entire bereavement committee; even Luba, who believed she had seen everything, was not unshaken. When they entered the room, the overripe steaming up of rot seized them more pungently than ever. She had already been placed inside the coffin, upon the white sheet in which she would be wrapped, now thrown loosely over her. They were ordered to dispense with the purification rites, simply to wash the hands and face and feet. Drawing back the sheet, they were dazed by the raw markings of a freshly stitched autopsy incision, Y-shaped, starting at each shoulder and meeting between the breasts, then plumbing in a straight line down to the pubic zone; another sewn-up incision crossed her forehead, ear to ear. All of the organs had been returned to the cavity of the body, they were told, but as they went about their work, a mortuary-science specialist ambled into the room with a lumpy plastic bag and dropped it into the casket with a wet plop. She could not be lifted; her back had already begun to decompose, bacteria lying in ambush had been liberated to start the process, maggots were burrowing. Instead of dressing her, they laid the shrouds on top, then swaddled her as best they could in the white sheet. The women were never told her name or the name of her father, only that she would be buried at the edge of the cemetery, at a distance from other souls. They understood what this meant. She could not have been much more than thirty years old—my mother's age, Lola thought.

At the Utopia afterward, Lola could barely sip her tea. Even Luba's appetite was affected. "No *schlag* for me today, LaToya darling," she said to the waitress. They sat opposite each other in silence, plunged into themselves, broken at last by Luba, who began to tell Lola a story about a butcher, one of the wealthiest merchants in her hometown, who would put his children on the scale every Friday morning and weigh them, and then distribute their weight in meat to the poor for the Sabbath; it was considered a very high act of charity, and inscribed upon his tombstone. "I'm telling you, Lola darling, it's a losing battle. Meat—*fleisch!*—that's what it all boils down to in the end! In the end, the vermins always wins. You thinks you're in control, but I gots news for you, darling."

Luba, at least, was in control until the worms moved in and took over; she had her delegated representative, she had her Fernie to carry out her wishes. Whom did Lola have? Nobody, and nothing. As painful as it was for her to ask for something for herself, as mortifying as it was to even admit that there was something left that she actually still desired on this earth, she tore herself open and turned to Luba.

She needed to be buried next to her mother, in the old Jewish cemetery on Long Island, she said to Luba. She was asking this very great favor of Luba—to take charge when the time came, and make sure this was done. When the time came she would be helpless, at the mercy of others who didn't care two cents about her, that was why she was appealing to Luba, to be her designated driver, to navigate for her, to fight—fight!—on her behalf. She would be forever indebted—unable, of course, to express her gratitude in words when the time came, like the silenced women they prepared for burial, but she would find a way to thank Luba now, in advance, materially and spiritually, with an open hand from the depths of her heart. Instantly, Luba protested that with all the *schlag* in her pipes, she would be the first to go, for sure, whereas Lola's pipes were probably clean as a whistle; Lola was a hermit, a lady monk, like a Hindu in a diaper. No, Lola insisted, Luba was a life force. Luba was indestructible.

The problem was, Lola went on, the plot next to her mother was taken by a complete stranger. There was a narrow strip of earth, a margin at best, between the two plots, her mother's and the stranger's, enough to squeeze in a child maybe, a small child, a ten-year-old maximum—that's what the chief rabbi of the cemetery had told her. Put me in with my mother in the same plot, Lola had cried. The rabbi shook his head. No doubling, no stacking, we've already done mass graves. Even so, he had sold her the sliver of *karka*, as he called it, the mean piece of earth between the two graves, at full price, and she had paid for it joyously, she owned it, she had the receipt—it was her plot. A ten-year-old maximum would be buried there, she had promised him. They had had several meetings to finalize the arrangements, but the truth was, she didn't trust him—that's why she was turning to Luba, to act as her agent and advocate and executor at the appointed hour. During one of her meetings with the rabbi, a boy had walked in with a yarmulke on his head and a knapsack on his back, just returned from one of those youth pilgrimages to Poland. From the backpack he drew out a plastic bag filled with pieces of bone he had collected from a garbage dump at one of the death camps—she forgot which camp, maybe it was even Luba's, maybe they were even the bones of Luba's mama. The rabbi agreed to bury the bones in the cemetery—Yeah, yeah, don't worry, sonny, I'll take care of it, the rabbi said. When the boy left, the rabbi shoved the bag in his desk drawer. Lola believed the bones were still in the rabbi's desk. Lola believed she had already by now reduced herself, through self-denial, through physical discipline and the mortification of her flesh, through fasting and abstinence, to the size of a ten-year-old, maximum. She had been a very good girl; she had given up all sweets. By size, she was now of an age to no longer deserve to be separated from her mother. It was her heart's desire to be buried beside her mother—My mother, Bella. She had earned the privilege, she had already cleansed herself of all impurities and abominations, saving Luba and the rest of the *tahara* bereavement crew a good deal of work and aggravation, setting the record, maybe, for the smallest normal adult corpse they'd ever have to handle, they could process her in five minutes flat and jump right out for a snack. A ten-year-old's coffin customized for the designated space was already set up in her apartment—she fit into it very comfortably now, with lebensraum to spare. Luba would notice it right away when the time came; she couldn't miss it. It was all that remained in the bedroom, with instructions typed out.

She lay on her back inside her coffin, dazed from her mortal combat with sleep, attending to the rush of water from Luba's endless shower above her head. A grinding paralysis had overtaken her. Through the terrifying darkness of the unmoored panic hours, she observed herself struggling to move her limbs, but the dense weight of the air bore down upon her and the sense of impending deluge pressing in would not release her. A scream was lodged in the back of her throat, she labored to push it out, but it was stuck, stuck, she was hoarse from the effort. She must have been able to scream as a child—Sarah Heartburn, that's what her mother used to call her; it seemed the closest of memories. Could it really be so? Could she have ever once indulged in overdramatics, thrown a tantrum, actually treated herself to the redundancy, in her mother's phrase, of a conniption fit? Sarah Bernhardt, a Jewish girl too, also slept in a coffin—it was practice, practice, practice in anticipation of the great farewell performance, illuminating, in the purest sense, the essence of rehearsal. Lola had seen an old sepia postcard—the image of the actress elegantly posed in a pale flowing gown, hair draped around her, long stems of lilies accessorizing her supine form in grand style—a luxurious coffin, befitting a superstar, cushioned with satin. Lola's was the plain pine box of a child, to qualify for admission into the holy graveyard, to fit into her grudging slice of dirt alongside her mother, to pass the rigid standards of the chief rabbi, in strict adherence to Jewish law, it was the flimsiest of barriers against the elements and organisms, the hairy maggots, the coffin flies, the carrion beetles, no nails or metal clamps holding it together to give the illusion of permanence—but for now, for the nights of her own private rehearsals, she padded it with her old quilt, her sagged-out pillow folded under her head, her dear blanket drawn up to her eyes wide open in the darkness, the coldness of the grave more fearful than death itself.

The master magician Harry Houdini was also laid to rest next to his mother, Mrs. Weiss—that was his wish, his absolute goal; any other place would have been unthinkable—in the old Jewish cemetery in Queens, a station of death on the road to Long Island. Lola would read about Mrs. Weiss's wizard son to her girls sitting cross-legged on the rug in the story corner of their classroom in a circle that emanated from her, she slightly elevated in a child's chair, the book perched upright on her lap to face them, moistening her forefinger and hooking her arm to turn the pages from the far edge, slowly, slowly like a peep show, in delicious anticipation of what would be revealed. Mrs. Weiss's boy had them under his spell. Heads tilted upward, in concentrated seriousness, they gazed their fill when the picture of his dead body laid out inside his custom-made coffin was fully exposed, the same elaborate bronze model special ordered for his legendary escapes, airtight and impregnable, in which he would have himself sealed and lowered into the black depths. Water engulfed him, but this was not the place where his spirit could bear to come to rest, he had to break free.

She was struggling to break out, but it was as if she were bound up in invisible ropes. Heavy drops of water were falling on her from above with a hypnotic beat, lulling her through the night, streaming, splashing, puddling around her, swelling beneath her, setting her adrift in her little boat. She was hovering above herself, observing herself floating in her child's ark.

From the floor below came crashing noises, doors slamming, heavy rubber boots mounting the stairs. Men in thick leather belts with their gear dangling down, in gray rodent masks, swarmed around her, hissing, buzzing. She watched herself as on a screen pinioned in the dead center of their beams. She was the motherless child, Snow White, encircled by laborers with axes and spades, laid out in a glass coffin, frozen, preserved, awaiting the beloved's awakening kiss. Hector the super was leaning down toward her, white teeth bared. She could not move her lips. It's not coming from here, she wanted to tell them, it's coming from upstairs, the flood comes from upstairs, run upstairs, she needed to tell them, save her, save her.

Only one man remained now. He threw himself on top of her, crushing her beneath his weight, his mouth open over hers, pumping, pumping, ripping her apart. Panting, he lifted himself to catch his breath, then fell on her again, sucking, sucking. She saw herself under him, helpless and trapped, lashed down as on an altar. She listened as the crate in which she had so carefully packed herself splintered and fractured, cracked like an egg. The shell fell away; she was curled up inside the translucent membrane, powerless to break out, unable to scream. Her mother had instructed her, when cooking or baking, to crack the eggs in a separate bowl, one by one, to examine for blood spots. A blood spot is an impurity, the egg must be thrown out. Blood will soon flow out of your body, her mother had told her, from a place you do not even believe exists; it is a curse, out of your body and into the water. Never leave your baby alone in the water, her mother had warned her. Once upon a time there was a grandmother who called up her daughter on the telephone who left her baby alone in the bathtub to talk to her mother. The baby slipped quietly under the water, sank, and drowned. This is a true story, her mother had said; all stories are true, anything you can imagine can happen.

The men were now tramping and pounding their way across the floor above her, over her head, striking at walls, dragging large objects to scrape out a passageway. The roar of the gushing water, upon which she had tossed through the long night, was suddenly cut off. She detached from her body and flew into the air. Looking up, she saw through the ceiling, through the heavy tub, through the bloated form crumpled inside it, the skin soaked by water, ice blue and shriveled, straight through the masses of flesh to the fist of the untrustworthy heart, now flaccid and cold—the big mama, the survivor who saved only herself, collapsed in the shower. Looking down, she saw herself stretched out, captive and numb. A presence was bending over her as to a baby in a cradle drained and heaving from sobbing with loneliness all through the night. The face was ravaged, hollow eye sockets spilling slugs like tears. Ma, she wanted to cry out, Ma—but no sound came from her mouth. In vain, she tried to push against invisible barriers to stretch out her arms as the presence withdrew, as it shrank away to a point in the ether and receded out of reach. I am very far away from you, she heard it say, over and over again, Very, very far, away, from you—until the words could no longer be heard but hung suspended in the void, over the face of the water.

Three Poems
Juliana Leslie

PALIMPSEST

Everything inside of everything else
fox and sparrow

crocus and plumage
you make hibiscus
who is also rose of Sharon

though you are nothing compared to chrysanthemum
who travels 5,000 miles and then some

"For you"
"I have never felt so alive"

SOFTER MORE RADIANT SIGNAL

Tell me more about
crayons, contingency
and winter fruit
polyamorous structural
locations
we know aren't always the best
for human hands anyway
Tell me she is all worn out
from work
and thinking
the ghostly opposite
or optimistic messenger
a perpetual shoe shine
or softer

more brilliant
orange
I embrace
wherein love lies
like a human anatomy lesson
More palpable and more
more
Tell me we need
more rigor
more strings,
more
disclosure,
more collapsed lungs,
crooked teeth, broken
capillaries, tell me we need more
of what happens to bodies when bodies decide
to say what they want more of
More love in the vernacular
for example
More words like
longing, appetite, hunger
more bodies to willfully embrace
in summer kitchens
Tell me you want more sublimation
of history
by palpable whim
and fancy
More French in brunette
more four inside five
more singular features to render
clean of muscle, more
muscle
More of that feeling
that accompanies an unsettled
state of being
More of the condition of being
naturally disposed to several
different feelings
and tell me more about these words
turbulent, euphoria, indiscreet

Juliana Leslie

THERE IS MANIFEST AMONG US A DESIRE

If such a thought were in me
to provide movement at the level of writing

I would ride this train all over California
I would

and I would hum
I would sleep in both

A Home To Go Home To
S. G. *Miller*

HE HAS SHOWN ME the old adobe house outside and in and he has taken me riding across all the parceled acres of land that surround the house and he has told me the told-again stories born of the place and of his family and of him. And now it is me showing Son what I have come from, going south to north along the coast from one border town to another one yet, from forests petrified to those old conifered, from cottonwood to silver fir, diamondback to amanita, erg dune to tidal flat, and sandstone to agate, from what is to what has been, from memory to what might be.

Our start-up is done according to ritual, our send-off as to custom and trend. The town people gather in earnest and attend us bearing gifts, the golden aster is vased upon the altar, the pig turns out on the spit in offering. We say all the words supposed to be said and do all the things supposed to be done and we get all the things that one gets. We get suitcases lent to us and bills tucked into envelopes and we get stories of people's own and advice aplenty for living our life anew. We take all of it as given in the wholeheartedness that it is. We get wishes scribbled across the side of the pickup truck that we leave as a kind of flourish to our pilgrimage, keeping what's written through the new moon we are in, as that moon waxes crescent and quarters to full and as it wanes gibbous and fades on toward its end. The words as they are chalked, the sand and the dust, the grime and the duff and the tar and the oil and the mud, and whatever else of the earth we collect up along the way, will all be washed away in the moon after, once we are back to here where we are, so beginning at another beginning.

I had seen the old adobe house on the road back from Mexico. I had only otherwise heard talk of it about town. Murmurs from girls sitting behind me during school break out in the shade of the ramada would settle about in the air with the drift of their cigarettes and the pitch of the cricket shrill. There were remarks from certain evening regulars at the coffee shop who had a tendency as well to keep abreast of my business. And my mother was one to bring home common scraps of talk too, just as she fueled rumor with comments of her own.

I would break away early. Son would come by in his pickup truck to get me as was the plan. I would skip out of astronomy, though astronomy was my favorite class of any, maybe as we lived in the midst of the land of night sky and I could do my homework just by looking upward. More so, I had hopes of one day becoming a scientist, a doctor or a researcher of some kind. Certain ways of thinking were hard for me, but other things came naturally. The body, the earth, the universe—those mysteries unseen—I could somehow most easily see. Not because I was good at finding answers to equations, but because I loved the locked rooms of the questions themselves. I could imagine the workings and the designs of things. Pictures came to me frequently in layer and in boundary, in what is called surface and expanse, in drift and intent—or something like this anyway, though I know no better way to explain it. And there are laws to hold to, laws physical and universal, laws unchangeable as to truth until falsified, laws that make a person feel safe.

But today I was going with Son.

We drove through a grove of groomed fruit trees with the old adobe house out ahead of us commanding attention from the podium of earth it was built on. Son pointed an empty plot of shade out under the open cahon where he said the sedan was missing from. This meant it was only the old man at home, he said, that his mother, he said, would be gone shopping or to luncheon or gone to some function or other that she could do her hair and dress up for. I didn't ask him if our timing was planned or accident, I only wondered it.

The hill was lawned handsomely with Saint Augustine and today automatic sprinklers sprayed watery rainbows over the slopes. Desert poppy and dusty maiden grew in the beds along the walkway and a climbing rose laid claim over the portal. A shepherd kind of dog rose up from the welcome mat and sniffed at my fingers and slapped its dust whip of a tail against us in greeting. It leaned into Son's leg and he whumped the dog on the shoulder a couple of times in a language back. Son was about to open the door but the old man was there to open it before us. He came out and tipped his hat back off his forehead and said he was pleased to meet me and he did seem so. He took my hand as if to shake it and he pulled me forward to him to where when he spoke I could feel the prickle of his breath on my face. After an uncomfortable while like this, he chuckled and let me go.

He said lunch was just about ready. We went into the old adobe house and he led us through the many cool dark rooms of it and then on into the kitchen. We sat at a table in a nook next to a window where we could look out at a grove of old lemon trees, their trunks all whitewashed white and their leaves all trimmed to globes, the fruit on them hanging like holiday ornaments. The old man set out aluminum plates of frozen dinners for lunch for us—frozen green beans and frozen fried chicken and frozen mashed potatoes all steamed with heat now and biscuits just unwrapped from their own aluminum blanketing. I readied it all up myself, the old man said. You kids, dig in, he said. He put cold bottles of colas out to drink, asking me what about a glass and ice with that or why not a nip of whiskey and I said I'd pass at the whiskey as I had homework to do after. Then he passed napkins around and he took a seat and we set to eating, the old man talking the whole time in story, me and Son gnawing on our wings and sucking down our cold cola drinks.

My old man came west to these borderlands, said the old man, when he was but a young man. He came out and bought him all the acres around us here you see. And he hired many men and planted many trees, the trees of which bore the fruit to be sold towns and counties and states away. This made my father's wallet get fat pretty durned fast, as you can imagine. And so he bought more land. And with his profits from all the land he told the men to build him a hummock in the middle of all his acres. Then he had them collect the gumbo from just over the border to mix the adobe mud up with. And he had them build this here adobe house with it atop of the hummock we sit upon. He told the men to cement in the borrow pit and so they did and they painted a turquoise color inside it as he had said to and they filled it in with water to the brim. He told the men to clear the land south of the old adobe house and to build him a corral there, and stables there, an arena and cowshoots and a tack-house there too. And my father decided that fruit had been a fruit-ful living for him and so he would make it a bigger venture yet. He told the hired men to build him a melon shed out behind the old adobe house. Then all the acres around the melon shed were cleared and the soil made ready and the seed was sown in with the seed drill. And during this time he built the waterways—the mother ditches and the acequias and the regaderas. He put in the presitas, the floodgates and the water gates. And the water was pumped

357

through the fields in these man-made capillaries of his, these valves and these shunts of his.

And my father did indeed become a rich man.

And he became a favored man in town. And the people made him the town mayor. He had many friends and supporters and many functions and parties to attend to. He had all this but he had not a woman to share it with. Then it was at one of the many socials he did come to meet a woman from the county east. And they were married and soon after they begat me and we lived the three of us, a happy family as ever there was one, under the roof of this here adobe house. Even during the driest spells in the heat of the days we were happy. There were nights, I remember, it was fiercely hot and we would go to bed with wet sheets and the fans blowing on us to get through the night and the weather, he said.

Whoo-ee, he said.

And still, we did all right.

And then my mother died and my father mourned her for the rest of his years. And the town people had empathy for him and elected themselves a new mayor. And I took over running the working of the land for him when he could not sleep nor could he get out of bed either.

All of this when I was yet a young man.

And so indeed I too would need a wife. And good fortune was soon bestowed upon me when a new family came into town from back east. They were nesters who had come as many others had come and that was to better their health and thereby their lives in this dryland habitat. They bought acres just north of our land and they built themselves a fine house upon it. And they planted acres of bermuda and alfalfa and pastureland. And we paid them to let our horses and cattle graze on their acres. And lo and behold they should have a lovely daughter with the prettiest yellow hair a man might have ever seen. Anyone might have ever seen. And soon the howdy-dos were made and, yes, I was lucky indeed.

And speaking of which, the old man said.

And he lifted his hip an inch off the bench and took his wallet out and from his wallet he brought a dollar bill out.

How about a bit of gambling? he said.

You know this game of Liar's Poker?

We leave with the music playing, with the guests out on the dance floor in two-step and atwirl, with some filling their punch cups up from the spout of the fish mouth, with others at tables working seriously at their cake. We leave behind the bouquets of desert flowers and the decorations of maché, the piles of ribboned merchandise, all the bright and many-colored lights. We step outside the rented tent into the greater tent of a tinseled starlit night. Above our heads is a spread of lost heroes and creatures of make-believe, a spiral of spiraling galaxies, a curtaining glow of aurora, a soffit of planets and stars. In skies to come there will be more and different views and still but a speck of all there is, wombed inside this universe as we are, with our vision so hindered. Yet I look outward and am filled with pictures of the more and the what there might be for us. What can be for me and Son. Now is only the beginning.

Hold it while ye may, yet happy pair.

We freeze in the click of the shutter.

And time is burned in in a rupture of light.

The scene is a clumsy one with Son in the lead and staggering on to the pickup truck and me behind trying to make my way through a maze of suns that veer off and kilter about before my eyes. I gather my veil and train, hitched to a great weight of dress as I am, and climb up and in and slide over to the middle of the bench seat, pushing aside the cumulus mass of satin and tulle and organza and letting it pillow onto the floor and over the seat and spill up and out through the window. Son gets in beside me, halo'd as he is by yet the ghost of the flash. He is light and mass and heat and smile and I am alive in the high spirit of him, of us, and of all that is tonight. I wish not to forget, but it is too much, this present is, all too much for the senses—like the blaze of the sun that can't be looked at too long. That potent the moment is.

We are caught in the blind spots of one last picture. We blink and rub at our eyes and wait for the world to right itself again. Then Son turns the key and starts us up and we give our good-byes and take our good lucks and everyone waves, as everyone does.

There is space and time and color and sound.

How else might I tell you?

We are too young to be thinking of doing it. But Son told me his mother told him he ought to be doing it. He said she said it is not correct to be spending nights in a same girl's bed when you are not yet wedded to her. Son's mother was hushed after our promises were made. She said no more about Son leaving after roundup and supper each evening and his not coming back until morning feed and watering time. When nothing was different but for this ring I have got on my finger. The ring, which you could say too is thanks to his mother, as she told the old man to give Son the sum he needed to go into town to see Mr. Gomez at the jewelry shop with. And now look at me, here at my age, wearing a diamond ring on my finger. A bright solitaire to be joined with a thin gold band meant to fit right with it.

Son and me, we too fit together perfectly.

My legs are hitched up around the crest of his hips and he rocks us into the bed like this, moving us as one in this way, the whole bed awave in the rhythm of us. I cinch my arms around the roll and breadth of his shoulders. His breath and his words are buried in my hair. We move and we move without missing a beat and we are roused and soothed by the cadence we make. And I keep my eyes on the stone, the white hot sparkle of star inside it, hoping to take some kind of meaning or power in the hold of it. I let myself be carried off in watching it, in a thought that becomes no thought at all.

By the law, I am a child. I am not legal age to be married. My mother told us she is happy to go down to the courthouse and sign for me for the license. She told us she is happy to have Son for a son. When he is around her her movements quicken and her lashes flutter and her voice turns sweet as her cakes and her drinks can be. She will tongue the icing off the knife blade and fill tall glasses with ice cubes and ice tea for us. And we will sit out in her patio of shade and she will flush and bat a napkin at her face. As she will talk about who has taken ill in the hot spell or what succulents in the beds have succumbed from it. As she will talk about the modern coolness of the new stucco church at the plaza and the kinds of flowers that will hold up inside it. Styled in the Spanish style, she will say, and inside a fancy archway beneath which the baptisms are given and the matrimonial vows exchanged.

Son will make jokes about robbing cradles.

She will slice another slice of cake for him and lick the knife another time. And he will say how nice my mother's legs are and this gets her to throw her head back and laugh like a young girl does again.

So I would ask her about her dress.

And you would ask me. You would say, why go and do a thing such as getting married when I am too young to be thinking of doing it? I

360

can only explain it like this—that whatever you believe it is is supposed to come true for you, well, one day you think it just does. Though if you were to ask me here, I could not tell you what the true I believe in is.

The unease was gone from me by evening. It was gone before the handshakes and the laughing and the fandango had begun. I was calmed during the song and the long walk down to where he was waiting for me at.

The spell, or whatever it was you might say it was, had passed.

Likely it was fear that started it. Or it might have been girlish habit or tendency. Or it could have been being mixed up or overwhelmed or even being just tired. Or maybe any number of things. Whatever the feeling was it came over me like some great alter in the weather when I got into the backseat of the station wagon. My mother put her foot to the gas and we were off in a kick-up of dust. She paid no heed to my abrupt quiet, as she must have been deep in some daydream of the notice that lay in store for her that day. She didn't look back at me. I didn't speak. I couldn't say anything without something inside me breaking up and coming out in some kind of strange animal sound. We moved down the road inside a cloud of whirling earth, my stomach rocking in unsettling waves and my mouth watering up with a worrisome acid taste. I took long deep breaths in to make the dizzy go away and the faint stop. I sat looking out at the world as it went wheeling by outside the window, feeling weepy, undone. I was overcome by a reckoning is what I was, some kind of knowing, some kind of something that made me hesitate, made me want to say wait—say, can't I maybe stay a child for just a little time longer yet. Yet knowing too it was too late to back up and turn around now.

I cleared my throat.

I hoped to stop shaking.

We rode down Main Street. It seemed the longest ride I had ever taken and yet we were already turning into the alameda before it seemed we should have been there. My mother parked the car in the shade of desert sycamore and we got out and I gathered my train up and we walked in the hot open sun of the plaza. Right then a diamondback rattled out in front of us onto the footpath and my mother and I cried out and shot back as the thing went slithering off into the nopal.

You'd better decide to take it as a good-luck sign, she said.

We hurried on into the courtyard and were soon inside the cool reprieve of the sanctuary. Chiseled figures hovered in the stillness above while on the ground busy women floated about with great concern for certainty, for detail and timing. I stood amidst all this in the foyer, trembling in vaulted shadow during the entire wait of the gathering, an upheaval of feelings welling up inside my chest. I stood alone in a thicket of confusion and a stir of goings-on, in the hard lope of my heart, a pounding so loud others surely could have heard it too. Then the building up of who knows what it was broke apart inside the swelling hold of my throat. It spilled out when my mother, dressed for this occasion in a prom dress of mine, one that I would never wear now, came up to me and spoke a few sentimental and commonly said words to me right before the step and assemble of the ceremonial party started.

I couldn't keep it reined in anymore. The dark poured forth from my eyes and splotched the bodice of the already stained dress. The dark matted my lashes together and rolled down my cheeks, turning the world abog and my face and dress a mess. Dark blotches would mark up all the photographs of us that were made in testament to this day. And I would see me standing upright and smiling in the biddings to be fertile as the earth and happy until death.

You are pale as a ghost, my mother said.

There were all the people there. There were all the names that had been written in the book. There were the words we had been told to speak. There was the thin gold band ready to be fit up against the bright solitaire meant for it. There were all the wishes prepared for us, all the gifts set out on a table, a feast on display, a great fiesta awaiting. The band was ready to play.

And there was Son at the far other end from where I was, dressed up in a stiff formal outfit not his, tugging at his shirt cuffs. But I cannot here recall having seen his face enough as my mother was suddenly walking off ahead of me and blotting him out, coupled and arm and arm as she was with her young escort. Now there was a humming commotion among the guests, a resonance as of insects. Then a soprano'd voice cued me to move and all the many heads turned back to watch as I walked toward them. And I thought right then but too late that the song that had hooked me once was the wrong one to choose for today.

I tossed the thought out. I would let the melody calm me.

The girls started out ahead, their gowns proudly homemade, their

362

hair done up and laced with heliotrope and adam-and-eve. And then it was me. I walked alone. It was my way of doing things. I had said I wanted to walk it alone, as I had written but never heard back, though I held to the chance that my father might show at the last minute. Yet knowing I was only born a daughter and not a son—an old and piddling story, one too I know, too many times told.

So I walked alone now in the weight of that dress and in parched afternoon light, the dress so heavy and the air so dense it seemed I moved in slow motion, as though it were something out of sleep I was harnessed to and trying to make my way forward in. I walked down that long aisleway, past all the town people who had come for the show and that I mostly did not know, their faces looking to me all one and a single blur of questioning. I walked on and on for what seemed a long time. I walked in that wrong song. Pillars of dusty light filtered in through the tall windows and settled on the heads of the attending, bestowing them with a kind of otherworldliness. You should have seen everyone, the way they had come dressed up in their finery and niceties and frills, though I wouldn't see any of this in detail until I looked at the pictures on record for us later. The women had come powdered and feathered and gloved, their hair twisted and braided and coiled, and there were pillboxes and bonnets and mantillas among them. The men wore their best-yoked jackets and leather vests, their silver bolo ties and turquoise studs, their tooled belts and rodeo buckles, their dress boots of lizard or snakeskin. They scratched at their starchy collets. They covered their crotches over with the flat of their felt hats.

All were upstanding now.

And we went on with what had been decided.

What we had decided.

My mother called the sheriff the first go-round. He showed up at the trailer and told me to get into his car and I argued that I would not and he said you had better and he said or else and he said a few words more he added to all this too. So I got in, mad as I was, and the sheriff delivered me back to her.

This is some months before Son.

Let me thank you, my mother said to the sheriff, personally.

Why tack a personally on for, I said, not asking a question.

My mother's way of keeping me with her was to say she was grounding me. She said I was to take the bus straight to campus and then after classes I was to go directly to the coffee shop for evening shift and then she would come pick me up and it was home only after that and that was it every night after work no matter what. Her dictum lasted one week. Then the anger began to stir about from where it was seated not so deeply and it spiraled up and out of me like a dustdevil. My mother was one great spouting horn of her own—coming at me with threats the way she did and with a pot lid in her one hand and a spatula raised above her head with the other. I fired some words at her hoping to knock her back and this must have worked as she was stopped in her fury and her face went suddenly deadpan. She wiped the froth off her chin with the back of a hand and she drove a cold hard look sharp as knives into my eyes that I won't soon forget. Then she put the pot lid and the spatula down and turned away.

Just go, she said.

The trailer I found is on the far edge of town, parked on desert pavement out on a deserted lot. The earth is barren and hard, having been winnowed over the years by the sand and the wind here. A gasoline station sits next to the lot and with a telephone booth there if I would have needed it.

I believed I wouldn't need it.

It was hot in the trailer on hot days out. It was hot in the trailer even on not hot days. I sat out on the front stoop of it with a hand saluted to my forehead to keep the burn of the sun off my face. I listened to a fiery wind huffing through the bitterbrush and mesquite. A high-pitched screeching of crickets came from everywhere and who knows where, going on and on as they will in their constant song and trill of courtship and territory. I sat in thought of better days to come as hot gusts of wind scarved dust across the lot. I imagined lush woodlands and wild rivers and grassy fields. I thought of boys who played guitars and sang to me. I thought of all there was that had been left or lost or simply tossed away and forgotten.

There was a dumpster that sat out across the lot. There would be picked-over bones and blackened peels and soiled diapers and such spilling up out of it, no matter if the garbage had just been emptied from it or not. There was not much else around. Just a billboard at the side of the road and a cowboy pictured in it who held a coiled rope in his fist and a cigarette between his teeth. I thought about someday getting braces thinking how that might change everything for me in the right direction. I added money to come and counted the weeks up. I thought about the days and the places and the people I was gone from and that were now far away and I wondered if any of what it all was was still there.

I picked a stick up. I tossed it to shoo a raggedy crowbird off the strewn garbage and it kwoked and lifted and paced. I swatted the flies away from my head. I looked for shade, a cool place. A truckload of fieldhands passed and there were those hisses and clucks you get and I picked a rock up and squailed it at their wake of hopeless noise, choking on the cloud of dust they left behind.

I was thirsty.

I would get up and wander over to the gasoline station to buy a soft drink. There was an old card table and some half-broken fold-down chairs under a single pecan tree there and I would sit and drink my drink in the shade of it. I would use the sweat of the cold bottle to wipe the dust off my face with and then I might rest my eyes on the empty booth ahead of me, at the lovers' names painted and scratched on the glass, at the book of pages yellowed and hanging abandoned inside on the chain, thinking how often I would mistakenly hear the telephone in it ringing. Thinking how I would be sickened by someone feeling as sorry for herself as I was feeling sorry for me.

We make the first stop the trailer where the clothes I left are waiting arrayed for me on the bed. It is almost too small a space in this aluminum alleyway of what some call a home, though not space or home enough for me and all this dress I'm fettered in along with it. It takes a long time for Son to unbutton all the hundred tiny buttons down the back of it. Such frippery, he says. He is drunk on wedding punch and he stumbles back and forth and the whole trailer rocks from side to side with us. His tongue is thick in his mouth and his fingers none too nimble and he mumbles and knits along the length of my spine, tail to nape, impatiently. He undoes the last button and holds up the heft of the dress and I free myself from within and climb out and under from inside it. Then there is a *whoosh* of fabric to the floor, the tent of it collapsing in release, a great rush of breath as of a wind gust through desert brush.

Son takes hold of me. He says, C'mon, we should let's do it here, but I tell him I want to do it as these things are done on such a day as this. What we do will be held in memory, I say. For always, I say. So? he says. That's good any way it goes, isn't it? he says. But he shrugs and his hands fall away from my waist. He picks up the borrowed suitcase of my things and carries it out to the truck. And I follow close behind, closing the door of the trailer the one last time.

The night sky is filled brimful as a night sky can be, lit brightly as it is with clusters of planets and pulsating stars and marriages of galaxies, all of it within a wobble of dust and gas and debris unseen. There are the Dippers little and big tonight, a lovely Pleiades, a throbbing red star like a tiny heart out. This is the matter of which we are made, I say to Son, all that is of us is above us. We stand together looking upward, our jaws loose hinged and our mouths hung open, as if to swallow what's above us down into us. Looking out at the past in its far distance, where from there, here we are not.

Let's get a get-go, he says.

He lets the bed down in a screech of metal and hinge. There is a thump of a suitcase tossed in, a jingling ring of ringed keys, Son humming that wrong song the wrong way. He opens the door of the truck and acts to doff a hat and I take the keys from him, telling him he has too much punch in him to be driving out on the highway and when the fun is just beginning for us. He says, Okey-dokey, you are the wifey. And we hop up and into the pickup truck and I pull us out of that empty lot, leaving the trailer behind, the dumpster, the billboard, the gas station, the card table, and the fold-down chairs, leaving the lot of it behind.

We drive past the outskirts with the lights veiled upon the town and atwinkle behind us. We take the highway west and come soon into a great arenal of darkness, a kind of nothingness that goes on and on for miles and miles, making a person uncomfortable, distrustful. It is darker than dark in the night. After a time our headlights begin to flood saguaro and organ pipe and ocotillo. Bright coyote eyes wink like stars along the roadside and startles of jackrabbits take cover in the brush. Desert rats dart to and fro in a rush to their middens—fur, bone, teeth, shell, cob and toy and fay, and whatever else they may be home to. Creeping things unnamed go every which way in a dash to sand hole or desert nest—timid creatures frightened by the rouse of our engine and the ricochet of our lights.

And Son goes into a story about rabbit hunting with boyhood chums. He laughs about getting drunk and shooting twenty-twos from out the windows of a pickup truck.

My father always said keep my eyes out the window on the broken line ahead if I was feeling carsick and queasy, I say.

Son slaps some kind of drum routine out on the dashboard.

Why do guys always have to do that? I say.

Do what? he says.

He rolls his window down and lets the cool desert air in and we sit in silence for a while. In not too long a time we come into a sea of rippled sand waves that crest and pyramid at our sides and attend us like guests for miles ahead. In the foreland in the distance lie a combering of dark foothills, seeming to be beasts fallen to extinction at the earth line. We make bets on how far away we are in minutes from here to the pass and our game carries us along for a good stretch of highway. After a time we start naming the names of places to come we have seen on the map, names such as Spring Valley and Torrey Pines, Oceanside and Riverside, and Santa Clarita, Santa Rosa, Santa Jacinta and Santa Whatnot, and we remember Petaluma and Fortuna and Ventura, Red Bluff and Coos Bay, and not to forget yet Lincoln City or Fall City, Tumwater or Winslow, nor Astoria. We will move through names. We will move through valley and mesa, playa and canyon, past chaparral and fumarole and peninsula, along urban parks and grazing fields and sea stacks, going on into shrubland and grassland and woodland, old growth and talus slopes, clearcut and cindercone, and we will move onward into all that world out in front of us we don't know. Who might possibly be as happy as we are?

A scratching of melody comes from the radio, chords rising open as the land that holds us, rhythm mimicking our passage down the road, harmony making this life seem it should only be that. We sing along to songs about what songs have always been about—beginnings, going on, breaking up, forgiving. We sing in fallen words and broken phrases as glints of tiger moths fly at us like snow, streaking the windshield over.

In time we begin to climb. We come to the top of the pass and into blue spruce, dwarf cedar, juniper. Just off the highway, lit up among a hush of trees, is the small lodge, a place that is just the beginning of all the places I say I am going to take us. Yet knowing there is no more joy in the getting there than there is in the going. Or maybe only half believing this to be so.

Hold it while ye may.

We get out of the pickup truck and breathe the incense of pine air and wood smoke in. Our breath pales the dark and goes ghosting off between us. Above us is a canopy of trees and through the tree holes there shines a luminous star, though this one we can't for sure be sure of. Yet the stillness is certain. Compared to nights upon nights glutted with a constant racket of crickets—that hum in the ears that will cause a buzz of the nerves. Except for the riffling of the creek alongside us now, the quiet is like something from out of a dream, making us want to whisper at one another in the dark to hold to the silence better, as if not to be waked from the time and the place we are in. A desire path cuts through the grass and I point to it that we should take this shortcut way instead of the steps laid out ahead. There, the way through the trees, I say. Son takes off on the path into the dark ahead of me and I turn to run and catch him when there comes a *thwok,* like the sound of a softball hit against a bat, and Son has run smack into the overhanging branch of a rambling tree. He is laid out flat on the ground. Even sober he could not have seen it coming. I cover my mouth to mute my laughing and I wait for Son to get up. But he doesn't. Don't be kidding around, I say. And still he is quiet. C'mon, I say, you have had your fun. But he is quiet still and now you see I am not laughing anymore. I bend down and he is cold silent. I touch his face and feel the wet trickle of blood. And my heart tumbles in my chest like a stack of children's blocks toppled to the floor.

Son, I say. I shake him.

A light inside the lodge goes on.

And he opens his eyes and smiles.

What are you doing just staring there, girl? the old man says. He finds me standing in the afternoon ticking of the grandfather clock, in the cool dark parlor of the old adobe house, in front of a fireplace meant more for fancy than for function. I stand at the mantel, handling the fewtrils placed just so and studying the pictures there in front of me, and I tell you, I could stay standing here this way the entire rest of the day, and on into the evening, throughout the night even. And I could do it all over the very next day for the entire day again. That is how much in awe I am of Son's growing-up days I see before me in the pictures, how in awe of the ways of his family I am, so foreign as they are to me. I am taken by the history of him. I am taken by the flesh and the hair and the teeth of him, of all that I see, so much so my bones ache as though to burst up out of me.

But I don't tell the old man any of this.

That boy sure knows how to set a horse, don't he, he says.

He picks one of the pictures up and puts his nose to it with his eyes asquint as if he were seeing something in it for the very first time. Then he puts it back down.

You kids, he says, and he chuckles the way he does.

Anyways, I need to skeedaddle into town to see a man about a new saddle for the bay, if you maybe want to ride along, he says.

Son says for me to wait on him, I say, and the old man okey-dokeys me and leaves me standing at the mantel. I go back to looking at the pictures there, all handsomely framed as they are and carefully arranged between candlesticks and Navajo bowls and pottery vases and those kinds of things set there by the old man's wife. There is a photo of Son when he was at the age of still being a Sonny, a small boy in cowboy hat and boots and holding a rope coiled in his kid-gloved hand. There is a picture of him as a 4-H'er standing proud beside his show cow and next to it the purple ribbon won and hung in another frame. There is a picture of Son grown some, in uniform with numbers on his chest and a ball in the hook of his arm, and I am struck with a worry now about others that might have loved him before me, names of girls I've heard from him that come back to me, visions before me that give me this sinking feeling.

And I shake the crazy thoughts away.

I look at the picture of him most recently, on horseback and dressed in vest and hat and badge, his chest out and held proud as a dancer does it, with the old man at his side and with the rest of the posse back in the background. Then I look all the photographs over again, who knows how many times. Until I notice something about the look on Son's face, how the look is the same, no matter what age or situation, in each of the pictures.

There is something that is off in him.

What is it I see? Is it boredom? Or seriousness? Or conceit? Is it impatience I see? Or what? Is it Son's being posed to be what's right in the eyes of others? Is it his trying to fit with certain attitudes and virtues they find most redeeming?

Will that look be changed in photographs to come of us?

How could I doubt it?

I will not to doubt it.

I am so much in love these days I take pity on anyone who isn't us. I look at everyone throughout the day, couples young and old, people here and there, alone or with others, smiling or talking or whatnot, and I cannot see a single face of anyone who could possibly be as happy as I am. It is only us who really know love, me and Son.

The wound on his head adds to the sanctity of this night, to the ritual of it, as if the clout were a sacrifice to powers unseen to ensure the blessings of our marriage. Son laughs when I tell him this, says I'm loco, says I'm loony in my cabeza, is what I am. But I tell him I will treasure whatever scar might likely be there to remind me for the rest of our days. I say I will cherish each day I am graced to see it. I'm looking at Son and staying my eyes on him trying to hold on to what I see. From this moment on, I will myself to hold on to everything here, this night, our beginning. I wonder about the whirl of time we are in and how it will spill out into memory someday and how it will all be lost or be changed. I want what is now to be always what it is. I want the here to remain always in my keeping. I cling to the words of every song that plays on the radio. I study the arrangement of the bed in the room we are in, where the door is, where the bathroom is, how the suitcase rests open, how the shoes are kicked off, the way the keys splay from the toss, the way the flower in the lapel begins to fail. I press at my temples to stay all that's before me inside my head. The smell of the perfume on me, on him, I savor it to save it. The feel of the silk of this nightgown that slips from my shoulders and down past my hips, the way the fabric of it puddles as it does to the floor, I will the imprint in. I want Son's chest in my keeping, his mouth, his hands on me, always to feel it all as I feel it now. I want always this happiness of wanting. This happiness of having.

Remember this moment, I say.

I wondered too late too about the luck of the dress.

It was my mother's, the one she had worn with my father, the one she had on just the one time on that one day, before all the bulk of it got packed up into my grandmother's hope chest, where it would stay boxed and wrapped and mysterious until there was serious claim enough for it to be brought out to life again. I had seen the dress only in the photograph, the one my mother had kept for whatever reason, as it was my father in the picture with her, and not any man of hers recent. The photograph is also kept inside a hope chest, but this being my mother's, one of the few items of furniture she will drag along with her from place to place. On slow afternoons I would open the hope chest to study that picture of my father and my mother, thinking if I had been my mother I would have lived a different story given that dress.

Given my father.

It is a white satin dress with a long train. There is a pale stain my mother left beneath the layer of tulle on the lap of it. But we do not see this until it is too late to get another dress and so I wear it the way it is, stain or no stain. I cover the stain over with a manner of moving my hands or with a gather of the organza or with the collar and flower of bouquet.

My mother would carry a bouquet again too, though a small one compared to mine, more a nosegay or a posey, you might say, as though her hopes or her enthusiasm or her something or other had waned along with the size of her blossomed arrangement. And of course she wore no gown or fancy dress this time nor any kind of altered rendering of one as she had with some of the men at the nuptials in between. She even left the posing out as far as we could see from the snapshot she sent to us from the gambling town north of us. We saw her with a new man in hand, him trailing a couple of steps behind her and her turning in a hurry to go, as if she had to get out of that chapel before someone up in the blue told her no, told her you can't be going out running around and getting married this many times over and over again.

We leave the lodge with mist rising like smoke from the dew and with sunrise embering in pink through the trees. Flycatchers and grackle chitter and whistle and acrobat about in a tangle of branches and tuckamore. The wind sways boughs and rustles bracken and skitters twigs and leaves and it slaps a cold wake-up at our faces.

We are day one married.

We are restless with readiness to get back onto the highway. We are soon moving westward to the coast where we will from there make a turn right and go straight the rest of the way up toward the northern border. Our journey up lasts half a moon's phase and it is rapturous and ordinary, detailed and blurry, seeming to go on and on for a long time and it is too soon over as the way all time can be. Just as in my telling this, present tense to past, just as long and as quick as that.

We do many things in many places. We sit atop a marine terrace eating abalone and vinegared chips with breakers striking at the cliffs and Son speaking of the old man's infidelities. We stop at a famous place in Angels City and I am lucky they don't card me and we drink whiskey and dance a-go-go at a disco, confident as if we should be locals in the place, even with Son dressed in cowboy boots and with the faded ring of snuff tin on the hip pocket of his dungarees. We take rides to the moon and we startle at alligators and we climb up into tree houses and we spin about in teacups all in a fantasyland, spending day until night there as if we were still young kids again. We pass through clots of dust and sheets of chaff and we pass through cloud and fog and hail and rain and we travel through warm fronts and humidity, choke points and wind shear. We drive over golden and stone and floating bridges, over river and channel and bay. We chug the truck up to the top of a silent volcano and we throw snowballs and pee yellow holes and get cold too soon, lacking proper coats. We take to the beach, the truck curmurring through scour and berm, and we stop to dig razor clams and geoduck and the tires out. We pick blue mussels and dogwinkles off rocks and we collect sea stars and sand dollars in jars. Each night we stop at a motel with the something-dollar same name—all the motels pinned along the interstate—and each day we start at one of the breakfast places in a coffee-shop chain. We drink our coffee sugared and creamy and we eat our bacon crispy and our eggs over easy. Every day is filled with the smell of a beginning, with the sweet wet smell of just-washed skin and hair and the old-spicy smell of Son's aftershave and sometimes the air is gritty with windblow or it is minerally of seaweed or it is resinous of pine. There are lingering tastes of salt air in the fog or cut hay in the heat, and some days there is bitter carbon on the lips from the diesel that rises off the highway, and at times a taste of metal, like car parts, or some days there is a taste of rain cloud or artichokes or burnt leaves and even a taste of wet dog somehow. There is on and on the thrill of a song that comes over the radio and marks our days to be remembered this way. There is the harmony of our voices in the to and the fro of our words, as we tell of places we have been and of places we would someday like to go, as we talk of accidents that have happened to us, good and bad and neither, as we speak of the still few people we have been through or would like to know, and we take all of what's said each to the other and shape it into something new to put inside a place that fits right and holds inside us.

Our journey turns a great blessing in its perfection. Within each day upon day there is suppleness and reflex, as in the movement of youth, all within the changing and the staying the same. And the knowing, or whatever it was it was—the thing that had risen up from inside me on the way to the church—just leftover material of some kind, you could say, like a comet—it's just rocketed out and away.

S. G. Miller

Why should I have been so afraid?

Yes, we are yet the happy pair, we are. And not a thing to mar any day of all the days on the road for us. Save for a comment about my not eating all the breakfast on my plate. Save for the fall and the clout to Son's head.

We come to my father's place, arriving into a terrain of mountains and waterway and evergreen, a wilderness that was a beginning for me, a childhood place and so of innocence, a paradise that way. We come to my father's house just outside the borderline of town, an old log abode built close to the shores of the sound and buried deeply in forest. A great western hemlock stands at the edge of the woodlot and serves as witness tree, its coned crown and fluted trunk and drooping leader bearing claim through generations to this family's parcel of land. The hemlock has been witness too to my imaginings, as I played hero or captured or saved in the woods for the countless hours of lost days. There are still the worn paths where in the past I have ambled alongside my father, picking wild blackberries or Indian plum with him, or I have stooped with him to brush the duff off chanterelles and fiddleheads to know them and pick them too.

To be safe, my father would say, and he would blow on the underside of the mushroom. Look here, he would say, these split gills will always tell you. And then we might fill our coffee cans full to the top with berries, him reminding me to pick only the tiny wild ones, leaving the fat Himalayas for the bear and the deer behind. And he might tell me other things that would stay inside my head too. He might say, let the clams you dig sit in a bucket of their water overnight until they have spit the sand out of their shells. Or he would say, carry a stick when walking down a lonely road so if you should come upon a mean dog all you need do is shake the stick in the dog's face, and mean it, to keep him away. Or he would say, walk fast when there are other people around and they will leave you be because they will think that you are busy.

There is a light in the cabin window on and we knock and find my father there and his wife there. My father opens the door and puts a face of welcome surprise on. He has a scruffy beard as has always been his habit. He has a bigger, rounder belly now. He smells like chopping wood. He shakes Son's hand and gives me a pat on the back and he offers us drinks and we follow him into the kitchen. His wife is pale and thin of hair and flesh and her smile is cool and thin too.

373

She says her name and flutters her arms and then she pivots and disappears somewhere.

My father makes a joke about marriage and the bump and the gash on Son's head. And Son says, he hates to say it, but he's had a headache ever since the wedding day. And I say I hope that husbands aren't like reading glasses, where after a time you get to rely on them so you can't manage without. Son says something cliché about love being blind which doesn't make much sense or fit right with what's said and my father seems embarrassed for him but laughs anyway and then he goes on quickly to one-up Son with another of his own. I look at Son, who now looks smaller than ever I had before seen him, even though he rises a good half foot or more over my father.

My father takes a bottle of wine from the refrigerator and screws the top off. He puts the screwtop to his nose and sniffs it.

Good week, he says.

I breathe in the home smell of maple bacon and cherry tobacco and wood smoke. I leave my father and Son in the midst of their polite and disquieted talk and I go and stand over at the sink and look out the window. I can see the smokehouse outside my father built for the curing and drying of fish and meat. Next to it there is a large vegetable garden, neatly rowed and tended, with bulging heads of lettuce and lazing squashes and beans vining their way up teepee'd poles. There is the swing still hung from the alder and I can see me there now on the wood seat of it hanging on tightly for life, afraid and thrilled at how far up in the air I am flying, calling out, *Higher, higher.* And there is the thick dark wilderness out there surrounding it all—the swing, the garden, the smokehouse, the house. The wild of all that wilderness out there, the shelter and hush in it, the surprise in it, the hide, the seek, the find in it.

Go play, I can hear my father say, prodding me out.

From here where I stand at the window I also see the add-on my father added as the family grew. I can see out and into the window to the bedroom across the way there. There where my father's wife stands looking in the mirror brushing her pale, thin hair and putting lipstick on her pale, thin lips. She stands in the bedroom that used to be my room. She looks in the mirror that used to be mine too.

Yet it was me who left my father's house, after all.

Wasn't it?

The rain comes and the rain ends and the woods are left gauzed in pockets of mist. We walk out into air soft as baby hair, air that has a weight to it too, air that makes ferns and leaves and needles shimmer in droplets that tick wet to the earth. We say our farewells and get settled back up into the pickup, sitting quietly with the truck warming and humming, and then Son wipers the windshield over and U-turns us around. I rub the vapor off the glass with a sleeve and through the blur I see a door close and a light go out inside the house. Take it slow, I say, and Son does, moving over the rooted-over driveway to keep the rattle of us down. He pulls us out onto the road and toward the way we have come from, taking a left at the crossroad, and from there to head down along the coast highway to the interstate and so back to Old Border Road, a place to be called home, a place to begin another beginning.

Desire with Digressions
Brian Evenson

IN THE END, SUFFERING and not knowing what else to do, I left her abruptly and without warning, taking only the clothes on my back. She was out behind our isolated house, near the meadow, the creek just beginning to rise as it did every year, and I went out and looked at her a final time as she sat in the grass looking at the creek, facing away from me.

Watching her, after all she had said to me, I felt that if her head were to turn toward me then I would see not her face but an unfeatured facelessness, as inhuman and smooth as a plate. And then, standing there, I realized I could not even imagine what her face looked like, nor recall ever having seen it at all, and this feeling grew until it became a form of panic. In the end, not knowing what else to do, not daring to risk seeing her face, I turned and walked through the house and out the front door and was gone.

Do you love me? her voice was saying in my head as I walked up the dirt road and then up the gravel road and then down the paved road until I found a car I could steal. *Do you love me?* it was saying as I drove quickly away, not knowing where I was going. But even in my head I could not bring myself to answer her, and when, finally, to stop her voice from saying it, I finally said, *Yes*, I could not even in imagination lift my eyes to meet her unimaginable face.

So began what proved to be days in orbit, with myself both afraid to go back and afraid to get too far away from her. I knew what I had felt about her face could not be natural, could not have anything to do with any reality connected to her. I could rationalize my fear away, and yet I still could not bring myself to return and look her in the face. I drove, I stole for food and gas, drove some more. Each time I seemed about to go far enough that I would no longer be able to think of going back, I found the car coaxed by my hands into a slow arc, an orbit with her at its center. *Why not simply go back?* I asked myself, at night, sleeping on the ground beside a guttering fire or sleeping curled in the car's backseat. And I would tell myself, *Yes, I will go back.* But when morning came, the sun a blank and burning round such as I feared her face to be, I could only continue my dim and erratic orbit.

Until at last I was forced to abandon the car, engine smoking and radiator stuttering, at the height of a mountain pass and to continue forward alone and on foot, shivering my way over the summit and plodding down the other side. I tried to thumb a ride, but cars were few and none stopped, and in the slow and beautiful descent from mountain to valley I began, ignored again and again, to think of myself as a ghost. What was it she had said to me, that day before she had abandoned me to sit beside the creek and grow strange? And how had I responded? Why could I not recall?

Midway downslope into the high valley was a graveled pullout and a small bar, little more than a shack fallen into poor repair. The door was sticky at first, and I thought for a moment in forcing it that it was locked, but then suddenly it gave way and I tumbled in. It was a dim place, lit by little more than the evening light streaming through its single window. It seemed nearly as cold inside as outside, the wind whistling through the walls. There was nothing behind the bar but two bottles of cheap scotch and a weathered keg of beer. A grizzled and toothless barmaid merely stared at me as I approached.

"What you want?" she finally asked.

Nothing, I claimed, only to get out of the cold for a moment and warm up before—

"We got beer, whiskey," she said. "Which suits?"

Both suited, I told her, but I was at the moment fallen in the cracks of life and a little short on funds.

"Got to drink to stay," she said, and so I dug around in one pocket and came up with a few coins. She looked at them and counted them and then poured me just enough whiskey to wet the bottom of a shot glass. "Get on with you," she said.

I carried the shot glass over to the table and sat down. The old woman at the bar kept her eyes on me. I tried to look at anything else but her.

Still, I had been there quite some time before my eyes adjusted sufficiently to make out, in one dark corner, another man. When he realized that I had noticed him, he nodded slightly. I nodded back, then lifted my shot glass and let the little that was in it trickle down my throat, licking the glass clean afterward. When I finally put it back down, I found him still to be watching me.

"What you want?" the barmaid barked, and it took me a moment to realize she was speaking to me.

I was fine, I told her, I didn't want anything.

"Got to drink or split," she said.

And so I stood up and made my way out, moving down the road in the fading sunlight.

I had gone nearly a half mile before I realized that I was not alone, that the man in the bar had followed me out and was now a little distance behind. I stopped and turned to him. He stopped as well.

"What is it?" I asked.

He just shook his head and shyly smiled.

I turned and started down again. When I looked back he was still there, still following.

"What?" I said again, and this time took a few steps back toward him.

"Nothing," he said.

"What do you mean, nothing?" I asked.

"I'm still trying to decide if you're the man."

"The man for what?"

"There's something," he said, "needs getting done. One man can't do it alone. It needs two. I'm trying to decide if you're the second."

"What's in it for me?" I asked.

He smiled. "Maybe you are the man," he said, and came closer.

I stayed as the light died and listened to him, watching the glints of his eyes, and tried to read the dimming lines of his face. It would, he claimed, take only a day or so, a quick trip up into the mountains, and then we would come back down, our fortunes made. *And what is it?* I asked. But he merely shook his head. I would have to trust him, he said.

I shrugged. What, in fact, I wondered, did I have to lose? At the very least this was a distraction from my own life. And so I agreed.

He took me by the arm, began to tug me slowly off the road, into the slush and snow.

"Wait," I said. "Let's wait for the morning."

But no, was I not the man after all? I had to trust him, we had to go now, there was not a moment to lose. And what, finally, did I care? Another day of shivering and cold? I would have it sooner or later, so why not sooner? So I allowed myself to be led off the road and away.

We trudged through the night, my hands gone blue with cold, my feet so numb I could hardly feel them. When he saw how I was suffering he drew from around his shoulders an old blanket that I wrapped around myself, feeling at least slightly less cold.

We stopped near dawn and he cleared a spot of snow and ice, and, with a solitary match and pine needles, started a small fire, slowly feeding them into a blaze. My feet, out of my wet shoes now, at first stayed numb and then felt as if they were being repeatedly stabbed. It was almost more than I could bear.

"Just a little more," he said to himself. In the firelight I could see just how haggard his face really was. "Just a little more," he said again.

And I looked at him and saw in his eyes a look closer to death than to mere exhaustion. A shadow had settled into his face and it lay there, just beneath the skin, blurring his features.

"Perhaps," I said, "we should go back."

He gave a little start, and then his eyes settled on me and he slowly smiled. "Just a little more," he said again. "Just a little more."

And so, just a little more. A slow tramp up into the mountains, the snow no longer slush but deep and powdery now, sticky, and the two of us tramping forward, he pushing a path through the snow and I following, the going slower as the sun slipped lower in the sky.

Until at last, past exhaustion, he seemed to glimpse what he was looking for, and we made for it.

It was a small miners' shack. Inside it was empty, not even wood for a fire. We were, both of us, too exhausted to trudge back out and go in search of dry timber, so instead we worked our way into a corner and huddled together, our bodies tight around one another, as the wind whistled around us.

I felt his face next to mine grow slowly cold, the heat draining out of him. And then I fell into a state between waking and sleeping and perhaps as well between death and life. In that state I saw myself again staring at her back, again afraid that she might turn around and reveal her face in a terrible way. But she did not turn around. It was as if she were frozen: she neither moved nor breathed. This made me even more afraid than if she were to turn around.

When the wind fell and morning light struck again, I opened my eyes to see my companion's lips gone blue, his face turning blue as well. He could open his eyes and move them, but hardly more than that.

And now what? I asked him. He was in no condition to go on, I argued. Now that we were here, would he not tell me what it was we had come in search of?

He regarded me torpidly through half-closed eyes. Slowly his mouth opened itself, his lips pulling apart only reluctantly, as if his face were being slowly torn, but then, instead of speech, a dim, wracked sound issued from his throat, and he died.

There is, in every event, whether lived or told, always a hole or a gap, often more than one. If we allow ourselves to get caught in it, we find it opening into a void that, once we have slipped into it, we can never escape. The void here—only one of several in what, from the wandering of love, my life had become—was this notion of some vague treasure awaiting me, something waiting to be taken, if only I could figure out what it was. I searched my companion's pockets, my fingers trembling with cold, but found nothing to indicate what we had been looking for, nor anything to tell me who, exactly, my companion had been. I searched the shack itself carefully, but found nothing to indicate the nature of what we had been searching for and no signs of a hiding place. I stripped him to see if he had any tattoos or hidden markings that might reconfigure my sense of the world, and found nothing. But rather than putting the clothes back on him, I put them on my own body, over my own clothing, so as to keep warm, so as to disguise myself.

Since I was in a miners' shack, perhaps whatever it was I was meant to find was in the mine. But coming out of the shack I could see no sign of a mine. I could, I thought, search until I found something, but I had no food, did not know what I was looking for. This was, I convinced myself, the hole that was opening into a void for me: a desire for some unknown riches that I might not even recognize were I to see them was coaxing me forward and into my own oblivion, offering to make me not rich but dead.

And it was with this realization that her face sprang up before me at last. In my head I saw her turn away from the creek and turn toward me and smile—her sparkling blue eyes, her high cheekbones, her beautiful full lips, her slightly skewed teeth: I could piece together little of her beyond that—whole regions of her face and head remaining unrendered and incomplete—but it was enough to fill me with a desire to see her again, a desire that pulled me out of the void and saved my life.

I kept her image before me as I moved back down the mountain again, along the trail we had blazed through the snow during our ascent. The journey seemed quicker this time, the crust of the snow already broken, the path already there to follow, the downward slope propelling me quickly forward. I kept putting one foot in front of the other, not stopping even after darkness fell. I kept plodding down, hardly conscious of anything around me until, not sure how many hours I had traveled, how many steps I had taken, I found myself at last on the road.

What immediately followed I have assembled after the fact and by inference. The few bits and pieces that I do remember feel less lived than observed from a distance. I was found delirious and shivering and nearly dead, by some car that stopped. I was taken to a facility, what seemed at first to me an asylum but which I have allowed myself over time to be convinced was a hospital. There, doctors in pale blue coats lopped off the toes on one foot and removed most of the other foot. A few fingers were cut free as well, while a few others still continue to itch and buzz with pain. I was asked who I was, without result: in my addled state I hardly knew the answer myself at first and then I chose to keep to myself the answers slowly coming to me. Eventually they stopped asking.

All the while I kept her image before me: the movement of her lips as she asked me, *Do you love me?* and I myself still unsure how or if I had responded, but knowing that now I would answer, *Yes.* And when, finally, I was coherent again, I lay in bed with my bandaged hands and stared at the ceiling and plotted how I would make my way back to her.

And then one day, abruptly and without warning, I simply climbed out of bed, slipped on my clothes, and left. I walked out the front door of the hospital and climbed into the first likely car I saw and not without difficulty hot-wired it and then, gripping the steering wheel with my bandaged hands, drove away. I could imagine her there, still by the creek, still waiting for me. I imagined how she would turn and face me and smile. *Where have you been,* I imagined her asking, and imagined myself shrugging and responding, *Nowhere,* though there was no place in my imagining for how her face might change once she saw my mangled hands and feet.

I drove through the night and I drove through the dawn, coming in from the west with the sun in my eyes. I left the car on the side of the paved road in place of the first car I had stolen, then walked the rest of the way up the paved road, down the gravel road, down the dirt road. The house looked just as I had left it, and I banged my way through the screen door and in, calling her name, receiving no response.

The house was still, the floors and furniture dim with dust, and I wandered from room to room, confused. Finally I went out the back door and into the meadow.

I could see her there instantly, sitting just as I had left her, and I started quickly toward her, calling her name again.

But once I went a little farther I found myself slowing, stopping. For I could see that what I had thought was her arm was only the bones that had once structured the arm, the flesh mostly gone. And I saw that part of her on the other side too was in the process of grimly disarticulating itself with the aid of vermin and time, and I remembered what, out of love or hate, had happened and why I had left in the first place.

And then what choice was there but to turn about in my dead man's clothes and leave, to go through the house and out the front door and get into the car again, to set off again, to fling myself free of her gravitation and, this time, to never, never come back.

Eclipse

Carole Maso

The way you glisten
in the distance
the way you shimmer
and glow
The way you keep flickering
and fading
The way you keep shrinking (a diminishing figure)
The way you break, pixilate

The way you keep fading and blurring when you are needed most
That vast detachment, that infinite indifference,
The breach of—
Promises, promises, Madame sings, doing a little soft shoe,
the god rag
The god gap
The bloat
doting and without—
this is a deserted place, the apostles whisper
and it is already late.
—hope

But here at the Palace, 4 a.m.
where we dare each other into ecstasy—
into welter and darkness
oblivion lovers
eclipse chasers
the child twirling until she falls
in the circular room
this vertigo
hobbling after the glow
following the glow
ringing like the inside of a bell
the tenderness of the inner bell

lobed
when all we ever wanted was the god sound
the ear of the deaf
the mercy seat,
the free fall
fervor for flowers and fifty kinds of forever.

In *The Book of Radiance* the force of light will erase us.

The way you keep burning
smoke at the periphery of the world
The way you keep turning to vapor

the oblivion lovers
in the center of the god beauty
when all we ever wanted was the god music.
I hear you and then I do not hear you so well.
the way you imperceptibly in the distance
from this last bed sing
Fueled by your transcendent hiddenness
I see you and then I do not see you so well.

a fluttering on the tongue
something sweet—the wine, the heat, a leap of faith
in the circular room, past midnight where we danced
wiping our brows in astonishment with the god rag.

dust of the end
wanting salvation or just
the way in
the way he looked that night on his knees. In a kind of prayer.

wailing in blue light
at the cistern
at the bed
at the grave
at the moment before the moment of death
at the apples and roses and snow
as they continue to fall
as they continue now to fall
every preposterous

outrageous
delicious
stupendous—
before the blur.

He carried a fish on a gleaming platter. The eye glistened. Evening. South of
France. Bright as day. I was quite burned by the sun. A sun that seemed to
refuse to set. In the distance the blue of the Méditerranée.

the god boat
the portal
We're at sea
afloat
The way you break. The way you keep breaking
up into sound
and light
over water.
Sound effects and a light show—
the god light.

Strands of syntax and
gene theory—endless proofs toward your existence.
blue flame
human hatred
All the things in the world that can burn

Is the god in the blue cup?
Is the god in the delicately curved ear
straining to hear

A little voice coming now from beneath the debris
the wrath of and
now Baghdad in flames

One of the seraphim flew to me, holding an ember that he had taken with tongs
from the altar

A voice coming from beneath the debris.

sing to me

Carole Maso

something smoky
Something smoldering
go for broke
light me up
on the screen
ash fierce
debilitating
hunger-valve
skin color

black man waving a white flag from the rooftop.
"Nearer, My God, to Thee"
sing a little song
Something bluesy
but not too sad . . .

Weight of gladiolas in the market.
The Hutu slaughter the Tutsi and you yawn
The prophets say: I see a conflagration
and you turn the page
The revelers say: at the Palace at 4 a.m., we danced
and you say whatever
how has even that passion flower turned so gaunt?
virus without end.

In the god wilderness.
If we demanded to see him.

If we insisted
with something
like god lust
when all we ever wanted was the god music
Thirst for the god song
god dirge
sing to me

gleaned from the TV:
a sign of some sort reading *Someone help us* can now be discerned from the
rooftops, where people have climbed to avoid the encroaching water, *Help us*,
written on bedsheets, yes, the people gesturing to the sky

Whimsical god who might locate Louisiana on a map have mercy on us

in the government forsaken
in the flood

What is this omniscient narrator trying to prove exactly?
the know-it-all, the god grip. Better perhaps to wander into that amorphous
forest dense with disappearance, wrong turns, dead ends, mists. Exactly what?

We want (but why) that narrator
the god without end. Before last light
after last light
more
we want more
last call
heard from beneath the debris
drunk on the god idea
we're in the dark
past midnight

Ordeal of ever after
ordeal of world without end
for ever and ever
amen.

the god brag

We're small in the night
and from beneath the debris of two towers
glimpsed in the mercury glass: his sudden departure.
glimpsed in the giant fallen orb

The god tunnel (no light)
the storm's eye
the funnel cloud

a central mystery around which events madly whirl
the vortex of no god

where's the punch line?

Carole Maso

Rosmarie Waldrop:
I asked him how he reconciled being an atheist with constantly writing about
God. He said it was a word his culture had given him, a metaphor for
nothingness, the infinite, silence, death, for all that calls us into question.
For the ultimate otherness . . . the very condition of his freedom: not to be.

Elusive is the god

Event spinning off and around a central mystery. Without beginning, without
end, and with no idea where the middle is or what it's all about in particular.

Faith is a miracle, a gift from god whereby eternal truth enters time in the
instant.

God is accessible only through Bach, he had said
Beginnings and endings only through Bach.

From the blue light of the screen, a voice: *somebody rescue us*

Blue shadow in the milk
Blue angel in the whir of the propeller
blue rays emanating from the radiation light
in little blue light
live
in galloping furious
in save us I beg you implore you
beseech you
petition you

the god test

Slowly, the office window, high above Manhattan, where one day he would be
forced to jump, grew dark.

the god fire
the god send
the god flight
despise not our petitions

As you are detraining: there is a space between the platform and the train
take care

Carole Maso

take charm
take hope

mind the gap . . .
take heart.

Ava Klein, tell me if you know
Before world's end
before land's end
the tide's suck and drag
the sand, whistle of stones, in the take away
the gasping of fish
and little ones.
How do birds find their way? From beneath the debris . . .
mignon
minnow
darling lost one
minna, minna, minna
unintelligible alphabet anymore
language that cannot capture this
But once.

Once I watched her, that elegant, intelligent creature, that goddess on the
night of the eclipse. Witnessed her balancing speech in grace against so much
silence and dark. Once. With her human pulse and cadence, as if the world with
her saying it, her seeing it, began anew each time. In a small way, of course.

The god instant

She asked Jabes how he reconciled being an atheist with constantly writing
about God.

Man is so lonely. Searches eastward.

Dependent on you for salvation we shimmy up to you once more.
Curly lamb of—
flaxen
fertile
nurturing
sing to me
when all we ever wanted was that music

Carole Maso

the screen lights up
and voila:
god.com
and the quiet.

For a mystical experience to occur, brain regions that orient you in space and
mark the distinction between self and world must go quiet.

Different regions of the brain are now as we speak disengaging from one
another.

We wave as we go quiet, as we go dark, one by one, and we are offered for a
moment something like peace.

The right side stays quiescent a while and the left side interprets this as a
sensed presence, as the self departing the body, or of
god—is that you then?

Waving one white flag
waving two checked flags
waving one white flag in surrender
waving dark stars and stripes
a nightmare of codes

I was banging my head against the great wall of god

the mournful horn of god

Near is and
Difficult to reach
The God
—Hölderlin

the boundaries of god

I know, Carlos, that all you ever wanted was the god light. One night of pure
paradise. Armed with a blindfold, a noose, a cup of thorns.

A cup of thorns at the foot of the bed. Lacerations supplications
that bleeding iconic hand—cut on the punch bowl. *Oh your poor paw!*

You rise before me now holding an ember
our safe word waiting for when we got there. Even now I hesitate to reveal it,
Carlos, don't ask me why.

Ava Klein, surely you are not dying yet.

This is a deserted place and it is already late.

How do birds find their way?

Acquaintances who told the couple that the death of their daughter was part
of a grand plan by a benevolent god offended them. Those who tried to offer
comfort by speaking of an afterlife offended them. But most of all they were
offended by those who were unable to face the death of a child. Who turned
away when they were needed most.

who thought the world of you

who would never have wanted to hurt you, ever

the god starves the fever

chattering incoherently
if you could make one wish
the child's Bible
a mother-of-pearl cover
for C, on the occasion of her first communion
a tiny missal
meant to be help
in the hand of a child

How do birds find their way? she had asked.

the terrible pulling away

the hand slips from hers

the god loss

(your back is turned)

Carole Maso

the dormant (hibernating?)
the door mat
the god door
dormouse
(I think god must be a little mouse, the child smiled.)

the door is open, the door is closed (you choose)
I wish for fish.
The _____ is _____. You choose.

the god portal
the place from which the children flung their small bodies
that brief interval through which they slipped
on the train bound for A.

Suddenly they found themselves on the ground and the train that carried their
deaths grew smaller and smaller and then disappeared in the night. And then
the sound quite remarkably of a flute or—no—a piccolo—
in the snow

Subjective truth is found in the intensity of the passion. It ends in faith,
which overthrows reason altogether. Soren, my friend as of late, says the
highest pitch of any passion is to will its downfall. In faith that passion has
been realized—reason has been overcome in the face of the absurd.

How are you feeling, Ava Klein? We do not suppose that you are dying yet.

The plot becoming increasingly irrelevant just as it begins to cohere. This relic
from an already receding past. Don't go. Stepping through the portal.

The window is (open) flooded yes, with light, early morning.

He does, he certainly does seem to love us.

Ava Klein, turn over on your side.

green grass
blue sky
white cloud, etc.
what can still be predicted
relied on (the god turns away)

(but not every time)
the sun is yellow

What can be seen out of this very window just now:
He came from out of nowhere. We were having drinks outside with the women.
I was quite burned by the sun. His name was Jean-Pierre or Jean-Luc or Jean-Paul. I was wearing a white dress with the straps down. We were about to cook a French fish we did not know the name of. I remember its shape on the plate. Anatole was already dead.

The harshness of the sun. The admittedly superficial conversation. The games of Pony and Innuendo and Despair. And all so very French. When he appeared out of nowhere we went off together to dance. I lacked discretion, the French couple said.

When all we ever wanted was world without end.
there in the distance.
and the shimmer.

Well, it was one of those ungodly summer days—the ones that never seemed to end, bright as midday at 10 p.m.,

and then, as if suddenly, darkness
the sun is cold
the sun is black
lamb of god who takes away the sins of the world
the sun is so cold and black
as if suddenly—but when had it happened?

In the god gap you bitterly laugh

Have mercy on us

Where have you gone? (he loves us not)

Just as man has forgotten his love for god,
so god has deserted man
leaving him to wander through the night
like an orphan.

And yet, Hölderlin seems to say, yes he does seem to be saying that the disappearance of god may be his most mysterious gift.

Made radiant by his very departure
Felt most extravagantly: his absence.

How to describe the light that came from this body that night—past midnight—bright as day? That evanescence. Paradise.

a field of hope
a field of pain
a field of song
a field of singing things listen:
birds lift toward the god fire
the darkening blue light
and her little dress drenched

Everything is going to fail Hölderlin and he sees it coming. Almost forty years of madness

In the lapse

Dear Francesco,
Much is expressed in the interval. Do not worry so much about our silences when they come. I hear you even then.

In the gap

the portable Virgin Mary perched on my night table.
How you keep shrinking. How you fit so nicely now inside my pocket.

Little Saint Francis with arc of birds (protect the child)
And the Little Flower, Saint Therese says
You instruct me in darkness and in silence.

feather nest
the _____hole

some soft place

some place soft (should the child come to term)

some place safe

the loving god bathes us in the hormones for pain

bathes us in hormones for birth

the god embrace
god bathes us, he does

in the hormones for death
for heartbreak

this chemical bath—as I feel it coming on now.

Anatole, we lost the child.

Towers crumble
people, whole countries are destroyed
the god cares not.

Slowly the window from where he would one day be forced to jump drew
dark.

A memorial concert for the victims of September 11 played without conductor.

The god comes no closer.

And the children ask over and over again
ou est la porte?
straining for the context.
Ou est la porte?

oh so they are looking for the door

or the god phone
or the god dome or

Standing at the grave, her husband's untimely death, the Croatian nanny
and I paw the earth—What does this say I ask pointing to the words engraved

on the stone. It says, Ivan Grbesic, God be with you. The word for God in Croatian is Bog then?
Yes.

Bog be with us. She offers Bog a gold watch and fob. Bog be with us. Despise us not.

From behind the closed door I implore thee

I am reminded at this juncture of my own Carlos. The black sand of his hourglass. Five burnings. The god lust.

Year after year the lovers slur into one another, holding their safe words, when all they ever wanted was to feel the edge, the distances where you glimmer. . . .

One celestial body obscures another

Where have you gone?

when all we wanted all we ever wanted was the god light

a cup of thorns at the foot of the bed, the seraphim, the ember

what does it mean? I do not understand.

Whether you understand or not is no concern of Bog's.

oblivion in the wave of a hand

all I ever wanted or loved or feared

I repeat is no concern of Bog's

Bring them on:

Wandering in now from out of nowhere, completely soaked, a little black girl tugs at a sleeve. "Don't stop the music," she says, "or I'll tell my father."

The Romanian (half hallucinating, but unbowed) swerves into the god space with his two sinister monks and his two starving men. One of the men the monks declare will be fed if he accepts God, the other if he denies God. And so it goes.

The quaintness of the plot.

Dear Bog,
For the war in Bosnia Herzegovina
For the war against Iraq
And for all wars

Falling into welter and waste and darkness.

What has happened to us here on earth?

Tell me if you know. . . .

Dear Bog,
Despise not our petitions.

The Vienna Philharmonic plays without conductor at Saint Patrick's Cathedral to commemorate the victims of the September 11 attack on the World Trade Center.

From the window where he would one day jump he now stood with his iBook and iPod and his whole life.

Madame in a pool of light doing a little soft shoe points to the horizon.

Floating in air the gipper glimmers. Who's that?

The child marvels. An ocean liner—the gipper waves

An inkling in light

It is late and this is a deserted place.

What stands always between us and the god? Obscuring the view.

Near is and difficult to reach the God.
—Friedrich Hölderlin

Carole Maso

He watched the world from the window where he would one day jump begin to glisten.

Think of the piccolo player who injects a little flourish, improvised on the spot in the safety created by the conductor. It may be that having a conductor— a good one, at least—to follow and to resist gives players a greater liberty, the critic suggests.

He watched the world begin to glow. An ember at the foot of the bed.

The gipper in a white dinner jacket puts down his baton.

Saint Rose opens *The Book of Radiance.*

For this—the inheritance of the saints in light—we thank you

In the moment before we are erased

—and for the silence now that seems to permeate this al fresco scene—on the part of the planet we called France, 10 p.m.:

this most mysterious gift

Desire levitating the fish slightly from the silver platter so that it is suspended in a kind of hover—retrieved, rescued for an instant.

Look how burned I am still and how willingly I go for salve—off with him one last time to the circular room to dance. . . .

Self-Portrait with Beach
Frederic Tuten

THE BEACH, THE SEA, the blue umbrellas. A sail. Then another, like a long arm climbing the horizon. She stretched out on a blanket beside me in the dreadful hot sand. A sheet of gulls wheeling and diving, a form emerging from under the flat sea. Flat, feverless, an ocean too exhausted to make waves, an ocean that had seen too much travel. I was thinking this when she asked: "Is the body the house for the soul, or are body and soul one and inseparable?" She slipped off her bikini top, exposing her breasts to the sky, to the gaze of the sea.

"Your body is my soul," I said. She laughed, in a friendly way, as if to assure me that in spite of what seemed my exaggeration, she was pleased.

"Poor you," she said finally, "stuck with a soul bound for decay."

"Nothing of you will decay," I said, "not as long as I'm alive." And in love, I wanted to add, for the truth of it. But certain truths are better left at home, under a pillow, nesting among the feathers.

The beach was filling up with little clusters of families staking their territories with umbrellas and chairs. Young couples, hungry to burn their bodies, marked their separate terrain, spreading mats and towels under the raw sun.

Out of nowhere, a young man in white cap, white jacket, and creamy white pants appeared, crooning the virtues of his homemade beverages, kept in a white box he shouldered. He was a white thing itself come from out of the blue.

"Where did you come from?" I asked, not having viewed him before he materialized in whiteness and smiles.

"Out there," he said, nodding to the ocean. "A cold beverage?" he asked. Cold. Cold like love gone cold, I was sure he added, but knew he had not.

"Maybe later," I said. "Try us again later when it gets really hot."

We should buy now, he said, because his was a special home-brewed drink—it had unique powers.

"Do you have any to make one young again?" I asked, feeling

ancient, like a sea who has washed up on too many shores.

"Yes, and beautiful as well," he replied. "I have many sorts of flavors and specialties. This one, for example," he said, drawing a small bottle from his jacket pocket, "is to keep your woman faithful."

"Oh! Fidelity," she said. "I'm surprised it hasn't already exploded in your pocket," she added playfully.

"This one never explodes," he said, "the body explodes before this does." He had a wonderful grin, white like his hair.

"I don't require the fidelity drink," she said, looking at me.

"But I would like the youth-restorative flavor," I said. "Give me three if you have them."

"I'm all out," he said, rummaging through his box. "It's an all-time favorite."

"Come back when you have more," she said. "We'll be here all day; we'll wait here for years."

"Of course, I would do the same," he said, giving her a sweet, devouring look that made me jealous. I could see her blush, even through the blanching sunlight. Another smile, wider than the first, then he sauntered away, all the while singing the praises of his magical beverages.

"You only love me because you find me beautiful," she said, "and so when that's gone, I'm gone too. Right?"

"Of course not," I said, half lying.

"And if I were a real soulless bitch, you'd still love me because I was beautiful. Right?"

"Let's not go into metaphysics," I said as if I had meant it.

Her long smooth legs, her strong feet, bronzed, like the rest of her, by the sun. Her beauty that I loved and wanted always to stay the same, through aging and death, at least through the next few years. I was superficial about wanting her to remain young forever—never more than her twenty-eight perfect years, never less than perfect.

Superficial in other ways as well, she would say—had said. We can find beauty everywhere, I once proclaimed, and in everything—even in the decay of roses and in the corpses of dead seagulls on the beach, in the scars on otherwise smooth flesh, but there is no beauty like the body of any creature in its perfect, healthy form. A perfect body shields all the blemishes and corruptions of the soul, makes them irrelevant to our regard, I once—late at night in bed, in an after-love drowse—had announced to her, to my regret.

A single-engine plane, trailed by a banner selling a fleet of desires, flew sleepily by, the propeller's old-fashioned hum bringing me back to my childhood on the beach, to my mother, bringing me to her tender smile under her wide yellow hat that defied the sun. Her breasts were full then and beautiful with the fullness of youth not yet overripened. The bodies we feast upon as children dominate the future landscape of our desire, imprinting forever all our dreams of beauty—and of unsightliness.

The sun was now on her thighs, spread discreetly, like temple gates in Arcadia. I had sketched her while she slept that morning, exhausting five large sheets of good paper before I realized—once again—how she always eluded me. I had turned her legs into the pillars of Hercules, her breasts into small bread loaves. The rest of her I had converted into a birch tree without branches.

Courbet would have painted her richly, her ripe thighs open to creating the world, if he had not viewed her—as he did women—as a metaphor. Renoir would have made her stupidly fleshy, a bourgeois bred on pastries, though she was lean like boundaries on a map. Gauguin would have transformed her into a child of the jungle, when she was nothing of nature except for her desires.

I myself had failed at it completely, as I had so many other things in life. My paintings rendered just the bare image of her but not the paradigms of her in my heart. The canvas was often left bare, with a few lines here and there to consecrate the quixotic memory of my ambition. More than any photograph, those lines etched her image in my mind, gathered up her scent, her voice, her twisted hairpins on the pillow. Of course, these are fancy words to cover my inability to draw a line that hinted at her soul, her true immortal form.

"I had a dry period after you left the last time," she said, turning over on her stomach.

"Did it last long?" I asked, fearful of knowing about her life without me. Wanting never to leave her, always leaving her and taking my chances that she would be there when I returned. And fearful too of her answer, I began studying the curve of her breasts as if for the first time, with the wonder of the first time.

"Until you returned," she said, like the friendly breeze that had come from the sea. She smiled and reached her hand out to mine, which was not far away, waiting, as it were, for hers.

Three teenagers sauntered by, loving themselves in a fidgety, insecure way, amazed by the newfound power of their bodies to unhinge reason and jolt planets from their orbits. They gave us a passing glance, and, seeing nothing but age, did not see us.

She rose on her elbows, trailing my field of vision, the two of us following them until they were no longer significant in our view.

"How long do you think I have?" she asked. "Staying passable, I mean."

"Aphrodite lives forever," I said.

"How long is that?" she asked.

"Five years for others, a hundred for me."

"Five years?" she said. "Five minutes, then. Five waves of the hand."

"Even when the young men stop looking," I said consolingly, "others will take their place, the older ones."

The vendor returned, promoting his drinks, walking back and forth, and every once in a while he would give her a long look, taking her in with evident, unaffected joy. How wonderful that one can give so much pleasure to another, without effort, merely by being, I thought. But not without feeling jealous that the young man's gaze, like a magnet, had drawn some part of her youth, her beauty, into himself, leaving less her for me. The voyeur is always a thief. I'm a prince of such thieves.

"Sometimes when you were gone I thought of sleeping around. Although 'around' sounds too vast a territory for a girl to cover." She laughed. I did too, but mirthlessly.

Some clouds appeared out of the blue, literally. Giant, swollen gray bags they were, like frisky blimps looking for a port. I would have loved to be with them—away from all jealousy—floating up there, sailing from harbor to harbor.

"Did you?" I asked, dreading her answer.

"What harm would it have done, after all, what would it have mattered once I'm in the grave?"

"I thought you intended to be cremated," I said, trying to lighten the clouds.

"What comfort to my ashes then?" she asked, shaking sand from her hair.

"'Ashes they shall become, but ashes in love.' Do you know that poem of Quevedo's?"

"You always quote it," she said. "I should know it by heart now. Is that how you love me, like an ash?"

"Always a glowing one," I said. "Glowing for you," I added for good measure, overflowing the cup. The three teenagers who had passed by earlier passed by again, but now they were middle-aged, with soft bellies and drooping chins, with children who had grown up and gone away, with husbands gone to younger women or gone to the grave. I could see that in them, their disappointments buried beneath their tans.

"I'm baked and I'm thirsty," she said, just as the vendor cast his handsome shadow over us. A strange shadow, considering that the sun, in some tricky maneuver, had darkened its complexion.

"I'm brewing up a new batch of drinks," he said. "Come up to the canteen for a fresh cup or two."

"The good stuff?" I asked. "The stuff of dreams?"

He smiled, like a flash of lightning. He smiled at her.

When we arrived at the canteen we saw a long line stretching back down to the shore. Hundreds of people, some holding their huge beach umbrellas over their heads, were waiting silently for the canteen doors to open. We had no desire to wait and were about to leave when he called out to us from the veranda.

"No, no, come here," he said, waving aside those at the top of the line to make way for us.

He sat us down at a wooden table under a thatched roof. He told us we would not have to wait long for his marvelous concoction to be ready, bringing us in the meanwhile a pitcher of ice water and a bowl of olives. That was a strange combination, I said, water and olives. It was his canteen, he said; he could bring us anything we wanted. Even music, if we were lonely for music.

Lonely for music, what a notion, I thought. But I suddenly realized that I was lonely for a music that would take me from the beach and its heat, for a music that would suit the mood of longing, as I was then feeling, to have back my life from the start, when I was young enough to believe I would never grow old, would never die. As if on cue, two birds began singing. I could see their still forms lurking above us in the straw roof, the birds singing of desire and love, of love eternal, of love beyond the bodily frame, beyond the cells, as they ecstatically crashed into blindness, silence, and death.

"How odd," she said. "Birds singing in German."

"Yes," I said. "More so that they have human voices."

"I overlooked that nuance," she said.

"*Tristan und Isolde*," we said simultaneously. Then she added, "No, wrong. *Ariadne auf Naxos*."

"It's the same thing," I said, "passion, death, funeral pyres, love, besotted smoke ascending to the gods."

The singing ceased; voices rose from outside the veranda. The line had grown even longer, extending far down and along the shore, which had turned a squalid gray, like the gray sky and sea. There was grumbling in the line and some pressed themselves against the canteen walls as if to break them down. No one was young.

"Look," he said, "look at the lovebirds." He held up a pair of golden metal nightingales by their metal tails. "I have musical chips for every mood, even Puccini if you prefer the sweetness."

"Oh!" she said. "Mechanical birds with chips for every mood."

I hated the deflation in her voice. She was still young and not steadied for disappointments.

"They are not expensive," he said. "I could let you have them for a price." He smiled at me in a reassuring way as he would to her uncle, then at her. "For a kiss," he said.

"I'd rather have the drinks," she said in a polite way that carried other meanings.

"Which you both shall have," he said, covering her rebuke with a face of smiles.

"And the others waiting out there?" I asked.

"They have had their share many times," he said, "while you have had none." Suddenly, his voice was that of an older man and not that of the youth who earlier had paraded the beach hawking his wares. He looked older, his skin gone dry, his body stooped over our table.

"I don't think we want your drink," she said, turning away as she spoke. "Do we?"

"I don't know," I said lightly. "I wouldn't mind trying the youth restorative. What harm could it do?"

She gave me a long look, as if to say: Why waste time on this charlatan? Why give away a moment of life that is not a moment spent together, when every second in this world steals us away from each other? And finally and perhaps to the core of it all: why let him flirt with me?

"What harm?" I repeated lamely, feeling, indeed, that in wanting, now more than ever, his magic drink, I had gone lame, at least in her eyes if not in mine.

"Stay," she said. "I'll take a walk along the beach and find you back at our umbrella."

The sky was darkening in an unfriendly way. I wanted to point that out to her, as if the weather was my concern, when what I really wanted to say was: don't leave, don't take that walk without me, don't shut down your heart from me for even a second, but then I thought of how wonderful being young again would be and I said, "I won't be long."

I watched her leave—without a kiss—watched her walk away slowly, so that by the time he had brought me my drink, she was far away, growing smaller, a diminishing dot against the blustery sky.

I was back in my beach chair but no longer needed the umbrella, as the sun was walled in by the darkest clouds. I kept the umbrella open so that she might better see me in the distance and also because as the beach began to empty, slowly at first and then at a faster pace, the rain drizzled down from the clouds. It would take a half hour or so, he said, before I would feel the effects of the drink, and then maybe an hour or two longer before the results were visible.

Little hints of change at first, such as an improvement in my hearing and sight, or a feeling of tightness of the skin under my chin, which had begun its slide with gravity. And then if all went well, in a matter of a few more hours I would be returned to my optimum moment of health and youth, back to my golden age, give or take a year or two.

The sea was rising and gulls were screaming at the waves. The swimmers had long ago returned to shore. The sea was empty, the beach emptier. Not a chair, not an umbrella, not a person in sight. I looked and looked in the direction of where I had last seen her walk and saw nothing but darkening space in retreat. Then the rain began in earnest, drowning the sea and the beach and flooding the canteen, which had already locked its doors and fastened the shutters, looking long ago abandoned. I was the only soul on the beach, the only soul on earth. I should pick myself up, I thought, and leave the beach, but I could not, did not wish to move, or change my place for any place in the world, waiting, under an umbrella in a deluge, as I was, for the return of my youth.

NOTES ON CONTRIBUTORS

CHIMAMANDA NGOZI ADICHIE was born in Nigeria. Her first novel, *Purple Hibiscus* (Anchor), won the Commonwealth Writers' Prize and the Hurston/Wright Legacy Award, and her newest novel, *Half of a Yellow Sun*, was published last fall by Knopf. A 2005–2006 Hodder Fellow at Princeton University, she divides her time between the United States and Nigeria.

AIMEE BENDER is the author of *The Girl in the Flammable Skirt, An Invisible Sign of My Own,* and *Willful Creatures* (all Anchor).

MEI-MEI BERSSENBRUGGE's selected poems, *I Love Artists,* was published by the University of California, and *Concordance,* a collaboration with Kiki Smith, was published last year by Kelsey Street. She lives in New York City and northern New Mexico.

ROBERT OLEN BUTLER has published ten novels and four volumes of short fiction, one of which, *A Good Scent from a Strange Mountain* (Grove Press), won the 1993 Pulitzer Prize for Fiction. His most recent book, *Severance* (Chronicle Books), is a collection of short short stories in the voices of recently severed heads. *Intercourse,* one hundred short short stories in the voices of fifty couples engaged in intercourse, will appear in 2008.

MARY CAPONEGRO's most recent collection of fictions is *The Complexities of Intimacy* (Coffee House). She is currently finishing a collection of stories and a novel.

H. G. CARRILLO is the author of *Loosing My Espanish,* a novel (Anchor Books), and his short stories have appeared in numerous journals. A PhD candidate and instructor in the Department of English at Cornell University, he divides his time between Ithaca, New York, and San Juan, Puerto Rico.

JOHN D'AGATA is the author of *Halls of Fame* (Graywolf).

RIKKI DUCORNET is currently completing a new collection of *Butcher's Tales* for the Dalkey Archive and will exhibit her new paintings at the Pierre Menard Gallery in Cambridge, Massachusetts, in May 2007. In 2004 she received the Lannan Literary Award for Fiction.

BRIAN EVENSON is the author of seven works of fiction, most recently *The Open Curtain* (Coffee House), which was named one of the ten best books of 2006 by *Time Out New York,* and is a finalist for an Edgar Award. He is the director of Brown University's Literary Arts Program.

MARY GAITSKILL is the author of the novels *Two Girls, Fat and Thin* (Poseidon) and *Veronica* (Pantheon), as well as the story collections *Bad Behavior* (Poseidon) and *Because They Wanted To* (Simon & Schuster). She teaches at Syracuse University. The author is grateful to Nuruddin Farah for kindly granting use of an excerpt from his novel *Secrets*.

ELIZABETH HAND's newest novel is *Generation Loss* (Small Beer Press in association with Harcourt).

SIRI HUSTVEDT is the author of three novels, *The Blindfold, The Enchantment of Lily Dahl,* and *What I Loved* (all Henry Holt/Picador), and two books of essays, *A Plea for Eros* (Picador) and *Mysteries of the Rectangle* (Princeton Architectural Press).

ROBERT KELLY's recent books include *May Day* (Parsifal), *Threads* (First Intensity), *Sainte-Terre* (Shivastan), *Lapis* (Black Sparrow/Godine), and *Shame/Schám* (McPherson). Some of the Faust workings in this issue were triggered by Bettina Mathes's study *Verhandlungen mit Faust* (Helmer Verlag) and her essay on Busoni and Freud.

JULIANA LESLIE is the author of the chapbooks *Pie in the Sky* (Braincase Press) and *Questions for Trees* (Minus House). She lives in Santa Cruz, California.

JONATHAN LETHEM's seventh novel, *You Don't Love Me Yet,* was published by Doubleday in March.

This year, KEVIN MAGEE's "to write as speech" appeared in *The Capilano Review.* In 2006, *Proletariaria,* in two volumes, became available in the *Blue Lion* print-on-demand series.

CAROLE MASO is the author of nine books, including *AVA, The American Woman in the Chinese Hat* (both Dalkey Archive), and *Defiance* (Dutton). "Eclipse" is an excerpt from her novel in progress, *The Bay of Angels.*

SHENA McAULIFFE is a recent graduate of the Writing Program at Washington University in St. Louis. Her work has appeared in the *Land-Grant College Review* and *Cutbank.*

S. G. MILLER's work will appear in *Best Stories from the Southwest,* forthcoming this fall. "A Home To Go Home To" is part of a novel in progress.

ANDREW MOSSIN is the author of the book-length poem *The Epochal Body* (Singing Horse), and his poetry and critical prose have appeared in numerous journals. He has just completed a memoir, *The Presence of Their Passing,* and is currently at work on a book of critical essays on the poets Robert Duncan, Robin Blaser, Charles Olson, and Nathaniel Mackey.

JOYCE CAROL OATES is the author, most recently, of *The Gravedigger's Daughter, Black Girl/White Girl,* and *High Lonesome: New and Selected Stories 1966–2006* (all Ecco). A frequent contributor to *Conjunctions,* she is the Roger S. Berlind Distinguished Professor of Humanities at Princeton University and a member of the American Academy of Arts and Letters.

407

ROSAMOND PURCELL is an internationally renowned artist and photographer. Her books include *Special Cases: Natural Anomalies and Historical Monsters* (Chronicle Books), *Owls Head*, and *Bookworm* (all Quantuck Lane Books), as well as collaborations with Stephen J. Gould. *Dice: Deception, Fate and Rotten Luck*, with Ricky Jay, is also available from Quantuck Lane Press. Her work is in many permanent collections around the world. She lives outside Boston.

TOVA REICH is the author of the novels *The Jewish War* (Pantheon), *Master of the Return* (Harcourt), and *Mara* (Farrar, Straus & Giroux). Her new novel, *My Holocaust*, will be published in 2007 by HarperCollins.

DONALD REVELL's most recent book is *Pennyweight Windows: New and Selected Poems*, published by Alice James, which will also publish his forthcoming new collection, *A Thief of Strings*.

LUC SANTE is the author of *Low Life* and *Evidence* (both Farrar, Straus & Giroux), and *The Factory of Facts* (Pantheon). *Kill All Your Darlings: Pieces 1990–2005* (Yeti Books/Verse Chorus Press) will be published later this year, as will his translation of Félix Fénéon's *Novels in Three Lines* (New York Review Books). He teaches writing and the history of photography at Bard College.

REBECCA SEIFERLE's fourth poetry collection, *Wild Tongue*, is forthcoming from Copper Canyon Press. Her previous collection, *Bitters* (also Copper Canyon), won the Western States Book Award, and in 2004 she was awarded a Lannan Literary Fellowship.

WILL SELF's fiction includes three short-story collections, *The Quantity Theory of Insanity* (winner of the Geoffrey Faber Memorial Prize), *Grey Area*, and *Tough, Tough Toys for Tough, Tough Boys*. His book *Cock and Bull* consists of two novellas, and he is the author of four novels, *My Idea of Fun, Great Apes, How the Dead Live*, and *Dorian*. His nonfiction includes *Perfidious Man* (with photographs by David Gamble), *Sore Sites*, and two collections of journalism, *Junk Mail* and *Feeding Frenzy*. His latest novel is *The Book of Dave*, published by Bloomsbury, which will also publish his selected stories, *The Undivided Self*, in the fall.

REGINALD SHEPHERD's five books of poetry include *Fata Morgana, Otherhood*, and *Some Are Drowning*, winner of the 1994 Associated Writing Programs' Award in Poetry (all University of Pittsburgh). He is editor of *The Iowa Anthology* (University of Iowa), and his book *Orpheus in the Bronx: Essays on Identity, Politics, and the Freedom of Poetry* is forthcoming from the University of Michigan.

DAVID SHIELDS's new book, *The Thing About Life Is That One Day You'll Be Dead*, is forthcoming from Knopf in 2008; *Reality Hunger: A Manifesto* is forthcoming from Vintage in 2009.

ELENI SIKELIANOS is the author of five books of poetry and one hybrid memoir, including, most recently, *The California Poem* (Coffee House) and *The Book of Jon* (City Lights). *Body Clock* is forthcoming next year from Coffee House.

SUSAN STEINBERG is the author of *Hydroplane* and *The End of Free Love* (both FC₂). She teaches at the University of San Francisco.

COLE SWENSEN's latest book is *The Glass Age* (Alice James Books). Previous volumes have received the Iowa Poetry Prize, the San Francisco State Poetry Center Book Award, and a National Poetry Series selection. A 2007 Guggenheim Fellow, she teaches at the Iowa Writers' Workshop.

ANNE TARDOS has published five books of poetry and the multimedia performance work and radio play *Among Men*. She is the editor of *Thing of Beauty: New and Selected Works*, by Jackson Mac Low, forthcoming in the fall from the University of California Press.

FREDERIC TUTEN's novels include *Tintin in the New World*, *Van Gogh's Bad Café* (both Black Classic Press), *The Adventures of Mao on the Long March* (New Directions), and, most recently, *The Green Hour* (W. W. Norton). "Self-Portrait with Beach" will appear in a book of photographs by Mona Kuhn, forthcoming from Steidl.

LEWIS WARSH's most recent books are *Origin of the World* (Creative Arts) and *Touch of the Whip* (Singing Horse). Two new books, *A Place in the Sun* (Spuyten Duyvil) and *Inseparable: Poems 1995–2005* (Granary), are forthcoming this year. He is director of the MFA program in creative writing at Long Island University in Brooklyn.

PAUL WEST is the author of numerous works of fiction and nonfiction. His most recent book is *Sheer Fiction VI* (McPherson). *The Shadow Factory*, an account of his recent stroke, is forthcoming from Lumen.

This is MICHAEL WHITE's first published fiction. He teaches English at the ASA Institute in Manhattan.

DELILLO FIEDLER GASS PYNCHON
University of Delaware Press
Collections on Contemporary Masters

UNDERWORDS
Perspectives on Don DeLillo's *Underworld*

Edited by Joseph Dewey, Steven G. Kellman, and Irving Malin

Essays by Jackson R. Bryer, David Cowart, Kathleen Fitzpatrick, Joanne Gass, Paul Gleason, Donald J. Greiner, Robert McMinn, Thomas Myers, Ira Nadel, Carl Ostrowski, Timothy L. Parrish, Marc Singer, and David Yetter

$39.50

LESLIE FIEDLER AND AMERICAN CULTURE

Edited by Steven G. Kellman and Irving Malin

Essays by John Barth, Robert Boyers, James M. Cox, Joseph Dewey, R.H.W. Dillard, Geoffrey Green, Irving Feldman, Leslie Fiedler, Susan Gubar, Jay L. Halio, Brooke Horvath, David Ketterer, R.W.B. Lewis, Sanford Pinsker, Harold Schechter, Daniel Schwarz, David R. Slavitt, Daniel Walden, and Mark Royden Winchell

$36.50

INTO *THE TUNNEL*
Readings of Gass's Novel

Edited by Steven G. Kellman and Irving Malin

Essays by Rebecca Goldstein, Donald J. Greiner, Brooke Horvath, Marcus Klein, Jerome Klinkowitz, Paul Maliszewski, James McCourt, Arthur Saltzman, Susan Stewart, and Heide Ziegler

$35.00

PYNCHON AND *MASON & DIXON*

Edited by Brooke Horvath and Irving Malin

Essays by Jeff Baker, Joseph Dewey, Bernard Duyfhuizen, David Foreman, Donald J. Greiner, Brian McHale, Clifford S. Mead, Arthur Saltzman, Thomas H. Schaub, David Seed, and Victor Strandberg

$39.50

ORDER FROM ASSOCIATED UNIVERSITY PRESSES
2010 Eastpark Blvd., Cranbury, New Jersey 08512
PH 609-655-4770   FAX 609-655-8366   E-mail AUP440@ aol.com

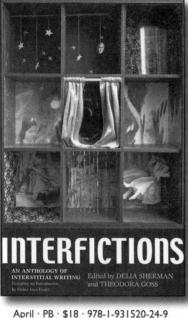

April · PB · $18 · 978-1-931520-24-9
Distributed to the trade by Consortium
www.interstitialarts.org

What is interstitial art?

Work that falls in the interstices—
between the cracks—of recognized
commercial genres. Interstitial Art wan-
ders across borders without stopping at
Customs to declare its intent.

So who are you and what are you doing?

The Interstitial Arts Foundation is dedicated to bringing together readers, writers, scholars, critics, listeners, musicians,
viewers, artists, performers, audience
and participants to celebrate and further
explore work that resists categorization.

What are the rules of crafting Interstitial work?

Interstitial Art is a moving target, it's work
that demands you engage with it on its
own terms. Interstitial artists don't make
rules—we debate and interrogate them.
Interstitial fiction is an umbrella term for
a wide variety of writing that does not
preclude or discount the use of other
terms. The IAF is not creating a new
movement; we're a barometer, measuring
(and celebrating!) what already exists.

Looking for something
unusual to read between
the Spring and Fall issues of
Conjunctions?

INTERFICTIONS
An Anthology of Interstitial Writing

Edited by Delia Sherman and Theodora Goss

In the first piece of art from the
Interstitial Arts Foundation, 19 new
and established writers dig into the
imaginative spaces between conventional genres—realistic and fantasti-
cal, scholarly and poetic, personal
and political—and bring up gems of a
new type of fiction: interstitial fiction.

Features an afterword by the editors, an introduction by Heinz Insu
Fenkl (professor of creative writing,
and director of ISIS: The Interstitial
Studies Institute at SUNY, New Paltz)
and fiction from the USA, Canada,
Australia, and the UK, and translated
from Spanish, Hungarian, and French.

Interfictions will inspire and provoke readers, reviewers, and artists of
all stripes.

∼

Delia Sherman earned a Ph.D. in Renaissance
Studies at Brown and taught at Boston
University and Northeastern. She is the author
of the novels *The Porcelain Dove* (Mythopoeic
Award winner), and *Changeling*. Sherman
cofounded the Interstitial Arts Foundation,
dedicated to promoting art that crosses genre
borders.

Theodora Goss was born in Hungary. She teaches
at Boston University, is completing a PhD, and is
introducing classes on the fantastic tradition in
English literature. She is the author of a short
story collection, *In the Forest of Forgetting*.

Cleopatra Haunts the Hudson
Sarah White
ISBN 978-1-933132-29-7 $13.00

Sarah White juggles spots of time like lit torches.
They shed light, for our pleasure, on
landscapes imagined and real, inner and outer.

MARIE PONSOT

SPUYTENDUYVIL.NET
AND BOOKSENSE.COM

Fission Among the Fanatics
Tom Bradley
ISBN 978-1-933132-33-4 $16.00

Tom Bradley is one of the most
criminally underrated authors
on the planet.

ANDREW GALLIX, 3 AM MAGAZINE

Strange Evolutionary Flowers
Lizbeth Rymland
ISBN 978-1-933132-21-1 $14.00

Part Zen poet, part temple priestess, Liz
Rymland writes with a style reminiscent
of Jack Kerouac and Alexandra David-Neel.

THOMAS LYTTLE, "PSYCHEDELIC
MONOGRAPHS AND ESSAYS, "PSYCHEDELICS REIMAGINED"

Black Clock

Aimee Bender / Francesca Lia Block / Tom Carson
Wanda Coleman / Samuel R. Delany / Brian Evenson
Janet Fitch / Tara Ison / Yxta Maya Murray
Geoff Nicholson / Joy Nicholson / Rachel Resnick
Lisa Teasley / Lynne Tillman

number 7

edited by Steve Erickson
designed by Gail Swanlund

blackclock.org

PUBLISHED BY CALARTS IN
ASSOCIATION WITH THE MFA
WRITING PROGRAM

Catherine Imbriglio
PARTS OF THE MASS

This first book of poems juxtaposes contemporary physics, personal and public history, and a passion for the sound of words with the structural arc of the Roman Catholic mass. The poems invest both in wordplay and in inquiry, wonder, disagreement, dissatisfaction and ethical urgency. This "mass" is attuned to turmoil and to the challenges of our day.

"Formally exploratory as her poems are, poetry is for her not a formal exercise but a necessity, a way to understand the world and the words with which we know it"—Reginal Shepherd

Poetry, 64 pages, offset, smyth-sewn, ISBN13: 978-1-886224-81-0, original paperback $14

Craig Watson
SECRET HISTORIES

Poems that map the nexus of history, language and political consciousness through the lens of an elusive present tense. The focus is on the way history is constructed as an active engagement with a non-negotiable future, as opposed to the passive receipt of past "truths." Subject matter reaches from the ancient Mongol Empire to the last days of mankind. In fragments and disjointed observations, the book tries to replicate and in fact become the process of "making" history.

Poetry, 80 pages, offset, smyth-sewn, ISBN13: 978-1-886224-83-4, original paperback $14

Recently published:
Erica Carpenter: *PERSPECTIVE WOULD HAVE US*

"an excellent, wonderful book... a celebration of subtlety in an age of bluntness" —Ron Silliman. Poetry, 72 pages, ISBN 1-886224-76-5, $14

Elizabeth Robinson: *UNDER THAT SILKY ROOF*

Poems concerned with "the brick floor from which the/kingdom of God extends/or could extend." 80 pages, ISBN 1-886224-71-4,$14

Jean Grosjean: *AN EARTH OF TIME*

[Serie d'Ecriture, No. 18; translated from the French by Keith Waldrop]

Between lyric and meditation on Biblical themes, the poems work up to a personal apocalypse. Poetry, 96 pages, ISBN 1-886224-79-x, $14

Suzanne Doppelt: *RING RANG WRONG*

[Serie d'Ecriture, No. 19; translated from the French by Cole Swensen]

Juxtaposed with her precise and abstract photographs, Doppelt's prose considers astronomy, weather, the five senses, plant life, the insect world, the nature of time — all in an implicit dialogue with the pre-Socratics.
Text and Photographs, 80 pages, ISBN 1-886224-80-3, $14

Gerhard Roth: *The Will to Sickness*

[Dichten =, No. 8; translated from the German by Tristram Wolff]

A fiercely experimental novel. 120 pages, ISBN 1-886224-78-1, $14

Orders: Small Press Distribution 1-800/869-7553, www.spdbooks.org; in Europe, www.h-press.no
www.burningdeck.com

FICTION COLLECTIVE TWO

FC2

http://fc2.org

FC2: A Literary Alternative Since 1974

formally adventurous fiction

FC2 is among the few alternative presses in America devoted to publishing fiction considered by many of the largest publishers to be too challenging, innovative, or heterodox for the commercial milieu. FC2's mission has been and remains to publish books of high quality and exceptional ambition whose style, subject matter or form push the limits of American publishing and reshape our literary culture. FC2 continues the commitment of its founders to unsettle the bounds of literature and broaden the audience for adventurous writing.

SPRING 2007

The Possibility of Music - Stephen-Paul Martin
Like Blood in Water - Yuriy Tarnawsky
Was - Michael Joyce

New From Parsifal Editions

www.parsifal-editions.com

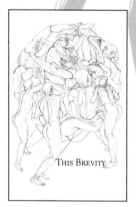

May Day
Poems by Robert Kelly
ISBN 0-9739960-1-3
109 Pages (paper)
$13.95 US
$16.00 CAD

> Midnight came and stayed. Sappho
> kissed me
> lightly on the corner of my mouth
> I touched her hip it was enough
> to get the brightness started.

from "Making Gold"

May Day continues Kelly's search for meaning, with poems born of a spiritual need and a perennial relationship with language which Jung describes as "...a deep presentiment that strives to find expression. It is like a whirlwind that seizes everything within reach and, by carrying it aloft, assumes a visible shape." The poems of *May Day* speak like sirens, both types, and are wrought from song and warning.

This Brevity
Poems by Gianmarc Manzione
ISBN 0-9739960-0-5
69 Pages (paper)
$13.95 US
$16.00 CAD

> Who isn't betting
> on some eventual adjustment
>
> heralding the end of regret?
> Look, even a day's carriage of leaf-shadows
>
> implies a kind of inconstancy.

from "Weather of Days"

This Brevity, Gianmarc Manzione's debut collection of poetry, bares a concentration of everyday occurrences, that "continual fever of circumstance / no one knows the end of", and questions each end with an honesty so vivacious that even death becomes an opportunity for the heart to revisit its losses. With discipline and ardor, his interrogations discover possibilities that assemble themselves into moments where loss, desire, and understanding, like Ashbery's trees, surprise us with a meaning that is at once calculated and unhinged.

NOON

A LITERARY ANNUAL

1324 LEXINGTON AVENUE   PMB 298   NEW YORK   NEW YORK   10128

EDITION PRICE $9 DOMESTIC $14 FOREIGN